Peter Lehn

data management and file structures

data management and file structures

second edition

Mary E. S. Loomis

PRENTICE HALL, Englewood Cliffs, New Jersey 07632

Library of Congress Cataloging-in-Publication Data

LOOMIS, MARY E. S.
Data management and file structures/Mary E.S. Loomis.—2nd ed.

    Includes bibliographies and index.
    ISBN 0-13-198342-3
      1. Data base management. 2. File organization (Computer science)
I. Title.
QA76.76.D3L66 1989
005.74—dc19   88-23258
               CIP

Editorial/production supervision and
   interior design: John Fleming
Cover design: Diane Saxe
Cover Photo: © 1985 Genigraphics Corporation
Manufacturing buyer: Mary Noonan

 © 1989, 1983 by Prentice-Hall, Inc.
A Division of Simon & Schuster
Englewood Cliffs, New Jersey 07632

Printed in the United States of America
10 9 8 7 6 5 4 3 2 1

ISBN 0-13-198342-3

Prentice-Hall International (UK) Limited, *London*
Prentice-Hall of Australia Pty. Limited, *Sydney*
Prentice-Hall Canada, Inc., *Toronto*
Prentice-Hall Hispanoamericana, S.A., *Mexico*
Prentice-Hall of India Private Limited, *New Delhi*
Prentice-Hall of Japan, Inc., *Tokyo*
Simon & Schuster Asia Pte. Ltd., *Singapore*
Editora Prentice-Hall do Brasil, Ltda., *Rio de Janeiro*

To Allison and Eleanor
—and Missed Opportunity . . .

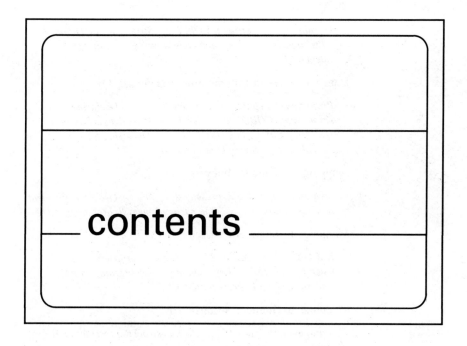

contents

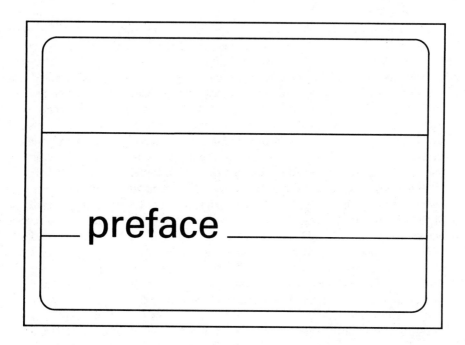

preface

This book is about structuring and organizing data—a fundamental aspect of designing and implementing computing software. Data structures determine the logical linkages between data elements, and affect the physical processing of data. All software programs use data structures of some kind; many use files as well. Data structure knowledge is required of people who design and develop software for either commercial or technical applications. It is also required of people who design and develop systems software, e.g., operating systems, language compilers, database management systems, and communications processors. Data structures and file organizations are primary factors that determine program performance.

There are two main parts of the text: the first (Chapters 1 to 9) deals with the area traditionally known as data structures; the second (Chapters 10 to 16) focuses on management and processing of files. The reader is guided from the most basic aspects of data management (including stacks, queues, and linked lists) through more complex data structures (trees and graphs) into processing of files (sequential, relative, indexed sequential, and multi-key organizations) and the elements of complex database management systems (DBMSs). DBMSs are increasingly important. They are ubiquitous on mainframes and minis, and are more and more prevalent on workstations and personal computers. The heart of a DBMS is data structuring and file processing logic.

The book will be most meaningful to readers who have at least an introductory knowledge of computer systems and programming, for example Course CS1 (Introduction to Programming Methodology) from the ACM Curriculum Committee on Computer Sciences "Curriculum '78–Recommendations for the Undergraduate Program in Computer Science" (*Comm. ACM*, 22(3), March 1979).

A good deal of the book concerns algorithms for building and manipulating data structures and file organizations. These procedures generally are presented in flowcharts and either COBOL or Pascal. COBOL was selected because of its prevalence in today's data management environments. Pascal represents the family of increasingly popular block-structured languages, has nice data-typing features, and conveniently exhibits the logical structure of algorithms. You need not know both (or even either) of these languages to find the book quite readable. If you are beginning with knowledge only of C or FORTRAN (or Basic or PL/I or an assembler language or . . .) and you spend a little time with the code presented in the text, you will be able to finish the book with not only an understanding of the principles of data management and file processing, but also reasonable introductory knowledge of COBOL and Pascal. Only standard COBOL (ANSI X3.23–1974, ISO 1989–1978, also known as COBOL74) and fundamental Pascal constructs have been used. The appendix includes documentation of the meta-language used to describe the COBOL syntax. It is not necessary for you to have a mathematical background, but a basically logical approach to problem-solving certainly would be helpful.

Each chapter ends with a brief summary (which also masquerades as an introductory overview if read prior to the chapter), a list of terms, and a set of review exercises. The terms include words that were introduced in the chapter or were especially important to understanding of the text material. You will benefit from testing yourself on the meanings of these terms and perusal of the definitions in the Glossary at the end of the book.

Some of the review exercises require only short answers. Others suggest programs and projects to assist you in strengthening your understanding of the material. In general, the simpler, recall exercises appear first, followed by the more interesting, "action" exercises. Answers to selected questions are included after the Glossary.

The text is appropriate to support Course CS2 (Program Design and Implementation—for details see Koffman, E. B., D. Stemple, and C. E. Wardle, "Recommended Curriculum for CS2, 1984," *Comm. ACM*, 28(8), August 1985), as well as Course CS5 (Introduction to File Processing) and the less mathematical aspects of Course CS7 (Data Structures and Algorithm Analysis) from the ACM Curriculum Committee on Computer Sciences "Recommendations for the Undergraduate Program in Computer Science" (*Comm. ACM*, 22(3), March 1979). At the graduate level it supports Course CS32 (Information Storage and Access) from the same committee's "Recommendations for Master's Level Programs in Computer Science" (*Comm. ACM*, 24(3), March 1981). It also is appropriate to support Course IS2 (Program, Data, and File Structures) from the ACM Curriculum Committee on Information Systems "Information Systems Curriculum Recommendations for the 80's: Undergraduate and Graduate Programs," *Comm. ACM*, 25(11), November 1982.

I have used the book in a two-semester undergraduate course sequence in a Management Information Systems (MIS) program in a College of Business and Public Administration, and in a one-semester graduate course in the MIS and Computer Science programs.

My fundamental objective in writing this book has been to structure and draw together the principles of data management and file processing in a readable presentation. The intent has been to preserve the essence of more rigorous mathematical treatments of the subject matter, while not bogging down the unsuspecting reader with too many details. My background in the text material comes from teaching it, extending it through various research endeavors, and using it in industry, both to build commercial and technical applications and database management systems. I hope to have drawn successfully on this background to present in this book a useful blend of theoretical concepts and practical applications.

The second edition differs from the first in several ways. The organization of topics has been changed to emphasize better the interrelationships of sorting, searching, and structuring techniques. There is greater emphasis on the performance characteristics of various data and file structures, making it easier to understand when to apply each. The glossary and exercises have both been extended. The material in general is presented more clearly, with more patience evident in the difficult parts.

Upon completion of the book, the reasonably motivated reader prepared with programming skills will be able to analyze the trade-offs of the data-handling needs of a particular problem situation, select the appropriate data structure or file organization, build the structure, retrieve selected data, update and maintain the structure, *and understand* what is going on. The book will give you a firm foundation for growing with the evolving technology of the complex information-handling field. You will be well prepared for follow-up study in database management techniques.

ACKNOWLEDGMENTS

The first edition of this book benefited from the feedback of many students in the Department of Management Information Systems at The University of Arizona, especially Clayton Curtis and Fred K. Nelson. The reviewers commissioned by Prentice Hall, especially Robert P. Burton, have helped to shape this Second Edition. The text materialized with the never-tiring support of vi, with occasional assistance from sharp scissors and sticky tape.

I thank my family for their continual and vocal encouragement for me to finish this work. Perhaps I should also acknowledge their encouragement for me not to start another one.

Mary E. S. Loomis

```
  ┌─────────────────────────────────────────┐
  │  ╭───────────────────────────────────╮   │
  │  │                                   │   │
  │  │ ___ chapter one _____          │   │
  │  │                                   │   │
  │  │                                   │   │
  │  │ ___ introduction to ___           │   │
  │  │     data structures ___           │   │
  │  │                                   │   │
  │  ╰───────────────────────────────────╯   │
  └─────────────────────────────────────────┘
```

chapter one

introduction to data structures

The first part of this book discusses the major types of data structures and tells how they are managed by computer programs. This introductory chapter should give you an understanding of what a data structure is and why data structures are important in information systems, as well as general knowledge of several simple data structures.

THE USE OF DATA

Before starting our discussion of data structures, let us first consider what data are and how they support information systems. Fig. 1–1 illustrates the roles that data play in the events of any organization. The large circle labeled ''data'' represents the overall data resource of the organization. This resource is an active participant in the organization's operations and planning. The small circles represent individual elements or items of data. These elements can be considered to be raw facts. They are aggregated and summarized in various meaningful ways to form information. Decisions are made on the basis of this information; we hope that the decisions we make *are* informed ones. The results of decisions are actions, which in turn generate more data. These data then can be incorporated into another cycle of the decision-making process.

1

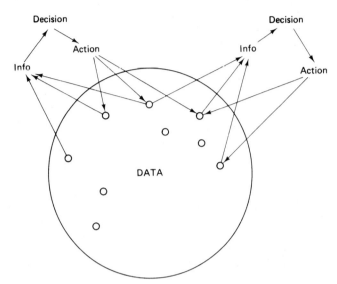

Figure 1-1 Data—An essential ingredient in taking action based on informed decision-making.

Sources of Information

Note that any given data element may participate in the generation of multiple "pieces" of information. It is important that there be flexibility in the ways that data items can be aggregated and summarized, so that meaningful information can be produced to support the decisions at hand. Note also that some data elements in an organization's data resource may have resulted from actions taken by forces or bodies external to the organization. The actions of competitors, the behavior of customers or clients, and the forces of legal requirements all enter into an organization's decision-making process.

Kinds of Decisions

The data resource must support several types of decision-making. It is convenient to recognize three levels of decisions:

- *Operational* decisions, which govern the daily activities of the organization.
- *Control* decisions, which determine the way the organization executes its designated "mission." These decisions are sometimes called *tactical* decisions.
- *Planning* decisions, which develop and define the organization's "mission." These decisions are sometimes termed *strategic* decisions.

Data and Decisions

The same element of data may participate in the production of information to support all three levels of decision-making. For example, one data element, the number of green telephone handsets produced by plastic-stamping machine #12345–78, could be used in answering each of the following questions:

1. How many green telephone handsets should machine #12345–78 be set up to produce today? (Operational)
2. Based upon production, failure, and repair data, should we purchase three more plastic-stamping machines for making telephone handsets? (Control)
3. Should the firm acquire a subsidiary company that produces plastic-stamping machines, thus increasing its ability to respond to changing market forces? (Planning)

Data must be structured correctly to be accessible and responsive to these various types of questions.

DATA MANAGEMENT

Data are expensive. They must be managed in such a way that they are correct and are available to produce needed information. Aspects of data handling include the following:

- Measurement
- Collection
- Transcription
- Validation
- Organization
- Storage
- Aggregation
- Update
- Retrieval
- Protection

Data Management Objectives

The objective of a data management system is to make the data resource resilient, flexible, and adaptable to supporting an organization's decision-making processes. Four useful guidelines for a data management system are

1. Data must be *represented* and *stored* so that they can be accessed later.
2. Data must be *organized* so that they can be selectively and efficiently accessed.
3. Data must be *processed* and *presented* so that they support the user environment effectively.
4. Data must be *protected* and *managed* so that they retain their value.

We will be discussing primarily the representation, storage, and organization of data by data structuring and file organization techniques. These techniques are important because they are primary factors in determining how well a data management system meets its objectives.

A CLASSIFICATION OF DATA STRUCTURES

We initially approach the study of data representation, organization, and processing from the viewpoint of data structures. A *data structure* is a class of data that can be characterized by its organization and the operations that are defined on it. Data structures are sometimes called *data types*.

Logical Data Structures

Data structures are very important in computer systems. In a program, every variable is of some explicitly or implicitly defined data structure, which determines the set of operations that are legal upon that variable. The data structures that we discuss here are termed *logical data structures*. There may be several different physical representations on storage possible for each logical data structure. For each data structure that we consider, several possible mappings to storage will be introduced.

Primitive and Simple Structures

Table 1–1 categorizes some of the data structures that are discussed in this book. Some are *primitive*: that is, they are not composed of other data structures. We will consider briefly examples of three primitives: integers, booleans, and characters. Other data structures can be constructed from one or more primitives. The *simple data structures* built from primitives that we will consider are strings, arrays, and records. Many programming languages support these data structures.

Linear and Nonlinear Structures

Simple data structures can be combined in various ways to form more complex structures. The two fundamental kinds of more complex data structures are linear and nonlinear, depending on the complexity of the logical relationships they represent. The linear data structures that we will discuss include stacks, queues, and linear linked lists. The nonlinear data structures include trees and graphs. We will find that there are many types of tree structures that are useful in information systems.

File Organizations

The data structuring techniques applied to collections of data that are managed as "black boxes" by operating systems are commonly called *file organizations*. A file carries a

TABLE 1–1.   WHICH DATA STRUCTURES ARE DISCUSSED IN WHICH CHAPTERS?

Primitive data structures	Simple data structures	Compound data structures			File organizations
			Nonlinear		
		Linear	Binary	N-ary	
Integer (1)	String (1)	Stack (4)	Binary Tree (8)	Graph (7)	Sequential (11)
Boolean (1)	Array (2)	Queue (5)	Binary Search	General Tree (8)	Relative (13)
Character (1)	Record (3)	Linked list (6)	Tree (8)	M-way Search Tree (14)	Indexed Sequential (15)
				B-Tree (14)	Multikey (16)
				B*, B + -Tree (14)	
				Trie (14)	

name, contents, a location where it is kept, and some administrative information, for example, who owns it and how big it is. The four basic kinds of file organization that we will discuss are sequential, relative, indexed sequential, and multikey file organizations. These organizations determine how the contents of files are structured. They are built on the data structuring techniques.

PRIMITIVES

Integers

You are probably already familiar with a number of primitive data structures because they are supported by nearly all the programming languages. One primitive data structure is the *integer*. An integer is a member of the following set of numbers:

$$\{\ldots, -(n + 1), -n, \ldots, -2, -1, 0, 1, 2, \ldots, n, n + 1, \ldots\}.$$

The fundamental operations on integers are familiar: addition, subtraction, multiplication, division, exponentiation, and so forth. These operations all work on pairs of numbers; they are binary operators. A unary operator has only one operand. Negation, which changes a number's sign, is a familiar example of a unary operator.

Booleans

A second example of a primitive data structure is the *boolean*, which is also called a *logical*. A boolean data element can have one of two values: *true* or *false*. The defined set of operations on this data structure is different from the legal set of operations for integers. The three basic boolean operators are *not*, *and*, and *or*. Table 1–2 shows the results of applying each of these operators to each of the valid boolean values. Note that *or* and *and* are both binary operators, while *not* is a unary operator. *Not* has precedence over *or* and *and*: that is, in the absence of parentheses which change the order of evaluation, *not* is evaluated before *and* or *or*. For example, in evaluation of the expression

    A and not B,

B is first negated, and the result is *and*ed with *A*.

TABLE 1–2 BOOLEAN OPERATORS

Value of first operand	Value of second operand	and	or	not*
true	true	true	true	false
true	false	false	true	false
false	true	false	true	true
false	false	false	false	true

* Applied to first operand.

The values *true* and *false* can also result from what are known as *relational operators*. Relational operators do not have boolean operands; rather they are operators with boolean results. These operators include $<, >, =, \le, \ge, \not\le, \not\ge, \ne$. For example, $<$ may operate on two integers, with the result being a boolean data value: $6 < 12$ is *true*.

Characters

A third primitive with which you are probably already familiar is the *character*. A character is an element taken from a set of symbols. One example set of symbols is

$$\{0,1,2,3,4,5,6,7,8,9,A,B,C,D, \ldots ,X,Y,Z, ,?,.,*,+,-,/\}$$

which includes the numeric digits, the alphabetic characters, and some special characters. A language compiler recognizes a particular character set.

STRINGS

One example of a data structure that is constructed from a more primitive data structure is the *string*, which is a finite sequence of symbols taken from a character set. The character set used to generate strings is called an *alphabet*. The set of strings that can be derived from the alphabet $A = \{C,D,1\}$ includes the following: 'CD1,' 'CD,' 'DDC,' '1D111,' and so forth, including the null or empty string. We typically delineate the beginning and the end of a string by the quote marker.

The string is an important data type and is widely used. For instance, strings are the basic medium in which programs are written and transmitted to a computer. They are the principal medium of exchange of information with users. Strings are used in files to store information. They are used in programming languages to name variables, labels, and procedures. In a more general context, it is via strings that humans communicate with each other.

The set of all possible strings that can be derived from an alphabet is called a *vocabulary*. The vocabulary V which is derived from alphabet A is sometimes denoted $V_A = A^*$. An alphabet need not contain only characters from our familiar alphabet $\{A,B,C,...,Y,Z\}$; it may contain any valid symbols. If the alphabet is $\{0,1\}$, then the obtainable strings are commonly called *bit strings*.

Definition

More formally, let us define a string S that is derived from the alphabet A by

$$S := {}'a_1a_2 \ldots a_N{}'$$

(eq. 1–1)

where each character $a_i \epsilon A$, for $1 \le i \le N$.

Every string has an attribute called its *length*, which is the number of characters in the string.

The operations that are legally defined upon strings are different from those that are legally defined for integers. The three major operations on strings are

1. Length,

2. Concatenation,

3. Substring.

String Length

The length operator gives the value of the string's length attribute. It has one operand, of type *string*, and produces a result of type *integer*. We can apply Length to the string S defined by eq. 1–1, giving result N by writing

$$N := \text{Length}(S).$$

String Concatenation

Concatenation operates on two strings, placing them end to end to produce a resultant string. The concatenation operator has two operands, both of type *string*, and produces a result of type *string*. If S is defined by eq. 1–1 and S^0 is defined by

$$S^0 := \text{'}b_1 b_2 \ldots b_M\text{'}$$
where each character $b_i \epsilon B$, for $1 \le i \le M$

on alphabet B, then

$$\text{Concat}(S, S^0) \text{ is } \text{'}a_1 a_2 \ldots a_N b_1 b_2 \ldots b_M\text{'}.$$

The length of the resultant string is the sum of the lengths of the component strings:

$$\text{Length}(\text{Concat}(S, S^0)) = \text{Length}(S) + \text{Length}(S^0).$$

The concatenation of the string with value 'STOVE' and the string with value 'PIPE' results in the string 'STOVEPIPE.'

Substring

Substring has a single string as one of its operands and generates a new string as its result. In order to specify fully the substring operation, one must specify not only the operand string, but also the starting point within that string and how many characters are to be taken from that string to form a new one. The substring operator has one operand of type *string*, two operands of type *integer*, and produces a result of type *string*. If S is defined by eq. 1–1, then

$$\text{Substr}(S, i, j) \text{ is } \text{'}a_i, a_{i+1}, \ldots a_{i+j-1}\text{'}$$
where i is the starting point,
$$0 < i < \text{Length}(S)$$
j is the number of characters to take,
$$0 < j < \text{Length}(S)$$
and $0 < i + j - 1 < \text{Length}(S)$,
for i, j of type *integer*.

The Length(Substr(S, i, j)) is j.

The substring operator can be used to undo the effects of concatenation:

$$\text{Substr}(\text{Concat}(S,S^0),1,\text{Length}(S)) \text{ is } S$$

and

$$\text{Substr}(\text{Concat}(S,S^0),\text{Length}(S) + 1,\text{Length}(S^0)) \text{ is } S^0.$$

Composite Operations

There are other composite operations that are legal for strings. For example, the insertion operator has two operands of type *string*, one operand of type *integer*, and produces a result of type *string*. Insert(S,S^0,i) inserts the string S^0 into the string S, such that the first character of S^0 is the ith character of the result.

$$\text{Insert}(S,S^0,i) \text{ is } \text{Concat}(\text{Concat}(\text{Substr}(S,1,i-1),S^0),\text{Substr}(S,i,\text{Length}(S) - (i-1)))$$

$$\text{where } 1 \leq i \leq \text{Length}(S) + 1.$$

The deletion operator has one operand of type *string*, two operands of type *integer*, and produces a result of type *string*. Delete(S,i,j) deletes from S the substring of length j that starts at the ith character.

$$\text{Delete}(S,i,j) \text{ is } \text{Concat}(\text{Substr}(S,1,i - 1), \text{Substr}(S,i + j,\text{Length}(S) - (i + j - 1)))$$

$$\text{where } 1 \leq i \leq \text{Length}(S)$$
$$0 \leq j \leq \text{Length}(S)$$
$$0 \leq i + j - 1 \leq \text{Length}(S)$$

for i,j of type *integer*.

Strings and Integers

We have distinguished between an integer value and a string value by delimiting the latter with the quote markers. In order to distinguish between integer and string values, programming languages commonly use the same convention. If 1234 is an *integer*, it is written 1234. If 1234 is a *string*, it is written either '1234' or ''1234''. In the same way, programming languages distinguish between string values and names of variables. For instance, ELMER may be ELMER the name of a variable, or ELMER the string. The string ELMER is written 'ELMER' or ''ELMER''; the variable name ELMER is written ELMER.

These three string operators—length, concatenation, and substring—cannot meaningfully be applied to variables that are of the integer data type. If we want to put the integer 12 together with the integer 34, we probably are not referring to concatenation with result 1234, but rather to addition with result 46. However, it is certainly valid to concatenate string '12' and string '34' with result a third string '1234' of length 4. Integers are sometimes converted to strings and manipulated as strings, then converted back to integers.

DATA STRUCTURES IN PROGRAMMING LANGUAGES

Programming languages give the programmer the means to assign a structure to each variable. A variable must have values taken from the set of defined values for its data structure and only those operations that are defined as being legal for that data structure should be performed upon the variable. Various programming languages have different ways of assigning data structures to variables; some compilers take more seriously than do others the responsibility of verifying adherence to the rules that characterize a particular data structure. For example, some compilers really do not care whether or not a program moves an alphabetic character like 'Q' to an integer field; they will even let the program go ahead and add 'Q' to something else, with no warning or notice of possibly meaningless results. Other compilers generate a compile-time error or execution-time error depending upon when the event occurred.

Some languages, such as Pascal and COBOL, require that the programmer explicitly declare the structure of every variable used in the program. Other languages, for example FORTRAN, have some implicit data typing. For instance, variables whose names start with I, J, K, L, M, or N are integers unless explicitly declared otherwise.

In some languages, such as COBOL, there is a special division of a program whose primary purpose is assignment of data structures. In some other languages, for example Pascal, the structure of a variable merely has to be declared prior to the first use of the variable. PL/I has the DECLARE statement for data definition; Pascal has the var statement; FORTRAN programmers use INTEGER, REAL, and DIMENSION statements.

Programmer-defined Data Structures

Most programming languages offer the programmer a predefined set of data structures. Others, for example Pascal with its type statement and the C language with its struct statement, enable programmers to define and name their own data structures. Sometimes this feature is used to give a programmer-defined name to a composite of system-defined primitives, but more creative data structuring by the programmer is also supported. In later chapters we will discuss some commonly used data structures that most programming languages do not support directly.

One of the notable differences between language-supplied, predefined data structures and programmer-defined data structures is the extent to which the operations on a data structure are validated. An exception is object-oriented programming languages which let the programmer explicitly declare the set of operations allowable on a programmer-defined data structure (commonly called a *class* in these languages). The compiler then enforces the restriction that only those operations can be used to manipulate instances of those structures.

Declaring Primitives in COBOL

Following are the ways in which a COBOL programmer would define variables that are integer, boolean, and character data structures. Assume the integer variable is to be named COUNT and to have a maximum of three digits; the boolean variable is to be named

SWITCH; the character variable is to be named BETA. The program's DATA DIVISION would include

```
01  COUNT PICTURE S999.
01  FLDA PICTURE X.
    88 SWITCH VALUE 'Y'.
01  BETA PICTURE X.
```

The *S* in COUNT's PICTURE clause represents a signed value. The sign is needed to allow negative values to be stored in a numeric variable. COBOL does not have a data type called boolean; instead the condition-name feature can be used to associate words with the values that a data item can assume. Those condition-names can then be used in conditional statements. For example, here, the 88-level condition-name SWITCH is defined to have the boolean value *true* when FLDA equals 'Y' and the boolean value *false* for all other values of FLDA. The programmer then can code

```
IF SWITCH THEN...
ELSE...
```

instead of

```
IF FLDA = 'Y' THEN...
ELSE...
```

The X pictures on FLDA and BETA indicate that values are to be taken from the full COBOL character set; the 9 picture on COUNT indicates that values are to be taken from the numerics.

Declaring Primitives in Pascal

A Pascal programmer declares primitive data structures using the <u>var</u> statement. For example, the following declares an integer variable named count, a boolean variable named switch and a character named beta:

```
var count: integer;
    switch: boolean;
    beta: char;
```

The number of digits in count could be controlled by format in read and write commands; variable switch can be assigned the value *true* or *false*.

Declaring Strings in COBOL

Strings can be defined easily in COBOL. To declare a variable named ADDRESS to be a string with length of 25 characters:

01 ADDRESS   PICTURE X(25).

The alphabet for deriving strings is the full character set supported by the compiler.

Declaring Strings in Pascal

Declaration of string variables in Pascal is somewhat more cumbersome:

var address : packed array [1..25] of char;

Here each element of the array called address holds one character of the string. The array must be packed if it is desirable to refer to the string as a whole; otherwise only the component characters of the string could be referenced. We consider arrays in some detail in the next chapter.

Pascal allows the programmer to give a name to a new composite data structure and then to assign that new type to variables. For example, the data structure formed from the primitive *char* could be given the name string25:

type string25 = packed array [1..25] of char;

Then the programmer could specify that variables name and address both have this structure:

var name, address : string25;

String Operations

Some languages have built-in operators for manipulation of variables that are string data structures. PL/I has LENGTH, SUBSTR, and || (concatenation). COBOL has STRING and UNSTRING. Pascal does not have these fundamental operators. The programmer who needs to perform string operations must write the corresponding routines or extract them from a library of codes. Some languages, notably SNOBOL, UCSD Pascal, and LISP, are specialized to enable the programmer to handle string data easily.

MAPPINGS TO STORAGE: INTEGERS

One characteristic of a logical data structure is that it may have several possible storage mappings or physical representations. In this section, some alternatives for mapping integers to storage are discussed. Some compilers make all the necessary decisions about which physical representations to use. Others allow the programmer to select from a set of predefined options.

Sign and Magnitude Representation

One possible storage mapping for integers is the *sign-and-magnitude* form. This is the conventional form for number representation by humans. Positive integers are identified by a plus sign and a string of digits which represent the magnitude; negative integers are identified by a minus sign and a string of digits which represent the magnitude. The plus sign is frequently omitted in our everyday use of numbers. However, it must be retained with the number for processing by the computer. The magnitude of a number is the natural value of the string of digits. In everyday usage by humans, a number's magnitude is represented in its base 10 (decimal) form. In computer memory, we represent magnitude in its base 2 (binary) form.

Humans nearly exclusively use the sign-and-magnitude form. If we were to develop computer algorithms for adding numbers in sign-and-magnitude form, we would find that when the operands have unlike signs, addition actually requires subtraction, which becomes complicated. To circumvent this problem, another storage mapping called *complement* representation was developed.

Two's-Complement Representation

Given the nonnegative integers X, X', and R, we define X' to be the *complement of* X *with respect to* R or *the* R*'s complement of* X when $X + X' = R$. In complement representation, the integers X are called *true forms* and the integers $X' = R - X$ are called the *complement forms*.

In a binary computer, one practical choice of the complementation constant R is as a power of 2:

$$R = 2^N.$$

The choice of N determines the range of integers that can be represented. The largest value representable in 2^N's complement form is 2^{N-1}. Mapping systems that use $R = 2^N$ are referred to as *two's-complement* systems. Table 1–3 illustrates the binary sign-and-

TABLE 1–3 TWO METHODS FOR REPRESENTATION OF INTEGER VALUES: BINARY SIGN-AND-MAGNITUDE AND TWO'S-COMPLEMENT

Integer	Binary Sign-and-Magnitude	Two's-Complement	
−7	−111	1001	
−6	−110	1010	
−5	−101	1011	
−4	−100	1100	complement forms
−3	−011	1101	
−2	−010	1110	
−1	−001	1111	
+0	+000	0000	
+1	+001	0001	
+2	+010	0010	
+3	+011	0011	
+4	+100	0100	true forms
+5	+101	0101	
+6	+110	0110	
+7	+111	0111	

magnitude representation and a two's-complement representation (using $R = 2^4$) of the integers in the range -7 to $+7$. The complement form $X' = R - X$ represents the negative integer $-X$; the true form X represents the positive integer X.

The algorithms used to perform arithmetic on integers represented in complement form are more convenient for the computer than are the algorithms to manipulate integers represented in sign-and-magnitude form. Thus, if much computation is to be performed on an integer variable, it may be advisable to represent it in storage using a complement form.

One's-Complement Representation

A second practical choice of the complementation constant R is

$$R = 2^N - 1.$$

These mapping systems are commonly referred to as *one's-complement* systems. One of the exercises at the end of the chapter suggests that you construct the one's-complement representation (using $R = 2^4 - 1$) of the integers in the range -7 to $+7$. The one's-complement systems provide the same advantages over the sign-and-magnitude form as do the two's-complement systems. Some arithmetic algorithms are more complex for two's-complement form than for one's-complement form; others are more complex for one's-complement form.

Basically, both the sign-and-magnitude and complement forms represent integers by theme and variation on the number's magnitude. An alternative is to map integers to storage using a digit-by-digit approach, treating each digit as a character.

MAPPINGS TO STORAGE: CHARACTERS

There are many schemes in use today for the representation of character data. The two most prevalent encoding schemes are the Extended Binary Coded Decimal Interchange Code (EBCDIC) and the American Standard Code for Information Interchange (ASCII).

EBCDIC

EBCDIC is an 8-bit code; 8 bits are required to represent any character in the character set. With 8 bits there are 2^8 (i.e., 256) possible combinations. The character set that the EBCDIC code can generate includes both upper- and lower-case alphabet letters, the numeric digits, and many special characters.

ASCII

ASCII is a 7-bit code. There are 2^7 possible combinations, which is half the number of characters offered by EBCDIC. The trade-off is that each character consumes less storage and can be transmitted more quickly.

TABLE 1–4 HUFFMAN CODE FOR A PARTICULAR APPLICATION

Charac- ter	Frequency of occurrence (%)	Code	Number of bits
0	55.5	0	1
1	6.7	1000	4
2	4.5	1100	4
8	3.5	10010	5
3	3.3	10100	5
A	3.2	10101	5
5	3.0	10110	5
6	2.7	11100	5
4	2.7	11101	5
9	2.2	11110	5
7	1.9	100110	6
F	1.5	101110	6
B	1.2	111110	6
Blank	1.1	110110	6
D	1.0	110100	6
E	0.9	110101	6
Z	0.7	1011110	7
P	0.6	1111110	7
N	0.5	1101110	7
u	0.4	10011110	8
C	0.4	10011100	8
H	0.4	10011101	8
R	0.3	10111110	8
M	0.3	11111110	8
L	0.3	11111111	8
S	0.25	11011110	8
I	0.20	100111110	9
T	0.15	110111110	9
K	0.15	110111111	9
Y	0.13	1001111110	10
X	0.12	1001111111	10
G	0.10	1011111100	10
J	0.10	1011111101	10
O	0.06	10111111100	11
Q	0.03	10111111101	11
V	0.03	10111111110	11
W	0.03	101111111110	12
.	0.01	1011111111110000	16
-		1011111111110001	16
?		1011111111110010	16
&		1011111111110011	16
/		1011111111110100	16
+		1011111111110101	16
<	below	1011111111110110	16
)	0.001	1011111111110111	16
(		1011111111111000	16
%		1011111111111001	16
=		1011111111111010	16
#		1011111111111011	16
?		1011111111111100	16
,		1011111111111101	16
@		1011111111111110	16
		1011111111111111	16

Average character length =
$0.555 \times 1 + 0.112 \times 4 + 0.206 \times 5 + 0.76 \times 6 + 0.018 \times 7 + 0.24 \times 8 + 0.005 \times 9 + 0.0045 \times 10 + 0.0017 \times 11 + 0.0003 \times 12 + 0.0001 \times 16$
= 2.91 bits per character

Source: J. Martin, *Computer Data-Base Organization*, 2nd ed. (Englewood Cliffs, N.J.: Prentice-Hall, Inc., 1977), Fig. 32.8.

Special-Purpose Schemes

Among the other encoding schemes available are some special-purpose codes, such as the family of Huffman codes. In this type of code, characters are represented by a variable number of bits depending upon the relative frequency of occurrence of the character in the vocabulary of the application. It is desirable to represent the most frequently occurring characters with the shorter bit patterns and less frequent characters with the longer bit patterns. For the example shown in Table 1–4, the character 0 is represented by a single bit 0; the character A is represented by a 5-bit pattern 10101; the character % is represented by a 16-bit pattern 1011111111111001. A trade-off to the resultant compressed storage requirement is the processing necessary to encode and to recognize characters.

Code Usage

Many compilers provide only a default mapping of characters to storage. Some compilers, however, will allow a programmer to specify that several codes are to be used within a single program. For example, a COBOL program might read or write some data to files using EBCDIC for tape drive compatibility. Other data might be read or written in ASCII, probably for input/output on terminal devices. Other data might be represented using an internal display code, if they are not to be shared with processes on any other equipment. Any particular data element can be encoded using only one scheme.

Representing Numeric Data

Files to be exchanged between computers are typically written in EBCDIC or ASCII, whether they are on tape or transmitted over a communications link. Thus, character-encoding schemes are commonly used to represent integers. A plus or minus sign is stored with the representation of the digits to indicate whether the value is positive or negative. Generally this sign is stored to the right of the low-order digit of the number.

Packed-Decimal Representation

Many compilers offer additional options and variations on these codes for integer representation. Perhaps the most widely used alternative is the *packed-decimal* format. This

TABLE 1–5 EXAMPLES OF CHARACTER-ORIENTED NUMERIC REPRESENTATIONS

Code		+903		
EBCDIC	11111001	11110000	11110011	01001110
ASCII	0111001	0110000	0110011	0101011
Packed-decimal	10010000	00111100		

Code		−903		
EBCDIC	11111001	11110000	11110011	00100000
ASCII	0111001	0110000	0110011	0101101
Packed-decimal	10010000	00111101		

scheme represents numeric data more concisely by storing two digits per 8 bits, rather than one digit per 8 bits (EBCDIC). The right-most 8 bits contain not only the low-order digit of the number, but also the sign of the number. Table 1–5 illustrates the representations of the integers $+903$ and -903 using various character-oriented schemes.

MAPPINGS TO STORAGE:STRINGS

Now that we have discussed how individual characters are represented, let us consider alternatives for representing strings of characters. The discussion in this section is limited to representation of strings in contiguous space; storage of a string of length N will require physically adjacent space for N characters.

In order to describe the contiguous storage mapping of a string, it is necessary to indicate both where the string's space starts and where it ends. In each of the following conventions, at least one auxiliary variable of type *pointer* is required. More will be said about the pointer data type later; for now suffice it to say that the value of a pointer variable is an address; i.e., the pointer identifies a storage location.

Storage Alternatives

There are at least three simple ways to describe string variables stored in contiguous space. We use as our examples two strings: STRING1 = 'ABCDEFG' and STRING2 = 'BCD'.

1. Keep a table of the following information for each string variable: its name, its starting address, its length. For example,

NAME	START	LENGTH
STRING1	PTR1S	7
STRING2	PTR2S	3

The corresponding storage format could be

```
A B C D E F G B C D
↑                 ↖
PTR1S             PTR2S
```

or (overlaying the strings)

```
A B C D E F G
↑   ↖
PTR1S   PTR2S
```

2. Keep a table of the following information for each string variable: its name, its starting address, its terminating address. For example,

NAME	START	TERM
STRING1	PTR1S	PTR1T
STRING2	PTR2S	PTR2T

The corresponding storage format could be

or (overlaying the strings)

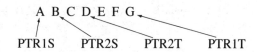

3. Keep a table of the following information for each string variable: its name and its starting address. Use an end-of-string marker (e.g., ξ) in storage to delimit the string. For example,

NAME	START
STRING1	PTR1S
STRING2	PTR2S

The corresponding storage format could be

$$A \ B \ C \ D \ E \ F \ G \ \xi \ B \ C \ D \ \xi$$
$$\uparrow \qquad\qquad\qquad \uparrow$$
$$PTR1S \qquad\qquad PTR2S$$

Packed-String Representation

Another consideration in the representation of strings in storage is whether that representation is to be packed or unpacked. Given a particular encoding scheme, and assuming a word-oriented machine, the *packed representation* of a string consists of placing each of the successive codes for the characters in successive storage words, with as many of the characters as possible in any given word. The string 'BINDERSTWINE' with four character-per-word packing is given in Fig. 1–2.

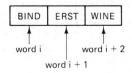

Figure 1–2 Example of four character-per-word packing.

Generalizing, with K characters per word, the number of words required to store string S is $\left\lceil \dfrac{\text{Length(S)}}{K} \right\rceil$, where $\lceil \quad \rceil$ is the ceiling function.* Sometimes the character codes fit words evenly; if there are 32 bits per word or 16 bits per word, EBCDIC with 8 bits per character fits very well. However, ASCII, with 7 bits per character, will allow two characters in a 16-bit word with two unusable bits remaining, or four characters in a 32-bit word with four unusable bits remaining.

Unpacked-string Representation

The *unpacked representation* for a string consists of storing one to a word the character codes for each of the successive characters. Each character is generally placed in the high-order bits of its word. The string 'BINDERSTWINE' stored in unpacked format is given in Fig. 1–3.

Figure 1–3   Example word from Fig. 1–2, in unpacked representation.

The number of words required to store string S in unpacked format is Length(S).

Which of the two types of string representation is better? It depends upon the objectives at hand. Packed representation is ideal for situations where minimizing storage utilization is paramount; however, operations are generally slower upon the packed representation than upon the unpacked representation. The unpacked representation requires no shifting, masking, or conversion when the contents of the words are manipulated.

SELECTION OF APPROPRIATE MAPPINGS

The previous sections should have convinced you that there are indeed several possible mappings of the example data structures to storage. The determination of which option is the most appropriate mapping to use is based upon (1) how the variable will be manipulated, (2) the range of values that the variable will have, and (3) the characteristics of the computer and memory that will process and store the variable.

The choice of one's- and two's-complement form implies that the arithmetic algorithms used are less complex for the computer than if a sign-and-magnitude representation were used. Algorithms to compute with integers represented in a digit-by-digit code are even more complex than are the sign-and-magnitude algorithms. In fact, many compilers convert numbers from a digit-by-digit form to either sign-and-magnitude or complement representation prior to performing arithmetic.

If calculations are so much less efficient with the digit-by-digit representations, why do they exist? The basic reason for the importance of coding schemes such as EBCDIC and ASCII is their capability to represent nonnumeric characters. Additionally, if numeric

* The ceiling function yields the first integer value greater than or equal to the operand. For example [3.16] is 4; [3] is 3.

data are to be displayed on a terminal screen or written on a report intended for human consumption, they must be represented in a displayable code. EBCDIC and ASCII are also commonly used to encode data on tape or to be transmitted over a communications link between processors.

Why are there so many coding schemes? The primary reason is that they have been developed by different groups for various purposes. Some machines, such as many IBM and DEC computers, use 32-bit words. An 8-bit character code (e.g., EBCDIC) is very convenient for representing data with that word size. The DEC System 10 has 36-bit words. A 7-bit character code (e.g., ASCII) conveniently represents five characters per word, with room for 1 sign bit. Large CDC computers, like the CYBER 175 and CDC 7600, have 60-bit words. These machines are well suited for scientific computing because of the greater precision made possible by the relatively long word length. A 6-bit character code (e.g., BCD) conveniently represents ten characters per word. Some space-saving codes are used when memory space is tight or communications capacities are quite limited.

The most widely used codes today for data exchange between machines are EBCDIC and ASCII. Many compiler vendors offer both these options. Additionally, nearly all the terminal vendors supply equipment with processors that accept one or both of these codes.

SUMMARY

This chapter began with a review of the importance of data to organizations' decision-making processes. Guidelines for data management systems were proposed. The concept of data structure was then introduced and the various data structures that will be discussed in this book were categorized.

Integers, booleans, and characters were introduced as examples of primitive data structures. A compound data structure called string and its fundamental operators (length, concatenation, and substring) were introduced.

The methods for declaring integers, booleans, characters, and strings in COBOL and Pascal were reviewed. These two languages will be used throughout the book to illustrate the types of support provided to programmers for data structure definition and manipulation.

There are several alternative ways to map any logical data structure to physical computer storage. Sign-and-magnitude and complement representations of integers were discussed. EBCDIC and ASCII were introduced as techniques for mapping character data to storage and then were extended to use for character-oriented mapping of integers to storage. Finally, the packed-decimal representation of integers was introduced.

The mapping of a string to storage involves both (1) the representation of each character of the string and (2) the representation of the combination of characters to form the string. Alternatives for storing information needed to find the beginning and ending symbols of a string were proposed; then the distinction between packed- and unpacked-string representation was made.

The selection of the most appropriate mapping scheme for any particular data structure should be based on the manipulations to be performed on that data, the characteristics of the values that the data structure will have, and the characteristics of the computer and the memory that will process and store the data structure. Some of the elementary trade-offs among mappings were introduced.

Data structures are essential to information systems. To be able to design efficient support for the data resources of an information system, one must have an understanding of how data are represented and manipulated. The data types that are used in a program help determine what the storage requirements are of that program, what its processing requirements are, what the input-output requirements are, what the response time will be, and so forth. A multiplicity of data structures is available primarily because different types of data are used in different ways. The data structures used actually define the access paths that are supported between data elements. The orientation of this book is toward understanding how the various data structures can be used in solving problems efficiently and effectively.

TERMS

alphabet	logical
ASCII	object-oriented programming
bit string	language
boolean	packed-decimal representation
boolean operator	packed-string representation
character	primitive
complement representation	sign-and-magnitude representation
concatenation	string
data structure	string length
data type	substring
EBCDIC	unpacked-string representation
integer	vocabulary

SELECTED REFERENCES

BASTANI, F. B. and S. S. IYENGAR. "The effect of data structures on the logical complexity of programs," *Comm. ACM*, 30(3):250–259, March 1987.

BOYER, R. S. and J. S. MOORE. "A fast string searching algorithm," *Comm. ACM*, 20(10):762–772, Oct. 1977.

CHOCK, M., A. F. CARDENAS, and A. KLINGER. "Manipulating data structures in pictorial information systems," *Computer*, 14(11):43–50, Nov. 1981.

HALL, P. A. V. and G. R. DOWLING. "Approximate string matching," *ACM Computing Surveys*, 12(4):381–402, Dec. 1980.

TURBA, T. N. "Length-segmented lists," *Comm. ACM*, 25(8):522–526, Aug. 1982.

REVIEW EXERCISES

1. List the various aspects of data handling that are required in an information system. Of these functions, which are likely to be the most expensive? Why?

2. Give five examples of integer values.

3. Give as many examples as you can of boolean values.

4. What is the result of each of the following operations where boolean variable FIRST has value *true*, variable SECOND has value *false*, and variable THIRD has value *true*?

   (a) *not* FIRST
   (b) FIRST *and* SECOND
   (c) FIRST *and* THIRD
   (d) FIRST *or* SECOND
   (e) FIRST *or* THIRD
   (f) *not* FIRST *or* THIRD
   (g) *not* (FIRST *or* THIRD)
   (h) *not* FIRST *and* SECOND
   (i) *not* (FIRST *and* SECOND)
   (j) FIRST *and not* SECOND
   (k) *not* (FIRST *and not* SECOND)

5. What is the result of each of the following operations, where string variable *S1* has value 'PIE,' variable *S2* has value 'MAGIC', and variable *S3* has value 'WHEEL'?

   (a) Length(*S2*)
   (b) Length(*S3*)
   (c) Concat(*S2*,*S1*)
   (d) Substr(*S3*,4,3)
   (e) Concat(Substr(*S2*,1,3),*S1*)
   (f) Concat(Substr(*S2*,1,3),*S3*)
   (g) Substr(Concat(*S1*,*S2*),1,Length(*S1*))
   (h) Substr(Concat(*S2*,*S1*),Length(*S2*) + 1,Length(*S1*))
   (i) Insert(*S1*,Substr(*S3*,6,1),3)
   (j) Delete(*S2*,2,2)
   (k) Insert(*S1*,Delete(*S3*,1,3),1)

6. Construct the one's-complement representation (with $R = 2^4 - 1$) of the integers in the range -7 to $+7$.

7. What is the minimum value of R needed to represent the R's complement of values between (a) -10 and $+10$? (b) -100 and $+100$?

8. What is the minimum value of R needed to represent the two's-complement of values between (a) -10 and $+10$? (b) -100 and $+100$?

9. How many bits are required to represent values in two's-complement form with $R = 2^N$?

10. How many bits are required to represent values in one's-complement form with $R = 2^N - 1$?

11. What are the largest and smallest values that can be represented in two's-complement form with (a) $R = 32$? (b) $R = 256$? (c) $R = 2^N$?

12. What are the largest and smallest values that can be represented in one's-complement form with (a) $R = 31$? (b) $R = 255$? (c) $R = 2^N - 1$?

13. What techniques are used to map integers to storage by the compilers available to you?

14. What techniques are used to map characters to storage by the compilers available to you?

15. Find charts that give the EBCDIC and ASCII character codes.

16. Give the EBCDIC representation of your name and address.

17. Give the ASCII representation of your name and address.

18. Represent your social security number or some other identification number using EBCDIC, ASCII, and packed decimal.

19. Give at least three possible storage representations of the three string values 'MAGPIE', 'PIE', and 'MAGENTA'.

20. What are the basic trade-offs to be considered in overlaying string representations in storage?

21. What are the basic trade-offs to be considered in packing string representations in storage?

22. What are the basic trade-offs to be considered in using (a) a length indicator to terminate a string representation, (b) a pointer to terminate a string representation, and (c) an end-of-string marker to terminate a string representation?

23. Explain how an object-oriented programming language differs from a conventional programming language in the area of data structure operations.

24. What is the full character set used by your Pascal (or COBOL or FORTRAN or PL/I or . . .) compiler?

25. Find out how to format character string input for your local Pascal compiler.

26. Write a program that reads and writes five character strings, each of length 10.

27. Modify your program to read and write N character strings, each of some unknown length. What are the required inputs to the program?

28. Write a program that implements the Length, Concat, and Substr operators.

29. Augment your program from 28 to implement the Insert and Delete operators.

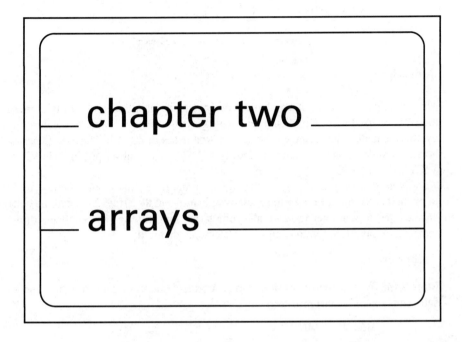

chapter two

arrays

This chapter discusses the common data structure known as the array. Arrays are basic building blocks for more complex data structures. Nearly every kind of complex structure can be represented indirectly using an array. We first define simple and multi-dimensional arrays. Then the facilities for declaring array variables in COBOL and Pascal are reviewed. Much of the chapter is devoted to discussion of how one- and multi-dimensional arrays are mapped to storage. Finally, a discussion of techniques for representing triangular and sparse arrays closes the chapter. We will find that arrays are used extensively in structuring data in a program's working memory, and in structuring data in more permanent files and databases.

ONE-DIMENSIONAL ARRAYS

An *array* is a finite, ordered set of homogeneous elements. The ordering property means that the first, second, third, . . . , n^{th} element of an array can be identified. The elements of an array are homogeneous, i.e., they all have the same data type. One array might be comprised of elements that are all strings; another might be comprised of elements that are all integers. The elements of an array may also each be arrays. Arrays are also commonly referred to as *tables*.

The simplest form of array is a *one-dimensional array*, or *vector*. A one-dimensional array named VICTOR, which consists of N elements, can be depicted as in Fig. 2–1.

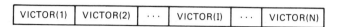

| VICTOR(1) | VICTOR(2) | · · · | VICTOR(I) | · · · | VICTOR(N) |

Figure 2–1 Example one-dimensional array.

Subscripts

The *subscript*, or *index*, of an element designates its position in the array's ordering. In the notation used here, a particular element is identified by the name of the array followed by the element's subscript enclosed in parentheses, i.e., VICTOR(I). Other possible notations to designate the element of array VICTOR with subscript I include VICTOR[I], $VICTOR_I$, and $VICTOR^I$.

Note that only the array itself is given a name. Elements of an array are referred to by their subscripts, i.e., by their relative positions in the array. This naming convention enables the programmer to write algorithms that loop through the elements of an array, rather than having to name each of the elements distinctly.

Definition

More formally, the one-dimensional array A with elements of data structure type T having subscripts extending from L through U is

$$A(L:U) = \{A(I)\}$$
$$\text{for } I = L, L + 1, \ldots, U - 1, U$$
$$\text{where each element } A(I) \text{ is a data structure of type } T.$$

The notation $A(L:U)$ indicates that A's subscript value ranges from L through U.

The number of elements in an array is called its *range*. The range of array $A(L:U)$ is $U - L + 1$. The range of array $B(1:N)$ is N.

Examples

As an example, a one-dimensional array might contain the temperatures recorded in a city for every hour during a 24-hour period. These elements are ordered by their corresponding time of the day. All elements are of the same kind; each is a temperature.

The minimum allowable value of an array's subscript is called its *lower bound*; the maximum allowable value is called its *upper bound*. In our formal definition of an array, L is the lower-bound and U is the upper-bound of A's subscript range. In the temperature-record example, a natural lower bound is 1 and upper bound is 24. Call the array TEMP. TEMP(I) is the temperature recorded at hour I, for $1 \leq I \leq 24$.

Another example of a one-dimensional array is a table of average state incomes. Name the array AVG-INCOME. The element AVG-INCOME(I) is the average income of the Ith state, where the states are ordered sequentially, say alphabetically. Thus AVG-INCOME(1) is the average income of Alabama and AVG-INCOME(50) is the average income of Wyoming.

For some applications it is more natural to use a lower bound that is not equal to 1. For example, temperatures of an experiment that are recorded every ten seconds from time zero might more conveniently be stored in an array with lower bound 0. The lower bound may even be negative. This is commonly the case for arrays that store data to be displayed graphically, such as on an axis of points ranging from -100 to $+100$.

MULTI-DIMENSIONAL ARRAYS

A two-dimensional array is an array in which each element is itself an array. An array named B which consists of M elements, each of which is an array of N elements can be depicted as an M-by-N table, as shown in Fig. 2–2.

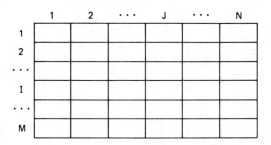

Figure 2–2   Example M-by-N array.

Subscripts

It is necessary to specify two subscript values in order to identify an individual element of a two-dimensional array. By convention, the first subscript refers to a *row* of the array, while the second subscript refers to a *column* of the array. That is, $B(I,J)$ is the element of B that is in the Ith row and J^{th} column of array B, as indicated in Fig. 2–3.

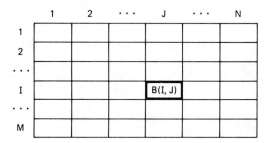

Figure 2–3   Element B(I,J) in a two-dimensional array.

Definitions

More formally, the two-dimensional array B with individual elements of type T having row subscripts extending from 1 to M and column subscripts ranging from 1 to N is

$$B(1:M, 1:N) = \{B(I,J)\}$$
$$\text{for } I = 1, \ldots , M \text{ and } J = 1, \ldots , N$$
$$\text{where each } B(I,J) \text{ is a data structure of type } T.$$

Array B is said to be of dimensions M by N. There are N elements in each row and M elements in each column of B; thus the total number of elements in array B is $M*N$.

In general, a two-dimensional array B with its first subscript having lower bound L_1 and upper bound U_1 and its second subscript having lower bound L_2 and upper bound U_2 is defined as

$$B(L_1:U_1, L_2:U_2) = \{B(I,J)\} \text{ for } L_1 \leq I \leq U_1$$
$$\text{and } L_2 \leq J \leq U_2$$
$$\text{where each } B(I,J) \text{ is a data structure of type } T.$$

The number of elements in a row of B is $U_2 - L_2 + 1$ and the number of elements in a column of B is $U_1 - L_1 + 1$. Thus the total number of elements in array B is $(U_2 - L_2 + 1)*(U_1 - L_1 + 1)$.

Examples

Two-dimensional arrays are quite common. For example, the Chamber of Commerce of your city might keep track of the number of hours of fair weather in each day of the year. These data can be stored in an array with dimensions 365 by 24. Call the array W. Values of W could be determined by

$W(I,J) = 1$ if it is fair during the Jth hour of the Ith day of the year
0 otherwise, i.e., if it snows, rains, sleets, drizzles, etc. during the Jth hour of the Ith day of the year.

All elements of the array are of the same kind; each is a boolean.

Another example of a two-dimensional array is one that contains data about the grades of students in a class on the four semester-exams. This array, called GRADE, would have dimensions M by 4, where M is the number of students. Then GRADE(I,J) is the grade achieved by the Ith student on the Jth exam. The value of I must be between 1 and M inclusive; J must be between 1 and 4 inclusive. Each element of the array is a grade; they could all be integers, or all be fixed-point numbers with two decimal places, or all be characters, depending on the convention adopted.

Cross-section

A *cross-section* of a two-dimensional array is obtained by holding one of the subscripts constant while varying the other through its entire range of values. The notation that is commonly used to denote a cross-section is an asterisk (*) for the subscript value that is to be allowed to take on its entire range of values. For example,

$B(*,4)$

refers to the fourth column of the array B pictured at the beginning of this section. That is,

$B(*,4) = \{B(1,4),B(2,4),B(3,4), \ldots , B(M,4)\}.$

Similarly,

      $B(I,*)$

is the Ith row of the array B;

      $W(47,*)$

is the row of W values recording the weather conditions on the 47th day of the year;

      GRADE(*,3)

is the column of GRADE values for recording exam grades for all students on the third exam. A cross-section of a two-dimensional array is essentially a slice taken from the array.

Transpose

The *transpose* of a two-dimensional array is obtained by reversing the subscript positions. The transpose of an *M*-by-*N* array is an *N*-by-*M* array. The transpose of array *B* is commonly denoted B^T. The transpose of the array *B* pictured at the beginning of this section is shown in Fig. 2–4.

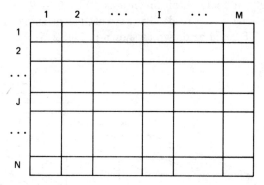

Figure 2–4   Transpose of the array in Fig. 2–2.

By definition,

      $B(I,J) = B^T(J,I)$.

For example,

      $B(3,8) = B^T(8,3)$.

The element in row 3, column 8 of array *B* is the same as the element in row 8, column 3 of the transpose of array *B*.

Extensions to More Dimensions

An array can be defined to be three-dimensional, four-dimensional, *N*-dimensional. The concepts of subscript range and number of elements can be directly extended from one-

and two-dimensional arrays to these higher-order arrays. In general, an N-dimensional array requires that the values of N subscripts be specified in order to identify an individual element of the array. An N-dimensional array A could be identified as

$$A(L_1:U_1, L_2:U_2, \ldots, L_N:U_N).$$

An individual element of array A could then be specified by $A(I_1, I_2, \ldots, I_N)$ where each subscript I_k is within the appropriate bounds $L_k \leq I_k \leq U_k$, for each $k = 1, 2, \ldots, N$. The total number of elements in array A is

$$\prod_{k=1}^{N} (U_k - L_k + 1)$$

which could alternatively be written

$$(U_1 - L_1 + 1) * (U_2 - L_2 + 1) * \ldots * (U_N - L_N + 1).$$

An example of a three-dimensional array is one containing data about the number of students in each of a university's six classifications of students (freshman, sophomore, junior, senior, graduate, unclassified), by sex, for all of a university's ten colleges. Such an array might be called COLLEGE-CT and could be of dimensions 6 by 2 by 10. (Alternatively, it could be of dimensions 10 by 6 by 2, or 10 by 2 by 6, or 2 by 6 by 10, etc., as long as the reader knows what the meaning of each dimension is.) Array COLLEGE-CT could be drawn as shown in Fig. 2–5.

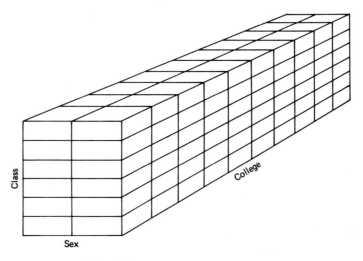

Figure 2–5 Example 3-dimensional array.

The value of element COLLEGE-CT(I, J, K), then, is an integer representing the number of students in class I of sex J for college K. To be valid, I must be 1,2,3,4,5 or 6; J must be 1 or 2; K must be between 1 and 10 inclusive.

It is difficult to draw pictures of arrays with more than three dimensions.

A cross-section of a multi-dimensional array is formed by holding one or more subscript values constant and varying each of the other subscripts through its entire range of values. For example,

> COLLEGE-CT(5,*,3)

is the "row" of COLLEGE-CT containing the number of students in the fifth class (graduate) of college 3, for both sexes. COLLEGE-CT (*,*,3) is the "plane" of COLLEGE-CT containing the number of students in college 3, for each class and both sexes.

ARRAYS IN COBOL AND PASCAL

One-dimensional Arrays

The most common programming languages all use the same approach to declaration of variables that are arrays. Three things need to be specified to declare an array: (1) the array name, (2) the subscript range, and (3) the type of data structure for the array elements. Consider first declaration of a one-dimensional array named TEMP with subscripts ranging from 1 to 24. Assume each element of the array is an integer, with range of values 0 degrees to 99 degrees.

In COBOL, in order to refer to the Ith temperature as TEMP(I), the programmer has to introduce a grouping name for the array elements. It is convenient simply to append TABLE to the application's array name. The program's DATA DIVISION would include

> 01   TEMP-TABLE.
>   02   TEMP   OCCURS 24 TIMES
>   PICTURE 99.

In Pascal there is no need for the artificial grouping variable. The array is declared in a var statement:

> var temp: array [1 . . 24] of integer.

Pascal allows a subscript's lower bound to be other than 1. For example,

> var graphpts: array [− 100 . . 100] of integer.

In COBOL arrays, a subscript must start from 1. The OCCURS clause indicates the subscript's upper bound.

To refer to the Ith element of the array above, COBOL uses the notation: TEMP(I). Pascal uses square brackets rather than parentheses about the subscript: temp[i].

Two-dimensional Arrays

The declaration of an array to contain scores of 40 students on 4 exams would be as follows.

In COBOL two grouping names are introduced

```
01   GRADE-TABLE.
   02   STUDENT OCCURS 40 TIMES.
      03   GRADE OCCURS 4 TIMES
                PICTURE 99V9.
```

In Pascal,

$$\text{var grade: array } [1 . . 40, 1 . . 4] \text{ of real.}$$

In COBOL, the grade for the Ith student on the Jth exam is GRADE (I,J). Pascal uses square brackets instead of parentheses: grade $[i,j]$. The subscript values must be within their valid bounds.

More Dimensions

The maximum number of dimensions that can be declared for a COBOL array is three. For example,

```
01   COLLEGE-CT-TABLE.
   02   CLASSF OCCURS 6 TIMES.
      03   SEX OCCURS 2 TIMES.
         04   COLLEGE-CT OCCURS 10 TIMES
                   PICTURE 9(5).
```

Attempts to declare four or more dimensions will be trapped by the compiler.

In Pascal the three-dimensional array would be defined by

$$\text{var collegect: array } [1 . . 6,1 . . 2,1 . . 10] \text{ of integer.}$$

In some languages, such as FORTRAN and COBOL, storage space is allocated to arrays at compile time. Thus the bounds must be specified explicitly when an array is defined. In other languages, such as PL/I, space can be allocated dynamically at execution time.

Operations on Array Elements

COBOL and Pascal (and other languages that allow programmers to declare arrays) have facilities for manipulation of individual elements of an array. The set of legal operations is defined by the data structures of the elements. For example, substring and concatenation operations may be performed on elements of an array defined to be strings. Arithmetic calculations may be performed on individual elements of an array of integers or of decimals. For example, in COBOL,

COMPUTE TOTAL-PAY (I) = HRLY-RATE (I) * HRS-WORKED (I)

where each of the three variables is an array element.

Operations on Arrays

Some programming languages also have array operations. For example, if A were declared to be an array in PL/I, then $A = A + 2$; would add 2 to each element of A. If A and B were declared to be arrays with the same dimensions, then in PL/I, $A = A * B$; would multiply each element of A by the corresponding element of B (i.e., by the element with the same subscripts), placing the result in A. This array multiplication is *not* matrix multiplication.

In PL/I, operations can be performed on cross-sections of arrays. For example,

$$GRADE(20,*) = 0;$$

sets each of the GRADE elements in the twentieth row to have value zero.

$$VECTOR(*) = ARRAY1(I,*) * ARRAY2(*,J);$$

multiplies the elements of the Ith row of ARRAY1 by the elements of the Jth column of ARRAY2. The arrays must be declared to have compatible subscript range values. For example, if the second subscript of ARRAY1 ranges from value 0 through 25, then the first subscript of ARRAY2 must also range from value 0 through 25, as must the subscript of VECTOR. The above multiplication then has the same effect as does the following loop:

```
DO K = 0 TO 25;
    VECTOR(K) = ARRAY(I,K) * ARRAY2(K,J);
END;
```

MAPPINGS TO STORAGE: ONE-DIMENSIONAL ARRAYS

As with other data structures, there are several ways to represent arrays in memory. These representation schemes can be evaluated on the basis of four characteristics: (1) the simplicity of element access, (2) ease of traversal along various paths, (3) storage efficiency, and (4) ease of growth. It is not possible to optimize all four of these factors simultaneously.

Lower Bound: One

Let us initially consider storage mappings for a one-dimensional array named EMP-NO with subscript lower bound 1 and subscript upper bound N. One way to store this array is so that the physical order of elements is the same as the logical order of elements. Storage for element EMP-NO($I + 1$) will be adjacent to storage for element EMP-NO(I), for $I = 1, \ldots, N - 1$.

In order to calculate the starting address (i.e., the location) of element EMP-NO(I), it is necessary to know

1. The starting address of the storage space allocated to the array.
2. The size of each element in the array.

Denote by B the array's starting address, also known as its *base location*. Assume that each element of the array occupies S bytes. Then the location of the Ith element of the array is

$$B + (I - 1) * S \hspace{4cm} \text{(eq. 2–1)}$$

because $I - 1$ elements, each of size S, physically precede the Ith element. The compiler needs to be able to determine element locations; they can be of use to a programmer using a memory dump to debug.

Generalizing the Lower Bound

Let us now extend eq. 2–1 to find the location of the Ith element of an array which has its subscript lower bound not equal to one. For instance, consider the array declared $Z1(4:10)$. Taking a specific case, the starting address of $Z1(6)$ is

$$B + (6 - 4) * S$$

because $6 - 4$ (i.e., 2) elements precede $Z1(6)$. For an array declared $Z2(-2:2)$, the location of $Z2(1)$ is

$$B + (1 - (-2)) * S$$

because $1 - (-2)$, or three, elements ($Z2(-2)$, $Z2(-1)$, and $Z2(0)$) precede $Z2(1)$.
    In general, the element ARRAY(I) of the array defined as ARRAY($L:U$) is at location

$$B + (I - L) * S \hspace{4cm} \text{(eq. 2–2)}$$

This formula is correct whether the lower-bound L is positive, negative, or zero.

MAPPINGS TO STORAGE: MULTI-DIMENSIONAL ARRAYS

Row-major Order

Because computer memory is linear, a multi-dimensional array must be linearized as it is mapped to storage. One alternative for linearization is to store first the first row of the array, then the second row of the array, then the third row, and so forth. For example, the array defined by *RATE* (1:4,1:6), which logically appears as shown in Fig. 2–6, appears physically in *row-major order* as shown in Fig. 2–7.

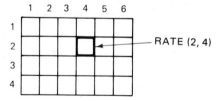

Figure 2–6   Example two-dimensional array.

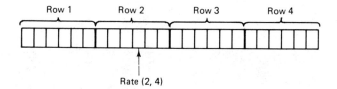

Figure 2–7   Array of Fig. 2–6 linearized in row-major order.

This is the storage-allocation scheme used for arrays declared in most implementations of COBOL, Pascal, C, and PL/I.

Assuming that B is the array's base address and that each element of the array is of size S, the starting address of the element $RATE(I,J)$ is

$$B + (I - 1)*6*S + (J - 1)*S$$

because there are $I - 1$ rows, each of length $6 * S$, which precede the row that element $RATE(I,J)$ is in, and there are $J - 1$ elements, each of length S, which precede element $RATE(I,J)$ in row I. Element RATE(2,4) is located at $B + 9*S$.

Generalizing, the element $ARRAY(I,J)$ of array defined by $ARRAY(L_1:U_1, L_2:U_2)$ is at location:

$$B + (I - L_1)*(U_2 - L_2 + 1)*S + (J - L_2)*S \qquad \text{(eq. 2–3)}$$

because there are $I - L_1$ rows, each of length $(U_2 - L_2 + 1)*S$, which precede the row that element $ARRAY(I,J)$ is in, and there are $J - L_2$ elements, each of length S, which precede element $ARRAY(I,J)$ in row I.

Illustrating this, the array defined by $Z(-2:2, 4:6)$ can be depicted logically as shown in Fig. 2–8.

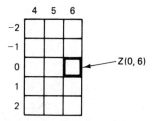

Figure 2–8   Example two-dimensional array.

This array appears physically in row-major order as shown in Fig. 2–9.

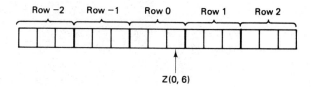

Figure 2–9   Array of Fig. 2–8 linearized in row-major order.

There are two rows (row -2 and row -1), each of length $3 * S$, preceding row 0. In row 0, there are 2 (i.e., $6 - 4$) elements, each of length S, preceding element $Z(0,6)$. That is, the starting location of $Z(0,6)$ is

$$B + (0 - (-2))*(6 - 4 + 1)*S + (6 - 4)*S,$$

which is $B + 8*S$.

With an N-dimensional array, row-major order varies the subscripts in right-to-left order. For example, for array

$$A(L_1:U_1,L_2:U_2,\ldots,L_N:U_N)$$

the elements are stored in the following order:

$A(L_1,L_2,\ldots,L_N)$
$A(L_1,L_2,\ldots,L_N + 1)$
$\ldots$
$A(L_1,L_2,\ldots,U_N)$
$A(L_1,L_2,\ldots,L_{N-1} + 1,L_N)$
$\ldots$
$A(L_1,L_2,\ldots,L_{N-1} + 1,U_N)$
$\ldots$
$A(L_1,L_2,\ldots,U_{N-1},U_N)$
$\ldots$
$A(U_1,L_2,\ldots,L_{N-1},L_N)$
$A(U_1,L_2,\ldots,L_{N-1},L_N + 1)$
$\ldots$
$A(U_1,L_2,\ldots,U_{N-1},U_N)$
$\ldots$
$A(U_1,U_2,\ldots,U_N)$

Column-major Order

Another alternative for linearization of a two-dimensional array is to store the elements in *column-major order*, i.e., store first the first column, then the second column, then the third column, and so forth. The RATE array mentioned earlier in this section appears physically in column-major order as shown in Fig. 2–10.

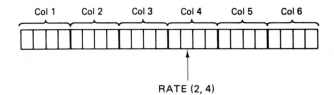

RATE (2, 4)

Figure 2–10 Array of Fig. 2–6 linearized in column-major order.

This is the storage allocation scheme used for arrays declared in many implementations of FORTRAN.

Assuming that B is the array's base address and that each element of the array is of size S, the starting address of the element RATE(I,J) is

$$B + (J - 1)*4*S + (I - 1)*S$$

because there are $J - 1$ columns, each of length $4*S$, which precede the column that element RATE(I,J) is in, and there are $I - 1$ elements, each of length S, which precede RATE(I,J) in column J. Element RATE(2,4) is located at $B + 13*S$.

Generalizing, the element ARRAY(I,J) of the array defined by ARRAY($L_1:U_1,L_2:U_2$), with column-major storage, is at location

$$B + (J - L_2)*(U_1 - L_1 + 1)*S + (I - L_1)*S. \qquad \text{(eq. 2–4)}$$

Compare this equation to eq. 2–3.

With an N-dimensional array, column-major order varies the subscripts in left-to-right order. For example, for array

$$A(L_1:U_1,L_2:U_2,\ldots,L_N:U_N)$$

the elements are stored in the following order:

$A(L_1,L_2,\ldots,L_N)$
$A(L_1 + 1,L_2,\ldots,L_N)$
...
$A(U_1,L_2,\ldots,L_N)$
$A(L_1,L_2 + 1,\ldots,L_N)$
$A(L_1 + 1,L_2 + 1,\ldots,L_N)$
...
$A(U_1,L_2 + 1,\ldots,L_N)$
...
$A(L_1,L_2,\ldots,L_N + 1)$
$A(L_1 + 1,L_2,\ldots,L_{N+1})$
...
$A(U_1,L_2,\ldots,L_{N+1})$
...
$A(L_1,L_2,\ldots,U_N)$
...
$A(L_1,U_2,\ldots,U_N)$
...
$A(U_1,U_2,\ldots,U_N)$

Selecting a Linearization Technique

In order to determine whether it is more advantageous to store an array in column-major order or in row-major order, it is necessary to know in what order the array elements are to be referenced. In fact, the available programming languages do not give the programmer a choice of array storage technique. Rather, especially in a virtual memory environment, the programmer should make a concerted effort to tailor the pattern of array element references to the storage pattern. For example, consider a procedure to calculate the average value of the elements in a 50-by-225 array named *A*. With column-major storage, the following reference pattern should be used:

In COBOL:

```
COMPUTE TOTAL = 0.
PERFORM SUM-UP VARYING J FROM 1 BY 1 UNTIL J > 225
            AFTER I FROM 1 BY 1 UNTIL I > 50.
```

where

```
SUM-UP.
    TOTAL = TOTAL + A (I,J).
```

This algorithm adds all the elements of one column before proceeding to the next. The same approach in Pascal is

```
total := 0;
for j := 1 to 225 do
    for i := 1 to 50 do
        total := total + a[i,j];
```

On the other hand, with row-major storage, which is more common for COBOL and Pascal, the following reference pattern is preferable. The algorithm adds all the elements of one row before proceeding to the next.

In COBOL:

```
COMPUTE TOTAL = 0.
PERFORM SUM-UP VARYING I FROM 1 BY 1 UNTIL I > 50
            AFTER J FROM 1 BY 1 UNTIL J > 225.
```

where

In Pascal:

```
SUM-UP.
    TOTAL = TOTAL + A(I,J).
```

```
total := 0;
for i := 1 to 50 do
    for j := 1 to 225 do
        total := total + a[i,j];
```

When it is necessary to pass arrays between FORTRAN routines and routines written in other languages (e.g., COBOL, PL/I, Pascal), it is extremely important that the programmer be aware of the combination of linearization techniques used.

TRIANGULAR ARRAYS

In the preceding section we discussed linearization of multi-dimensional arrays. In this section we consider some aspects of the linearization of a special type of array: triangular arrays.

Definitions

A triangular array may be either *upper-triangular*, as shown in Fig. 2–11, or *lower-triangular*, as shown in Fig. 2–12, where all elements below (or above) the diagonal are zero. An array is called *strictly upper-* (or *lower-*) *triangular* if the elements of the diagonal are also zero.

$$
\begin{bmatrix}
X & X & X & X & X & X \\
0 & X & X & X & X & X \\
0 & 0 & X & X & X & X \\
0 & 0 & 0 & X & X & X \\
0 & 0 & 0 & 0 & X & X \\
0 & 0 & 0 & 0 & 0 & X
\end{bmatrix}
\qquad
\begin{bmatrix}
X & 0 & 0 & 0 & 0 & 0 \\
X & X & 0 & 0 & 0 & 0 \\
X & X & X & 0 & 0 & 0 \\
X & X & X & X & 0 & 0 \\
X & X & X & X & X & 0 \\
X & X & X & X & X & X
\end{bmatrix}
$$

Figure 2–11 Upper-triangular array.   **Figure 2–12** Lower-triangular array.

In a lower-triangular array with N rows, the maximum number of nonzero elements in the Ith row is I. The total number of nonzero elements thus is no more than

$$
\sum_{I=1}^{N} I = \frac{N(N + 1)}{2}
$$

This expression is also true for an upper-triangular array with N rows. For large N, it would be desirable not to have to store all of the array's zero-valued elements.

Linearization

One approach to this problem is to linearize the array and store only the elements of the nonzero triangular portion. Let us store the upper-triangular array T by rows in a one-dimensional array named S with subscript bounds 1 through $N(N + 1)/2$. Element $T(1,1)$ is stored as element $S(1)$, element $T(1,2)$ is stored as element $S(2)$, and so forth up to element $T(1,N)$ which is stored as element $S(N)$. Then element $T(2,2)$ is stored as $S(N + 1)$, because $T(2,1)$ is zero. Element $T(N,N)$ is stored as $S(N(N + 1)/2)$. In general, where in S is $T(I,J)$ stored? Note that $I \leq J$ for all elements in the nonzero part of T.

Sharing Space

Sometimes a program requires the use of more than one triangular array. If two of these arrays are of essentially the same dimensions, then it is a relatively straightforward task to store them in a manner that conserves space. Assume that array A is upper-triangular and N by N, and that array B is lower-triangular and $N - 1$ by $N - 1$. Then A and B

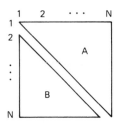

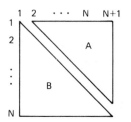

Figure 2–13 Upper-triangular and lower-triangular arrays sharing an N-by-N space.

Figure 2–14 Upper-triangular and lower-triangular arrays sharing an N-by-N + 1 space.

can be stored together in an N-by-N array C as shown in Fig. 2–13. Elements $C(I,J)$ where $I \leq J$ are elements of A, and elements $C(I,J)$ where $I > J$ are elements of B. In fact, element $A(I,J)$ is stored as $C(I,J)$ for $I \leq J$, and element $B(I,J)$ is stored as $C(I + 1,J)$ for $I \geq J$.

Let array A be upper-triangular, let array B be lower-triangular, and let both be N by N. Then array C must be N by $N + 1$ in order to contain both A and B as shown in Fig. 2–14. Here element $A(I,J)$ is stored as $C(I,J + 1)$ for $I \leq J$ and $B(I,J)$ is stored as $C(I,J)$ for $I \geq J$.

Consider now the case in which two upper-triangular arrays, say A and AA, both of which are N by N, are to share the same array space. One approach is to transpose one of the triangular arrays, say AA, such that instead of being upper-triangular, it appears to be lower-triangular. That is, array AA is transposed to form array AA^T, and element $AA(I,J)$ becomes element $AA^T(J,I)$. Then A and AA^T can be stored together in an array C with dimensions N-by-$(N + 1)$ as shown in the preceding paragraph. Element $A(I,J)$ is stored as $C(I,J + 1)$, and element $AA(I,J)$ is stored as $C(J,I)$.

Accommodating Change

One problem with all of these linearization techniques arises when elements are made nonzero in the lower part of an upper-triangular array. The array then is no longer upper-triangular. If it shares the space of a square array with a lower-triangular array, there will be an obvious conflict. One solution is to not allow an upper-triangular array to be updated if that would cause the array no longer to be upper-triangular. Another approach is to recognize the change in array characteristics and move it to its own space.

SPARSE ARRAYS

Definition

Another special type of array which arises commonly in applications is a *sparse array*. It is actually difficult to draw the dividing line between those arrays that are sparse and those that are not; loosely, an array is called sparse if it has a relatively high density of

$$
\begin{bmatrix}
0 & 0 & 0 & 0 & 1 & 0 & 0 & 2 & 0 & 0 \\
0 & 1 & 0 & 0 & 0 & 0 & 0 & 0 & 0 & 0 \\
1 & 0 & 0 & 0 & 0 & 0 & 0 & 0 & 0 & 0 \\
0 & 0 & 0 & 0 & 0 & 0 & 0 & 0 & 0 & 0 \\
0 & 0 & 0 & 4 & 0 & 0 & 0 & 0 & 0 & 0 \\
0 & 0 & 0 & 0 & 0 & 0 & 0 & 2 & 0 & 0 \\
0 & 0 & 0 & 0 & 0 & 0 & 0 & 0 & 0 & 0 \\
2 & 1 & 0 & 0 & 0 & 0 & 0 & 0 & 0 & 0
\end{bmatrix}
$$

Figure 2–15   Example sparse array.

zero elements. For instance, the array in Fig. 2–15, which has 8 nonzero elements out of 80, is sparse; it is 90% zero.

Linearization

Multi-dimensional sparse arrays can be linearized through the techniques presented earlier in this chapter; however there would be much wasted space. Let us now consider two alternative representations that will store explicitly only the nonzero elements.

Vector Representation

Each nonzero element in a two-dimensional sparse array can be represented as a triple with the format (row-subscript, column-subscript, value). These triples then can be ordered by increasing row-subscript major and column-subscript minor, and can be stored as a vector. For example, using this approach, the 8-by-10 sparse array shown in Fig. 2–15 is represented by vector V, shown in Fig. 2–16.

	row	column	value
V(1):	1,	5,	1
V(2):	1,	8,	2
V(3):	2,	2,	1
V(4):	3,	1,	1
V(5):	5,	4,	4
V(6):	6,	8,	2
V(7):	8,	1,	2
V(8):	8,	2,	1

Figure 2–16   Vector representation of the sparse array of Fig. 2–15.

This storage mapping uses more space to represent any particular nonzero element but avoids representing the zero elements.

If the sparse array were one-dimensional, each nonzero element would be represented by a pair. In general, each nonzero element of an N-dimensional array is represented by an entry with $N + 1$ values.

Operations on the vector representation of the two-decimal sparse array must use the row and column information to determine where each value resides. One inconvenience with this form of representation is handling addition of nonzero elements to the array or changing previously nonzero elements to have zero value. The problem is not in changing the element's value, but in maintaining the order of nonzero elements in the representation vector. For example, if the above array were updated so that the element with subscripts (1,8) were to have value zero, then vector elements V(3) through V(8) should be shifted to become elements V(2) through V(7). Similarly, if the element with subscripts (4,6) were to be updated to have value 9, then vector elements V(5) through V(8) would need to be shifted to become elements V(6) through V(9) and V(5) would be the triple (4,6,9).

Linked-list Representation

Another representation for sparse arrays is to use linked lists. We defer consideration of that important alternative until Chapter 6, which discusses linked lists.

SUMMARY

An *array* is a finite, ordered set of homogeneous elements. The elements of an array are referred to by their positions, as specified by subscripts. The composition of arrays in which each element is an array results in multi-dimensional arrays. The chapter introduced the declaration of arrays in COBOL and Pascal programs.

One-dimensional arrays can be mapped to storage in a straightforward linear way. In order to calculate the starting address of a particular element, it is necessary to know the base location of the array and the size of each preceding element in the array.

Multi-dimensional arrays must be linearized as they are mapped to storage. The most common linearization techniques for a two-dimensional array are to store the elements in row-major order (COBOL, Pascal, C, and PL/I) or in column-major order (FORTRAN).

The chapter terminated with a discussion of two special types of arrays: triangular arrays and sparse arrays. Use of the conventional array-linearization techniques generally results in excessive space requirements for these array types. Linearization techniques that are tailored to the characteristics of triangular and sparse arrays include storing two triangular arrays together in a single square array and representing only the nonzero elements of a sparse array.

Techniques for addressing into arrays are covered in detail in Chapter 13 in the sections on address calculation techniques for relative files.

TERMS

array	sparse array
base location	strictly triangular array
column-major order	subscript
cross-section	table
index	transpose
lower bound	triangular array
lower-triangular array	upper bound
range	upper-triangular array
row-major order	vector

SELECTED REFERENCES

DeMillo, R. A., S. C. Eistenstat, and R. J. Lipton. "Preserving average proximity in arrays," *Comm. ACM* 21(3): 228–231, March 1978.

Greenberg, H. J. and R. P. O'Neill. "Representing super-sparse matrices with perturbed values," *Comm. ACM* 24(7): 451–456, July 1981.

Hellerman, H. "Addressing multidimensional arrays," *Comm. ACM* 5(4): 205–207, April 1962.

MacVeigh, D. T. "Effect of data representation on cost of sparse matrix operations," *Acta Informatica* 7(4): 361–394, 1977.

Pooch, U. W., and A. Nieder. "A survey of indexing techniques for sparse matrices," *ACM Computing Surveys* 5(2): 109–133, June 1973.

Rosenberg, A. L. and L. J. Stockmeyer. "Hashing schemes for extendible arrays," *Jour. ACM* 24(2): 199–221, April, 1977.

Rosenberg, A. L., and L. J. Stockmeyer. "Storage schemes for boundedly extendible arrays," *Acta Informatica* 7(3): 289–303, 1977.

Rosenberg, A. L. "Allocating storage for extendible arrays," *Jour. ACM* 21(4): 652–670, Oct. 1974.

Standish, T. A. "Arrays," Chapter 8 in *Data Structure Techniques*, Reading, Mass.: Addison-Wesley Publishing Co., pp. 348–376, 1980.

Tarjan, R. E. and A. C. Yao. "Storing a sparse table," *Comm. ACM* 22(11): 606–611, Nov. 1979.

REVIEW EXERCISES

1. In an array with columns numbered from 4 through 13 and rows from 6 through 12, what is the maximum number of elements that can be stored?

2. What is meant by the terms "row-major order" and "column-major order"?

3. How many elements are in the array SPACE($A:B,C:D$)?

4. How many elements can be held by an array with dimension A($1:N$)? B($-N:0,3$)?

5. The array TEST($1:10,1:5$) is stored in memory by columns. If base location $B = 0$ and element size $S = 1$, what is the address of element TEST(7,2)?

6. Given ARRAY(10:30, 10:100), with base location = 50 and element size = 8 bits
   (a) How many elements are in ARRAY?
   (b) What is the starting location of ARRAY(21,75) if ARRAY is stored by row?

7. Given array A(50:100, 50:75), what is starting location of A(62,56)?

8. Write an expression to find the address of the jth element in the ith row of the array IVAN ($B: A,D:C$), where each element in the array takes up n words of memory. Assume the starting location is 0.

9. Consider array Q($A:B,C:D,E:F$), base location = X, length of element = L.
   (a) Find the total number of elements of the array.

(b) Find the starting location of $Q(I,J,K)$. What have you assumed about how the array is linearized and stored?

10. What is the maximum number of dimensions available for arrays in COBOL?

11. Given the COBOL array

```
01   TABLE.
     03   TABLE-ROW OCCURS 50 TIMES.
          05   TABLE-COL OCCURS 4 TIMES.
               07   TABLE-DEPTH OCCURS 6 TIMES PIC XX.
```

How many elements does the table contain?

12. Illustrate and describe one method of representation for sparse arrays.

13. Write an algorithm to transpose an array.

14. Write a transpose for the following sparse array where you store the array as a vector of (row-subscript, column-subscript, value) triples.

$$\begin{bmatrix} 0 & 0 & 1 & 0 & 0 & 0 \\ 2 & 0 & 0 & 0 & 3 & 0 \\ 0 & 0 & 0 & 9 & 0 & 1 \\ 0 & 16 & 0 & 0 & 0 & 0 \end{bmatrix}$$

15. Write an algorithm to compute the product of two sparse matrices each represented as an array.

16. Show how two triangular arrays can be stored together.

17. What are the trade-offs to be considered when storing two triangular arrays in one square space?

18. Show that an upper-triangular array with N rows has no more than $N(N + 1)/2$ nonzero elements.

19. Consider storage of a lower-triangular N-by-N array T by rows in a one-dimensional array S with subscript bounds 1 through $N(N + 1)/2$. What is the subscript in S of element $T(I,J)$? (Difficult!)

20. A regularly occurring type of sparse array is a "tridiagonal" array, where all elements except those on the main diagonal and the diagonals immediately above and below the main diagonal are zero. A 5-by-5 tridiagonal, for example, has the structure

$$\begin{bmatrix} a_{11} & a_{12} & 0 & 0 & 0 \\ a_{21} & a_{22} & a_{23} & 0 & 0 \\ 0 & a_{32} & a_{33} & a_{34} & 0 \\ 0 & 0 & a_{43} & a_{44} & a_{45} \\ 0 & 0 & 0 & a_{54} & a_{55} \end{bmatrix}$$

Consider storing a tridiagonal array in a singly subscripted array $B(I)$, with a_{11} in $B(1)$, a_{12} in $B(2)$, a_{21} in $B(3)$, a_{22} in $B(4)$, a_{23} in $B(5)$, etc. What is the subscript in B of element a_{ij}?

21. Write a program that traverses a maze. The maze is a two-dimensional 12-by-12 table with values of 1 indicating possible paths and 0s indicating walls. Figure P2–21 is an example maze.

0	0	0	0	0	0	0	0	0	0	0	0
0	0	0	0	0	0	1	1	0	0	0	0
0	1	0	0	0	0	1	1	1	0	0	0
0	1	0	0	0	0	1	0	1	0	1	0
1	1	0	0	1	1	1	0	1	1	1	1
0	1	1	1	0	0	1	0	0	0	1	0
0	1	0	1	0	0	1	0	0	0	0	0
0	0	0	1	0	1	1	1	1	0	0	0
0	1	1	1	1	0	1	0	0	0	1	0
0	1	0	0	0	0	1	0	0	0	1	0
0	1	0	0	0	0	1	0	0	0	1	0
0	1	1	1	1	1	1	1	1	1	1	0

Figure P2–21 Example maze.

There will be a single element in the first column with the value 1 and that will be the starting point. There will also be only a single value in the last column that is 1, which will be the ending point. The maze will be read in with one row per line. The row's values will be in the first 12 columns of the line.

Make up your own maze for testing purposes, then use the above example.

Output should consist of the path (excluding wrong turns), specified by row and column of the elements traversed, from the beginning to the end of the maze. You cannot traverse diagonals.

22. There is a data type known as a variable-length string, which has a length attribute that may take on different values over time. Consider an array of variable-length strings, for example the array MONTH(1:12), where each element is a string of 0 to 9 characters, whose value is the name of the corresponding month. One way to store this array is to allocate space for 9 characters for each element, regardless of how much space is actually used. How could this array be stored so that the amount of empty space allocated to the array is minimized? Does your technique work if there will be modification of the values of the elements of the array?

23. Why do the conventional algorithms for finding array elements require that all elements be of the same data structure type?

24. Some programming languages, for example COBOL and FORTRAN, use 1 as the default lower-bound for arrays. Others, for example C, use 0 as the default lower-bound. Suggest programming practices that might help to avoid difficulties in subscripting that might be encountered in converting a FORTRAN program to C (or vice versa).

25. Some programming languages like FORTRAN, store arrays in column-major order. Others, like C and COBOL, store arrays in row-major order. Illustrate by example the problems encountered in passing arrays between FORTRAN and C or COBOL programs.

26. Consider array Q ($-1:1,1:2,1:3$).
    (a) How many elements are in Q?
    (b) List the sequence of elements if Q is stored in row-major order.
    (c) List the sequence of elements if Q is stored in column-major order.

```
┌─────────────────────────────────────────────┐
│  ┌───────────────────────────────────────┐   │
│  │                                       │   │
│  │                                       │   │
│  │                                       │   │
│  │ ── chapter three ──────               │   │
│  │                                       │   │
│  │                                       │   │
│  │                                       │   │
│  │ ── records ─────────                  │   │
│  │                                       │   │
│  │                                       │   │
│  │                                       │   │
│  └───────────────────────────────────────┘   │
└─────────────────────────────────────────────┘
```

This chapter introduces a simple data structure that is of major importance: the record. The record data structure is defined and compared with the other data types that have already been introduced, then facilities for declaring records in COBOL and Pascal are reviewed. The record data structure is a composite of other data structuring techniques and this chapter is quite brief. The mapping of record variables to storage is straightforward and the operations on records will be already familiar.

Records are the basic components of files and of databases. The record data structure introduced in this chapter will be an elementary construct used in the remainder of the text.

DEFINITIONS

A *record* is a finite, ordered collection of possibly heterogeneous elements that are treated as a unit. A record is distinguished from an array in that all elements in an array must have the same structure, but the component elements of a record may have different data structures. A record is sometimes referred to simply as a *structure*. The elements of a record are commonly called fields. A *field* is a specified area of a record used for a particular kind of information.

Forming Records

A unit of information derives at least some of its meaning from its relationship to other information. The record data structure enables a set of elements of logically related information to be explicitly grouped. For example, the string field named JOB-TITLE with value 'ANALYST' does not bear much information on its own. However, more information is conveyed when the JOB-TITLE field is coupled with other logically related fields, such as EMP-NO of type *string* with value '123456789' and PAY-RATE of type *decimal* with value 15.93. These heterogeneous elements cannot form an array because they are different data structures. They can, however, be grouped to form a record of employee information, as shown in Fig. 3–1.

JOB-TITLE	EMP-NO	PAY-RATE
ANALYST	123456789	15.93

Figure 3–1   Example record.

Examples

An element of a record may be a composite data structure, like another record or an array. For example, an employee's record might contain NAME and OFFICE-ADDR fields, as shown in Fig. 3–2.

JOB-TITLE	EMP-NO	PAY-RATE	NAME			OFFICE-ADDR	
			LAST	FIRST	INIT	BLDG	ROOM
ANALYST	123456789	15.93	MUD	JOE	N	CSC	403

Figure 3–2   Example record.

It might also contain an array of PROJECT-CODES, as shown in Fig. 3–3.

JOB-TITLE	EMP-NO	PAY-RATE	NAME			OFFICE-ADDR		PROJECT-CODES				
			LAST	FIRST	INIT	BLDG	ROOM					
ANALYST	123456789	15.93	MUD	JOE	N	CSC	403	18	40	41	50	53

Figure 3–3   Example record containing an array.

A field with no subordinate fields is called an *elementary item*; a field with subordinate fields is called a *group item*. OFFICE-ADDR and NAME are group items in the example above.

Composite records like this are quite common. It is also possible to have an array of elements of type record within a record. For example, an employee record might have an array of two TELEPHONE-NO group items, as shown in Fig. 3–4.

JOB-TITLE	EMP-NO	PAY-RATE	NAME			OFFICE-ADDR		PROJECT-CODES					TELEPHONE-NO			
			LAST	FIRST	INIT	BLDG	ROOM						AREA	LOCAL	AREA	LOCAL
ANALYST	123456789	15.93	MUD	JOE	N	CSC	403	18	40	41	50	53	202	2991673	301	6263116

Figure 3–4   Example record containing arrays and sub-records.

This EMPLOYEE record data structure is composed of the fields named JOB-TITLE, EMP-NO, PAY-RATE, NAME, OFFICE-ADDR, PROJECT-CODES, and TELE-PHONE-NO, each, of course, with its own data structure. The variable EMPLOYEE can take on various values over time.

Identifying Keys

A record generally contains an identifying field. Continuing the above example, a particular employee's EMPLOYEE record occurrence is identified by the value in its EMP-NO field. The identifying field of a record is called its *key* field. The key of a record may be either an elementary item or a group item. For example, a particular class's COURSE record might be identified by the value of its DEPARTMENT, NUMBER, and SECTION fields.

Files

A collection of logically related record occurrences that are treated as a unit is called a *file*. Usually all of a file's record occurrences are of a single record format. Sometimes, however, there are several record formats on one file. For example, an EMPLOYEE record occurrence might be followed by several record occurrences of type PROJECT-RESPONSIBILITY, each detailing the employee's efforts on a particular project.

A major portion of this text is devoted to the topic of organizing files of records in such a way that they can effectively support applications processing. Although most files are stored on secondary-storage media, some relatively small, commonly used files are stored in primary memory.

The operations that are legal upon records are those that are defined upon the contained fields, based upon their data structures.

RECORDS IN COBOL AND PASCAL

Let us consider now the facilities that allow declaration of record variables in COBOL and Pascal.

COBOL

COBOL uses a system of *level-numbers* to indicate the structures of records. A record description begins with the record name, which is always at the 01 level, and includes then the specifications for the fields contained in the record. For example, the EMPLOYEE record of the preceding section would be declared in the DATA DIVISION of a COBOL program as follows.

```
01  EMPLOYEE.
    02  JOB-TITLE           PICTURE X(7).
    02  EMP-NO              PICTURE X(9).
    02  PAY-RATE            PICTURE 9(2)V9(2).
    02  NAME.
        03  L-NAME          PICTURE X(12).
        03  F-NAME          PICTURE X(8).
        03  INIT            PICTURE X.
    02  OFFICE-ADDR.
        03  BLDG            PICTURE X(3).
        03  ROOM            PICTURE 9(3).
    02  PROJECT-CODES OCCURS 5 TIMES PICTURE 9(2).
    02  TELEPHONE-NO OCCURS 2 TIMES.
        03  AREA-CODE       PICTURE 9(3).
        03  LOCAL           PICTURE 9(7).
```

Each item description is preceded by a level-number taken from the set {01, 02, 03, . . ., 49}*; the combination of these level-numbers describes the hierarchical structure of the fields in the record. An increase in level-numbers, as from 01 to 02 between EMPLOYEE and JOB-TITLE and from 02 to 03 between NAME and L-NAME, between OFFICE-ADDR and BLDG, and between TELEPHONE-NO and AREA-CODE, indicates subdivision of a group item into its component fields. The group-item EMPLOYEE comprises JOB-TITLE, EMP-NO, PAY-RATE, NAME, OFFICE-ADDR, PROJECT-CODES and TELEPHONE-NO. The group-item TELEPHONE-NO, which is an array with two occurrences, comprises AREA-CODE and LOCAL.

Note that only the elementary items have PICTURE clauses. This data-typing information is not used on group items, because their structures are defined by the elementary items they contain.

A deeper hierarchy in COBOL would require use of greater level-numbers. For instance, the LOCAL part of the telephone number could be subdivided into two elementary items named EXCHANGE and NUMB.

```
    02  TELEPHONE-NO OCCURS 2 TIMES.
        03  AREA-CODE       PICTURE 9(3).
        03  LOCAL.
            04  EXCHANGE    PICTURE 9(3).
            04  NUMB        PICTURE 9(4).
```

Note that LOCAL no longer includes typing information because now it is not an elementary item.

PL/I uses level-numbers in essentially the same way as COBOL does, except that PL/I uses level 1 instead of level 01, level 2 instead of level 02, and so forth.

---

* Level-numbers from 01 to 09 can be written without the leading 0. Special meanings are given to the additional level-numbers 66, 77, 88.

Pascal

Pascal uses a blocking facility rather than the level-number convention to define record structures. Each entry to be subdivided is bracketed by record and end, to indicate the grouping of data elements.

```
type name = record
                lname : packed array [1 . . 12] of char;
                fname : packed array [1 . . 8] of char;
                init : char
            end;
     addr = record
                bldg : packed array [1 . . 3] of char;
                room : integer
            end;
     localphone = record
                exchange : integer;
                numb : integer
            end;
     phoneno = record
                areacode : integer;
                local : localphone
            end;
     employeerec = record
                jobtitle : packed array [1 . . 7] of char;
                empno : packed array [1 . . 9] of char;
                payrate : real;
                empname : name;
                officeaddr : addr;
                projectcodes : array [1 . . 5] of integer;
                telephoneno : array [1 . . 2] of phoneno
            end;
```

This example shows the definition of new data types, here name, addr, localphone, phoneno, and employeerec. This type statement could be followed by the definition of variables with the defined structures.

```
var employee : employeerec;
```

Qualified Names

To refer to a particular element of a record structure, a uniquely identifying variable name must be used. If the simple field name is unique, then it suffices. If the field name is not unique, then some form of qualification must be used to make it unique. For example, consider the following COBOL record structure.

```
01   STUDENT.
     . . .
     02   BIRTH-DATE.
          03   MM              PICTURE 99.
          03   DD              PICTURE 99.
```

```
                         03   YY                    PICTURE 99.

                 . . .
                 02  UNDERGRAD.
                         03   MATRIC-DATE.
                                 04   MM          PICTURE 99.
                                 04   DD          PICTURE 99.
                                 04   YY          PICTURE 99.
                         03   DEGREE-DATE.
                                 04   MM          PICTURE 99.
                                 04   DD          PICTURE 99.
                                 04   YY          PICTURE 99.

                 . . .
                 02  GRAD.
                         03   MATRIC-DATE.
                                 04   MM          PICTURE 99.
                                 04   DD          PICTURE 99.
                                 04   YY          PICTURE 99.
                         03   DEGREE-DATE.
                                 04   MM          PICTURE 99.
                                 04   DD          PICTURE 99.
                                 04   YY          PICTURE 99.

                 . . .
```

The data name YY is not unique, but it can be qualified to show which YY in the structure is referred to, for example YY OF BIRTH-DATE. However, YY OF MATRIC-DATE is not unique and further qualification is necessary: either YY OF MATRIC-DATE OF UNDERGRAD or YY OF MATRIC-DATE OF GRAD. A fully qualified variable name refers all the way back to the 01 level; for example YY OF MATRIC-DATE OF GRAD OF STUDENT.

Pascal uses a slightly different convention for qualification of variable names. The examples of the preceding paragraph would be the following.

> birthdate.yy
> undergrad.matricdate.yy
> grad.matricdate.yy
> student.grad.matricdate.yy

Traffic Flow Example

Fig. 3–5 is another example of a record data structure and its declaration in COBOL and Pascal. The record contains information about traffic flow at an intersection.

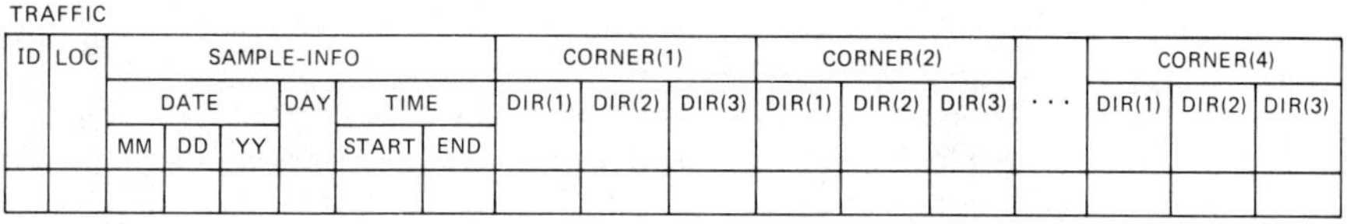

TRAFFIC

ID	LOC	SAMPLE-INFO						CORNER(1)			CORNER(2)				CORNER(4)		
		DATE			DAY	TIME		DIR(1)	DIR(2)	DIR(3)	DIR(1)	DIR(2)	DIR(3)	· · ·	DIR(1)	DIR(2)	DIR(3)
		MM	DD	YY		START	END										

Figure 3–5   Example traffic-flow record.

In COBOL this record could be declared as

```
01  TRAFFIC.
    02  ID                          PICTURE 99.
    02  LOC                         PICTURE X(5).
    02  SAMPLE-INFO.
        03  SAMPLE-DATE.
            04  MM                  PICTURE 99.
            04  DD                  PICTURE 99.
            04  YY                  PICTURE 99.
        03  SAMPLE-DAY              PICTURE X(3).
        03  SAMPLE-TIME.
            04  START-TIME          PICTURE 9(4).
            04  END-TIME            PICTURE 9(4).
    02  CORNER OCCURS 4 TIMES.
        03  DIR OCCURS 3 TIMES      PICTURE 9(6).
```

In Pascal the declaration could be

```
type date = record
              mm: integer;
              dd: integer;
              yy: integer
            end;
     time = record
              starttime: integer;
              endtime: integer;
            end;
     sampleinfo = record
                    sampledate: dates;
                    day: packed array [1 . . 3] of char;
                    sampletime: time
                  end;
     trafficrec = record
                    id: integer;
                    loc: packed array [1 . . 5] of char;
                    trafficsample: sampleinfo;
                    dir: array [1 . . 4, 1 . . 3] of integer
                  end;
var traffic: trafficrec;
```

FORTRAN does not have a facility for declaration of record variables. Rather, each of the component elementary items is defined separately; their grouping to form a record is only implicit. Program logic or documentation should indicate that a group of fields actually forms a record.

MAPPINGS TO STORAGE

Records are nearly always mapped linearly to storage. Memory is allocated to each of the elementary items in the record, in order and contiguously by order of appearance in the declaration. For instance, in the above TRAFFIC record, the memory layout would be as shown in Fig. 3–5.

This linear mapping technique often causes data elements to begin off word boundaries. On some machines, certain types of processing require that data be aligned on a certain type of boundary: halfword, fullword, or doubleword. In order to ensure correct alignment in these cases it may be necessary for the programmer to insert space containing no meaningful data between data elements. This filler space is called *slack bytes* or *padding*.

Proper alignment of data elements and natural boundaries can result in more efficient execution of some arithmetic and subscripting operations. When data elements appear between word boundaries or if they cross word boundaries, they may need to be moved elsewhere in order to execute some machine operations. Synchronization can be accomplished by recognizing word boundaries and organizing data appropriately using padding in the data structure, or, in COBOL, by using the SYNCHRONIZED clause. See a COBOL language manual for details of this clause.

SUMMARY

A *record* is a finite, ordered collection of possibly heterogeneous elements, which may themselves be composite structures (records or arrays). The primary purpose of the record data structure is to group together for input/output purposes logically related fields. The elements of a record can be referred to individually within a program, and the entire group of elements in the record can be treated collectively for input/output operations.

The operations that can be performed on the elements of a data structure are defined by their individual data types.

The mapping of a record to storage is generally simple and linear. Sometimes padding space is inserted within a record for purposes of enhancing the efficiency of certain arithmetic operations. This space can be inserted explicitly or by use of a programming language feature such as the COBOL SYNCHRONIZED clause.

Records are important because they can preserve the natural logical structure of related items of information.

TERMS

elementary item	level-number
field	padding
file	record
group item	slack bytes
key	structure

SELECTED REFERENCES

COBOL, PL/I, and Pascal textbooks and language manuals.

MARCH, S. T. "Techniques for structuring database records," *ACM Computing Surveys* 15(1): 45–79, March 1983.

REVIEW EXERCISES

1. What is the difference between an array and a record? Can an array be part of a record? Can a record be part of an array?

2. Why might a programmer decompose a field into component pieces?

3. Two programs access the same file of records. One program treats *phoneno* as an elementary item, while the other program considers *phoneno* to be a group item. Why the discrepancy?

4. Just based on the contents of this chapter, why do you think FORTRAN has been considered not to be a business-oriented programming language?

5. What are the trade-offs to be considered in brute-force use of padding and use of the COBOL SYNCHRONIZED feature?

6. Find out what the structure of records is on your local student or employee file.

7. Study several examples of record declarations in COBOL or Pascal programs.

8. Write a program to read data into the structure of the EMPLOYEE record used as an example in this chapter.

9. Commonly all the record occurrences in a file have the same data structure. Sometimes, however, there are several record structures in a single file. What are the trade-offs between (a) mixing STUDENT and CLASS records in a single file, and (b) putting each kind of record in its own file? Give a situation where option a) would be more appropriate, and one where option b) would be more appropriate.

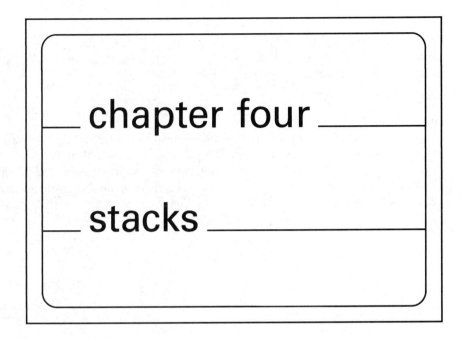

chapter four

stacks

One of the most commonly used linear data structures is the stack. The operations that define the stack data structure are introduced; then the facilities for declaring and manipulating stacks are discussed. Much of this chapter is devoted to examples of the use of stacks.

DEFINITIONS

Linear List

A *linear list* is a data structure comprised of an ordered set of elements; the number of elements in the list can vary. We will denote the linear list named A comprised of T elements as

$$A = [A_1, A_2, \ldots, A_T].$$

If $T = 0$, then A is said to be an empty or null list. An element can be deleted from any position in the linear list and a new element can be inserted into any position in the list. The list can grow or shrink over time.

Stack

A *stack* is a special case of linear list in which insertion and deletion operations are restricted to occur only at one end, which is referred to as the stack's *top*. We denote by Top(S) the top element of the stack S. For stack S, where

$$S = [S_1, S_2, \ldots, S_T]$$

the Top(S) is S_T.

We use Noel(S) to denote the number of elements in stack S. Noel(S) is an attribute of stack S and has an integer value. For the stack S above. Noel(S) is T.

The Noel[th] element of a stack is the top element. We can draw logical pictures of stacks such that their tops are to the up or the down direction, or draw them horizontally such that their tops are to the left or the right direction (Fig. 4–1).

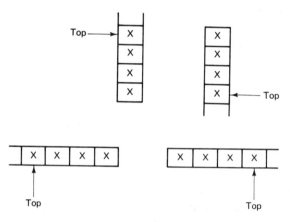

Figure 4–1   Drawings of stacks.

It does not really matter, as long as we are consistent for any particular stack. Here we generally use the convention of having the top in the up direction.

In any case, for stack

$$S = [S_1, S_2, \ldots S_{Noel}]$$

we will say that element S_I is above element S_J, for $I > J$. S_I is more accessible than the elements that it is above, that is, S_I will be taken off the stack before any element that is below it. S_I has been in the stack for less time than any of the elements that it is above.

Any picture that we draw of a stack is really only a snapshot in time. The top element changes as the stack grows and shrinks; the bottom remains fixed.

Examples

A common example of a stack is a pile of trays in a cafeteria. The trays are supported by a spring mechanism in a casing such that only the top tray is visible and available for removal (Fig. 4–2). Adding another tray to the top of the stack compresses the spring; removing a tray lightens the load on the spring so that the next tray appears at the counter level.

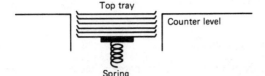

Figure 4–2   Example stack of trays.

Another example of a stack is a railway system used to shunt cars from one position to another (Fig. 4–3).

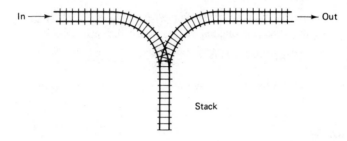

Figure 4–3   Tracks forming a stack.

The last railcar placed on the stack is the first one that can be taken off the stack.

Stack Operations

There are four basic operations that are legal for data type *stack*:

1. Create (stack)
2. Isempty (stack)
3. Push (element, stack)
4. Pop (stack)

The Create(S) operator returns an empty stack with name S. By definition

Noel (Create(S)) is 0
and   Top (Create(S)) is null.

The Isempty operator determines whether or not a stack is empty. The operand is a stack; the result is a boolean. Isempty(S) is true if stack S is empty (that is, if Noel(S) = 0) and false otherwise. Note that Isempty (Create(S)) is true.

Adding an element to a stack is called pushing the stack. Push(E,S) adds element E to the top of stack S. The result is the augmented stack. Note that

Top(Push(E,S)) is E.

Push(E,S) also increments Noel(S). The result of pushing an element onto any stack cannot be an empty stack:

> Isempty(Push(E,S)) is false.

Removing an element from a stack is called popping the stack. Pop(S) removes an element from the top of stack S. The result is the decreased stack. If the popped element should be saved, action to do so should be taken prior to the pop operation. Note that Pop(S) decrements Noel(S). It is an error to try to pop an element from an empty stack:

> Pop(Create(S)) yields an error condition.

In the absence of such an error, Pop(S) decrements Noel(S) and changes Top(S).
The pop operator undoes the results of the push operator:

> Pop(Push(E,S)) is S.

You might find it useful to derive other tautologies from combinations of the elementary stack operators.

Example

Let us start with an empty stack and consider the effects of a sequence of pushes and pops. We represent the empty stack S pictorially in Fig. 4–4(a).

S   Noel(S) = 0, Top(S) undefined.   **Figure 4–4(a)**

First push on the element A, giving S = [A], (Fig. 4–4(b)):

S   Noel(S) = 1, Top(S) = A,   **Figure 4–4(b)**

then push on the element B, giving S = [A,B], (Fig. 4–4(c)):

S   Noel(S) = 2, Top(S) = B,   **Figure 4–4(c)**

then push on the element C, giving S = [A,B,C], (Fig. 4–4(d)).

S   Noel(S) = 3, Top(S) = C.   **Figure 4–4(d)**

We could pop an element, giving S = [A,B], (Fig. 4–4(e)):

S   Noel(S) = 2, Top(S) = B,   **Figure 4–4(e)** then perhaps push on two more elements, say D then E, giving S = [A,B,D,E], (Fig. 4–4(f)):

E
D
B
A
S   Noel(S) = 4, Top(S) = E.   **Figure 4–4(f)**

We might then want to pop an element off the stack, giving S = [A,B,D], (Fig. 4–4(g)):

D
B
A
S   Noel(S) = 3, Top(S) = D,   **Figure 4–4(g)**

and so forth. The stack is said to operate in a *last-in-first-out* (LIFO) manner. Elements are removed in the reverse of the order in which they were inserted onto the stack.

STACKS IN COBOL AND PASCAL

Housing Stacks in Arrays

Although stacks are widely used, most programming languages do not have a built-in *stack* data structure. In order to program a solution for a problem that calls for use of a stack, the programmer must use the language's existing features to simulate the stack's operation. There are several ways to represent stacks. Perhaps the simplest way to represent stacks is to house them in arrays. In this section we introduce this method of handling stacks in COBOL and Pascal.

A stack can be housed in an array, but it is essential to recognize that a stack and an array are two different data structures with different rules. First, recall that there are no restrictions on where elements can be inserted into or deleted from an array. Thus it is the *programmer's* responsibility to enforce the LIFO rules for a stack that is housed in an array. Second, housing a stack in an array immediately constrains the stack to contain homogeneous elements. There is nothing in the concept of a stack that prevents it from holding a variety of types of elements. Another artificial constraint is imposed when the programmer must specify the upper bound on the array's subscript values. A stack variable has no constraint on the maximum number of elements that it may contain at any given time. (We could conceivably have an infinitely tall stack of cafeteria trays or poker chips.) However, a stack variable housed in an array is confined to the space allocated to that array. In fact, a stack grows and shrinks over time, but an array has a constant size.

Declaring Stacks

Let's consider the declaration of a stack variable named S. Assume that each element of S will be an integer and that S will have a maximum of 100 elements. In addition to declaring the array that will house S, we must declare a variable TOP-PTR whose value will be the subscript of the present top element of the stack. We name the combined array and top indicator the STACK-STRUCT. With this representation, Noel(S) = TOP-PTR. Isempty(S) is true when TOP-PTR = 0 and is false when TOP-PTR > 0.

In COBOL:

```
01   STACK-STRUCT.
     02   S                        OCCURS 100 TIMES
                                   PICTURE 9(5).
     02   TOP-PTR                  PICTURE 9(3).
```

In Pascal:

```
type stackstruct =
        record      stack: array [1..100] of integer;
                    topptr: integer
        end;
var     s: stackstruct;
```

If there were several stacks used in the same program, each would need its own top indicator. (Note that we used TOP-PTR because TOP is a COBOL reserved word.)

Stack Operations

A compiler will not detect violations to the LIFO rules of operation for a stack housed in an array. The programmer must be careful not to index into S anywhere except using the value of TOP-PTR.

The operations of pushing and popping S can be programmed as follows. We use EON to be the element to be pushed onto S and EOFF to be the element popped off of S. Note that we save EOFF. We will use the variable NOEL-MAX to be the maximum number of elements that S's array can accommodate; here NOEL-MAX = 100. Throughout we indicate that the application determines the actions to be taken when an overflow condition (attempt to push onto a full stack) or an underflow condition (attempt to pop an empty stack) occurs.

In COBOL paragraphs:

```
PUSH.
     IF TOP-PTR < NOEL-MAX
     THEN COMPUTE TOP-PTR = TOP-PTR + 1
            MOVE EON TO S (TOP-PTR)
     ELSE overflow-condition.
POP.
     IF TOP-PTR > 0
     THEN MOVE S (TOP-PTR) TO EOFF
            COMPUTE TOP-PTR = TOP-PTR - 1
     ELSE underflow-condition.
```

In Pascal procedures:

```
procedure push (eon:integer);
begin if (s. topptr < noelmax)
    then begin s.topptr : = s.topptr + 1;
                   s.stack [s.topptr] : = eon
          end
      else OVERFLOW-CONDITION
end;
procedure pop (var eoff:integer);
begin if (s.topptr > 0)
    then begin eoff : = s.stack [s.topptr];
                   s.topptr : = s.topptr − 1
          end
      else UNDERFLOW-CONDITION
end;
```

We have assumed that S is a globally known variable.

It is important to caution again that the integrity of a stack must be maintained by the programmer when the stack is housed in an array. It is the programmer's responsibility to ensure that only the top pointer is used as the point of reference into the stack.

There are other ways to represent a stack variable even when there is no built-in stack data structure. We will discuss these representations later, as in chapter 6 on linked lists.

EXAMPLE APPLICATIONS OF STACKS

Stacks are used extensively in solving a wide variety of problems. They are used by compilers, by operating systems, and by applications programs. In this section we outline several uses of stacks; there are many others. We will look at three examples and will use one of our illustrative languages (COBOL or Pascal) in each.

Example: Matching Parentheses

One task of a compiler is to verify that the programmer has adhered to the grammatical rules (syntax) of the programming language. Consider the syntax verification problem of ensuring that for each left parenthesis there is a corresponding right parenthesis. A stack can be used to facilitate the matching procedure.

The algorithm is simple. We scan the string elements left to right. Whenever we encounter a left parenthesis, we push it onto a stack. Whenever we hit a right parenthesis, we check the state of the stack. If it is empty, then we have found a right parenthesis that does not close a left parenthesis and have an error. If the stack is not empty, we have found a pair and merely pop the stack. If the stack is not empty at the end of the string, then there is at least one unclosed left parenthesis. At any point in the scan, the number of elements in the stack is the nesting depth of the parenthesis. A given program statement

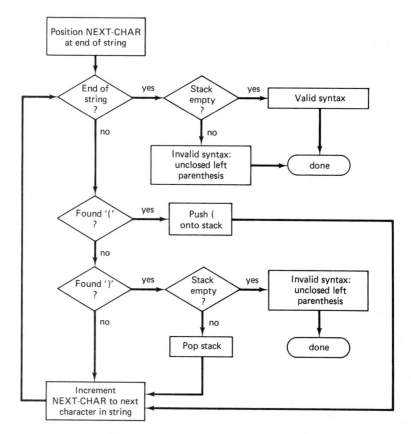

Figure 4–5 Logic for matching parentheses.

has a parenthesis nesting depth that varies, depending upon how far through the statement the scan has proceeded. A flowchart for this algorithm is given in Fig. 4–5.

We program this routine in COBOL. The string to be scanned is stored character-by-character in an array STRING. The stack is housed in an array STACK. Assume we know that 80 is the maximum number of characters in the string and that the actual string terminates with a semicolon (;). The data structures are defined by

```
01  STACK-STRUCT.
    02  STACK              OCCURS 80 TIMES
                           PICTURE X.
    02  TOP-PTR            PICTURE 99 VALUE 0.
01  STRING.
    02  CHAR               OCCURS 80 TIMES
                           PICTURE X.
01  NEXT-CHAR              PICTURE 99.
```

These structures are manipulated by the following code:

```
PERFORM SCAN-NEXT-CHAR
        VARYING NEXT-CHAR FROM 1 BY 1
        UNTIL NEXT-CHAR > 80
            OR CHAR(NEXT-CHAR) = ";".
IF TOP-PTR = 0
    valid syntax
ELSE invalid-syntax-unclosed-left-parenthesis.
```

where

```
SCAN-NEXT-CHAR.
    IF CHAR(NEXT-CHAR) = "("
        PERFORM PUSH
    ELSE IF CHAR(NEXT-CHAR) = ")"
        PERFORM POP.
PUSH.
    COMPUTE TOP-PTR = TOP-PTR + 1.
    MOVE CHAR(NEXT-CHAR) TO STACK(TOP-PTR).
POP.
    IF TOP-PTR = 0
        Invalid-syntax-no-matching-left-parenthesis
    ELSE COMPUTE TOP-PTR = TOP-PTR - 1.
```

Actually, for the purposes of this problem, in which we never look at elements as they are popped off the stack, it suffices just to keep track of the number of elements that are in the stack at any given time. The stack can be virtual.

A more interesting syntax-verification problem is the construction of an algorithm for matching not just left and right parentheses, but also left and right square brackets and left and right curly braces in the same string. For instance, the algorithm should be able to have the following string for input and determine whether or not the bracket symbols are properly matched:

$$(\{A + B*C/([D + E - (F + G)*(A + B)])*(F - G + B)\}/(D - E - (A + B))).$$

Developing and coding the algorithm are left as an exercise. How many stacks are needed?

In this problem, as in many others that call for the use of stacks, the stack contains a record of postponed obligations which need to be attended to in LIFO order.

Example: Recursion

Stacks are commonly used to keep track of where a program is when it contains procedures that call themselves. These procedures are known as *recursive* procedures.

For example, consider the problem of becoming a millionaire. To have a million dollars 25 years from now, how much money do you need to deposit in the bank today at an annually compounded interest rate of 8%? One way to program this problem is to use a recursive procedure. Let's approach the problem in the following way: Assume that you're sitting comfortably 25 years in the future and now have one million dollars. How

much money did you have in the bank in year 24? At that time, you had that amount
which at a rate of 8% would yield one million dollars in one year. That is, one million
divided by 1.08. How much did you need to have in the year 23? And so forth.

The following Pascal program uses a recursive procedure called *compound* to calculate the amount that you need to deposit in year 1 in order to reach a goal of one million
in 25 years.

```
     program retire(output);
     const goal = 1000000; rate = 0.08;
     var nowhave:real; yr:integer;
1    procedure compound(var yr: integer); {determines amount in
     savings 1 year earlier}
2    begin if(yr > 0)then
3        begin nowhave : = nowhave/(1.0 + rate);
4            yr : = yr − 1;
5            compound(yr) end;
6    end; {compound}

7    begin yr : = 25; {main program block}
8        nowhave : = goal;
9        compound(yr);
10       write(nowhave); writeln;end;
11   end.
```

The value of the variable yr changes each time the procedure named compound is called,
starting at 25 and going to 0 at the termination of the program. A stack is used by the
system to keep track of where the retire program is at any given time during execution.
Each time that procedure compound is invoked, the calling address is pushed onto the
stack. Each time that compound is exited, the stack is popped and control returns to the
address that was on top. The first call to compound is in statement 9, and the control
stack is as shown in Fig. 4–6(a).

TOP-PTR ⟶ | 9 |

Figure 4–6(a)

The second invocation of compound is from statement 5 when yr has the value 24. The
control stack is as shown in Fig. 4–6(b).

TOP-PTR ⟶ | 5 |
           | 9 |

Figure 4–6(b)

The third call to compound is from statement 5 when yr has value 23. The control stack
then becomes as shown in Fig. 4–6(c).

TOP-PTR ⟶ | 5 |
           | 5 |
           | 9 |

Figure 4–6(c)

After 25 calls to the procedure compound, the stack is as shown in Fig. 4–6(d).

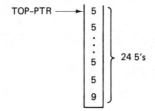

Figure 4–6(d)

There have been 24 calls from statement 5, and yr finally has the value 0. Now the stack comes into play as the calls are unraveled. Each invocation of compound needs to be returned from in sequence (LIFO) until the original call is reached. Return from the last call to compound results in popping the stack such that it is as shown in Fig. 4–6(e).

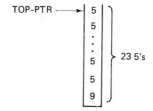

Figure 4–6(e)

Eventually, all of the addresses are popped off the control stack and we return to statement 9. The next statement writes the determined value of nowhave, which is the amount you need to deposit.

In this example, the Pascal compiler established the need for a stack and provided the instructions for properly pushing and popping the stack. In the prior example, the COBOL programmer carried all responsibility for handling the stack.

Some compilers are not able to handle recursive procedure calls because they do not have the needed stack mechanisms. Before programming one and expecting it to work (especially in COBOL or FORTRAN), check your local language manuals. Unfortunately, recursive procedures in these languages commonly compile apparently correctly but go haywire during execution.

Example: Postfix Notation

A third application of stacks is in the compilation of arithmetic expressions in high-level programming languages. The compiler needs to be able to translate from our usual form of representation of arithmetic statements (called *infix notation*) to a form that can more easily be used for generation of object code. For binary operators, such as addition, subtraction, multiplication, division, and exponentiation, the operator in infix notation appears between the two operands, e.g., $A + B, E \uparrow F$. Stacks can be used to transform this notation to what is known as *postfix notation*, in which both operands appear before the operator, e.g., $A B +, E F \uparrow$. This form is easier for the compiler to handle, as we shall see.

Consider the following algorithm, which converts expressions from infix to postfix notation. A stack is used to retain infix operators until their operands have been scanned. The expression is scanned left to right. There are four basic rules.

1. If the symbol is "("
   it is pushed onto the operator stack.

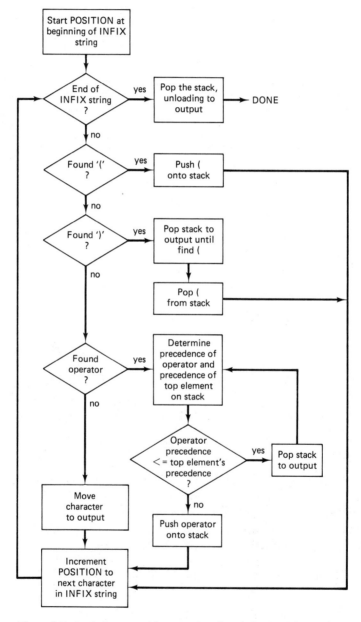

Figure 4–7 Logic for converting expressions from infix to postfix notation.

2. If the symbol is "')''

it pops everything from the operator stack down to the first "(." The operators go to output as they are popped off the stack. The "(" is popped but does not go to output.

3. If the symbol is an operator,

then if the operator on the top of the operator stack is of the same or higher precedence, that operator is popped and goes to output, continuing in this fashion until the first left parenthesis or an operator of lower precedence is met in the operator stack. When that situation occurs, then the current operator is pushed onto the stack.

4. If the symbol is an operand,

it goes directly to output.

The terminating symbol, here the semicolon, pops everything off the stack. A flowchart of the algorithm is shown in Fig. 4–7.

Let us first consider use of this algorithm with just three operator precedence levels.

Highest: Exponentiation ($\uparrow$)

Middle: Multiplication (*), Division (/)

Lowest: Addition (+), Subtraction (−)

Figure 4–8 shows the operator stack and the output as each character of the infix arithmetic expression

$$((A + B) * C/D + E \uparrow F)/G;$$

is scanned.

Time point	1	2	3	4	5	6	7	8	9	10	11	12	13	14	15	16	17	18
Character scanned	(	(	A	+	B	)	*	C	/	D	+	E	↑	F	)	/	G	;
Operator TOP → stack	(	(	(	+	+	(	*	*	/	/	+	+	↑	↑		/		
		(	(	(	(		(	(	(	(	(	(	+	+				
				(	(								(	(				
Output			A		B	+		C	*	D	/	E		F	↑+		G	/

Figure 4–8 Operator stack contents as each character is scanned.

The resultant postfix expression is

$$AB + C * D/EF \uparrow + G/.$$

Note that all parentheses have been removed from the expression. The parentheses were needed in infix notation to indicate the desired precedence of operators. In postfix notation, operator precedence is indicated solely by operator order. The postfix string can be scanned from left to right, setting up intermediate expressions which involve only binary operations as follows.

Step 1. $T_1 = AB+$ String becomes: $T_1\, C*D/EF \uparrow + G/$

Step 2. $T_2 = T_1\, C*$ String becomes: $T_2\, D/EF \uparrow + G/$

Step 3. $T_3 = T_2\, D/$ String becomes: $T_3\, EF \uparrow + G/$

Step 4. $T_4 = EF \uparrow$ String becomes: $T_3\, T_4 + G/$

Step 5. $T_5 = T_3\, T_4+$ String becomes: $T_5\, G/$

Step 6. $T_6 = T_5\, G/$ String becomes: T_6

You should note that no operator is scanned until after its two operands have been scanned. If you are familiar with an assembler-level language, it may be obvious the type of code the compiler would generate to implement the above six steps.

This algorithm can be programmed in COBOL as follows. The variables are declared in the *DATA DIVISION*.

```
01  OP-STACK.
    02  STACK OCCURS 100 TIMES      PICTURE X.
    02  TOP-PTR                     PICTURE 9(3).
    02  NOEL-MAX                    PICTURE 9(3)
                                        VALUE 100.
01  IN-STRING.
    02  INFIX OCCURS 100 TIMES      PICTURE X.
01  HOUSEKEEPING.
    02  POSITION                    PICTURE 9(3).
    02  NEXT-CHAR                   PICTURE X.
    02  EOFF                        PICTURE X.
    02  OP-PRECEDENCE               PICTURE 9.
    02  TOP-PRECEDENCE              PICTURE 9.
01  PRECEDENCE-RULE.
    02  CHAR-CHECK                  PICTURE X.
        88  LEVEL-0                 VALUE ' + ', ' − '.
        88  LEVEL-1                 VALUE '*', '/'.
        88  LEVEL-2                 VALUE ' ↑ '.
        88  LEVEL-3                 VALUE '('.
    02  PRECEDENCE-LEVEL            PICTURE 9.
```

In the *PROCEDURE DIVISION* the driver is

```
COMPUTE TOP-PTR = 0.
PERFORM SCAN-NEXT-CHAR
        VARYING POSITION FROM 1 BY 1
        UNTIL POSITION > NOEL-MAX OR INFIX (POSITION)
            = ';'.
PERFORM POP-STACK-TO-OUTPUT
        UNTIL TOP-PTR = 0.
```

and

```
SCAN-NEXT-CHAR.
      MOVE INFIX (POSITION) TO NEXT-CHAR.
      IF NEXT-CHAR = '('
            PERFORM PUSH-STACK
      ELSE IF NEXT-CHAR = ')'
            PERFORM POP-STACK-TO-OUTPUT
                  UNTIL STACK (TOP-PTR) = '('
            PERFORM POP-STACK
            ELSE IF NEXT-CHAR = ' ↑ ' OR '*' OR '/' OR ' + ' OR ' −
                  PERFORM FIND-OP-PRECEDENCE
                  PERFORM FIND-TOP-PRECEDENCE
                  PERFORM EMPTY-STACK-TO-LOWER-
                        PRECEDENCE UNTIL OP-PRECEDENCE >
                        TOP-PRECEDENCE
                  PERFORM PUSH-STACK
            ELSE DISPLAY NEXT-CHAR.
PUSH-STACK.
      COMPUTE TOP-PTR = TOP-PTR + 1.
      IF TOP-PTR > NOEL-MAX
            error-condition
      ELSE MOVE NEXT-CHAR TO STACK (TOP-PTR).
POP-STACK.
      IF TOP-PTR = 0
            error-condition
      ELSE MOVE STACK (TOP-PTR) TO EOFF
            COMPUTE TOP-PTR = TOP-PTR − 1.
POP-STACK-TO-OUTPUT.
      PERFORM POP-STACK.
      DISPLAY EOFF.
FIND-OP-PRECEDENCE.
      MOVE NEXT-CHAR TO CHAR-CHECK.
      PERFORM FIND-PRECEDENCE.
      MOVE PRECEDENCE-LEVEL TO OP-PRECEDENCE.
FIND-TOP-PRECEDENCE.
      IF TOP-PTR > 0
            MOVE STACK (TOP-PTR) TO CHAR-CHECK
            PERFORM FIND-PRECEDENCE
            MOVE PRECEDENCE-LEVEL TO TOP-PRECEDENCE
      ELSE MOVE 0 TO TOP-PRECEDENCE.
EMPTY-STACK-TO-LOWER-PRECEDENCE.
      PERFORM POP-STACK-TO-OUTPUT.
      PERFORM FIND-TOP-PRECEDENCE.
FIND-PRECEDENCE.
      IF LEVEL-0
            COMPUTE PRECEDENCE-LEVEL = 0
```

> ELSE IF LEVEL-1
>   COMPUTE PRECEDENCE-LEVEL = 1
> ELSE IF LEVEL-2
>   COMPUTE PRECEDENCE-LEVEL = 2
> ELSE IF LEVEL-3
>   COMPUTE PRECEDENCE-LEVEL = 3
> ELSE error-condition.

An alternative mode of representation of an arithmetic expression is *prefix form*, in which the operator precedes its operands, e.g., $+AB$, $\uparrow EF$. An exercise at the end of the chapter asks you to consider what changes need to be made to the postfix algorithm above in order to generate strings that are in prefix form rather than postfix form.

The exercises also suggest that you consider enhancement of the conversion algorithms to incorporate treatment of the relational operators ($<, <=, =, >=, >$), the boolean operators (*and, or, not*) and arithmetic unary operators (e.g., $-$, $+$). To assist your efforts, the usual operator precedences follow.

Level 6:   unary $-$, unary $+$, *not*
Level 5: $\uparrow$
Level 4: $*, /$
Level 3: $+, -$
Level 2: $<, <=, =, >=, >$
Level 1:   *and*
Level 0:   *or*

Note that we also assigned a high priority to (in the above COBOL routine. This facilitated handling of the stack.

We will return to consideration of prefix, infix, and postfix notation when we discuss binary trees in Chapter 8.

MAPPINGS TO STORAGE

We have already discussed the use of an array to house a stack. We have also seen that one-dimensional arrays are generally mapped to storage in a physically sequential manner. A contiguous set of addresses is allocated to array elements. The simplest mapping of a stack to storage uses the same approach. The stack is assigned a base location which remains fixed. The stack is then allowed to grow into adjacent locations.

Sharing Space

So far we have considered allocating storage only to a single stack. Assume now that we have two stacks that need to co-exist in memory. If stack S1 will have a maximum of M elements and stack S2 will have a maximum of N elements, they could be allocated memory as depicted in Fig. 4–9.

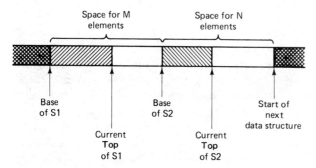

Figure 4–9 Allocation of space to two stacks.

This is not particularly efficient, especially if stacks S1 and S2 are never full at the same time.

Consider the case where we know that the number of elements in S1 and S2 *combined* will never exceed *N*.

$$Noel(S1) + Noel(S2) \leq N$$

For example, assume there are 500 people taking a programming aptitude test. Some are presently employed as computer professionals; the rest are not. We do not know before the tests are completed how many of the people are in each category. Yet we want to track the sequence in which people complete the tests, using one stack for each category. One approach is to allocate room for each of the stacks to grow to its maximum number of elements, say *N*, as above. At any given time there will be space allocated for at least *N* too many elements. An alternative approach will enable us to allocate room only for the combined maximum *N*. Face the two stacks such that they grow toward each other, as depicted in Fig. 4–10.

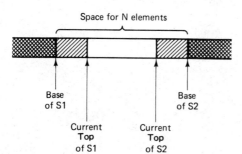

Figure 4–10 Alternative allocation of space to two stacks, growing toward each other.

S1 and S2 will never run into each other, yet neither of them will ever overflow; together they can accommodate up to *N* elements. Stack S1 grows to the right and stack S2 grows to the left.

Consider now the problem of allocating memory to three or more stacks such that (1) overflow will occur only when the total size of all the stacks together exceeds the space available, and (2) each stack has a fixed base location. In fact it is not possible to adhere to both these conditions simultaneously for three or more stacks. When it is necessary to allocate memory to several stacks, one or both of the conditions has to be relaxed.

Either more space has to be allocated or the stack bases may need to be moved around. One technique for efficient allocation of space when there are three or more stacks is called Garwick's technique, which periodically reallocates space to the stacks. At reallocation time, growth in each of the stacks is measured, and space is reapportioned so that each stack receives space proportional to its growth since the last reallocation. In this technique the stack bases move around; those stacks that tend to grow tend to get more of the space.

In Chapter 6 we will discuss ways to allocate stacks to noncontiguous memory by using linked lists. It is generally not possible to predict the maximum size that a stack will obtain; thus dynamic storage allocation schemes (such as Garwick's technique) and noncontiguous storage schemes are commonly used.

SUMMARY

A *stack* is a special case of linear list in which insertion (push) and deletion (pop) operations are restricted to occur only at one end, which is referred to as the stack's top. Stacks may be housed in arrays. This approach imposes several constraints on stack use but is commonly used. The integrity of a stack must be maintained by the programmer when the stack is housed in an array. It is the programmer's responsibility to ensure that insertion and deletion operations occur only at the stack's top. The chapter introduced the declaration and manipulation of stacks in COBOL and Pascal.

Examples illustrated that a stack can be used in the solution of problems that need a last-in-first-out data structure. An example of recursive calls to determine a desired investment amount showed the need to return to a calling location. A stack was used by the compiler to keep track of these locations in order by call. The postfix example used both a LIFO pattern for which operands pertained to a particular operator and a nesting pattern of parentheses.

The chapter terminated with a discussion of allocation of memory to multiple stacks.

TERMS

infix notation	push
last-in-first-out (LIFO)	recursive procedure
linear list	stack
pop	syntax
postfix notation	top
prefix notation	

SELECTED REFERENCES

GARWICK, J. "Data storage in compilers," *BIT*, 4: 137–140, 1964.

KNUTH, D. E. *The Art of Computer Programming, Vol. I, Fundamental Algorithms*. Reading, Mass.: Addison-Wesley Publishing Co., 1973, pp. 234–251.

KORSH, J. F. and G. LAISON. "A multiple-stack manipulation procedure," *Comm. ACM* 26(11): 921–923, Nov. 1983.

STANDISH, T. A. "Stacks and queues," Chapter 2 in *Data Structure Techniques*. Reading, Mass.: Addison-Wesley Publishing Co., 1980, pp. 28–41.

YEH, D. Y. and T. MUNAKATA. "Dynamic allocation and local reallocation procedures for multiple stacks," *Comm. ACM* 29(2): 134–141, Feb. 1986.

REVIEW EXERCISES

1. Draw a stack and indicate the direction of elements in and out.
2. Fill in the blanks:
   (a) If you pop an empty stack, you get a(n) _____ .
   (b) If you correctly push element i onto a stack, Top = _____ .
   (c) Top of an empty stack = _____ .
   (d) If you pop and then push element i, Top = _____ .
   (e) How many elements are in a newly created stack? _____ .
3. What are the results of the following assertions:
   (a) Isempty (Create (S)) is _____ .
   (b) Isempty (Push(i,S)) is _____ .
   (c) Pop(Create (S)) is _____ .
4. What is the result of Top(Push(i,S))? _____ .
5. What is the result of Pop(Push(i,S))? _____ .
6. How can a stack be implemented in FORTRAN?
7. Write an algorithm that adds elements to a stack.
8. Write an algorithm that deletes elements from a stack.
9. Write an algorithm that creates and loads a stack.
10. List three applications of stacks. For each give reasons why stacks would be preferable to arrays.
11. The algorithm PUSH checks for an overflow condition, and algorithm POP checks for an underflow condition. What is meant by overflow and underflow, and why would we want to check for such conditions? What might be the appropriate action to take under each condition?
12. What is the postfix form for each of the following?
    (a) $A * B - (C + D) - (E - F) + F/H \uparrow I$
    (b) $((B * C) + C/D \uparrow F) + G$
    (c) $A \uparrow B * C - D + E / F / (G + H)$
13. Write an algorithm for popping an item off a stack and assigning the value popped to variable x.
14. Write a program that uses a stack to check for matching left and right parentheses, left and right braces, and left and right brackets in a string of characters.
15. Write an algorithm that uses a stack to convert an arithmetic expression from infix to prefix notation.
16. Write a program to implement your infix-to-prefix conversion algorithm.
17. Write a Pascal program to convert an arithmetic expression from infix to postfix notation.

18. Write a program to convert an arithmetic expression from infix to postfix notation, where the arithmetic expression may contain the following operators: $<$, $<=$, $=$, $>=$, $>$, *and*, *or*, *not*, unary $-$, unary $+$, $\uparrow$, *, /, +, $-$.

19. STACK

3
4
1
8
5
6

Write an algorithm that will create a new stack containing the elements of STACK above in ascending order. Minimize the number of intermediary stacks used.

chapter five

queues

Another special case of the data structure *linear list* which was introduced in Chapter 4 is the *queue*. Whereas stacks are restricted such that elements are added to and deleted from only the top of the list, queues are restricted such that elements are added to the rear and deleted from the head. We are all familiar with queues as they commonly arise in our everyday lives. We stand in queues in supermarkets, banks, and post offices. Cars generally proceed in queues through intersections. Queues also commonly arise in computer-based information systems. Customer orders enter queues to be filled; products enter inventory queues; tasks enter queues in computers awaiting service from the CPU.

In this chapter the operations that define the queue data structure are introduced; then facilities for declaring and manipulating queues in COBOL and Pascal are covered. Several examples of applications that use queues are discussed at the end of the chapter.

DEFINITIONS

A *queue* is a special case of the general data structure defined in the preceding chapter as a linear list:

$$A = [A_1, A_2, \ldots, A_T].$$

In a queue, insertion is restricted to occur only at one end of the list, which we call the *rear*; deletion may occur only at the other end of the list, which we call the *front*. We denote by Front (Q) the front of the queue Q and by Rear (Q) the end of the queue Q. For queue Q where

$$Q = [Q_1, Q_2, \ldots, Q_T]$$

Front (Q) is Q_1 and Rear (Q) is Q_T.

We use Noel (Q) to denote the number of elements in queue Q. Noel (Q) is an attribute of queue Q and has an integer value. For queue Q above, Noel (Q) is T.

The Noel[th] element is at the rear of the queue; it is the element that has been in the queue the least amount of time. The first element of the queue is at the front of the queue; it is the element that has been in the queue the longest.

It does not really matter whether we draw a queue such that it grows from right to left (Fig. 5–1(a))

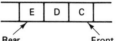

Rear   Front   **Figure 5–1(a)**   Drawings of a queue.

or from left to right (Fig. 5–1(b))

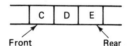

Front   Rear   **Figure 5–1(b)**

or vertically, as long as we are consistent in keeping track of the queue's front and rear.

In any case, for queue

$$Q = [Q_1, Q_2, \ldots, Q_{Noel}]$$

we will say that element Q_I is *before* element Q_J, for I < J. Q_I will be removed from the queue before any of the elements behind it. Q_I has been in the queue longer than any of the elements that it precedes. Clearly this is the way the people near the front of the post office line would like the order of service to be determined.

Queue Operations

There are four basic operations that are legal for data type *queue*.

1. Create (queue)
2. Isempty (queue)
3. Insert (element, queue)
4. Remove (queue)

Create (Q) returns an empty queue with name Q. By definition

> Noel (Create (Q)) is 0,
> Front (Create (Q)) is undefined,
> Rear (Create (Q)) is undefined.

The Isempty (Q) operator determines whether or not a queue is empty. The operand is a queue; the result is a boolean. Isempty (Q) is true if queue Q is empty (that is, if Noel (Q) = 0) and false otherwise. Note that Isempty (Create (Q)) is true.

Insert (E,Q) is the operator that inserts element E into queue Q. By definition, E is placed at the rear of the queue. The result of the operation is the augmented queue.

> Rear (Insert (E,Q)) is E

Noel (Q) is incremented by the Insert operation, and

> Q_{Noel} is E.

The result of inserting an element into any queue cannot be an empty queue:

> Isempty (Insert (E,Q)) is false.

In only one condition does inserting an element into a queue affect the front of the queue:

> If Isempty (Q)
> then Front (Insert (E,Q)) is E
> else Front (Insert (E,Q)) is Front (Q).

Remove (Q) removes the front element from queue Q. The result is the decreased queue. If that first element should be saved, action to do so should be taken prior to the removal operation. Noel (Q) is decremented by the Remove operation, and the previously second element of Q becomes the new front element.

It is an error to try to remove an element from an empty queue:

> If Noel (Q) = 0
> then Remove (Q) yields an error condition.

Note that

> Remove (Create (Q)) also yields an error condition.

In only one case does the removal of an element from a queue undo the immediately previous insertion of an element into the queue:

> If Isempty (Q)
> then Remove (Insert (E,Q)) is Q
> else Remove (Insert (E,Q))
> $\qquad$ = Insert (E, Remove (Q)).

If Q is not empty, the insertion and removal operators act independently and do not affect each other.

Example

For an example of the effects of a sequence of queue operators, let us start with an empty queue named Q. Q = [] can be represented by Fig. 5–2(a).

Noel(Q) = 0
Front(Q) undefined
Rear(Q) undefined   **Figure 5–2(a)**

First insert element A, giving Q = [A] (Fig. 5–2(b)),

| A |

Noel(Q) = 1
Front(Q) = A
Rear(Q) = A   **Figure 5–2(b)**

then the element B, giving Q = [A,B], (Fig. 5–2(c)),

| A | B |

Noel(Q) = 2
Front(Q) = A
Rear(Q) = B   **Figure 5–2(c)**

then the element C, giving Q = [A,B,C], (Fig. 5–2(d)).

| A | B | C |

Noel(Q) = 3
Front(Q) = A
Rear(Q) = C   **Figure 5–2(d)**

We could then remove an element from Q, giving Q = [B,C] (Fig. 5–2(e)),

| B | C |

Noel(Q) = 2
Front(Q) = B
Rear(Q) = C   **Figure 5–2(e)**

and then perhaps insert two more elements, say D then E, giving Q = [B,C,D,E] (Fig. 5–2(f)):

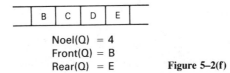

Noel(Q) = 4
Front(Q) = B
Rear(Q) = E   **Figure 5–2(f)**

We might then want to delete an element from the queue, giving Q = [C,D,E] (Fig. 5–2(g)),

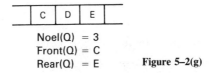

Noel(Q) = 3
Front(Q) = C
Rear(Q) = E   **Figure 5–2(g)**

and so forth. The queue operates in a first-in-first-out (FIFO) manner. Elements are removed in the order in which they were inserted into the queue. You should compare the activity of this example queue with that of the example stack in the preceding chapter. The same sequence of operations occurs in both cases, but the contents of the lists are quite different.

QUEUES IN COBOL AND PASCAL

Housing Queues in Arrays

Just as most programming languages do not have a built-in stack data structure, so they do not have a built-in data type queue. In order to program a solution for a problem that calls for use of a queue, the programmer must use the language's existing features to simulate the queue's operation. One of the simplest ways to represent a queue is to house it in an array. In this section we introduce this method of handling a queue in COBOL and Pascal.

Housing a queue in an array immediately imposes two artificial constraints on that queue. First, the elements that are inserted into the queue must be homogeneous, because that is part of the definition of an array. Second, the programmer must specify an upper bound on the number of elements in the queue when it is housed in an array. A queue variable has no logical constraint on the maximum number of elements that it may contain. (The queue for the Uptown Picture Show Emporium might wind around the block three and a half times on Saturday night.) However, a queue housed in an array is confined to the space allocated to that array. In fact, a queue grows and shrinks over time, but an array has constant size.

Housing a queue in an array has the additional difficulty that the integrity of the queue is the programmer's responsibility. It is up to the programmer to ensure that the queue operates on a FIFO basis. The compiler will not ensure that elements won't be inserted and removed willy-nilly from the middle of the data structure.

Declaring Queues

Let's consider the declaration of a queue variable named Q. Assume that each element of Q will be an integer and that Q will have a maximum of 100 elements. In addition to declaring the array that will house Q, we must declare variables that point us to the front and rear elements of the queue. FRONT and REAR will be integer variables whose values will be subscripts of the first and last elements of the queue, respectively. We name the combined array and its front and rear indicators the QUEUE-STRUCT.

In COBOL:

```
01  QUEUE-STRUCT.
    02  Q               OCCURS 100 TIMES
                        PICTURE 9(5).
    02  FRONT           PICTURE 9(3).
    02  REAR            PICTURE 9(3).
```

In Pascal:

```
type queuestruct =
    record queue: array [1 . . 100] of integer;
           front,rear: integer;
    end;
var q: queuestruct;
```

Queue Operations

Initially, we will set FRONT and REAR equal to 0 for the empty queue. The insertion and removal operators are actually quite simply implemented in COBOL and Pascal. The main complication is in checking that FRONT and REAR do not point outside of the bounds of the queue's array. We use the variable NOEL-MAX to be the maximum number of elements that the queue's array can accommodate; here NOEL-MAX = 100. Throughout we indicate that the application determines the actions to be taken when an overflow condition (attempt to insert an element into a full queue) or an underflow condition (attempt to remove an element from an empty queue) occurs.

Note that inserting an element into an empty queue requires moving both the FRONT and REAR pointers. When removing an element from a queue empties the queue, FRONT and REAR are reset to 0 so that insertion into the queue will then proceed from the low end of the array. We use EON to be the element inserted onto the queue and EOFF to be the element removed from the queue. Note that we save EOFF and assume that q is a globally known variable in the Pascal examples.

In COBOL:

```
INSERT.
    IF REAR = NOEL-MAX
        overflow-condition
```

```
            ELSE COMPUTE REAR = REAR + 1
                MOVE EON TO Q(REAR)
                IF FRONT = 0
                        COMPUTE FRONT = 1.
        REMOVE.
         IF FRONT > 0
            MOVE Q (FRONT) TO EOFF
            IF FRONT = REAR
                    COMPUTE FRONT = 0
                    COMPUTE REAR = 0
            ELSE COMPUTE FRONT = FRONT + 1
        ELSE underflow-condition.
```

In Pascal:

```
procedure insert (eon:integer);
begin if(q.rear < noelmax)
        then begin q.rear := q.rear + 1;
                    q.queue[q.rear] := eon;
                    if(q.front = 0)
                    then q.front := 1
              end
         else OVERFLOW-CONDITION
end;
procedure removeq(var eoff : integer)
begin if(q.front > 0)
        then begin eoff := q.queue[q.front];
                    if(q.front = q.rear)
                    then begin q.front := 0;
                               q.rear := 0
                         end
                    else q.front := q.front + 1
              end
         else UNDERFLOW-CONDITION
end;
```

The number of elements in the queue at any given time can be calculated from the values of the front and rear pointers.

```
If FRONT = 0
then Noel (Q) is 0
else Noel (Q) is FRONT − REAR + 1
```

Moving through Storage

Let us now examine a bit more carefully these algorithms and the use of an array to house a queue. Consider the successive insertion and removal of elements; for example, insert four elements (Fig. 5–3(a)),

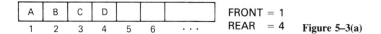

FRONT = 1
REAR = 4   **Figure 5–3(a)**

remove two elements (Fig. 5–3(b)),

FRONT = 3
REAR = 4   **Figure 5–3(b)**

insert three more elements (Fig. 5–3(c)),

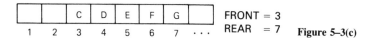

FRONT = 3
REAR = 7   **Figure 5–3(c)**

remove two more elements (Fig. 5–3(d)),

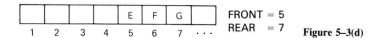

FRONT = 5
REAR = 7   **Figure 5–3(d)**

and so forth. The queue is traveling left-to-right through the array. What happens when
REAR = 100 and we need to insert more elements into the queue? We have hit the
boundary of the array. The queue is full only if FRONT = 1 and the maximum has been
reached, i.e., Noel (Q) = 100. However, it is probably more likely that the front of the
queue has migrated ''to the right'' due to removal of one or more elements and FRONT
> 1. It may even be the case that FRONT = 100 and there is only one element in Q
yet it appears as if Q is full.

One approach to solving this problem is to house the queue in a larger array. This
is not a terribly attractive solution unless we have an infinite amount of storage to devote
to that array or can take advantage of *a priori* knowledge of the queue's behavior over
time.

CIRCULAR QUEUES

A better approach is to arrange Q in a circular fashion, considering Q(1) as following
Q(NOEL-MAX), as in Fig. 5–4. (In the following we replace variable NOEL-MAX by
the variable N to make the diagrams easier to draw.) Now, depending upon how the
insertion and removal operators are implemented, the queue will use the circular array
differently. We present two alternatives here; other alternatives are left as exercises.

First, continue with our convention of having variable FRONT point to the first
element in the queue and variable REAR point to the last element in the queue. Various
configurations of the queue at several points in time are given in Fig. 5–5, where X marks

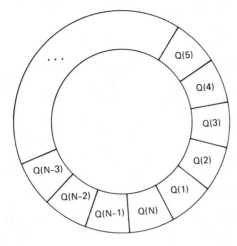

Figure 5–4   Circular queue.

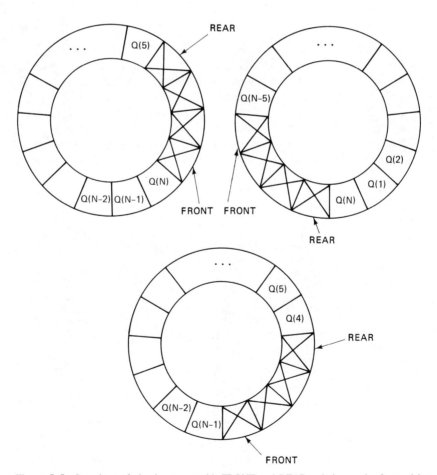

Figure 5–5   Snapshots of circular queue with FRONT and REAR pointing to the first and last elements, respectively.

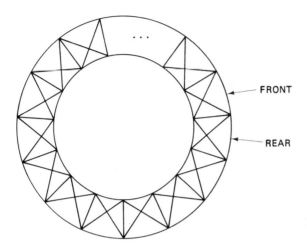

Figure 5–6 Full queue, using pointer conventions of Fig. 5–5.

a slot that is occupied by an element of the queue. Note that the queue's elements may span the boundary between Q(1) and Q(N), as shown in the third picture. The insertion and deletion operators must account for resetting of the FRONT and REAR pointers when they cross the boundary from value N to value 1.

The condition for an empty queue is FRONT = REAR = 0. A full queue is depicted in Fig. 5–6. Note that this queue "grows" in the counterclockwise direction. What does the queue look like when it contains just one element? Compare the positions of the FRONT and REAR pointers when the queue is full and when the queue contains just two elements, as shown in Fig. 5–7.

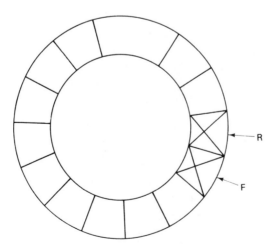

Figure 5–7 Queue with two elements, using pointer convention of Fig. 5–5.

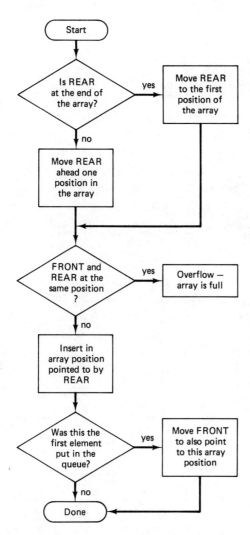

Figure 5–8 Logic for inserting an element in a circular queue.

Using Circular Queues

The algorithms for the Insert and Remove operators for circular queues are given in Figs. 5–8 and 5–9 respectively.

    The algorithms can be implemented in COBOL as follows.

```
INSERT.
    IF REAR = N
                COMPUTE REAR = 1
    ELSE COMPUTE REAR = REAR + 1.
```

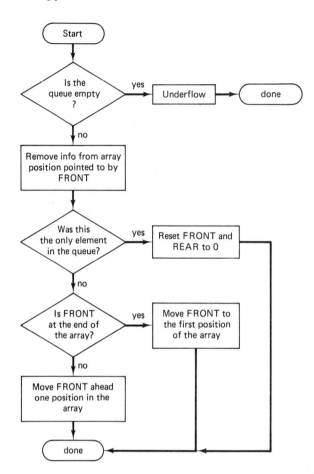

Figure 5–9 Logic for removing an element from a circular queue.

```
IF REAR = FRONT
            overflow-condition
ELSE MOVE EON TO Q(REAR)
      IF FRONT = 0
                  COMPUTE FRONT = 1.
REMOVE.
      IF FRONT = 0
            underflow-condition
ELSE MOVE Q(FRONT) TO EOFF
      IF FRONT = REAR
                  COMPUTE FRONT = 0
                  COMPUTE REAR = 0
      ELSE IF FRONT = N
                  COMPUTE FRONT = 1
      ELSE COMPUTE FRONT = FRONT + 1.
```

In Pascal:

```
procedure insert(eon:integer);
begin if(q.rear = n)
         then q.rear := 1
         else q.rear := q.rear + 1;
         if(q.rear = q.front)
         then OVERFLOW-CONDITION
         else begin q.queue[q.rear] := eon;
                     if(q.front = 0)
                     then q.front := 1
              end;
end;


procedure remove(var eoff : integer);
begin if(q.front = 0)
         then UNDERFLOW-CONDITION
         else begin eoff := q.queue[q.front];
                     if(q.front = q.rear)
                     then begin q.front := 0;
                                 q.rear := 0
                          end
                     else if(q.front = n)
                          then q.front := 1
                          else q.front := q.front + 1
              end;
end;
```

Variations

If we use the same algorithms but number the slots in a clockwise rather than counter-clockwise direction, the queue will appear to move in a clockwise direction. If we retain the counterclockwise numbering scheme but change the insertion and removal codes such that the REAR and FRONT pointers are decremented rather than incremented, the queue will appear to move in a clockwise direction.

Some programmers prefer to number the array slots from 0 to N − 1, rather than from 1 to N (Fig. 5–10). Now we can handle the transition over the $Q(N − 1) − Q(0)$ boundary using modulo arithmetic, which is a built-in function in Pascal, FORTRAN, and PL/I. A mod B in Pascal is the integer remainder resulting when A is divided by B. I := A mod B in Pascal is equivalent in result to COBOL's

DIVIDE A BY B GIVING C REMAINDER I.

The insertion and removal operations then can be implemented in the Pascal program as follows. Replace the code

if(q.rear = n)
then q.rear := 1
else q.rear := q.rear + 1

by

$$q.rear := (q.rear + 1)\bmod n;$$

in the insert procedure. Replace the code

if(q.front = n)
then q.front := 1
else q.front := q.front + 1

by

$$q.front := (q.front + 1) \bmod n;$$

in the remove procedure.

Actually, this change to the scheme of numbering slots makes it somewhat more difficult to detect an empty queue. FRONT = REAR = 0 now is indicative of a queue with one element, in the slot 0 (Fig. 5–11). Recall that when the queue's array is based at 1 instead of zero, FRONT = REAR = 0 means that the queue is empty.

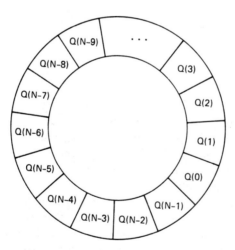

Figure 5–10 Circular queue space with base at array slot 0.

An Alternative Representation

To alleviate this difficulty, a second technique for representing a queue in a circular array is commonly used. Rather than having FRONT point *to* the front element of the queue, use FRONT to point to the slot *preceding* the one containing the front element of the queue. Examples are shown in Fig. 5–12. Now the queue is empty when FRONT =

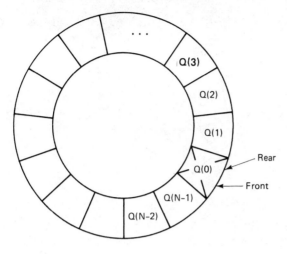

Figure 5–11 Circular queue space of Fig. 5–10 with FRONT = REAR = 0.

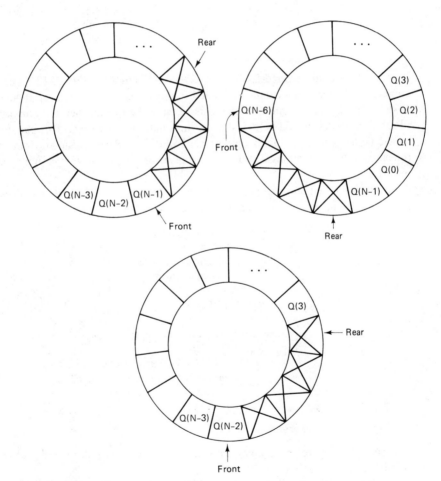

Figure 5–12 Snapshots of circular queue with FRONT pointing to the slot preceding the first element and REAR pointing to the last element.

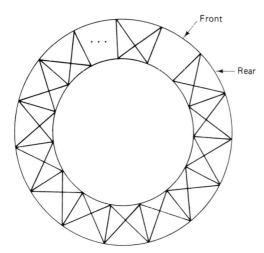

Figure 5–13 Full queue, using pointer convention of Fig. 5–12.

REAR, and it is full when REAR = (FRONT + 1) mod N (Fig. 5–13). The maximum number of elements that can be contained in this queue is N − 1, even though there are N slots. If we were to allow N elements to enter the queue, then the condition for full FRONT = REAR would be the same as the condition for empty. This paradox could of course be handled by recognizing whether FRONT = REAR resulted from an insertion (queue is full) or a removal (queue is empty), or simply by maintaining the value of Noel(Q).

The insert and remove operations in Pascal for a circular queue with indices 0 through n − 1 and front pointing in front of the first element follow.

```
procedure insert (eon:integer);
begin if(q.front<>(q.rear + 1) mod n)
      then begin q.rear := (q.rear + 1) mod n;
                 q.queue[q.rear] := eon
           end
      else OVERFLOW
end;
procedure removeq(var eoff:integer);
begin if(q.rear = q.front)
      then UNDERFLOW-CONDITION
      else begin q.front := (q.front + 1) mod n;
                 eoff := q.queue[q.front]
           end;
end;
```

You should compare these algorithms with the algorithms presented earlier for front pointing to the queue's first element.

An alternative representation would have REAR point to the slot one behind the

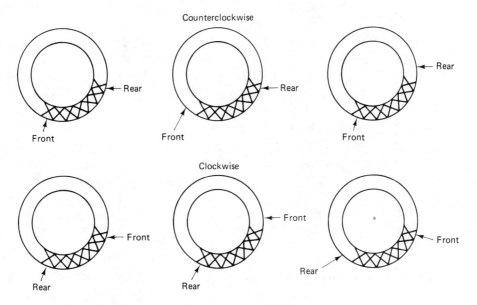

Figure 5–14   Alternative conventions for representing a queue in a circular array.

rear of the queue, with FRONT pointing to the first element. You should develop the insertion and removal algorithms for this approach.

Summary

Thus we have proposed at least six ways to represent a queue in a circular array (Fig. 5–14). The representation mode is determined by the way that pointers are handled in the insertion and removal algorithms used. In all cases it must be possible to detect when the queue is empty and when it is full. The algorithms for handling these various approaches are all of essentially the same complexity. We have presented the variety of techniques here because *all* are in extensive use; the maintenance programmer may very well have to deal with any and all of the techniques.

There are other ways to represent a queue besides housing it in an array. We will discuss these representations later, primarily in the next chapter on linked lists.

PERFORMANCE OF QUEUES

Queues are extensively used in applications that simulate the behavior of real systems in which there is FIFO activity. Queues build up in many commonplace situations: cars enqueue at a traffic light; patrons wait in line at the post office; shoppers queue up at checkout counters in grocery stores; messages queue up in communications networks; files are spooled to be delivered in FIFO order to a line printer; and so on.

Performance Parameters

Designers are often interested in improving the performance of such systems, where performance can be measured by parameters like the following:

- Average number of elements in the queue.
- Average time spent in the queue.
- Probability that queue length will be greater than some number.
- Probability that queued time will be greater than some number.
- Minimum and maximum queue length over a period of time.
- Minimum and maximum time in queue over a period of time.

There are three basic approaches to determining values for the above parameters: observation, simulation, and queueing theory.

Observation

Observation can be applied to study an existing system. For instance, you may have seen electronic counters at traffic lights observing the cars waiting and proceeding through the intersection. Observation is not appropriate to study systems that are still in the design phase or to study effects of proposed changes to existing systems.

Simulation

A powerful tool that can be used to study the behavior of systems is simulation. A simulation exercises a model of the system under study. For example, a simulator of a grocery store checkout system would generate arrivals to the checkout queues, would characterize each arrival by the amount of service it requires, would represent the rate of service rendered at each checkout stand, and so forth. The simulator would gather statistics during the operation of the model over some period of time. These statistics would characterize the behavior of the queues that develop.

In order to build a simulation model, it is necessary to have substantial statistics available to characterize the system under study. These statistics include arrival distributions, the means and standard deviations of service times, and so on. These data may be gathered by observation or may be hypothesized for a ''paper'' system that does not yet exist.

Once the simulation model is developed, its parameters can be adjusted and experimented with fairly easily. Effects of changes to the system can be investigated. For example, what happens to the system behavior if we set up an additional checkstand? What happens if we have two quick-check lines instead of one? What happens if we slightly slow down the rate of service, say by requiring that all customer checks be verified by the store manager?

Queueing Theory

Queueing theory is an analytic approach to studying behavior of systems that involve queues. A set of equations and curves has been developed with sound mathematical basis for estimating queue sizes, waiting times, probabilities of delay, and so forth. Just as is the case with simulation, assumptions regarding the characteristics of the system under study must be made in order to apply the results of queueing theory. For example, the arrival rate of entries to the queues must be established; the number of queues and the number of servers (who remove elements from queues) must be determined; the service discipline must be characterized (e.g., serve to completion—as in the grocery store— versus serve some quantum of time and then put the element at the end of the queue so it will be served again later—as in computer timesharing systems); and the distribution of service demands must be selected.

One of the interesting results of queueing theory shows that the queueing config- uration of multiple servers, each with its own queue (Fig. 5–15) has a longer average waiting time than does the same system configured with a single queue (Fig. 5–16), where the element at the front of the queue is serviced by whichever server happens to become available next. You may have seen this type of queue management implemented in your local post office or bank. Why is it not generally used in grocery stores?

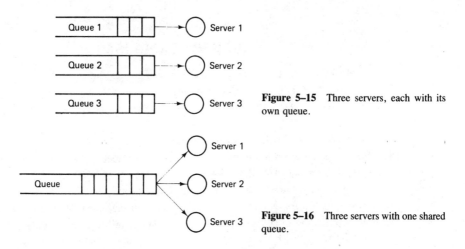

Figure 5–15 Three servers, each with its own queue.

Figure 5–16 Three servers with one shared queue.

SUMMARY

A *queue* is a special case of linear list in which insertions are restricted to occur only at one end of the queue, which is referred to as the queue's rear, and removals may occur only at the other end of the queue, which is referred to as the queue's front.

Queues are used extensively in computer operation; for instance, in selecting the next job to be serviced, in selecting the next file to be printed on the printer, in selecting the next packet to process from a communications line. Additionally, queues are extensively used for modeling purposes, as in the simulation of traffic patterns in grocery stores, post offices, barber shops, and so forth. A queue can be used in the solution of any problem that needs a first-in-first-out data structure. Inventories sometimes behave this way.

Queues can be represented in storage in much the same way as are stacks; by being housed in arrays. When stacks are housed in arrays, the integrity of a queue must be maintained by the programmer. It is the programmer's responsibility to ensure that insertion and deletion operations occur only at the queue's rear and front, respectively.

Because queues propagate through storage with successive insertions and removals, circular arrays are commonly used. The algorithms for managing queues are deceptively simple; the reader should be careful to build a sound understanding of them.

TERMS

array   queue
circular queue   queueing theory
first-in-first-out (FIFO)   rear
front   simulation
linear list   stack

REVIEW EXERCISES

1. Describe the similarities and differences between queues and stacks.
2. At which end of a queue is an insertion made? A removal?
3. Why are queues that are housed in arrays usually represented in circular rather than linear fashion?
4. Should a stack be circular? Why or why not?
5. In looking at an algorithm to insert an element into a queue, how can one tell if the queue is moving clockwise or counterclockwise?
6. When is the *mod* function convenient to use in circular queues?
7. How do you test for an empty queue? Describe your placement of the front pointer.
8. Write a procedure to add an element to a circular queue when the first element is designated FRONT and when REAR indicates the space just past the end of the queue.
9. Write an algorithm to count the number of items in a circular queue.
10. Write an algorithm for deleting an element from a circular queue when REAR points to the rear and FRONT points to one space ahead of the front.
11. Write an algorithm for adding an element to a circular queue when REAR points to the rear and FRONT points to the front.
12. Draw a queue of ten elements indicating the front and rear. Give the algorithm to check to see if a queue is full.
13. Write an algorithm to put two queues of varying lengths (but with a sum total length of N) into an array of N slots.

14. A CPU allows each transaction a maximum of 2 units of processing time; if that task is completed, then it is sent on for output to disk or to a terminal; if not, it is sent back to the rear of the queue that it came from for further processing. Given that all tasks are queued for the CPU and that 2 priorities exist—priority 1, which gets precedence, and priority 2, which is subordinate to priority 1—and given the following transactions,

Trans	Priority	Time of entry	Req. service
A	1	0	1
B	2	0	2
C	2	1	6
D	1	2	4
E	1	2	3
F	2	3	2
G	1	5	1

trace the history of the applicable queues and the CPU's processing in 1-unit intervals until all processing is completed.

15. (a) There is a bank with two tellers. One is experienced, one is new. The average transaction time for the new teller is twice as long as for the experienced teller. Write an algorithm to direct customers to the appropriate teller so that the average waiting time for both lines is equal.

(b) Now assume that the new teller "learns" after each transaction and his/her transaction time decreases by $\frac{1}{n}$ (where n = transaction time for the experienced teller) after each transaction. Write an algorithm to equate line waiting times for this situation.

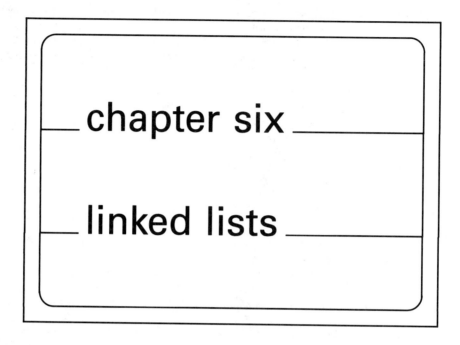

chapter six

linked lists

In this chapter we consider the use of linked lists to represent linear data structures: general linear lists, stacks, and queues. Later in the book we will address the use of linked lists to represent nonlinear data structures: trees and graphs.

LINKED LIST REPRESENTATION

Problems with Sequential Representation

In preceding chapters we represented stacks and queues by housing them in arrays. A basic constraint imposed by this mode of representation is that the amount of storage allocated to the stack or queue is fixed. The space is allocated regardless of whether the stack or queue is empty, and there is the possibility of overflow if the stack or queue becomes larger than expected. This is also a problem when an array is used to house a general linear list.

However, there is an even more severe constraint imposed in the general case. What happens when the 43rd element, say 'IGOR,' is removed from a linear list of 2492 names? Elements 1 through 42 are not affected, but elements 44 'IVAN' through 2492 'ZELDA' logically should each be shifted in the array; element 44 becomes new element 43, element

45 becomes element 44, . . . , element 2492 becomes element 2491. Now, what happens when a new element, say 'HORATIO,' is to be inserted after element 41, 'HORACE'? Elements 42 'HOWARD' through 2491 'ZELDA' logically need to be shifted "down" in the array to make room for the new element 42. The new element cannot just be tacked onto the end of the array, because the logical ordering of elements in the linear list is conveyed by the physical ordering of elements in the array.

Nonsequential Representation

A solution to the data movement problems encountered in using sequential representation is to instead use nonsequential representation. Sequential representation mirrors the logical ordering of elements in a linear list in physical storage; the logical ordering and the physical ordering are the same. With nonsequential representation, the logical ordering of elements and the physical ordering of elements need *not* be the same. The logical ordering is represented by having each element point to the next element; the elements of the list are linked together. To access the elements in logical order, these links are followed.

Basic Concepts

Fig. 6–1 is a picture of a linear linked list that contains four elements. We call each element of the list a *node*.

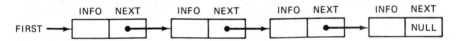

Figure 6–1   Example linked list.

There is a pointer to the first node of the list. Each node has a link to the next node of the list. The last node has a *NULL* pointer, which indicates that there is no next node. Each node actually has two parts: the data contents and the pointer field. Each node is a record data structure (see Chapter 3).

The linked nodes do not have to be physically adjacent. The list of four nodes in Fig. 6–1 might be as shown in Fig. 6–2.

A linear list with no nodes is called an *empty list*. The linked list representation of an empty list is merely a null first pointer. The operation of creating an empty list then is

        First : = Null.

Advantages

Recall that another constraint imposed by using an array to house a queue or stack is that the elements must be homogeneous. This constraint can be relieved by using the linked list representation scheme. Nodes with different data structures can be linked together.

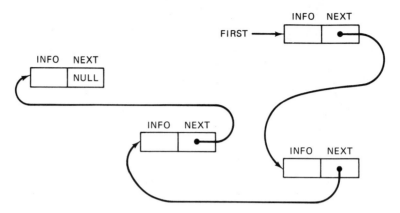

Figure 6–2   Example linked list, equivalent to Fig. 6–1.

The benefits of linked list representation become apparent when the insertion and removal operations are considered. To remove the 43rd node, say 'IGOR,' from a linear list with 2492 nodes (Fig. 6–3(a)), it is necessary only to change the pointer in the prior (42nd) node to point to the next (44th) node (Fig. 6–3(b)).

To insert a new node, say 'HORATIO,' after the 41st node, it is necessary only to change the pointer in the 41st node to point to the new node and to have the new node point to the 42nd node (Fig. 6–3(c)). No shifting of data is necessary.

Costs

The costs of using a linked list rather than sequential representation are basically two. First, space is required in the linked representation for the pointer fields. Second, it will usually take longer to search for a node in a linked representation than in a list housed in an array. Recall that there is a calculation that can be used to find the starting location of the Nth element in an array. In order to find the Nth node in a linked list (assuming no use of auxiliary pointers), the chain of the previous N-1 nodes must be visited. The Nth node cannot be located directly.

BASIC OPERATIONS ON A LINKED LIST

We consider now the basic operations on a linked list. Later we will see how linked lists are declared and manipulated in programs.

Notation

It is necessary to introduce some notation. Let P be a pointer variable. Its value is an address, i.e., the location of some other variable. The operations that are legal on pointer variables are the following:

Figure 6–3(a)   Example of a singly-linked list.

Figure 6–3(b)   Deletion of Igor from linked list in Fig. 6–3(a).

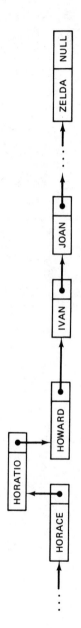

Figure 6–3(c)   Insertion of Horatio into linked list in Fig. 6–3(b).

1. Test for Null.

2. Test for equality with another pointer variable.

3. Set to Null.

4. Set to point to a node.

These are the only operations that we can do with pointers. Denote by

> Node(P)   the node pointed to by P;
> Info(P)   the value in the information portion of the node pointed to by P;
> Next(P)   the value in the link portion of the node pointed to by P.

Removing a Node

Consider the linked list of Fig. 6–4(a).

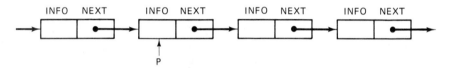

Figure 6–4(a)   Steps in removing a node from a linked list.

The algorithm to remove from the linked list the node following the one pointed to by P follows. We use Q as an auxiliary pointer variable and will first set it to point to the node to be removed.

(a) Q : = Next(P)

(b) Next(P) : = Next(Q)

(c) Free node Q's space for reuse.

Step (a) gives the structure shown in Fig. 6–4(b).

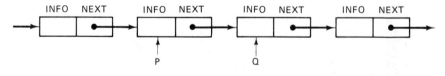

Figure 6–4(b)

Step (b) gives the structure shown in Fig. 6–4(c).

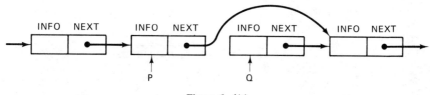

Figure 6–4(c)

Step (c) gives the structure shown in Fig. 6–4(d). Removing a node requires touching two nodes, the ones pointed to by P and Q. No other nodes need to be accessed or changed.

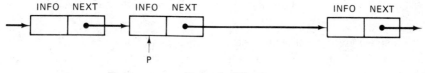

Figure 6–4(d)

This sequence of operations returns the removed node to be reused, except if P points to the last node of the list. How should the algorithm be modified to accommodate that situation?

Inserting a Node

The algorithm to insert the contents of a variable NAME into the linked list such that it follows the node pointed to by P follows. Again we use the auxiliary pointer Q, as well as another, called NEW.

(a) Get space for the new node, and make NEW point to it.
(b) Info(NEW) : = NAME
(c) Q : = Next(P)
(d) Next(P) : = NEW
(e) Next(NEW) : = Q

After steps (a) and (b), we have the structures shown in Fig. 6–5(a).

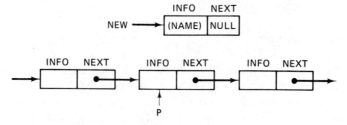

Figure 6–5(a)   Steps in inserting a node into a linked list.

After steps (c) and (d), we have the structures shown in Fig. 6–5(b).

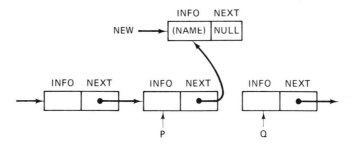

Figure 6–5(b)   Steps in inserting a node into a linked list.

Step (e) gives the structures shown in Fig. 6–5(c).

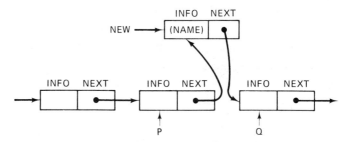

Figure 6–5(c)   Steps in inserting a node into a linked list.

It is important to recognize that links such as P, Q, NEW, and the NEXT variables all point to *nodes*, not just to the INFO part of nodes. An arrow in these diagrams points to an entire box. Inserting a node requires touching two nodes: the new node and the one pointed to by P. No other nodes need to be accessed or changed.

MANAGING AVAILABLE SPACE

We have already assumed the existence of two functions—one to create node space and one to return it for reuse—which we used in our insertion and removal algorithms. Now let us look at these functions in more detail.

The Storage Pool

The storage pool contains all space that is not in use. Assume that this space is formatted into units with the structure of nodes for our linked list. In fact a program may use several linked lists, with nodes of various formats, in which case we would have several pools of empty nodes. For purposes of simplifying our explanation, we assume for now that we have only one node type.

Managing Available Space   **101**

What is an appropriate structure for the storage pool? We probably do not want to use sequential representation, because nodes will be removed rather randomly from our linked list and we would like that space to be reusable. Therefore the storage pool will be represented using a linked structure. Logically, however, the storage pool is merely a linear list. We call the function that returns the location of the *next* free node in the storage pool Getnode.

Initially, when all "user" lists are empty, the storage pool contains all the available space. We will use Avail as the pointer to the first node on the list of available space (Fig. 6–6).

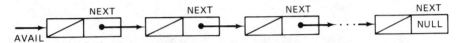

Figure 6–6   The list of available space.

Getting a New Node

When node space is needed, it is obtained from this list of available space by invocation of the Getnode function. The exception condition of not having any more available space must be handled correctly.

If Avail = Null
then out-of-free-space
(a)   else begin; Getnode : = Avail;
(b)   Avail : = Next(Avail);
(c)   Next(Getnode) : = Null;
         end;

Step (a) gives the structure shown in Fig. 6–7(a).

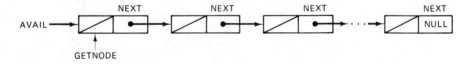

Figure 6–7(a)

Step (b) gives the structure shown in Fig. 6–7(b).

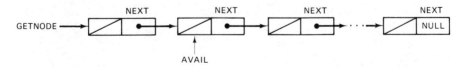

Figure 6–7(b)

Step (c) gives the structure shown in Fig. 6–7(c).

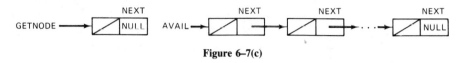

Figure 6–7(c)

Getting a node from the free-space list requires touching just one node (the one at the front of the list) and changing the Avail pointer.

Freeing a Node

We call the procedure that returns to the available space list a node that is no longer needed Freenode. This action makes that node's space reusable. The argument of Freenode is a pointer to the node that is to be placed into the storage pool. Quite simply, procedure Freenode (Q) is

   (a) Next(Q) : = Avail
   (b) Info(Q) : = Null
   (c) Avail : = Q.

Step (a) gives the structure shown in Fig. 6–8(a).

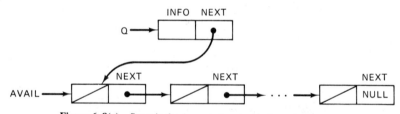

Figure 6–8(a) Steps in freeing a node, placing it on the Avail list.

After steps (b) and (c), we have the structure shown in Fig. 6–8(b).

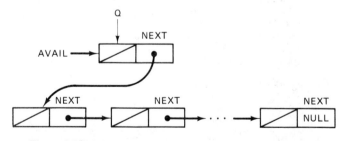

Figure 6–8(b) Steps in freeing a node, placing it on the Avail list.

Pointer Q will then be handled by the invoking routine in some appropriate manner. Q is probably an auxiliary pointer. The Info portion of the newly freed node has been slashed, as have the Info portions of other freed nodes in our diagrams, to indicate that it has been nulled and will be rewritten when eventually removed from the storage pool by a later Getnode invocation.

These Getnode and Freenode algorithms structure the storage pool not just as a linear list, but as a stack. In fact, the storage pool is sometimes referred to as the Avail *stack*. How would the algorithms be different if the storage pool were structured as an Avail *queue*?

After a sequence of insertion and removal operations on a user list, it and the Avail list might be quite intertwined physically, although the proper management of links keeps them logically untangled (Fig. 6–9).

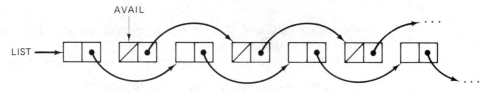

Figure 6–9 Avail list and user's list.

In the remainder of our treatment of linked lists we continue to assume the existence of Getnode and Freenode.

LINKED LISTS IN PASCAL, USING POINTER VARIABLES

Defining Linked Lists

We now turn to techniques for using linked lists in programs. In the preceding sections we made rather extensive use of pointers. Pascal has a built-in pointer data type and facilities for controlling dynamic storage. A single node can be declared in Pascal by

```
type nodeptr = ↑ nodetype;
     nametype = packed array [1 . . 10] of char;
     nodetype = record
                    info : nametype;
                    next : nodeptr
                end;
```

The notation ↑ *nodetype* indicates that *nodeptr* is a data type that points to things that have *nodetype* type. In Pascal a variable that is declared to be a pointer is constrained to contain the address of a particular type of data structure.

We declare p to be a *nodeptr* and node to be a *nodetype* structure,

```
var p : nodeptr;
    node : nodetype;
```

and we represent by

$$p \uparrow .info$$
$$\text{and} \quad p \uparrow .next$$

the info and next parts respectively of the node pointed to by p. The pointer p is given the Null value by p : = nil.

Managing Space

The following verbs are used by the programmer to control Pascal's space-management facilities:

new(p)   Allocates space for one of whatever type p points to and sets p to the address. This is Pascal's Getnode function.

dispose(p)   Frees the object currently pointed to by p. This is Pascal's Freenode procedure.

The Pascal run-time environment handles the free-space management.

Removing a Node

The algorithm to remove from the linked list the node following the one pointed to by p is coded in Pascal as follows. We place the info contents of the removed node in variable out, and we assume that node has been globally declared.

```
procedure removaf(p:nodeptr,var out:nametype);
      var q:nodeptr;
      begin if(p ↑ .next = nil)
            then UNDERFLOW-CONDITION
            else begin q : = p ↑ .next;
                        p ↑ .next : = q ↑ .next;
                        out : = q ↑ .info;
                        dispose (q)
                  end;
      end;
```

Only two nodes in the linked list have been touched: the ones pointed to by p and q. No other nodes need to be accessed or changed.

Inserting a Node

The algorithm to insert the contents of variable in into the linked list so that it follows the node pointed to by p is coded in Pascal as follows:

```
procedure inseraf(p:nodeptr,in:nametype);
      var q:nodeptr;
```

$$\underline{\text{begin}}\ \text{new(q);}$$
$$q \uparrow .\text{info} := \text{in;}$$
$$q \uparrow .\text{next} := p \uparrow .\text{next;}$$
$$p \uparrow .\text{next} := q$$
$$\underline{\text{end;}}$$

Only two nodes have been touched: the new one (pointed to by q) and the one pointed to by p.

As a safety check, prior to invoking these algorithms, the program should ensure that there actually is a node pointed to by p. In Pascal, p = <u>nil</u> would indicate that there is no such node.

LINKED LISTS IN COBOL AND PASCAL, WITHOUT USING POINTER VARIABLES

Using an Array

When using a programming language that does not have a built-in *pointer* data type, the code for declaring and manipulating linked lists is a bit more complex. We simulate pointer variables by housing a linked list in an array. The value of a pointer variable then becomes the value of a subscript.

Fig. 6–10 is a diagram of an array that houses a linked list of names. Each element of the array is a record with two fields: Info and Next. We use the value 0 to represent Null.

The Avail stack can share this same array of space (Fig. 6–11). Maintaining links between the available nodes makes management of the available space easier than if each had a null Next pointer. Fig. 6–12(a) shows the linked list after removal of the element following the one pointed to by P, where P = 5, and after insertion of 'HORATIO' in the proper alphabetic sequence (Fig. 6–12(b)).

	INFO	NEXT
1	IVAN	6
2	HOWARD	5
3		
4	HORACE	2
5	IGOR	1
6	JOAN	0
7		

FIRST = 4

Figure 6–10 Array housing a linked list.

	INFO	NEXT
1	IVAN	6
2	HOWARD	5
3		7
4	HORACE	2
5	IGOR	1
6	JOAN	0
7		0

FIRST = 4
AVAIL = 3

Figure 6–11 Array housing Avail list and user's linked list.

	INFO	NEXT
1	IVAN	6
2	HOWARD	1
3		7
4	HORACE	2
5		3
6	JOAN	0
7		0

FIRST = 4
AVAIL = 5

	INFO	NEXT
1	IVAN	6
2	HOWARD	1
3		7
4	HORACE	5
5	HORATIO	2
6	JOAN	0
7		0

FIRST = 4
AVAIL = 3

Figure 6–12(a) Linked list after removing Igor and inserting Horatio.

Figure 6–12(b) Linked list after removing Igor and inserting Horatio.

Because we are using arrays, we must establish an upper bound on the number of nodes that will be in the linked list; assume the maximum is 500.

Defining a Linked List

The array can be defined as follows. Note that the array holds both the user's linked list and a linked list of available space. In COBOL:

```
01   SPACE-ARRAY.
     02   NODE OCCURS 500 TIMES.
          03   INFO          PIC X(10).
          03   NEXTNODE      PIC 9(3).
     02   FIRSTNODE          PIC 9(3).
     02   AVAIL              PIC 9(3).
```

We use NEXTNODE and FIRSTNODE here because NEXT and FIRST are reserved words in COBOL. FIRSTNODE contains the subscript of the first node in the user's list; AVAIL contains the subscript of the first node in the list of available space.

Array storage can be used for a linked list in Pascal, although this is only rarely done. The pointer-variable techniques introduced in the previous section are preferable. In Pascal, array storage for a linked list would be declared as follows.

```
type nodeptr = 0..500;
     nametype = packed array [1..10] of char;
     nodetype = record
                     info: nametype;
                     next: nodeptr
                end;
var node: array [1..500] of nodetype;
    first, avail: nodeptr;
```

In all cases, when we house a linked list in an array, we use the value zero to represent null.

Removing a Node

The algorithm to remove from the linked list the node following the one pointed to by P requires that two nodes be touched: the one with subscript P and the next one logically following P, with subscript Q. Additionally, the index to available space has to be changed.
   In COBOL:

```
REMOVAF.
    IF NEXTNODE (P) = 0
        underflow-condition
    ELSE COMPUTE Q = NEXTNODE (P)
        COMPUTE NEXTNODE (P) = NEXTNODE (Q)
        output INFO (Q)
        COMPUTE NEXTNODE (Q) = AVAIL
        COMPUTE AVAIL = Q.
```

In Pascal:

```
procedure removaf(p:nodeptr);
var q:nodeptr;
begin
    if(node[p].next = 0)
    then UNDERFLOW-CONDITION
    else begin q := node [p].next;
            node[p].next := node[q].next;
            writeln (node[q].info);
            node[q].next := avail;
            avail := q
        end;
end;
```

Inserting a Node

The algorithm to insert the contents of variable IN into the linked list so that it follows the node pointed to by P requires touching two nodes, the one taken off the available-space list with subscript Q and the one with subscript P. The index to the next available node also has to be changed.

   In COBOL:

```
INSERAF.
    IF AVAIL = 0
    THEN overflow-condition
```

```
ELSE COMPUTE Q = AVAIL
     COMPUTE AVAIL = NEXTNODE (AVAIL)
     MOVE IN TO INFO (Q)
     COMPUTE NEXTNODE (Q) = NEXTNODE (P)
     COMPUTE NEXTNODE (P) = Q.
```

In Pascal:

```
procedure inseraf(p:nodeptr,in:nametype);
var q:nodeptr;
begin if(avail = 0)
      then OVERFLOW-CONDITION
      else begin q : = avail;
                 avail : = node[avail].next;
                 node[q].info : = in;
                 node[q].next : = node[p].next;
                 node[p].next : = q
           end;
end;
```

FURTHER MANIPULATIONS OF SINGLY LINKED LISTS

The basic operations of removing and inserting nodes in linked lists were detailed in the previous section. Here we develop algorithms to further manipulate linked lists and lead into a discussion of common enhancements to singly linked lists. Each algorithm is encoded in either COBOL or Pascal.

Finding a Particular Node

First, how can you find the Ith node in a list? If the list were housed in an array, a calculation using base location of the array and node size would yield the address of the desired node. If the list is represented in a linked manner, then we must step through the nodes, counting until we are positioned on the Ith one. Of course, it is necessary to check that there actually are at least I nodes in the list. The algorithm is shown in Fig. 6–13. To find the Ith node requires touching I nodes, unless the list contains fewer than I nodes. Then the entire list must be touched. The COBOL to implement the search follows, using the SPACE-ARRAY declaration from the preceding section.

```
COMPUTE PTR = FIRSTNODE.
PERFORM STEP-THRU-LIST
     VARYING J FROM 1 BY 1
          UNTIL J = I OR PTR = 0.
IF PTR = 0
     list has fewer than I nodes
ELSE output INFO (PTR).
```

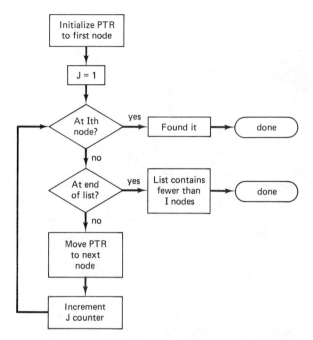

Figure 6–13 Logic to find the Ith node of a linked list.

where

STEP-THRU-LIST.
COMPUTE PTR = NEXTNODE (PTR).

    The algorithm to determine the number of nodes presently in a linked list is related and is left to the reader.

Inserting at the End of a List

The algorithm to insert a node at the beginning of a list has already been given in our discussions of the Avail stack. We have also seen the algorithm to remove a node from the beginning of a linked list, again in the discussion of the Avail stack. Let's consider now the algorithm to insert a node at the end of a linked list. The algorithm is shown in Fig. 6–14. All nodes in the list must be touched before the end can be found. We use the declarations from a previous section.

```
procedure inserend(first: nodeptr,in: nametype);
var newnode,q: nodeptr;
begin new(newnode);
      newnode ↑ .info : = in;
      newnode ↑ .next : = nil;
      q : = first;
      do while(q ↑ .next< >nil)
         q : = q ↑ .next;
      q ↑ .next : = newnode
end;
```

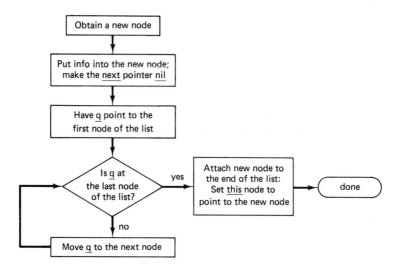

Figure 6–14   Logic to insert a node at the end of a linked list.

We use newnode as the name of the pointer to the new node because new is a reserved word. This code works except in the case where the initial list pointed to by first is empty. Fix the procedure such that it works correctly for all cases.

We now have seen how linked lists can be used to implement not just stacks but also queues. When a linked list is used to represent a queue, there should be a pointer directly to the rear of that queue, to avoid looping through all the nodes when there is occasion to find the last one. Let's call that pointer rear. The insertion algorithm then is shown in Fig. 6–15 and is coded in Pascal as follows.

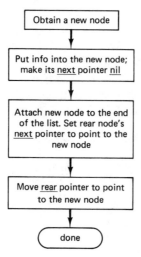

Figure 6–15   Logic to insert a node at the end of a linked list, with a pointer already set to the rear.

```
procedure inserend(in: nametype, var rear: nodeptr);
var newnode: nodeptr;
begin new(newnode);
        newnode ↑ .info : = in;
        newnode ↑ .next : = nil;
        rear ↑ .next : = newnode;
        rear : = newnode
end;
```

Only two nodes must be touched, the new one and the one that was the last one, pointed to by rear.

Reversing a List

An algorithm to reverse the elements in a linked list so that the last element becomes the new first element and the first element becomes the new last element involves stepping through each node of the list to change all the pointers. The algorithm is shown in Fig. 6–16. In COBOL (again using the SPACE-ARRAY):

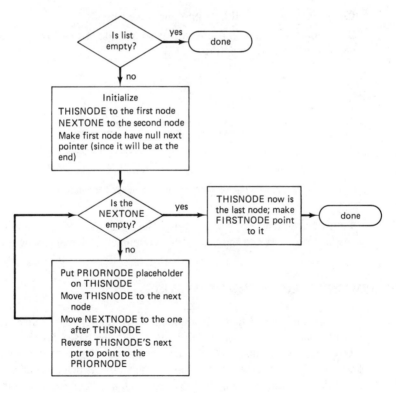

Figure 6–16 Logic to reverse the order of the nodes of a linked list.

```
01  AUX-POINTERS.
    02  THISNODE        PIC 9(3).
    02  PRIORNODE       PIC 9(3).
    02  NEXTONE         PIC 9(3).
REVERSE-LIST.
    IF FIRSTNODE NOT = 0
    THEN COMPUTE THISNODE = FIRSTNODE
        COMPUTE NEXTONE = NEXTNODE (THISNODE)
        COMPUTE NEXTNODE (THISNODE) = 0
        PERFORM STEP-THRU-LIST UNTIL (NEXTONE = 0)
        COMPUTE FIRSTNODE = THISNODE.
STEP-THRU-LIST.
    COMPUTE PRIORNODE = THISNODE.
    COMPUTE THISNODE = NEXTONE.
    COMPUTE NEXTONE = NEXTNODE (THISNODE).
    COMPUTE NEXTNODE (THISNODE) = PRIORNODE.
```

Other algorithms that you may find useful to develop yourself are the following:

- Concatenate two linked lists into one linked list.
- Split a linked list into two linked lists so that the last element in the first one is the element pointed to by P (Fig. 6–17).

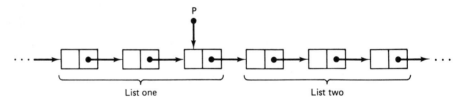

P

List one   List two

Figure 6–17   Splitting a linked list into two.

- Split a linked list into two linked lists such that the first list contains only elements where Info < M and the second list contains the elements where Info > = M.

CIRCULARLY LINKED LISTS AND HEAD NODES

Now that you understand these fundamental operations, we can investigate several enhancements that overcome various difficulties with the basic linked list.

One shortcoming that you may have noticed already is that given a pointer P into a linked list, it is not possible to reach any of the elements that precede Node(P). A simple change to the data structure will enable us to reach any node from any other node. Rather than storing a Null pointer in the Next field of the list's last element, have that last node

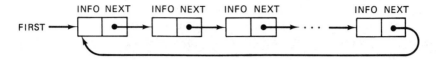

Figure 6–18   Circularly linked list.

point back to the beginning of the list (Fig. 6–18). This type of structure is called a *circularly linked list*.

You should investigate for yourself the changes that this modification to the list structure implies for the algorithms that were presented in prior sections.

The Josephus Problem

A famous problem that uses a circularly linked list is the Josephus problem. This problem has to do with selective deletion from a circularly linked list. There is a group of bandits in the Wild West who find themselves in a desperate predicament. The group is surrounded by the sheriff's posse and has no hope for mass escape. There is just one horse left. In order to select who shall take the horse and ride off with the booty, they (being a civilized group of bandits) do the following. Numbers are written on slips of paper and shuffled in a hat. The bandits stand in a circle. One is designated to be in the starting position (Fig. 6–19(a)).

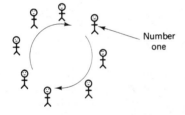

Figure 6–19(a)   The Josephus problem.

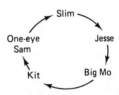

Figure 6–19(b)   The Josephus problem.

A number, say n, is drawn from the hat and the count begins around the circle (clockwise); the nth person is eliminated. He steps out of the circle; the circle's boundary is tightened. The count begins again with the man to his left being number 1. Again the nth person is eliminated. The process continues until only one bandit remains. He grabs the goods, jumps on the horse, and rides off into the sunset.

Assume the initial circle of bandits is as shown in Fig. 6–19(b) and Jesse is selected number 1 (he's the biggest). The number 4 is drawn, and One-eye Sam is the first bandit to be eliminated. The count begins again with Slim, and Kit leaves the circle. Again the count begins with Slim, and the number 4 falls on Slim. Jesse becomes first, and Big Mo loses as number 4. Jesse grabs the horse.

You should write a program that simulates this procedure. Input should be the list of names of bandits, ordered by their positions in the circle, and the drawn number n.

Output the names of the bandits as they are eliminated and the name of the winner. The obvious choice of data structure for this problem is a circularly linked list.

In the future we assume that all linked lists are circular unless noted otherwise.

Head Nodes

Now consider the problem of searching for a particular node, say the one that contains the name 'ELOISE,' in a circularly linked list. It's easy enough to get caught in an infinite loop while stepping through the list unless the programmer is very careful. Remember, the end of the list is no longer signaled by an element with a null Next pointer.

One common approach to this difficulty is to append a head node at the beginning or end of the list (Fig. 6–20).

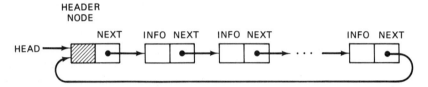

Figure 6–20   Circularly linked list with head node.

The head node may be distinguished from the other nodes in several ways:

- It may have a special value in its Info field which is invalid as data in the other elements (in this case we hash the Info field as in the above diagram).
- It may have a flag that marks it as a head node.

A designer may put meaningful data in a head node. For instance, the head could contain the number of nodes in the list, a user-oriented description of the list, a creation-date, or other information.

When a circularly linked list with head is empty, it still has its head node as shown in Fig. 6–21.

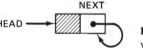

Figure 6–21   Empty circularly linked list with head node.

That is, Next(Head) = Head.

The algorithm for insertion of the contents of a variable NAME at the head of this list is

(a) Get space for a new node, and make NEW point to it.

(b) Put the contents of the variable NAME into the Info part of the new node.

(c) Make the new node point to the node that the head node used to point to.

(d) Make Head point to the new node.

How does the existence of a head node affect the other algorithms presented in this chapter? You should note the indispensable value of drawing pictures to simulate pointer handling as you develop and analyze algorithms.

Removing a Particular Node

You may have noted that our removal algorithms so far have all been specified so that the node *after* one pointed to is removed from the list. How can we remove the node pointed to by P? With only links to the next node, it is necessary that we step through the chain of nodes, comparing addresses until we are positioned on the one located at P, of course being careful not to fall off the end of a noncircular list. The algorithm is shown in Fig. 6–22. It is necessary not only to keep testing to see if the node pointed to by THIS is the node to be deleted, but also to keep track of what the prior node is so that

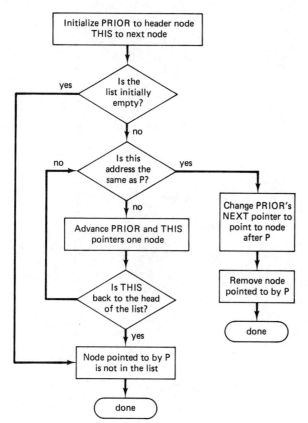

Figure 6–22 Logic for removing from a circularly linked list the node pointed to by P.

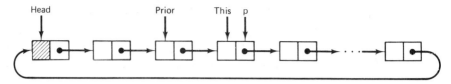

Figure 6–23   List with auxiliary pointers.

it can be linked to the node after THIS, if THIS happens to be equal to P (Fig. 6–23). On the average, removing the node pointed to by P requires touching half the nodes in the list. In the worst case, which occurs when the node pointed to by P is not in the list, all the nodes in the list must be touched. Compare this performance with that of the two algorithms presented earlier for removing the node after the one pointed to by P.

One way to code the algorithm in Pascal follows.

```
procedure removp(head:nodeptr,var p:nodeptr, out:nametype);
var prior, this:nodeptr;
    flag:0..2;
begin
    prior : = head;
    this : = head ↑ .next;
    flag : = 1; {search in progress}
    while flag = 1
        do begin
            if(this = head)
            then flag : = 2;   {have completed list, and not found node
                                        pointed to by p}
            if(this = p)
            then flag : = 0 {have found node pointed to by p}
            else begin prior : = this;
                        this : = this ↑ .next {step to next node}
                end;
        end;
if(flag > 0)
then NODE POINTED TO BY P IS NOT IN THE LIST
else begin {removal of node pointed to by p}
            prior ↑ .next : = p ↑ .next;
            out : = p ↑ .info;
            dispose(p)
        end;
end;
```

You might find it a useful exercise to develop the above algorithm for a noncircularly linked list and/or a linked list without a head node.

DOUBLY LINKED LIST

Basic Concepts

When it is desirable to be able to traverse a linked list backwards or to delete particular nodes, there are performance advantages to using a doubly linked rather than singly linked list. In a *doubly linked list* each node has not only a pointer to the next node but also a pointer to the prior node (Fig. 6–24).

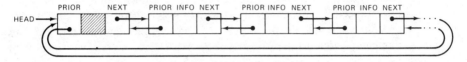

Figure 6–24   Doubly linked list.

Variations on a doubly linked list are to omit the head node and/or to not make the list circularly linked.

We called the pointer to the next node Next(Node); we call the pointer to the prior node Prior(Node). These pointers could be named the *right* and *left* pointers, the *successor* and *predecessor* pointers, *s-link* and *p-link* pointers, and so forth.

A fundamental property of doubly linked lists is that for any pointer P into the list,

$$Next(Prior(P)) = P$$

and
$$P = Prior(Next(P))$$

Taking a step backward from a node, then a step forward always positions you on the original node. Similarly, taking a step forward to the successor, then a step backward to the predecessor puts you back on the original node.

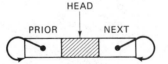

Figure 6–25   Empty doubly linked list.

An empty doubly linked list is as shown in Fig. 6–25. Both the Next and Prior pointers in the head node point to the head node; there are no other nodes in the list. That is,

$$Prior(Head) = Head$$

and
$$Next(Head) = Head.$$

Defining a Doubly Linked List

A doubly linked list structure can be declared as follows in Pascal using pointer variables.

$$\underline{\text{type}} \ \text{nodeptr} = \uparrow \text{nodetype};$$
$$\text{nodetype} = \underline{\text{record}}$$
$$\overline{\text{prior}} : \text{nodeptr};$$
$$\text{info} : \text{namctype};$$
$$\text{next} : \text{nodeptr}$$
$$\underline{\text{end}};$$

Because COBOL does not have pointer variables, COBOL programs use array storage for doubly linked lists. Just as we saw earlier in our discussion of using an array to house a singly linked list, the Avail list of empty space shares the doubly linked list's array. The Avail list is also doubly linked. The programmer must manage the indexes for the beginnings of each list, here done with the HEAD and AVAIL variables. In the following code, we assume a maximum of 500 nodes.

```
01   SPACE-ARRAY.
     02   NODE OCCURS 500 TIMES.
          03   PRIOR          PICTURE 9(3).
          03   INFO           PICTURE X(10).
          03   NEXTNODE       PICTURE 9(3).
     02   HEAD               PICTURE 9(3).
     02   AVAIL              PICTURE 9(3).
```

Fig. 6–26 shows an array housing a doubly linked list. Compare this example with the singly linked lists shown in Fig. 6–12.

	INFO	NEXT	PRIOR
1	IVAN	6	2
2	HOWARD	1	4
3		7	5
4	HORACE	2	0
5		3	0
6	JOAN	0	1
7		0	3

FIRST = 4
AVAIL = 5

Figure 6–26   Array housing doubly linked list.

Removing a Node

We can now reconsider our algorithms for removal and insertion of nodes in linked lists. First, for removal of the node pointed to by P from a doubly linked list, the pointers to that node from its successor and predecessor nodes must be reset (Fig. 6–27(a)).

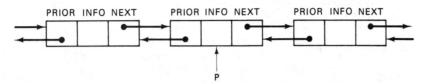

Figure 6–27(a)   Steps in removing a node from a doubly linked list.

The procedure is

(a) Set an auxiliary pointer to P's predecessor and one to its successor.

(b) Change the predecessor's Next pointer to point to P's successor, instead of to P.

(c) Change the successor's Prior pointer to point to P's predecessor, instead of to P.

(d) Free the space pointed to by P.

This algorithm requires touching three nodes, the one pointed to by P, its successor, and its predecessor. Compare this performance with that of the algorithm shown in Fig. 6–22, which removes the node pointed to by P from a singly linked list. Step (a) gives the structure shown in Fig. 6–27(b),

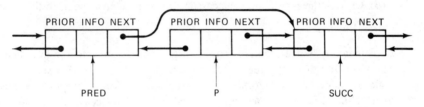

Figure 6–27(b)   Steps in removing a node from a doubly linked list.

and after step (c) we have the structure shown in Fig. 6–27(c).

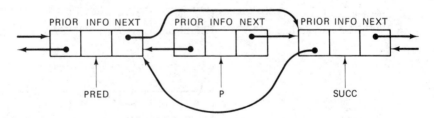

Figure 6–27(c)   Steps in removing a node from a doubly linked list.

In Pascal the algorithm can be coded as follows.

```
procedure removp(var p:nodeptr, out:nametype);
var pred,succ:nodeptr;
```

```
begin pred : = p ↑ .prior;
      succ : = p ↑ .next;
      pred ↑ .next : = succ;
      succ ↑ .prior : = pred;
      out : = p ↑ .info;
      dispose(p)
end;
```

Inserting a Node

To insert a variable IN into a doubly linked list such that it follows the node pointed to by P, we first establish the new node in the list, and then reset the pointers appropriately. The key to this algorithm is to not destroy pointers that are needed later. The procedure is

(a) Get a new node and fill it with the user's data.

(b) Set the new node's Next pointer to point to P's successor, and its Prior pointer to point to P.

(c) Change P's Next pointer to point to the new node.

(d) Change the new node's successor's Prior pointer to point to the new node instead of to P.

Implementing step d requires setting an auxiliary pointer to the new node's successor. The algorithm touches three nodes, the one pointed to by P, P's successor, and the new node. By contrast, the algorithm to insert a node to follow the node pointed to by P into a singly linked list requires touching just two nodes; P's successor did not need to be accessed. After step b, we have the structure shown in Fig. 6–28(a).

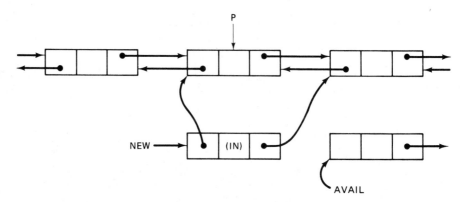

Figure 6–28(a)   Steps in inserting a node into a doubly linked list.

After step d we have the structure shown in Fig. 6–28(b).

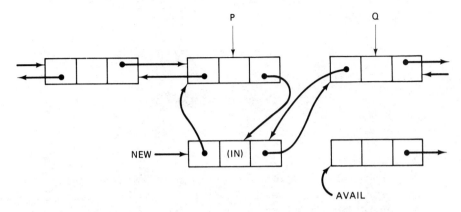

Figure 6–28(b) Steps in inserting a node into a doubly linked list.

In COBOL:

```
INSERAF.
        COMPUTE NEW = AVAIL.
        COMPUTE AVAIL = NEXTNODE (AVAIL).
        MOVE IN TO INFO (NEW).
        COMPUTE NEXTNODE (NEW) = NEXTNODE (P).
        COMPUTE PRIOR (NEW) = P.
        COMPUTE NEXTNODE (P) = NEW.
        COMPUTE Q = NEXTNODE (NEW).
        COMPUTE PRIOR (Q) = NEW.
```

Convince yourself that this algorithm works even when the list is initially empty.

Try developing for doubly linked lists the algorithms suggested in the preceding sections. The algorithms should be as generally correct as possible. That is, it should not be necessary to have one algorithm to do something to an initially empty list and another to do the same thing to an initially populated list. The algorithm itself should handle the "extreme" cases.

The basic trade-offs between use of singly linked and doubly linked lists are pointer storage and maintenance costs versus ease of list manipulation.

EXAMPLE APPLICATIONS OF LINKED LISTS

We now consider several applications that make good use of the linked list data structure. The first example uses linked lists to represent polynomials. The second example uses linked lists to represent alphabetically ordered string data. The third example shows how linked lists can be used to represent sparse arrays.

Polynomials

A polynomial is an algebraic expression of the form

$$a_n x^n + a_{n-1} x^{n-1} + \ldots + a_2 x^2 + a_1 x + a_0.$$

Each a_i is a coefficient of the corresponding power of the x variable. For example, in the polynomial

$$143x^4 + 201x^2 + 14x + 2$$

$a_4 = 143$, $a_3 = 0$, $a_2 = 201$, $a_1 = 14$, and $a_0 = 2$. Let's call this polynomial POLY1.

Polynomials are used in both scientific and business-oriented problems. General-purpose programming languages like Pascal, PL/I, COBOL, and FORTRAN do not have built-in data types or functions to manipulate polynomials directly. Rather, it is common to represent polynomials using arrays or linked lists. An appropriate node structure is (in Pascal)

```
type nodeptr = ↑ nodetype;
     nodetype = record
                    exp : integer;
                    coef : integer;
                    next : nodeptr
                end;
```

where exp is the variable's exponent, coef is the corresponding coefficient, and next links this node to the next node in the polynomial representation. Only the terms with nonzero coefficients need to be represented.

It is convenient to circularly link the nodes in order by decreasing exp values of the terms they represent (Fig. 6–29).

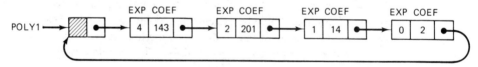

Figure 6–29   Example polynomial representation.

Addition (or subtraction) of two polynomials requires the addition (or subtraction) of the coefficients of terms with matching exponents. For example:

$$
\begin{array}{r}
143x^4 + \phantom{312x^3 + {}} 201x^2 + 14x + 2 \\
+ \phantom{143x^4 + {}} 312x^3 - 21x^2 + 42 \\
\hline
143x^4 + 312x^3 + 180x^2 + 14x + 44
\end{array}
$$

An algorithm to add polynomials POLY1 and POLY2 to form POLYSUM is introduced in Fig. 6–30. Implementation of the algorithm in Pascal follows. The head nodes are passed to the procedure polyadd. Poly1 and poly2 are pointers to the head nodes of

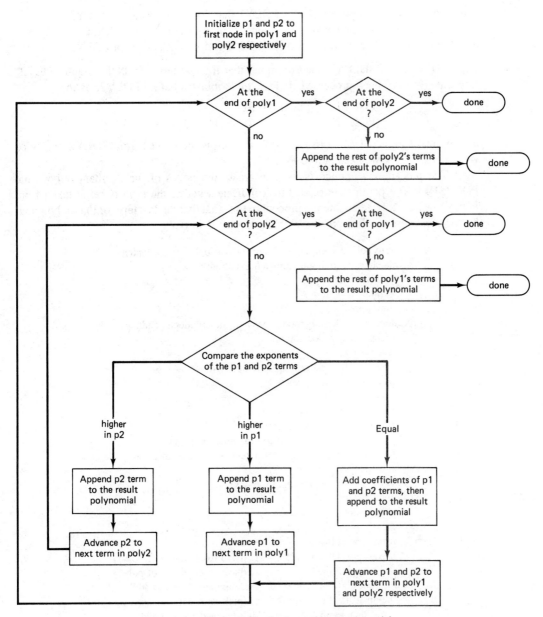

Figure 6–30 Logic to add two polynomials.

polynomials POLY1 and POLY2, respectively. Polysum points to the head node of the polynomial POLYSUM, which is constructed by the procedure. Pointers p1, p2, and psum are the addresses of the terms presently being considered in POLY1, POLY2, and POLYSUM, respectively. The *match* indicator is used to signal the following conditions:

exp1high: There is a power of x in POLY1 that does not appear in POLY2.
expmatch: There is a power of x that appears in both POLY1 and POLY2.
exp2high: There is a power of x in POLY2 that does not appear in POLY1.

The end1 and end2 flags are used to signal that the last terms of POLY1 and POLY2, respectively, have been processed. If POLY1 terminates before POLY2, as in

$$\begin{array}{lll} \text{(POLY1)} & 14x^4 + 3x^3 \\ + \quad \text{(POLY2)} & & 7x^3 + x^2 + 3 \end{array}$$

then terms of POLYSUM from exp = 2 on can just be copied from POLY2, and vice versa if POLY2 terminates before POLY1.

   The procedure sumnode is used to create the nodes of the resultant polynomial POLYSUM. The parameters passed to it indicate whether the term is being taken from POLY1 or POLY2 and enable the procedure to signal that the last term of that polynomial has been processed. Nodeptr is a globally known data type.

```
procedure polyadd(poly1,poly2:nodeptr;var polysum:nodeptr);
type match = (exp1high,expmatch,exp2high);
var p1,p2,psum:nodeptr;
      expflag:match;
      end1, end2: 0..1;
procedure sumnode(poly:nodeptr;var p,psum:nodeptr, endflag:0..1);
      {subprocedure declaration}
var pnew:nodeptr;
begin new(pnew); {add new node to sum list}
      psum ↑ .next : = pnew;
      psum : = pnew;
      psum ↑ .exp : = p ↑ .exp;
      psum ↑ .coef : = p ↑ .coef;
      p : = p ↑ .next; {move p to next node on poly}
      if p=poly then endflag : = 1 {check if at end of poly}
end; {sumnode}
begin end1 : = 0; {main program block}
      end2 : = 0;
      p1 : = poly1 ↑ .next;
      p2 : = poly2 ↑ .next;
      psum : = polysum;
      if(p1 = poly1)then end1 : = 1; {have reached end of poly1}
      if(p2 = poly2)then end2 : = 1; {have reached end of poly2}
      while (end1 =0 and end2=0) {there are still terms to add}
      do begin if(p1 ↑ .exp>p2 ↑ .exp) {pick term with greater exponent}
               then expflag : = exp1high {as next term to add}
               else if(p1 ↑ .exp=p2 ↑ .exp)
                    then expflag : = expmatch
                    else expflag : = exp2high;
            case expflag of
            exp1high: sumnode(poly1,p1,psum,end1); {add poly1
               term}
```

```
              expmatch: begin sumnode(poly1,p1,psum,end1); {add
                     poly1 term}
                                 psum ↑ .coef : = psum ↑ .coef + p2 ↑ .coef;
                                        {add poly2 term}
                                 p2 : = p2 ↑ .next;
                                 if p2 = poly2 then end2 : = 1 {end of
                                                poly2}
                          end;
              exp2high : sumnode(poly2,p2,psum,end2) {add poly2
                     term}
         end;
      end;
      {have reached end of at least one poly}
      while (end1 = 0) {have reached end of poly2}
      do sumnode(poly2,p2,psum,end2); {add rest of poly1 terms}
      while (end2 = 0) {have reached end of poly1}
      do sumnode(poly2,p2,psum,end2); {add rest of poly2 terms}
      psum ↑ .next : = polysum
   end;
```

This program can be modified to handle instead the subtraction of two polynomials. A useful exercise is to write a program to add two polynomials that are represented by linked lists that are housed in arrays rather than implemented using pointer variables. How would the algorithm be different if the linked lists were not circular? If they did not have head nodes? If they were doubly linked? Why was the singly linked list chosen as the data structure here?

What are the algorithms for multiplication of polynomials? For division of polynomials?

Consider now the problem of manipulating polynomials in two variables, say in x and y. Again, a linked list is an appropriate data structure to represent this abstract data type. Each term can be represented by a node of the following type.

```
type nodeptr = ↑ nodetype;
     nodetype = record
                       coef : integer;
                       xexp : integer;
                       yexp : integer;
                       next : nodeptr
                 end;
```

Only the terms with nonzero coefficients need to be represented.

Algorithms to manipulate these polynomial representations can be simplified by requiring that the terms be linked in some specific order, say in sorted order by x exponent major, y exponent minor. For example,

$$14x^3 + 82x^2y - 47y^4 + 12y^2 + 6$$

would be as shown in Fig. 6–31.

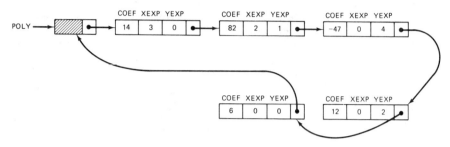

Figure 6–31   Example polynomial with two variables.

Develop an algorithm to add two polynomials in two variables. How does it differ from the algorithm presented here to add polynomials in one variable?

What is the appropriate node structure for terms of a polynomial in three variables? In *n* variables?

A Simple Multi-linked List

As we will discuss in more detail later, there are many cases where it is appropriate to use linked lists with more than two pointers per node. One simple example of a data structure with three pointers per node is a doubly linked list of variable-length string data where each node contains a pointer to the actual data rather than the data value (Fig. 6–32).

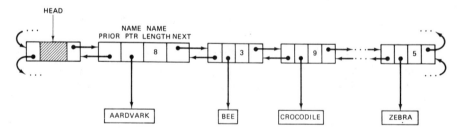

Figure 6–32   Example multi-linked list.

The major benefit of using this data structure here is that the nodes of the primary doubly linked list can be fixed in length. Each contains three pointer values and one integer. Management of fixed-length chunks of memory is significantly less complex than is management of variable-length chunks of memory. Of course, here we still have to contend with the actual names of animals, which are variable length.

Sparse Arrays

A common application of linked lists is to represent sparse arrays. Earlier we discussed sequential representations of sparse arrays. Linked representations of sparse arrays have the potential to significantly reduce storage requirements and to reduce the number of calculations performed in some array operations. Only the nonzero entries in an array will be represented.* The overhead introduced by the linked representation may outweigh the benefits if the array is not sparse enough.

One possible linked representation of a two-dimensional sparse array is the following. There is one linked list for each row and for each column of the array. Each of these linked lists has a head node and is circular, but is only singly linked. Each nonzero entry in the array is represented by an occurrence of a node of the form (in Pascal).

```
type nodeptr :  ↑nodetype;
     nodeptr = record
                 row : integer;
                 column : integer;
                 value : integer;
                 nextincol : nodeptr;
                 nextinrow : nodeptr
               end;
```

Each node contains an indication of the row and column in which the nonzero entry appears, the value of the entry, and two pointers. One pointer is to the next node in the same row; one pointer is to the next node in the same column.

For example, the following 5-by-4 array

1	0	0	0
0	−3	0	0
2	0	1	0
0	0	14	0
0	0	0	0

would have the representation shown in Fig. 6–33. Each nonhead node participates in two linked lists: one for its row and one for its column. In this example there are four nonzero rows and three nonzero columns; there are seven non-null lists. Here there are five nonzero entries in the array and nine head nodes. The fifteen zero entries have not taken up storage space.

This particular technique for representing a sparse array is quite satisfactory when there are frequent updates to the array. The linked structure makes it fairly easy to make changes in what is and is not a nonzero entry. For other approaches to representing sparse arrays, the interested reader should consult U. W. Pooch and A. Nieder, "A survey of indexing techniques for sparse matrices," *ACM Computing Surveys*, 5(2):109–133, June 1973.

You might develop algorithms to add two sparse arrays (i.e., matrices) and to perform matrix multiplication on two sparse matrices.

What would be an appropriate structure to represent a sparse three-dimensional array? A sparse n-dimensional array?

* These "sparse" techniques can also be applied when most of the elements of the array take on a particular nonzero value, say 1.

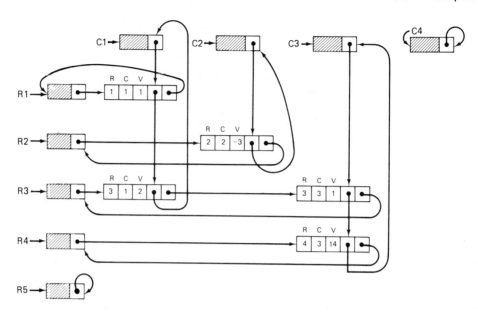

Figure 6–33 Linked representation of sparse array.

SUMMARY

A linked list is a nonsequential way to represent a linear data structure. Each node of a linked list contains at least one pointer, which links that node to the next node on the list. A linked list may be circular, in which case the last node points to the first node. Linked lists commonly are implemented with head nodes. In order to simplify algorithms to perform some insertions and removals from linked lists, pointers to prior as well as next nodes are often used. The resultant lists are called doubly linked lists.

When a given node can participate simultaneously in more than one linked list, the structure is said to be a multi-linked list. We will study these structures in more detail later.

We have seen how to use linked lists to represent not just general linear lists, but also special kinds of linear lists, notably stacks and queues. We have considered several representative applications that use linked lists. Singly linked lists are appropriate for representation of polynomials; a doubly linked list can be used to represent sorted variable-length strings; a two-dimensional multi-list structure can be used to represent a sparse array.

The basic benefit of using a linked list is that it does not require sequential storage. Thus it can be advantageous to use linked lists when there is significant insertion and deletion activity in a logically ordered data structure. It is also appropriate to use a linked list when it is necessary to logically order elements that are not physically sequential, e.g., to implement a stack of available chunks of space. The basic costs of using a linked list are the space requirements for pointers and the overhead of manipulating and managing pointers.

We use linked lists extensively in the rest of this book. They are fundamental to data management techniques.

TERMS

array	node
circularly linked list	null
doubly linked list	pointer variable
head node	queue
linear list	stack
linked list	

SELECTED REFERENCES

BERMAN, G. AND A. W. COLIJN. "A modified list technique allowing binary search," *Jour. ACM* 21(2):201–206, April 1974.

CLARK, D. W. "A fast algorithm for copying list structures," *Comm. ACM*, 21(5):351–357, May 1978.

COHEN, J. "Garbage collection of linked data structures," *ACM Computing Surveys*, 13(3):341–367, Sept. 1981.

FISHER, D. A. "Copying cyclic list structures in linear time using bounded workspace," *Comm. ACM*, 18(5):251–252, May 1975.

LINDSTROM, G. "Copying list structures using bounded workspace," *Comm. ACM*, 17(4):198–202, April 1974.

POOCH, U. W. AND A. NIEDER. "A survey of indexing techniques for sparse matrices," *ACM Computing Surveys*, 5(2):109–133, June 1973.

SCHNEIDERMAN, B. AND P. SCHEUERMANN. "Structured data structures," *Comm. ACM*, 17(10):566–574, Oct. 1974.

REVIEW EXERCISES

1. Fill in the Next pointers so that the following array representation of a linked list is in alphabetical order by Info field contents. What does the stack of available space look like?

```
        INFO    NEXT
    1 |  PEACH  |      |
    2 |  APPLE  |      |
    3 |         |      |
    4 |  CHERRY |      |
    5 |  GRAPE  |      |
```

Figure P6–1

2. A list of items appears in an array as follows.

```
        DATA    NEXT
    1 |  ITEM G |      |
    2 |  ITEM D |      |
    3 |  ITEM J |      |
    4 |  ITEM B |      |
    5 |  ITEM E |      |
    6 |  ITEM F |      |
    7 |         |      |
    8 |         |      |
    9 |         |      |
```

Figure P6–2

Show the contents of the Next fields to link the items alphabetically.

3. Insert items C, A, and Z to the above array such that the resultant linked list is still in alphabetic order.

4. Write an algorithm to find the jth node in a singly linked list.

5. Write an algorithm to return a circular linked list T to the pool of available nodes.

6. What is the result of Next(Prior(P)) in a doubly linked list?

7. Let X be a pointer to some arbitrary node in a singly linked list. Write an algorithm that will place '1234' in the Info field of an additional node and insert this additional node after the node pointed to by X.

8. Write an algorithm that will insert a node S into a doubly linked list immediately before node X.

9. Write an algorithm that will reverse a noncircular singly linked list. A doubly linked list.

10. Write the algorithms to get a node and to free a node for a storage pool that is structured as a queue.

11. How many links must be changed to delete an item from a doubly linked list?

12. Write the algorithms to add to an delete from a stack represented using a singly linked list.

13. Write the algorithms to add to and delete from a queue represented using a singly linked list.

14. Write a routine to concatenate two singly linked lists A and B.

15. How can the following sparse matrix be represented by linked lists?

```
0     0     5     2
0    10     4     0
0     0     0     2
0     0     0     0
```

16. Write an algorithm to delete the node containing 'CAT' from the linked list below.

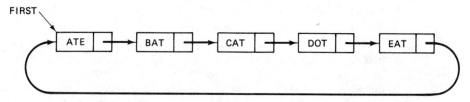

Figure P6–16

17. Write an algorithm to split the above linked list between 'BAT' and 'CAT' and attach head nodes from the Avail list to the start of the new list.

18. Why is a circular linked list appropriate for the Josephus problem? Write the algorithm to solve the Josephus problem.

19. Illustrate the use of linked lists to represent the polynomials $5x^3 + 7x^2 + 9$ and $3x^2 + 4x + 7$.

20. Show how linked lists can be used to represent the following polynomials.

$$7x^4y - 3x^2y^2 + 5y + 12y^2 - 2$$
$$9x^3y^2 + 2x^2y^2 - 11xy + 3y^3$$

21. Write an algorithm to count the number of nodes in a linked list.

22. Consider the use of an array to store a linked list of book inventory information. The array is defined as follows in COBOL.

```
01   BOOK-ARRAY.
     02   BOOK-NODE OCCURS 15 TIMES.
          03   AUTHOR              PIC X(20).
          03   NEXT-AUTHOR         PIC 99.
          03   TITLE               PIC X(30).
          03   NEXT-TITLE          PIC 99.
          03   STOCK-NO            PIC 9(5).
          03   NEXT-STOCK-NO       PIC 99.
          03   PRIOR-STOCK-NO      PIC 99.
          03   NEXT-AVAIL          PIC 99.

     02   HEADS.
          03   FIRST-AUTHOR        PIC 99.
          03   FIRST-TITLE         PIC 99.
          03   FIRST-STOCK-NO      PIC 99.
          03   LAST-STOCK-NO       PIC 99.
          03   AVAIL               PIC 99.
```

Entries are linked alphabetically by author's last name, alphabetically by first word of title, and in ascending order by STOCK-NO. Show the contents of the BOOK-ARRAY after completion of each of the following transactions.

Operation	Stock-no	Title	Author
INSERT	53526	CREATIVE PHOTOGRAPHY	F. STOP FITZGERALD
INSERT	98374	NEWSPAPER ORIGAMI	LINUS TYPE
INSERT	14683	COOL HAND LUKE	HADDA DUWITT
INSERT	23764	THE LONGEST YARD	LOWEN MAUER
INSERT	49261	LA MARKE DE LA FRANCAISE	ASCENT AGU
INSERT	19822	BEER BASTED HOT DOGS	DR. FRANK ANNSTEIN
INSERT	76482	FOUR-WAY ROMANCE	QUAD LAMOORE
INSERT	17760	COMPUTER SIMULATION	ARTIE ABACUS
INSERT	38641	BETSY WORE BLUE JEANS	DENN M. STRETCHER
INSERT	73920	FINGER LICKIN' GOOD	C. SANDERS
DELETE	14683		
DELETE	76482		

23. What advantages are there from having a head node on a list? What disadvantages?

24. What advantages does a circular singly linked list have over a non-circular singly linked list? What disadvantages?

25. What advantages does a circular doubly linked list have over a circular singly linked list? What disadvantages?

26. Consider an array of 500 nodes used to house a doubly linked list. Assume that the available nodes are linked together in a singly linked list.
    (a) Write an algorithm to remove a node from the doubly linked list.
    (b) Write an algorithm to insert a node into the doubly linked list.
    (c) What is the average number of nodes that are touched in your removal algorithm?
    (d) What is the average number of nodes that are touched in your insertion algorithm?
    (e) Compare your answers to (a)–(d) with the situation where the available nodes *are* also in a doubly linked list.

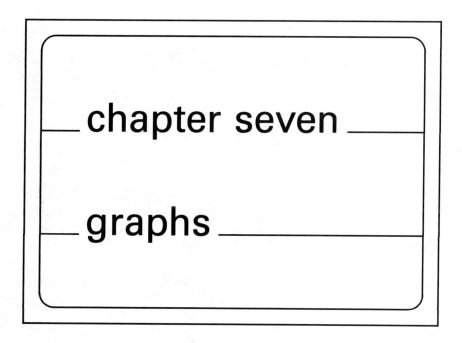

chapter seven

graphs

The data structures that have been discussed so far in this book have been linear structures. For each element, there has been a *next* element. This linearity is typical of strings, of elements along a single dimension of an array, of fields in a record, of entries in a stack, of entries in a queue, and of nodes in a simple linked list. In this chapter we begin our study of *nonlinear* data structures. In these structures each element may have several "next" elements, which introduces the concept of branching structures. These branching data structures quite appropriately are called *graphs* and *trees*.

We discuss graphs and their representation and operations in this chapter. Chapter 8 will start our discussion of trees, which are special kinds of graphs.

DEFINITIONS

Intuitively, a graph is a set of points and a set of lines, with each line joining one point to another. The points are called the *nodes* of the graph, and the lines are called the *edges*. We denote the set of nodes of a given graph G by V_G and the set of edges by E_G. For example, in the graph G of Fig. 7–1, $V_G = \{a,b,c,d\}$ and $E_G = \{1,2,3,4,5,6,7,8\}$. The number of elements in V_G is called the *order* of graph G. A *null graph* is a graph with order zero.

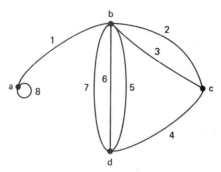

Figure 7–1 Example graph.

An edge is determined by the nodes it connects. Edge 4, for example, connects nodes c and d and is said to be of *form* (c,d). A graph is completely determined by its set of nodes and set of edges. The actual positioning of these elements on the page is unimportant. The graph of Fig. 7–1 is equivalent to the graph of Fig. 7–2.

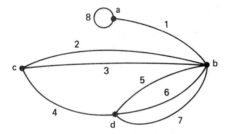

Figure 7–2 Equivalent graph to Fig. 7–1.

Note that there may be multiple edges connecting two nodes, e.g., edges 5, 6, and 7 are all of form (b,d). Some pairs of nodes may not be connected; for example, there is no edge here of form (a,c) or (a,d). Some edges may connect one node with itself; e.g., edge 8 is of form (a,a). These edges are called *loops*.

A graph G is called a *simple graph* if both of the following conditions are true:

1. It has no loops, that is, there does not exist an edge in E_G of form (v,v) where v is in V_G.

2. No more than one edge joins any pair of nodes, that is, there does not exist more than one edge in E_G of form (v_1,v_2) for any pair of elements v_1 and v_2 in V_G.

Fig. 7–3 depicts a simple graph derived from the example graph of Fig. 7–1.

A graph that is not a simple graph is sometimes called a *multigraph*. You will find that edges are sometimes referred to as *arcs* and nodes are sometimes termed *vertices*.

A *connected graph* is a graph that cannot be partitioned into two graphs without removing at least one edge. The graph of Fig. 7–4 is *not* a connected graph.

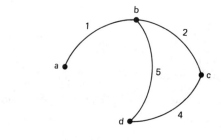

Figure 7–3 Example simple graph derived from Fig. 7–1.

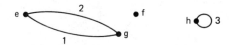

Figure 7–4 Example unconnected graph.

Paths

A *path* in a graph is a sequence of one or more edges that connects two nodes. We denote by $P(v_i, v_j)$ a path connecting nodes v_i and v_j. For $P(v_i, v_j)$ to exist, there must be in E_G a sequence of edges of the following form.

$$P(v_i, v_j) = (v_i, x_1) (x_1, x_2) \ldots (x_{n-1}, x_n) (x_n, v_j)$$

The *length* of a path is the number of edges that it comprises. In the simple graph of Fig. 7–3, the following are paths between nodes b and d:

$P(b,d) = (b,c) (c,d)$	length = 2
$P(b,d) = (b,c) (c,b) (b,c) (c,d)$	length = 4
$P(b,d) = (b,d)$	length = 1
$P(b,d) = (b,c) (c,b) (b,d)$	length = 3

In general, we are interested only in paths in which a given node is "visited" no more than once. This restricts our interest to only the first and third paths above. The second path visits both nodes b and c twice; the fourth path visits node b twice. We will always be interested in *not* traversing the same edge more than once in a path. This will prevent our algorithms from getting delayed retracing their steps.

Cycles

A *cycle* is a path in which both of the following conditions are true:

1. No edge appears more than once in the sequence of edges.
2. The initial node of the path is the same as the terminal node of the path; i.e., $P(v,v)$.

In other words, a cycle returns to where it started. The graph of Fig. 7–2 has several cycles, for example.

$$P(a,a) = (a,a)$$
$$P(b,b) = (b,c)\ (c,b)$$
$$P(b,b) = (b,c)\ (c,d)\ (d,b)$$
$$P(d,d) = (d,b)\ (b,c)\ (c,d)$$
$$P(d,d) = (d,b)\ (b,d)$$

A graph with no cycles is said to be *acyclic*. Figs. 7–5(a) and (b) both represent acyclic graphs.

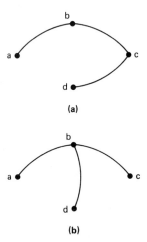

(a)

(b)   **Figure 7–5**   Example acyclic graphs.

Directed Graphs

Another special case of the general graph data structure is a *directed graph*, in which directionality is assigned to the graph's edges. An example is shown in Fig. 7–6.

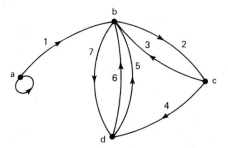

Figure 7–6   Example directed graph.

Each edge of a directed graph includes an arrow.

The *in-degree* of a node in a directed graph is the number of edges that terminate at that node; the *out-degree* of a node is the number of edges that emanate from that node. The *degree* of a node is the sum of its in- and out-degrees. For the example of Fig. 7–6 the values are

in-degree(a) = 1	out-degree(a) = 2	degree(a) = 3
in-degree(b) = 4	out-degree(b) = 2	degree(b) = 6
in-degree(c) = 1	out-degree(c) = 2	degree(c) = 3
in-degree(d) = 2	out-degree(d) = 2	degree(d) = 4

Throughout this chapter we refer to the nodes of graphs by their labels. In reality, a node may contain any kind of information. We will tend to ignore these node contents; you should not forget, however, that the ultimate purpose of graphs and trees is to represent the logical structure of this information.

GRAPHS IN PROGRAMS

As with some of the other data structures that we have studied, the common programming languages do not have a built-in data type called "graph." Instead, the graph's characteristics are simulated by housing it in another data structure. There are three major approaches to representing graphs: matrix representation, list representation, and multilist representation. After considering each of these, we delve into discussion of some of the more common operations on graphs: graph traversal and path analysis.

ADJACENCY MATRIX REPRESENTATION

Consider a graph G with set of nodes V_G and set of edges E_G. Assume the graph is of order N, for N >= 1. One approach to representing this graph is to use an *adjacency matrix*, which is a N-by-N array A, where

$$A(i,j) = \begin{cases} 1 \text{ if and only if edge } (v_i,v_j) \text{ is in } E_G \\ 0 \text{ otherwise.} \end{cases}$$

If there is an edge connecting nodes i and j, then A(i,j) = 1. The adjacency matrix for the undirected graph in Fig. 7–7 is

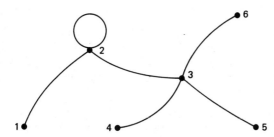

Figure 7–7 Example undirected graph.

i \ j	1	2	3	4	5	6
1	0	1	0	0	0	0
2	1	1	1	0	0	0
3	0	1	0	1	1	1
4	0	0	1	0	0	0
5	0	0	1	0	0	0
6	0	0	1	0	0	0

Directed Graphs

An edge of a *directed graph* has its source in one node and terminates in another node. By convention, edge (v_i, v_j) denotes direction from node v_i to node v_j.

The adjacency matrix for the directed graph of Fig. 7–8 is

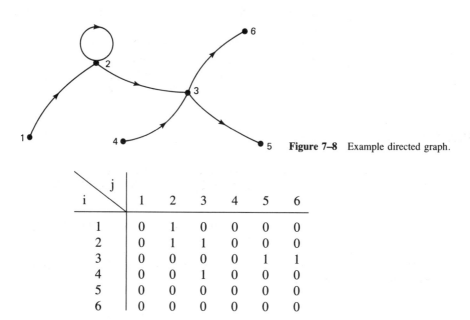

Figure 7–8 Example directed graph.

i \ j	1	2	3	4	5	6
1	0	1	0	0	0	0
2	0	1	1	0	0	0
3	0	0	0	0	1	1
4	0	0	1	0	0	0
5	0	0	0	0	0	0
6	0	0	0	0	0	0

Sparse Matrices

A graph of order N has an N-by-N adjacency matrix. In many cases these adjacency matrices are quite sparse and can be stored as sparse arrays. In these cases, the matrix representation approach generally is not as suitable as the linked approaches that we will introduce later in this chapter.

The adjacency matrix of an undirected graph is symmetric. Thus even if the matrix is not sparse, storage requirements can be cut almost in half by storing only the upper

(or lower) triangle of the matrix. Refer back to Chapters 2 and 6 to refresh your understanding of triangular and sparse arrays.

Defining Graphs in COBOL and Pascal

The following array definition can be used to declare a graph named GRAPH of order
24 in COBOL. The graph requires a 24-by-24 adjacency matrix.

```
01   GRAPH.
    02   ROW OCCURS 24 TIMES.
       03   COL OCCURS 24 TIMES.
          04   EDGE PIC 9.
```

EDGE (I,J) then has value 1 if an edge exists between nodes I and J and has value 0
otherwise.

Another way to interpret an adjacency matrix is as a boolean data type. For example,
in Pascal:

$$\text{type graph : array } [1 . . 24, 1 . . 24] \text{ of boolean;}$$

Here graph $[i,j]$ has value *true* if an edge exists between nodes i and j and has value
false otherwise.

Edge Calculations

It is often convenient to be able to do arithmetic on an adjacency matrix. For example,
the degree of node i in an undirected graph is

$$\sum_{j=1}^{N} A(i,j)$$

The in-degree of node i in a directed graph is the column-sum of the matrix

$$\sum_{k=1}^{N} A(k,i)$$

and the out-degree of node i is the row-sum of the matrix

$$\sum_{k=1}^{N} A(i,k)$$

We will discuss other common results of manipulating the adjacency data later in the
chapter. If the adjacency matrix is defined to be boolean, then these common manipulations
are not quite so straightforward. Instead of summation, they require series of boolean
operations (*and* and *or*).

Weighted Edges

There are many graph applications in which variations on the pure adjacency matrix representation are appropriate. Consider the graph shown in Fig. 7–9, which might be used in a trucking company's information system. This is an example of a graph with weighted edges. The nodes represent cities and the edges represent truck routes between cities. Each edge is labeled with the distance between the connected pair of cities. Rather than using a bit matrix to represent this trucking system, we instead might use weighted edge matrix representation (Fig. 7–10).

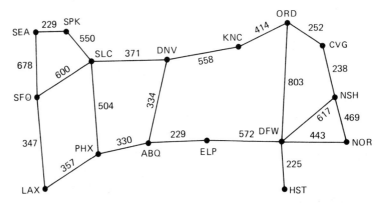

Figure 7–9   Example graph showing inter-city distances.

	1	2	3	4	5	6	7	8	9	10	11	12	13	14	15	16
1		0	0	334	229	0	0	0	0	0	0	330	0	0	0	0
2			0	0	0	0	0	0	238	0	252	0	0	0	0	0
3				0	572	225	0	0	617	443	803	0	0	0	0	0
4					0	0	558	0	0	0	0	0	0	0	371	0
5						0	0	0	0	0	0	0	0	0	0	0
6							0	0	0	0	0	0	0	0	0	0
7								0	0	0	414	0	0	0	0	0
8									0	0	0	357	0	347	0	0
9										469	0	0	0	0	0	0
10											0	0	0	0	0	0
11												0	0	0	0	0
12													0	0	504	0
13														678	0	229
14															600	0
15																550
16																

Figure 7–10   Weighted-edge matrix representation of Fig. 7–9.

where node 1 = ABQ	6 = HST	11 = ORD	16 = SPK
2 = CVG	7 = KNC	12 = PHX	
3 = DFW	8 = LAX	13 = SEA	
4 = DNV	9 = NSH	14 = SFO	
5 = ELP	10 = NOR	15 = SLC	

Weighted edges are used frequently. In transportation applications, the weights commonly represent distances, as above. In flow applications, the weights commonly represent capacities. For example, the nodes on a graph might represent the gallon/minute capacity of a pipe-line between the connected locations, or the bits/second capacity of a communications facility between the connected switching stations.

In other applications, the edge weights represent time. For instance, graphs can be used to represent networks of activities. Each edge represents a task or activity. The weight on the edge represents the amount of time required to complete the activity. Each node represents an event, the completion of the set of activities represented by the edges coming into the node. No activity on an out-edge can be started until all activities on in-edges to a node have completed. (Variations on the basic activity graph allow a completion event to be signaled by a subset of the incident activity edges.) We will consider activity graphs in more detail later in our discussion of critical path analysis.

LINKED REPRESENTATIONS

Representation of a graph using the adjacency matrix technique requires storage of edge information for each possible pair of nodes. For graphs of N nodes with few edges relative to the possible N^2 connections, a linked representation generally is more appropriate.

A new programmer on a project at the city's computer center discovered the hard way the benefits of selecting the appropriate representation for a data structure for the application. He was responsible for a COBOL program which was to be part of the transportation system. The program was to be used to keep track of traffic volumes on major city streets. The nodes on the graph were to represent intersections; the edges were to represent streets. Weights on the edges were to represent the traffic volumes. Each edge for a one-way street had only one weight; each edge for a two-way street carried two weights. Data were collected for 500 intersections. The programmer used an adjacency matrix to represent the traffic graph. Few of the intersections represented the confluence of more than four street segments. The vast majority of the adjacency matrix thus held zeroes; the program's storage requirements prevented it from fitting in the city computer's main memory. The programmer did not recognize the problem with the matrix representation, and instead spent many hours compacting the *PROCEDURE DIVISION* code. The program completion date passed (several times) and the code had never even been tested. Alas, the programmer left for greener pastures. An experienced programmer found the troublesome code on her desk, identified the gross storage requirements of the matrix, converted the program to use a linked representation, and completed the project.

In contrast to the adjacency matrix technique, which stores information about every possible edge, the linked representations store information about only those edges that exist. As edges are added or deleted from the graph, the linked representation must be modified accordingly. There are two fundamental types of linked structures to represent graphs; one is called the node directory representation and the other one is called the multi-list representation.

Node Directory Representation

The *node directory representation* includes two parts: a directory and a set of linked lists. There is one entry in the directory for each node of the graph. The directory entry for node *i* points to a linked list that represents the nodes that are connected to node *i*. Each record of the linked list has two fields: one is a node identifier; one is a link to the next element on the list. The directory represents nodes; the linked list represents edges.

A node directory representation of the undirected graph of Fig. 7–7 is given in Fig. 7–11.

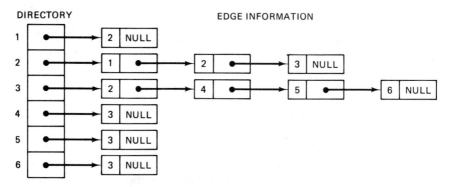

Figure 7–11   Node directory representation of Fig. 7–7.

An undirected graph of order *N* with *E* edges requires *N* entries in the directory and 2*E linked list entries, except that each loop reduces the number of linked list entries by one. (Why?)

A node directory representation of the directed graph of Fig. 7–8 is given by Fig. 7–12.

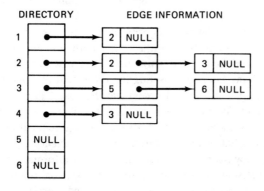

Figure 7–12   Node directory representation of Fig. 7–8.

A directed graph of order *N* with *E* edges requires *N* entries in the directory and *E* linked list entries.

The linked list headed by the *i*th directory entry corresponds to the *i*th row of the adjacency matrix representation. The directory entries are ordered sequentially by node identifier. Although we also have ordered the linked list entries by node identifier, they could have appeared in any order since each entry bears its node identity.

A COBOL declaration of the node directory representation of an undirected graph of order 24 with a maximum of 100 edges is

```
01   GRAPH.
     02   NODE OCCURS 24 TIMES
                      PICTURE 9(3).
     02   EDGES.
          03   LIST-ENTRY OCCURS 200 TIMES.
          04   NODE-ID PICTURE 99.
          04   NEXT-ENTRY PICTURE 9(3).
```

This approach requires N entries in the directory and $2*\text{max}(E)$ array entries, where N is the order of the graph and $\text{max}(E)$ is the maximum number of edges. $\text{Max}(E)$ could be as large as $N(N - 1)$, bringing the total number of entries in the directory and the array to N^2, which is the same as if an adjacency matrix been used.

Use of a language, like Pascal, that supports dynamic memory allocation, would reduce the space requirements. An undirected graph of order 24 and a maximum of 100 edges could be declared in Pascal by the following.

```
type nodeid = 0 . . 24;
     pedgeptr  =  ↑ edgeinfo;
     edgeinfo  =  record node : nodeid;
                         next : edgeptr end;
     directory  =  array [1 . . 24] of edgeptr;
```

Note that the maximum number of edges is immaterial to the declaration; the edgeinfo records are allocated as nodes are inserted in the graph. This approach requires N entries in the directory and $2*E$ edgeinfo records, where N is the order of the graph and E is the number of edges. The implementation matches the linked-list design presented earlier in this section. The COBOL array implementation approximates the linked-list design.

Weighted Edges

Representation of a graph with weighted edges requires making provision in the data structure for storage of those weights. Fig. 7–13 shows a directed graph with weighted edges. This particular example is an activity graph: each node represents an event and each edge represents a task whose completion helps to trigger the next event, which is the start of other tasks. Each edge's weight is its required time. This kind of graph is commonly used in project management systems.

A node directory representation for this graph is shown in Fig. 7–14. The record for each

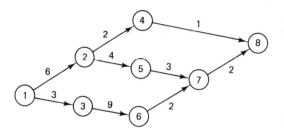

Figure 7–13 Example activity graph.

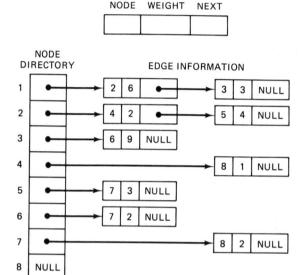

Figure 7–14 Node directory representation of Fig. 7–13.

edge entry contains the identifier of the destination node, the weight of the edge, and a pointer to the next edge with the same source node.

Edge Calculations

To determine the degree of a node in an undirected graph requires counting the number of entries on its linked list. The out-degree of a node in a directed graph also can be determined by counting the number of entries on its linked list.

Determining the in-degree of node i is more complex. Each of the linked lists must be accessed in order to detect whether or not node i appears as a destination node. To facilitate finding prior nodes and determining in-degrees, an auxiliary directory of edges coming into nodes may be maintained.

Some types of graph analysis are easier with the adjacency matrix representation than with linked representation. However, if storage space were the only criterion for selection, then the linked representation generally would require less space, unless the graph were highly connected. If a graph has a highly volatile structure, then it may require less work to add or delete edges in the adjacency matrix representation than in the node directory representation. Changing a matrix entry generally is faster than is adding (deleting) another entry to a linked list.

Multi-list Representation

In the *multi-list representation* of graph structures, there are again two parts: a directory of node information and a set of linked lists of edge information. There is one entry in the node directory for each node of the graph. The directory entry for node i points to a linked adjacency list for node i. Each record of the linked list area appears on two adjacency lists: one for the node at each end of the represented edge. Using the data structure of Fig. 7–15 for each edge entry (v_i, v_j),

NODE 1   NODE 2

ID   ADJ   ID   ADJ

| V_i | $NEXT_1$ | V_j | $NEXT_2$ |

Figure 7–15   Data structure for edge (v_i, v_j).

a multi-list representation for the example graph of Fig. 7–7 is Fig. 7–16. This is not the only multi-list representation for this graph. It is based on the set of edges $\{(1,2),(2,2),(2,3),(4,3),(3,5),(3,6)\}$. An alternative representation based upon the set of edges $\{(2,1),(2,2),(2,3),(3,4),(5,3),(3,6)\}$ is shown in Fig. 7–17. If the graph were directed, there would not be such flexibility in selecting identifiers for edges.

An edge weight can be stored with the other information recorded for the edge, just as was done in earlier examples of graph representations.

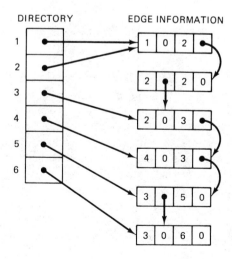

Figure 7–16   Multi-list representation of Fig. 7–7.

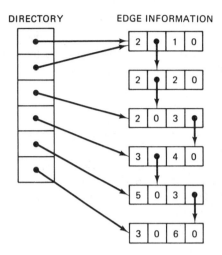

Figure 7–17 Another multi-list representation of Fig. 7–7.

A Pascal declaration of a multi-list representation for a weighted graph of order 24 follows.

```
type nodeid = 0 . . 24;
     nodetype  =  ↑ edgeinfo;
     edgeptr  =  ↑ edgeinfo;
     edgeinfo = record node1 : nodeid;
                        node2 : nodeid;
                        adjlist1 : edgeptr;
                        adjlist2 : edgeptr;
                        weight : integer
                 end;
     graph  =  array [1 . . 24] of nodetype;
```

GRAPH TRAVERSAL

In many applications it is necessary to visit all the nodes of a graph. For example, there could be a requirement to print a list of all the events in an activity graph (for example, Fig. 7–13), or to determine which cities are included in a distance chart (for example, Fig. 7–9), or to determine the total distance between cities in the distance chart.

The two basic graph traversal techniques that we present are breadth-first and depth-first. It is usually necessary to take precautions to visit each node and edge only once. Revisiting a node could cause it to be listed more than once; retracing an edge could lead to repeating our steps through the graph. There may be several paths between any pair of nodes. Graph traversal algorithms generally *mark* each node as it is visited. A previously marked node cannot be revisited. Alternatively, a graph traversal algorithm may mark each edge as it is followed. A previously marked edge cannot be part of another path. "Mark bits" can be stored with the other node or edge information.

Breadth-first Traversal

In *breadth-first traversal* of a graph, one node is selected as the start position. It is visited and marked, then all unvisited nodes adjacent to that node are visited and marked in some sequential order. Finally, the unvisited nodes immediately adjacent to these nodes are visited and marked, and so forth, until the entire graph has been traversed.

Breadth-first traversal of the graph of Fig. 7–13 results in visiting the nodes in the following order: 1, 2, 3, 4, 5, 6, 7, 8. The sequence 1, 3, 2, 6, 5, 4, 7, 8 is also a valid breadth-first traversal visitation order.

The traversal algorithm uses a queue to store the nodes of each "level" of the graph as they are visited. These stored nodes are then treated one by one and their adjacent nodes are visited, and so forth until all nodes have been visited. This terminating condition is reached when the queue is empty. A flowchart of the algorithm is given in Fig. 7–18.

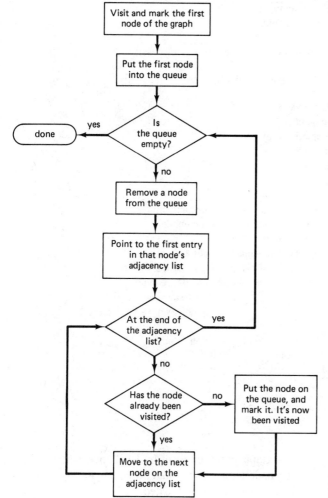

Figure 7–18 Flowchart of breadth-first graph traversal algorithm.

The algorithm can be implemented in Pascal as follows. Assume that the node directory representation that was discussed earlier is used, with mark bits added to the node information. The queuestruct data type and the insert and remove procedures were defined in Chapter 5.

```
type nodeid = 0 . . ordergraph;
     edgeptr = ↑ edgeinfo;
     nodetype = record mark : 0 . . 1;
                       adjlist : edgeptr
                end;
     edgeinfo = record node : nodeid;
                       weight : integer;
                       next : edgeptr
                end;
     graphtype = array [1 . . ordergraph] of nodetype;
var graph : graphtype;
    firstnode : nodeid;
```

The iterative procedure can be programmed as follows.

```
procedure breadth (firstnode:nodeid);
var : queuestruct;
    savenode : nodeid;
    adjptr : edgeptr;
begin {visit firstnode here}
    graph[firstnode].mark := 1;
    insert(firstnode);
    while g.f <> 0
    do begin remove (savenode);
             adjptr := graph[savenode].adjlist;
             {visit nodes adjacent to savenode}
             while adjptr <> nil
             do begin savenode := adjptr ↑ .node;
                      if (graph[savenode].mark = 0)
                      then begin insert(savenode);
                                 {visit savenode here}
                                 graph[savenode].mark := 1
                           end;
                      adjptr := adjptr ↑ .next
                end;
       end;
end;
```

Depth-first Traversal

Whereas breadth-first traversal of a graph proceeds level-by-level, depth-first traversal follows first a path from the starting node to an ending node, then another path from the start to an end, and so forth until all nodes have been visited.

Depth-first traversal of the graph of Fig. 7–13 results in visiting the nodes in the following order: 1, 2, 4, 8, 5, 7, 3, 6. A path is pursued until no unvisited nodes remain reachable; then the algorithm backs up to the last node that was visited that has an unvisited adjacent node. An equally valid sequence to result from depth-first traversal of the example graph is: 1, 3, 6, 7, 8, 2, 5, 4.

Breadth-first traversal was described easily using an iterative procedure; depth-first traversal lends itself well to recursive definition. A flowchart for recursive depth-first traversal is given in Fig. 7–19. Pascal code to implement the traversal for graphs represented by the node-directory structure declared in the preceding section follows.

```
procedure depth (var thisnode:nodeid);
var savenode : nodeid;
    adjptr : edgeptr;
begin {visit thisnode here}
    graph[thisnode].mark := 1;
    adjptr := graph[thisnode].adjlist;
    while adjptr <> nil
    do begin savenode := adjptr ↑ .node;
                if (graph[savenode].mark = 0)
                then depth(savenode);
                adjptr := adjptr ↑ .next
        end;
end;
```

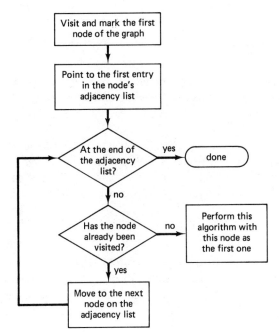

Figure 7–19 Flowchart of recursive depth-first graph traversal algorithm.

Comparisons

The exercises at the end of this chapter suggest that you write breadth-first and depth-first traversal algorithms for graphs that are represented by multi-list structures and for graphs that are represented by adjacency matrices. Let us now compare the relative time requirements of these traversal types with the linked and nonlinked representations.

In the breadth-first traversal, each node of the graph enters the node queue only once. Thus the outer *while* loop is executed N times, where N is the order of the graph (*ordergraph*). If the graph is represented by a linked structure, then only those nodes that are adjacent to the node at the front of the queue are examined. Thus the inner *while* loop is executed a total of E times, where E is the number of edges in the graph. Breadth-first traversal of a linked structure is therefore $O(N*E)$.

However, if the graph is represented by an adjacency matrix, then the inner *while* loop is executed once for each other node in the graph, since the entire row of the adjacency matrix must be examined. Thus breadth-first traversal of an adjacency matrix is $O(N^2)$.

The same type of logic can be applied to show that depth-first traversal of a graph represented by a linked structure is also $O(N*E)$, and breadth-first traversal of a graph represented by an adjacency matrix is also $O(N^2)$.

Thus linked representation saves space and produces shorter traversals, until the graph becomes more densely connected. As long as $E < N$, linked representation is more efficient. Recall that the maximum possible value for E is $N^2 - N$, which occurs when there is an edge between every pair of nodes.

How does one determine whether a depth-first or a breadth-first traversal should be conducted? This choice is typically determined by the logic of the application.

REACHABILITY AND SHORTEST PATHS

Graph analysis commonly involves following paths through the graph. There are many interesting problems in analysis of graph paths. We will consider just two in this section: reachability and shortest paths. Use of the adjacency matrix representation will facilitate the initial discussion.

In some problems edge weights are important. For example, determining the shortest path between a pair of cities in the graph of Fig. 7–9 uses the edge weights, which are distances. On the other hand, determining whether or not two nodes are connected need not consider edge weights. We initially assume that edge weights are all one.

Reachability

Figure 7–20 represents the adjacency matrix for the graph of Fig. 7–9. A non-zero entry for a city pair indicates that there is a path between them with no intermediate cities. Multiplying the adjacency matrix by itself will show for which city pairs there is a path with exactly one intermediate city. Call the adjacency matrix A. Conventional matrix

i \ j	1	2	3	4	5	6	7	8	9	10	11	12	13	14	15	16
1	0	0	0	1	1	0	0	0	0	0	0	1	0	0	0	0
2	0	0	0	0	0	0	0	0	1	0	1	0	0	0	0	0
3	0	0	0	0	1	1	0	0	1	1	1	0	0	0	0	0
4	1	0	0	0	0	0	1	0	0	0	0	0	0	0	1	0
5	1	0	1	0	0	0	0	0	0	0	0	0	0	0	0	0
6	0	0	1	0	0	0	0	0	0	0	0	0	0	0	0	0
7	0	0	0	1	0	0	0	0	0	0	1	0	0	0	0	0
8	0	0	0	0	0	0	0	0	0	0	0	1	0	1	0	0
9	0	1	1	0	0	0	0	0	0	1	0	0	0	0	0	0
10	0	0	1	0	0	0	0	0	1	0	0	0	0	0	0	0
11	0	1	1	0	0	0	1	0	0	0	0	0	0	0	0	0
12	1	0	0	0	0	0	0	1	0	0	0	0	0	0	1	0
13	0	0	0	0	0	0	0	0	0	0	0	0	0	1	0	1
14	0	0	0	0	0	0	0	1	0	0	0	0	1	0	1	0
15	0	0	0	1	0	0	0	0	0	0	0	1	0	1	0	1
16	0	0	0	0	0	0	0	0	0	0	0	0	1	0	1	0

Figure 7–20   Adjacency matrix for Fig. 7–9.

multiplication is used to find A^2. That is, the i,j^{th} element of A^2 is the result of multiplying row i by column j of A.

$$A^2_{ij} = \sum_{k=1}^{n} A_{ik}A_{kj}$$

$A^2_{ij} = 1$ if there is a path of length 2 from node i to node j; $A^2_{ij} = 0$ otherwise.
   In general, the mth power of the binary adjacency matrix is

$$A^m_{ij} = \begin{cases} 1 \text{ if there is a path of length } m \text{ from node } i \text{ to node } j, \\ 0 \text{ otherwise.} \end{cases}$$

For the city-distance example, A^m will show which city pairs have paths that require stops at $m - 1$ intermediate cities. The problem of determining whether or not pairs of nodes are connected thus can be solved by finding

$$\sum_{t=1}^{N} A^t$$

which results in a matrix called the *transitive closure of A*, commonly denoted A^+. Actually the summation need not be carried out N times, where N is the order of the graph, but rather only as many times as the length of the longest path. The transitive closure of A is also referred to as the *reachability matrix* of A.

Shortest Paths

In addition to determining if node j can be reached from node i, it is commonly of interest to find the shortest path from node i to node j. Development of the general algorithm is left as an exercise, but we do make two observations about shortest paths here. These points should help your development efforts. Refer again to the graph of Fig. 7–9. Following is a table of the shortest paths from DNV to each other city, listed in the order in which a shortest-path algorithm detects them.

Path	Distance
DNV-ABQ	334
DNV-SLC	371
DNV-KNC	558
DNV-ABQ-ELP	334 + 229 = 563
DNV-ABQ-PHX	334 + 330 = 664
DNV-SLC-SPK	371 + 550 = 921
DLV-SLC-SFO	371 + 600 = 971
DNV-KNC-ORD	558 + 414 = 972
DNV-ABQ-PHX-LAX	334 + 330 + 357 = 1021
DNV-ABQ-ELP-DFW	334 + 229 + 572 = 1135
DNV-SLC-SPK-SEA	371 + 550 + 229 = 1150
DNV-KNC-ORD-CVG	558 + 414 + 252 = 1224
DNV-ABQ-ELP-DFW-HST	334 + 229 + 572 + 225 = 1360
DNV-KNC-ORD-CVG-NSH	558 + 414 + 252 + 238 = 1462
DNV-ABQ-ELP-DFW-NOR	334 + 229 + 572 + 443 = 1578

There are several possible paths between many of the pairs of cities. Note that

1. The shortest paths are detected in nondecreasing order of their distances; i.e., the next destination node is the one with the minimum distance from the source node of all those nodes not yet selected.
2. The shortest path to that next destination node goes through nodes that have already been selected.

If the edge weights were to represent costs rather than distances, then the same algorithm could be used to detect cheapest paths. If the edge weights were to represent speeds (e.g., kilobits/second), then the algorithm could be modified easily to detect fastest paths.

CRITICAL PATHS

The graph of Fig. 7–13 represents an activity graph. Nearly all projects can be represented by such graphs. Quite good techniques have been developed to assist in the evaluation and analysis of activity graphs, e.g., the Critical Path Method (CPM), Performance Evaluation and Review Technique (PERT), and Resource Allocation and Multi-project

Scheduling (RAMPS) techniques. Here we introduce only the basic aspects of activity graph analysis.

The graph structure of a project can show that several tasks can be executed in parallel. For example, tasks from events 2 and 3 can proceed concurrently in Fig. 7–13. Of interest to the management of the project is determining which events are critical to timely completion of the project. An event is *critical* if slippage of its scheduled completion time causes the completion of the entire project to be delayed. The shortest possible completion time for the project is the longest path through the graph. The longest path is called the *critical path*; the critical events lie along this path. The length of this path is called the *critical path time*, CPT. An information system might include programs to find critical paths and CPT, as well as to draft and modify activity graph charts.

One way to detect the critical path and to determine allowed slippage times for events not on the critical path is to find earliest and latest start times for the events. The *earliest start time* of event i, EST_i, is the earliest possible trigger time for the event. For the graph of Fig. 7–13—

Event	EST
1	0
2	6
3	3
4	8
5	10
6	12
7	14
8	16

The EST_i is calculated from the longest path to node i from the start node. Note that tasks from both nodes 5 and 6 must complete before event 7 is triggered. More formally,

$$EST_i = \max_{j \in P(i)} \{EST_j + T(j,i)\}$$

where $P(i)$ is the set of immediate predecessors to node i

$T(j,i)$ is the weight of the edge from node j to node i.

The *latest start time* of event i, LST_i, is the latest possible time that event i can be triggered with the graph completing in critical path time. The set of LST_i are calculated backwards from the last event. For the graph of Fig. 7–13—

Event	LST
1	0
2	13
3	3
4	15
5	11
6	12
7	14
8	16

Formally,

$$LST_i = \min_{j \in S(i)} \{LST_j - T(i,j)\}$$

where $S(i)$ is the set of immediate successors to node i.

The difference between the LST_i and EST_i is the allowable slippage of event i.

Event	LST-EST
1	0
2	7
3	0
4	7
5	1
6	0
7	0
8	0

The critical events thus are represented by nodes 1, 3, 6, 7, and 8, which are on the longest path of the graph. These are the events that need to be controlled in order for the project to complete on time. Note that if a noncritical event were to slip beyond its allowable window, then the critical path through the graph would be changed.

SPANNING TREES

A *spanning tree* is a tree that contains all the nodes of graph and has no other nodes. Many applications call for the identification of the spanning tree for a connected graph. Figures 7–21 and 7–22 show two of the many spanning trees of the graph of Fig. 7–9. Each spanning tree shows a way to plan truck routes so that each city can be serviced. Can you construct others?

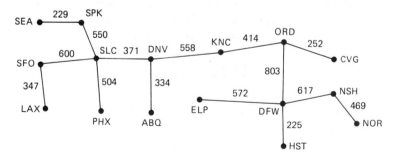

Figure 7–21 A spanning tree for Fig. 7–9.

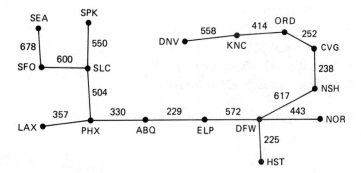

Figure 7–22 Another spanning tree for Fig. 7–9.

Of primary interest is the identification of a *minimal spanning tree* for a graph. The cost of a spanning tree is the sum of its edge weights. The cost of the spanning tree of Fig. 7–21 is 6845 miles; the cost of the spanning tree of Fig. 7–22 is 6567 miles. Neither of these happens to be the spanning tree of least possible cost.

Kruskal's Algorithm

One approach to finding minimal spanning trees is an algorithm developed by Kruskal. This algorithm considers inclusion of graph edges in order by increasing cost; an edge is included if it does not form a cycle. A cycle would mean that two paths exist between pairs of nodes. Applying Kruskal's algorithm to the graph of Fig. 7–9 proceeds as follows:

1. Lowest cost: DFW-HST (225)
2. Lowest cost: ABQ-ELP (229)
3. Lowest cost: SEA-SPK (229)
4. Lowest cost: CVG-NSH (238)
5. Lowest cost: ORD-CVG (252)

The developing minimal spanning tree now is as shown in Fig. 7–23(a).

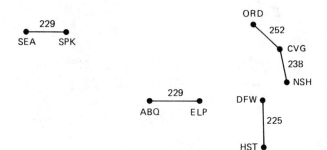

Figure 7–23(a) Initial steps in finding a minimal spanning tree for Fig. 7–9.

6. Lowest cost: PHX-ABQ (330)
7. Lowest cost: DNV-ABQ (334)
8. Lowest cost: SFO-LAX (347)
9. Lowest cost: LAX-PHX (357)
10. Lowest cost: KNC-ORD (414)

The minimal spanning tree now is as shown in Fig. 7–23(b).

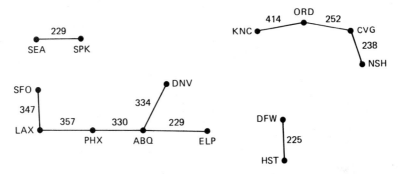

Figure 7–23(b)   Intermediate steps in finding a minimal spanning tree for Fig. 7–9.

11. Lowest cost: DFW-NOR (443)
12. Lowest cost: NSH-NOR (469)
13. Lowest cost: PHX-SLC (504)
14. Lowest cost: SLC-SPK (550)
15. Lowest cost: DNV-KNC (558)

We have been very lucky in avoiding cycles! The minimal spanning tree is shown in Fig. 7–23(c).

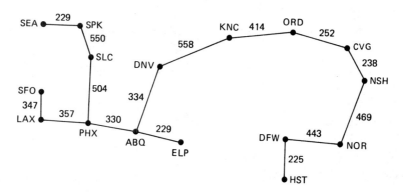

Figure 7–23(c)   Minimal spanning tree for Fig. 7–9.

In fact, we now have included all nodes and the minimal spanning tree is complete, with cost of 5479.

Assume for the moment that all nodes had *not* yet been included. Consideration of the next lowest cost edge (ELP-DFW) would detect a cycle. That edge would be rejected and the edge with the next lowest cost would be considered, and so forth until all nodes were included.

Minimal spanning trees thus are the least-cost way to connect the nodes of the graph. Cost, of course, can be measured in terms of distance, time, money, and so forth, depending upon the edge weight units. In the list of Selected References at the end of this chapter are materials that contain several algorithms for finding minimal spanning trees.

SUMMARY

In this chapter we discussed graphs in some detail. First the basic concepts of graph data structures were introduced. Three fundamental techniques for representing graphs were covered: adjacency matrix representation, and two forms of linked representation—node directory and multi-list. Use of an adjacency matrix tends to make graph analysis algorithms at least $O(N^2)$, while use of a linked representation tends to make graph analysis algorithms $O(N*E)$. Examples of declaring graphs in COBOL and Pascal were given.

Two basic graph traversal techniques were introduced: breadth-first and depth-first. These algorithms take precautions to visit each node only once by marking each node as it is visited or each edge as it is traversed. Breadth-first traversal generally is programmed as an iterative procedure, whereas depth-first traversal generally is programmed as a recursive procedure.

Several path analysis problems were discussed. Powers of a graph's adjacency matrix can be used to detect paths of a given length between node pairs and to determine if one node is reachable from another node. An example was used to illustrate the algorithm for detecting the shortest paths between one node and the other nodes. Critical path analysis was introduced, along with the concepts of earliest and latest start times. Finally, spanning trees and a technique (Kruskal's algorithm) for identifying a minimal spanning tree of a graph were introduced.

TERMS

activity graph

acyclic graph

adjacency matrix

arc

breadth-first

connected graph

critical path

cycle

degree (of a node)

depth-first

directed graph

earliest start time

edge

graph

in-degree
latest start time
loop
minimal spanning tree
multigraph
node
null graph
order (of a graph)
out-degree

path
path length
reachability matrix
simple graph
spanning tree
transitive closure
undirected graph
vertex

SELECTED REFERENCES

CHANDY, K. M. and J. MISRA. "Distributed computation on graphs: shortest path algorithms," *Comm. ACM*, 25(11):833–837, Nov. 1982.

CHIN, F. Y., J. LAM, and I–N. CHEN. "Efficient parallel algorithms for some graph problems," *Comm. ACM*, 25(9):659–665, Sept. 1982.

EBERT, J. "A versatile data structure for edge-oriented graph algorithms," *Comm. ACM*, 30(6):513–519, June 1987.

FORD, L. and D. FULKERSON. *Flows in Networks*. Princeton: Princeton UP, 1962.

LAWLER, E. L. "Comment on computing the k shortest paths in a graph," *Comm. ACM*, 20(8):603–604, Aug. 1977.

LITKE, J. D. "An improved solution to the traveling salesman problem with thousands of nodes," *Comm. ACM*, 27(12):1227–1236, Dec. 1984.

LOUI, R. P. "Optimal paths in graphs with stochastic or multidimensional weights," *Comm. ACM*, 26(9):670–676, Sept. 1983.

MINIEKA, E. "On computing sets of shortest paths in a graph," *Comm. ACM*, 17(6):351–353, June 1974.

QUINN, M. J. and N. DEO. "Parallel graph algorithms," *ACM Computing Surveys*, 16(3):319–348, Sept. 1984.

TARJAN, R. E. "Applications of path compression on balanced trees," *Jour. ACM*, 26(4):690–715, Oct. 1979.

WHITNEY, V. K. M. "Minimal spanning tree," *Comm. ACM*, 15(4): 273–274, April 1972.

REVIEW EXERCISES

1. Assume that a directed graph of order N is represented by an adjacency matrix, where *graph* $(i,j) = 1$ if an edge connects nodes i and j and is zero otherwise. What are the expressions for determining the following: (a) the in-degree of node i, (b) the out-degree of node i?

2. Draw a directed graph. What is its adjacency matrix? What is its reachability matrix? Represent the graph using a node-directory structure. Represent the graph using a multi-list structure.

Traverse the graph using the breadth-first approach. Traverse the graph using the depth-first approach. What is the minimal spanning tree of the graph?

3. Can there be a cycle in a simple graph? If so, give an example. If not, why not?

4. Draw several graphs. For each graph answer the following questions. Is the graph: (a) acyclic? (b) connected? (c) directed? (d) simple? (e) What is the order of the graph? What is the (f) in-degree, (g) out-degree, (h) degree of each node?

5. What kind of data structure is typically appropriate for storing an adjacency matrix?

6. One linked representation of a graph maintains a directory of nodes and corresponding linked lists of edges. Develop an alternative linked representation which maintains a directory of edges and corresponding linked lists of nodes. Analyze the storage requirements of your representation and compare them with the requirements of the linked representation given in the chapter.

7. Write programs to do (a) a breadth-first traversal and (b) a depth-first traversal of a graph represented by a multi-list structure.

8. Write programs to do (a) a breadth-first traversal and (b) a depth-first traversal of a graph represented by an adjacency matrix.

9. Write a program to find the critical path of a weighted graph represented by (a) an adjacency matrix, (b) a node-directory structure, (c) a multi-list structure.

10. Develop an activity graph for your own activities for the next week or month. Find the critical path through the graph.

11. Write a program to generate the set of shortest paths from node i to all other nodes in a graph of order n. Assume that the graph is represented by (a) an adjacency matrix, (b) a node-directory structure, and (c) a multi-list structure.

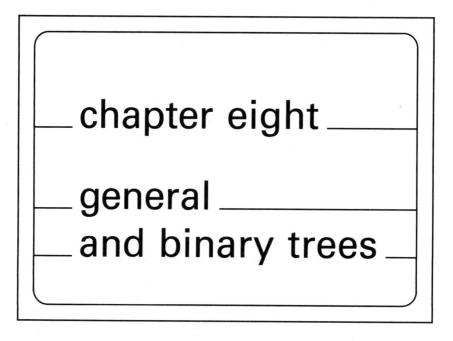

chapter eight

general and binary trees

An important class of graphs is those that are structured as *trees*. A tree is an acyclic simple, connected graph. A tree contains no loops and no cycles; there is no more than one edge between any pair of nodes. The graphs of Fig. 7–5 are trees; the graphs of the preceding figures in Chapter 7 are not trees.

GENERAL TREES

Our attention will be restricted to the class of trees known as *rooted trees*. A tree is said to be rooted if it has one node (called the *root*) that is distinguished from the other nodes. The root of tree T is denoted root(T).

More formally, a tree T is a finite set of zero or more nodes ($v_1, v_2, \ldots, v_n$) such that

1. There is one specially designated node (say v_1) called Root(T).
2. The remaining nodes ($v_2, \ldots, v_n$) are partitioned into $m \geq 0$ *disjoint* sets named $T_1, T_2, \ldots, T_m$ such that each T_i is itself a tree.

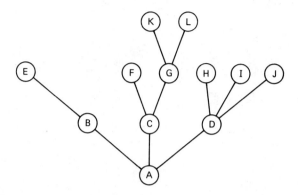

Figure 8–1 Example tree.

The sets $T_1, \ldots, T_m$ are called the *subtrees* of Root(T). Note the recursive nature of this definition; we have defined trees in terms of trees. A tree with no nodes is a null tree.

Fig. 8–1 shows a tree in which we have labeled each node by a letter within a circle. This is the notation we will usually use in drawing trees. Here Root(T) = A. The three subtrees of root A are rooted at B, C, and D respectively. B is the root of a tree with one subtree, rooted at E. That subtree has no subtrees. The tree rooted at C has two subtrees, rooted at F and G respectively.

We sometimes apply directional characteristics to a tree's edges. An edge goes *from* a root node *to* a subtree's root, as shown in Fig. 8–2. Here we have drawn the tree in the more typical fashion of data management texts, with its root on top and its edges (or *branches*) growing downward.

We have said that a tree has a specially designated node called its root. The root is not just randomly selected; rather it is a node distinguished by the property that

$$\text{In-degree}(v) = 0 \text{ for } v = \text{Root}(T).$$

The root has no incoming branches. Because a tree is a connected graph, there can be no more than one node with this property. Consider the subtrees of A from the tree of

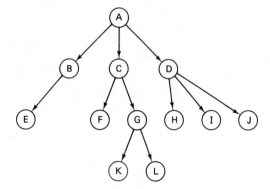

Figure 8–2 Tree with directed edges.

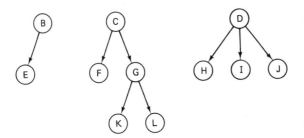

Figure 8–3   Three subtrees from Fig. 8–2.

Fig. 8–2, as shown in Fig. 8–3. Note that the edges connecting A to B, C, and D do not appear in these subtrees, because A is not one of their nodes.

The terminology used in talking about general trees is similar to that used with genealogical trees and live trees. If there is an edge (A,B), then A is said to be the *parent* of B; B is said to be the *child* of A. A child, thus, has only one parent node. Two nodes with the same parent are called *brothers* (or *sisters*), and so forth in the vein of family trees. The nodes with out-degree zero are called the *leaves* of the tree. The leaf nodes of the tree of Fig. 8–2 are E, F, K, L, H, I, and J.

The nodes of a tree are said to be on *levels*, where a node's level is determined by the length of the path from the root to that node. For example, in the tree of Fig. 8–2:

level 0	A
level 1	B, C, D
level 2	E, F, G, H, I, J
level 3	K, L.

The *height* of a tree is one plus the number of the highest level on which there are nodes. The *weight* of a tree is its number of leaf nodes. The height and weight of the tree of Fig. 8–2 are 4 and 7 respectively.

A collection of rooted trees is called a *forest*. Figure 8–3 shows a forest of three trees.

Forms of Representation

We have used one graphical notation to represent trees. Other graphical notations for tree structures include (1) nested sets (Fig. 8–4), and (2) nested parentheses

$$(A(B(E))(C(F)(G(K)(L))) (D(H)(I)(J)))$$

in which parentheses bracket the root and subtrees of each tree, and (3) indentation, as shown in Fig. 8–5.

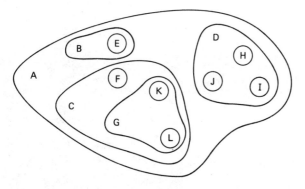

Figure 8–4 Nested-set representation of the Fig. 8–2 tree.

Figure 8–5 Indented representation of the Fig. 8–2 tree.

BINARY TREES

The most important class of general trees is binary trees. A *binary tree* is a finite set of nodes which either is empty or contains two disjoint binary trees that are called its *left* and *right* subtrees. Note that in addition to the requirement that the maximum out-degree of any node of a binary tree is 2, there is the additional constraint that leftness and rightness are imposed upon subtrees. The binary trees of Fig. 8–6(a) and (b) are *not* the same; they are two different trees, one with a left subtree and one with a right subtree. The tree of Fig. 8–6(c) is not a binary tree, because its subtree does not have leftness or rightness (only downness).

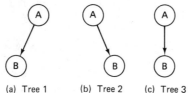

(a) Tree 1   (b) Tree 2   (c) Tree 3   **Figure 8–6** Example trees.

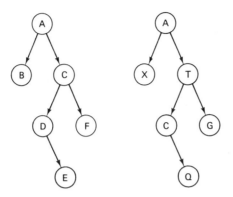

Figure 8–7 Two similar trees.

Two binary trees are said to be *similar* if they have the same structure, as exemplified in Fig. 8–7. Two binary trees are said to be *equivalent* if they are similar and contain the same information. The two trees of Fig. 8–7 are not equivalent.

We now consider some properties of binary trees that further distinguish them from general trees. Consider a binary tree with K levels, as depicted in Fig. 8–8. Note that we now begin to omit the arrows on the tree's edges, as there is no question about where the root is. A binary tree is said to be *complete* if it contains the maximum number of nodes possible for its height. How many nodes does a complete binary tree with K levels contain? The number of edges coming into any level (except level 0) is twice the number of nodes on the prior level. Thus the maximum number of nodes on the Ith level is 2^I. Therefore, a complete binary tree with K levels contains

$$\sum_{I=0}^{K-1} 2^I$$

nodes, which is $2^K - 1$. A complete binary tree with three levels contains seven nodes; a complete binary tree with ten levels contains 1023 nodes.

A binary tree with K levels is said to be *almost complete* if levels 0 through

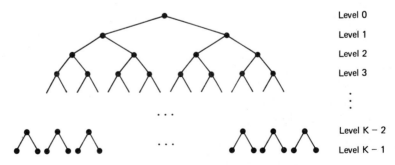

Figure 8–8 A complete binary tree with K levels.

$K - 2$ are full and level $K - 1$ is being filled left to right, as shown in Fig. 8–9, for a 5-level tree.

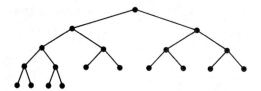

Figure 8–9 An almost complete binary tree with five levels.

The shortest maximum path length (denoted by PL_{max}) for a binary tree is achieved by making the tree as full (bushy) as possible. An almost complete tree has the minimum height for its set of nodes. The minimum height (denoted by H_{min}) for a binary tree with N nodes is

$$H_{min} = \lceil \log_2(N + 1) \rceil$$

where $\lceil x \rceil$ denotes the ceiling function, i.e., the smallest integer $\geq x$. When $N = 1$, then $H_{min} = 1$. When $N = 3$, level 1 is filled and $H_{min} = 2$. When $N = 7$, level 2 is filled and $H_{min} = 3$. (Recall that if $\log_2 X = y$, then $2^y = X$.)

The worst-case height is achieved when the binary tree is long and leggy, as shown in Fig. 8–10.

Figure 8–10 A long leggy tree, with maximum height.

Now the maximum height (denoted H_{max}) for a binary tree with N nodes is

$$H_{max} = N.$$

We will see that a major use of trees is to structure a collection of data in a manner that facilitates searching for a particular element. In general it will be desirable to arrange data in the tree in such a way that search path lengths are minimized. Almost complete trees are commonly used for this reason.

REPRESENTATION OF BINARY TREES

Binary trees are most commonly represented by linked lists. Each node can be regarded as having three elementary fields: an information area and pointers to the left and right subtrees. For example, the binary tree in Fig. 8–11 can be represented by linked lists as shown in Fig. 8–12.

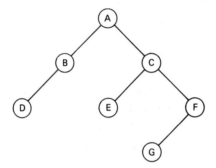

Figure 8–11   Example binary tree.

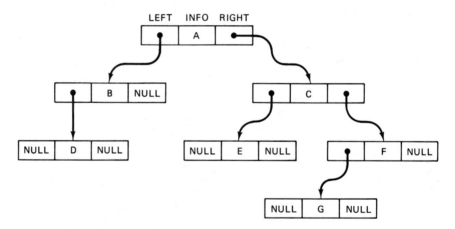

Figure 8–12   Linked-list representation of the Fig. 8–11 tree.

The topological placement of the boxes of the linked lists on the page is of course meaningless; storage for the nodes could be scattered throughout memory.

Defining Trees in Pascal

In Pascal, a binary tree data structure could be defined using pointers, just as we did in the chapter on linked lists. Let's assume that the information fields contain integer values.

$$\text{type nodeptr} = \uparrow \text{nodetype};$$
$$\text{nodetype} = \text{record}$$
$$\text{left:nodeptr};$$
$$\text{info:integer};$$
$$\text{right:nodeptr}$$
$$\text{end};$$

Each time a node is created, it has this structure. The program must set the values of the left and right pointer fields correctly to establish the interconnections between nodes forming the tree. Space can be allocated dynamically to the nodes as they are added to the tree; space can be freed dynamically as nodes are removed from the tree.

Defining Trees in COBOL

In COBOL, a binary tree with a maximum of 500 nodes could be declared by the following.

```
01   BINARY-TREE.
     02   NODE OCCURS 500 TIMES.
          03   LEFTN      PICTURE 9(3).
          03   INFO       PICTURE 9(5).
          03   RIGHTN     PICTURE 9(3).
```

Because COBOL does not provide built-in pointer variable support, the binary tree is housed in an array. We have used LEFTN and RIGHTN as names for the left and right pointers because LEFT and RIGHT are COBOL reserved words. To manage space in such an array would require use of an AVAIL list of empty (available) nodes, just as we discussed in the chapter on linked lists. Space must be allocated to hold the maximum tree size, since COBOL array space cannot be allocated dynamically.

BINARY TREE REPRESENTATION OF GENERAL TREES

It is considerably easier to represent binary trees in programs than it is to represent general trees. With a general tree, it is unpredictable how many edges will emanate from a node at any given time. Thus node space has to be managed in such a way that each node is allowed a variable number of subtree pointers or that each node is allocated space for a fixed number of subtree pointers, whether they are all needed or not. Binary trees are attractive in that each node has a predictable maximum number of subtree pointers: 2.

Fortunately, there is a straightforward technique for converting a general tree to a binary tree form. The algorithm has two easy steps:

1. Insert edges connecting siblings and delete all of a parent's edges to its children except to its leftmost offspring.
2. Rotate the resultant diagram 45° to distinguish between left and right subtrees.

For example, consider the general tree in Fig. 8–2, which is reproduced here as Fig. 8–13(a). This is not a binary tree. Some nodes have more than two subtrees; the subtrees do not have leftness or rightness. Step 1 of the transformation results in the structure depicted in Fig. 8–13(b). Note that there is *not* an edge inserted to connect E and F; they are not siblings in the original tree because they have different parents (B and C). Step 2 results in the binary tree shown in Fig. 8–13(c).

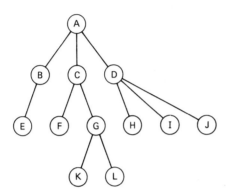

Figure 8–13(a)   Example general tree.

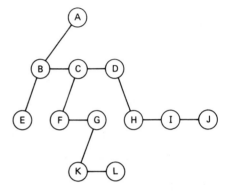

Figure 8–13(b)   Initial transformation of Fig. 8–13(a)'s general tree.

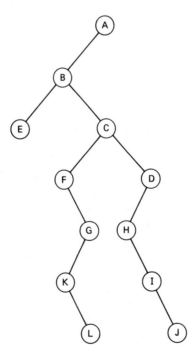

Figure 8–13(c)   Binary tree representation of Fig. 8–13(a) general tree.

In the resultant binary tree, left pointers are always from a parent node to its first (leftmost) child in the original general tree. Right pointers are always from a node to one of its siblings in the original tree.

Can the original general tree be reconstructed from the resultant binary tree? What

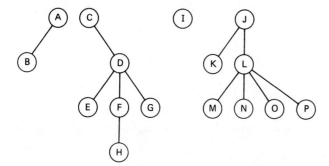

Figure 8–14(a)   Example forest.

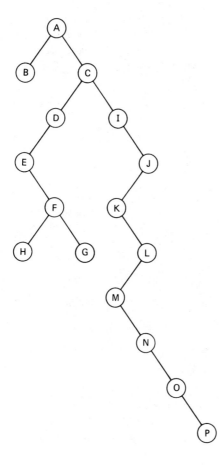

Figure 8–14(b)   Binary tree representation of Fig. 8–14(a) forest.

happens when this transformation is applied to a general tree that is already a binary tree?

This transformation algorithm can also be applied to convert a forest of general trees to a single binary tree by considering the tree roots to be siblings. For example, the forest of Fig. 8–14(a) can be represented by the binary tree of Fig. 8–14(b).

Binary trees generated by this type of conversion have fairly large heights for the number of nodes that they contain. Their search paths are relatively long, but memory management is not complicated.

EXAMPLE TREES

We will see that trees are commonly used to structure data to facilitate searches for particular nodes. Trees are also useful for representing collections of data that have branching logical structures. For example, binary trees 1 and 2 of Fig. 8–15 represent arithmetic statements. Each nonleaf node is an operator; its left and right subtrees are its operands. Compilers commonly build binary trees in the process of scanning, parsing, and generating code for evaluation of arithmetic expressions. Tree 3 of the figure represents a collection of data elements that are positioned in the tree such that if K is the label of a node, all labels of nodes in its left subtree are less than (or equal to) K and all labels of nodes in its right subtree are greater than K. This kind of tree is commonly used to structure collections of names, keys, or labels. Searching for a node in the tree can be considerably faster than searching the same collection sequentially. Let's consider this kind of tree in more detail.

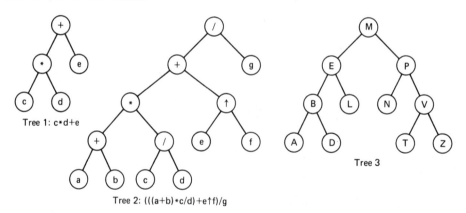

Figure 8–15   Example trees.

BINARY SEARCH TREES

A *binary search tree* over the collection of n records with keys $K_1, K_2, \ldots, K_n$ is a binary tree, each of whose nodes R_i bears one of the keys K_i, for $i = 1, \ldots, n$. The keys are the node identifiers. Searching for a particular node will be done by looking for its

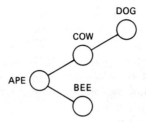

Figure 8–16 Example binary search tree.

key value. The nodes of the binary tree are arranged so that for each node R_i, the following properties hold:

1. All keys of nodes in the left subtree of R_i precede the key labeling R_i.

    If $R_j \in \text{left}(R_i)$
    then $K_j < K_i$.

2. The key labeling R_i precedes the keys of all nodes in the right subtree of R_i.

    If $R_j \in \text{right}(R_i)$
    then $K_i < K_j$.

In general we require that the keys in the collection be distinct, although this constraint sometimes is relaxed. The precedence of keys is determined by their linear ordering according to a collating sequence.

    For example, the binary tree of Fig. 8–16 conforms to the above properties and qualifies as a binary search tree over the keys APE, BEE, COW, and DOG.

    It is important to note that there are many possible ways to arrange the keys of a record collection so that valid binary search trees result. For example, Fig. 8–17 shows four additional binary search trees over the keys APE, BEE, COW, and DOG. Can you construct others?

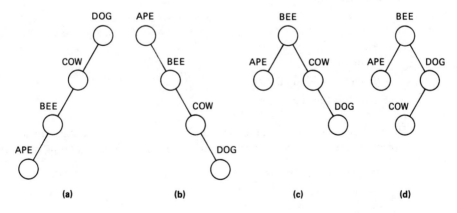

Figure 8–17 More binary search trees.

As you construct binary search trees, you should notice that once you have started the tree and have decided which key should be inserted next, there is no choice about where to place that key. The properties that define a binary search tree dictate the relationships between nodes and determine where the next node should reside. The structure of a particular binary search tree is determined by the order in which the nodes are placed into the tree. Unless we allow the tree to be restructured during the insertion process, a new node is always inserted as a leaf.

The node structure for a binary search tree can be declared in Pascal as

```
type nodeptr =  ↑ nodetype;
     nodekey =  packed array [1 . . 10] of char;
     nodetype = record
                     left: nodeptr;
                     key: nodekey;
                     info: integer;
                     right: nodeptr
                end;
```

for nodes with keys of ten characters and integer information.

SEQUENTIAL SEARCHES

The process of going through a tree in such a way that each node is visited once and only once is called *tree traversal*. When a tree is traversed, its entire collection of nodes is looked at. There are several well-known methods of binary tree traversal. Each imposes a sequential, linear ordering upon the nodes of a tree. A node is said to be *visited* when it is encountered in the traversal; whatever processing is desirable on its contents is done at that time.

The Algorithms

There are three kinds of basic activities in each of the binary tree traversal algorithms:

Visit the root.
Traverse the left subtree.
Traverse the right subtree.

The methods differ in the order in which these types of activities are performed. The algorithms we present here are all recursive; each is defined in terms of itself.

PRE-ORDER TRAVERSAL

1. Visit the root.
2. Traverse the left subtree in pre-order.
3. Traverse the right subtree in pre-order.

IN-ORDER TRAVERSAL

1. Traverse the left subtree in in-order.

2. Visit the root.

3. Traverse the right subtree in in-order.

POST-ORDER TRAVERSAL

1. Traverse the left subtree in post-order.

2. Traverse the right subtree in post-order.

3. Visit the root.

The nodes of the trees of Fig. 8–15 are visited in the following sequences when the trees are traversed according to the above-listed methods.

Tree 1:	Pre-order:	$+\,*cde$
	In-order:	$c*d+e$
	Post-order:	$cd*e+$
Tree 2:	Pre-order:	$/+*+ab/cd\uparrow efg$
	In-order:	$a+b*c/d+e\uparrow f/g$
	Post-order:	$ab+cd/*ef\uparrow+g/$
Tree 3:	Pre-order:	MEBADLPNVTZ
	In-order:	ABDELMNPTVZ
	Post-order:	ADBLENTZVPM

The results of these traversals of trees 1 and 2 may remind you of the example application of stacks in Chapter 4 for notation of arithmetic expressions. Post-order traversal results in a string representation in postfix form; an operator is preceded by its two operands. Pre-order traversal results in a string representation in prefix form; an operator precedes its operands. In-order traversal results in a string representation in infix form; an operator appears between its operands. Note that the prefix and infix representations may lose proper operator precedence if the original arithmetic expressions required use of parentheses to override natural precedence rules. In postfix notation, operator precedence is preserved and is indicated solely by operator order. For this type of example, post-order traversal appears to be the most useful.

By contrast, in-order traversal of tree 3 appears to yield the most useful results; the nodes are traversed in alphabetic sequence. Tree 3 is a binary search tree. In-order traversal is used to sequentially search a binary search tree.

Pre-order traversal is the most useful for other types of applications. One of the most important of these is traversal of the trees managed by hierarchical database management systems such as IBM's Information Management System (IMS). Pre-order traversal is equivalent to the IMS *hierarchic sequence* order.

Thus all three traversal techniques are important and have practical application. The technique most appropriate for a particular situation is determined by the way the information has been structured in the tree.

In-Order Traversal

A Pascal procedure to traverse a binary search tree in in-order follows. Note that this procedure, like the definitions for traversals, is recursive.

```
procedure inorder(var rootptr:nodeptr);
begin if rootptr < > nil
         then begin inorder(rootptr ↑ .left);
                     writeln(rootptr ↑ .info);
                     inorder(rootptr ↑ .right)
              end;
end;
```

The pointer types and node structure were defined earlier. It is relatively easy to write the corresponding recursive procedures to implement pre-order and post-order traversal. Pre-order and post-order traversals probably would not be used on a binary search tree but could be used for other kinds of binary trees.

Nonrecursive In-Order Traversal

In some implementations, nonrecursive routines that explicitly perform their own stacking and unstacking are more efficient than recursive routines. A nonrecursive algorithm to traverse a binary tree in in-order is shown in Fig. 8–18. Each node of the tree is pushed

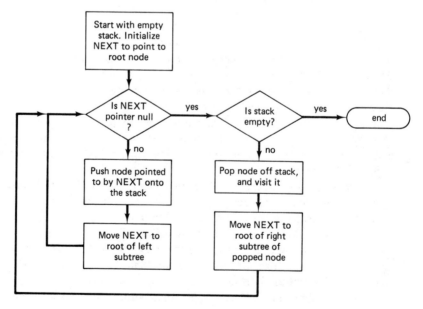

Figure 8–18   Nonrecursive in-order traversal algorithm.

onto a stack so that they are popped off in in-order. The algorithm first picks up the lowest left node, then its root, then the right node (which may have subtrees itself), then moves up a level (by going one level down into the stack) to visit that root and save its right node, and so forth until all nodes have been visited.

Pascal In-Order Traversal

A Pascal procedure to implement this algorithm follows. The procedure uses the built-in pointer variable type to implement the binary tree and an array to implement the stack that is needed to keep track of node locations in the tree during traversal. The pointer to the tree's root is rootptr.

```
procedure inorder(rootptr: nodeptr);
type stackstruct = record stack: array [1 . . 500] of nodeptr;
                          topptr: 0 . . 500
                   end;
var next: nodeptr;
    goflag: boolean;
    s: stackstruct;
begin s.topptr : = 0;
      next : = rootptr; {start at root}
      goflag : = true;
      while (goflag)
      do begin {build stack of pointers to nodes}
              {stop when encounter null left pointer}
          while (next< >nil)
          do begin s.topptr : = s.topptr + 1;
                   s.stack[s.topptr] : = next;
                   next : = next ↑ .left
             end;
          {visit node on top of stack}
          if (s.topptr > 0)
          then begin next : = s.stack [s.topptr];
                     s.topptr : = s.topptr − 1;
                     writeln (next ↑ .info);
                     {traverse right subtree}
                     next : = next ↑ .right
               end;
          else goflag : = false; {stack is empty}
         end;
   end;
```

COBOL Post-Order Traversal

A nonrecursive COBOL procedure to traverse a binary tree in post-order follows next. This procedure houses the binary tree and the stack in arrays. We assume that the binary tree has a maximum of 500 nodes and that the value 0 is used to simulate a null pointer.

The tree and stack are declared in the *DATA DIVISION*.

```
01  BINARY-TREE.
    02  NODE                OCCURS 500 TIMES.
        03  LEFTN           PICTURE 9(3).
        03  INFO            PICTURE 9(5).
        03  RIGHTN          PICTURE 9(3).
01  AUX-PTRS.
    02  ROOT                PICTURE 9(3).
    02  NEXTN               PICTURE 9(3).
01  STACK-STRUCT.
    02  STACK               OCCURS 500 TIMES
                            PICTURE 9(3).
    02  TOP-PTR             PICTURE 9(3) VALUE 0.
```

In the *PROCEDURE DIVISION*—

```
POSTORDER.
    MOVE ROOT TO NEXTN.
    PERFORM LOOP.
    PERFORM LOOP UNTIL TOP-PTR = 0.
```

where

```
LOOP.
    PERFORM SAVENODE UNTIL NEXTN = 0.
    MOVE STACK (TOP-PTR) TO NEXTN.
    COMPUTE TOP-PTR = TOP-PTR - 1.
    DISPLAY INFO (NEXTN).
    MOVE RIGHTN (NEXTN) TO NEXTN.
SAVENODE.
    COMPUTE TOP-PTR = TOP-PTR + 1.
    MOVE NEXTN TO STACK(TOP-PTR).
    MOVE LEFTN (NEXTN) TO NEXTN.
```

THREADED BINARY TREES

The nonrecursive procedures for binary tree traversal given in the preceding section are not trivial. In fact, the use of stacks to keep track of which nodes have and have not been visited (especially for post-order traversal) is really quite messy. In order to facilitate the traversal of a binary tree, we sometimes *thread* the tree with pointers that explicitly show a traversal ordering. Intuitively, the threads link the tree's nodes in the sequence of the traversal method.

There are two types of threads: a *right thread* links a node to its successor node in the traversal ordering; a *left thread* links a node to its predecessor node in the traversal ordering. From these definitions, it should be clear that a tree can be threaded according to only *one* traversal method; it is threaded in pre-order *or* in-order *or* post-order. (Of course multiple sets of threads could be used to multi-thread a tree.) A binary search tree is typically threaded in pre-order.

We represent threads in our figures by dashed pointers. Fig. 8–19(a) shows the three trees of Fig. 8–15 threaded in pre-order; Fig. 8–19(b) shows them threaded in in-order; Fig. 8–19(c) shows them threaded in post-order. Only right threads are illustrated.

Node Representation

One alternative for representing a threaded binary tree is simply to have each node structured as follows.

```
type nodeptr = ↑ nodetype;
     nodetype = record
                     left: nodeptr;
                     info: integer;
                     right: nodeptr;
                     rightthread: nodeptr;
                     leftthread: nodeptr
                end;
```

Each node has its usual left and right pointers, its information field(s), and its left and right thread pointers. All pointers are to other nodes with this same structure. If the tree were a binary search tree, each node would also have a key field.

In-Order Traversal

A nonrecursive procedure to traverse in in-order a binary tree which is threaded in in-order follows. The pointer firstin points to the first node of the tree in in-order. The right threads are followed from each node to the next.

```
procedure inorder(firstin: nodeptr);
var p: nodeptr;
begin p : = firstin;
      while p <> nil
      do begin writeln (p ↑ .info);
                p : = p ↑ .rightthread
         end;
end;
```

This is about as simple as a traversal algorithm can get!

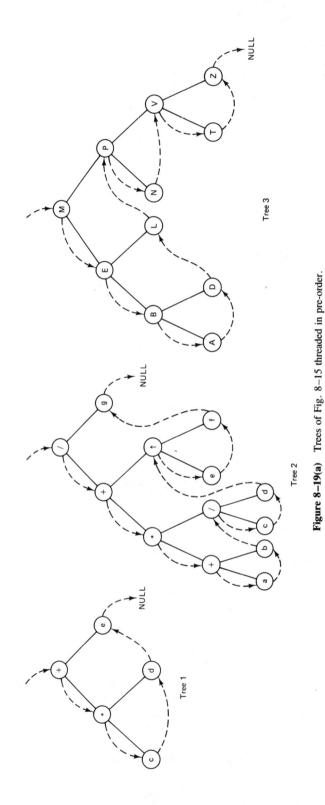

Figure 8-19(a) Trees of Fig. 8–15 threaded in pre-order.

Tree 1

Tree 2

Tree 3

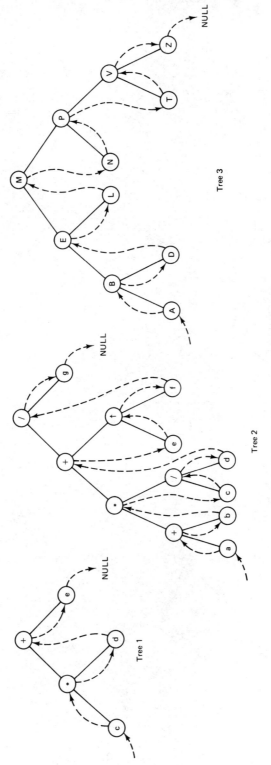

Figure 8–19(b) Trees of Fig. 8–15 threaded in in-order.

179

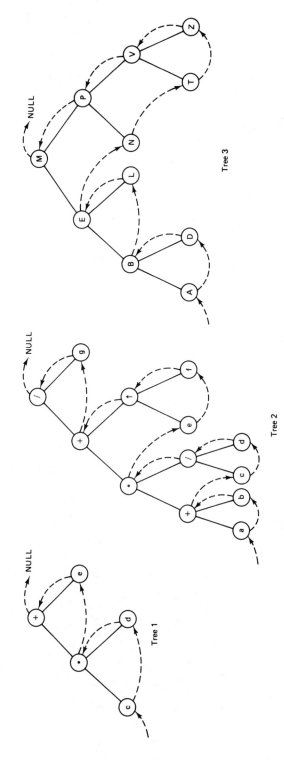

Figure 8–19(c) Trees of Fig. 8–15 threaded in post-order.

Tree 3

Tree 2

Tree 1

An Alternative Representation

A second alternative for representing a threaded binary tree requires less "overhead" storage for pointers but can make the tree management and traversal algorithms a little more complex. First, how many null pointers are there in an unthreaded binary tree with N nodes? Such a tree has a total of $2N$ (null and non-null) pointers: N pointers to left subtrees and N pointers to right subtrees. Of these, only $N - 1$ are non-null, since each node except the root has only one pointer to it. Thus there are always $N + 1$ null pointers. If you examine a tree that is threaded in pre-order, you will find that threads of nonleaf nodes parallel actual left pointers. There really is no need to duplicate these pointers. The leaf nodes, which need the threads, have null subtree pointers. We thus can represent a binary tree threaded in pre-order by having each node structured as follows.

```
type nodeptr = ↑ nodetype;
     nodetype = record
                   left : nodeptr;
                   threadflag : 0 . . 1;
                   info : integer;
                   right : nodeptr
                end;
```

To prevent confusion of threads and subtree pointers, threadflag can be set to value 0 when left represents a pointer to a left subtree and can be set to 1 when left represents a right thread. Alternatively, when a binary tree is housed in an array, left pointers can be represented by positive subscript values and right threads can be represented by negative subscript values, or vice versa. The trees in Fig. 8–15 threaded with single pointers are shown in Fig. 8–20.

   The pre-order traversal procedure then is as follows. The left pointers are followed from each node to the next. Sometimes these pointers are right threads, and sometimes they are real left pointers.

```
procedure preordthr(root : nodeptr);
var p : nodeptr;
begin p : = root;
         while p <> nil
         do begin writeln(p ↑ .info);
                      p : = p ↑ .left
               end;
end;
```

Note the similarity of this procedure to the one given for in-order traversal of a threaded tree.

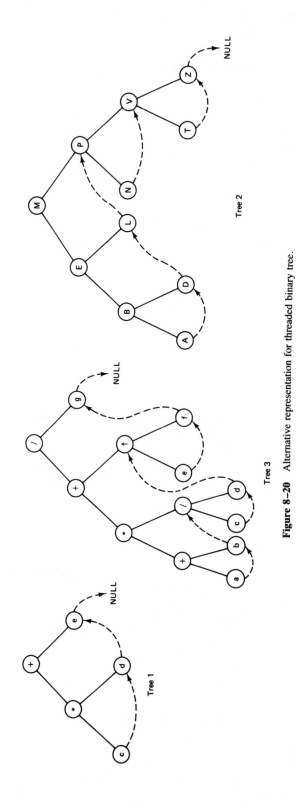

Figure 8-20 Alternative representation for threaded binary tree.

DIRECT SEARCHES

The properties of a binary search tree imply that there is a procedure for determining whether or not a node with a given key resides in the tree and for finding that node when it exists. To find the node with key k in the binary search tree rooted at R_i, the following steps are taken.

1. If the tree is empty, the search terminates unsuccessfully.
2. If $k = K_i$, the search terminates successfully; the sought node is R_i.
3. If $k < K_i$, the left subtree of R_i is searched, i.e., $R_i : =$ left(R_i).
4. If $k > K_i$, the right subtree of R_i is searched, i.e., $R_i : =$ right(R_i).

This algorithm is programmed here as a Pascal recursive procedure, where r initially points to the tree's root.

```
procedure search(k : nodekey, var r, foundnode : nodeptr);
begin if(r = nil)
        then foundnode : = nil
        else if (k = r ↑ .key)
            then foundnode : = r
            else if (k < r ↑ .key)
                then search (k,r ↑ .left,foundnode)
                else {k > r ↑ .key}
                    search(k,r ↑ .right,foundnode)
    end;
```

The search terminates with foundnode either pointing to the sought node if it exists or with null value if key k is not in the tree.

Finding a particular node in a tree that is not a binary search tree is usually done with a sequential search rather than a direct search, unless the tree is specially structured and the nodes have key fields. A sequential search of a tree with N nodes will require an average of $N/2$ node visitations to find a particular node. In the worst case, all N nodes will need to be traversed to determine that the sought node is not in the tree.

The effort required to find a particular record in a binary search tree depends upon the position of the record in the tree. We have seen that there are many possible binary search trees to organize a given collection of records. The farther the sought record is from the tree's root, the greater is the effort required to find the record. The search effort is measured by the number of comparisons made before the search terminates, either successfully or unsuccessfully.

For example, to find the record with name DOG in the various binary search trees of Fig. 8–17 requires the following numbers of comparisons:

tree (a)   1 comparison.

    (b)   4 comparisons.

(c)   3 comparisons.

(d)   2 comparisons.

If it were necessary often to find DOG, then tree (a) would probably be considered to be a better binary search tree than would tree (b). In general, though, how does one determine whether one binary search tree is better than another? What is a good binary search tree? How are good binary search trees constructed?

A binary search tree cannot be evaluated well on the sole basis of the search path that it provides to just one record. Rather, the search paths through the entire tree should enter into the evaluation; thus the expected (i.e., weighted average) length of a search path in the tree is useful.

Let s_i be the probability that key K_i is sought, where K_i $(i = 1, \ldots, n)$ is one of the keys in the tree, given that the search is a successful one. That is,

$$\sum_{i=1}^{n} s_i = 1.$$

Considering first just the successful searches, the expected search length for the binary search tree is

$$\sum_{i=1}^{n} s_i c_i$$

where c_i is the number of comparisons required to reach key K_i. $c_i - 1$ is the number of the level upon which node R_i resides. For example, if the access probabilities for the keys structured in the binary search trees of Fig. 8–17 were

APE	.2
BEE	.4
COW	.3
DOG	.1

the expected search lengths for those trees would be

	APE		BEE		COW		DOG		
(a)	.2*4	+	.4*3	+	.3*2	+	.1*1	=	2.7
(b)	.2*1	+	.4*2	+	.3*3	+	.1*4	=	2.3
(c)	.2*2	+	.4*1	+	.3*2	+	.1*3	=	1.7
(d)	.2*2	+	.4*1	+	.3*3	+	.1*2	=	1.9

Note that here in order to reduce the expected search length, the tree is structured so that the most frequently accessed names are placed as close as possible to the root.

To accomplish this, the keys must be inserted into the tree in the proper order. Clearly there are problems with this approach if the access probabilities are unknown! In these situations the designer sometimes can guess the relative frequencies of access, then restructure the tree after measures of actual usage have been gathered.

Note also that the expected path length of a binary search tree will change as nodes are inserted into the tree; what is today a good tree structure may tomorrow become a relatively poor tree structure because of node insertions and/or changes in the patterns of access to the tree's contents.

Before discussing how to accommodate these changes, we should also consider the effects of unsuccessful searches. Let u_i be the frequency with which an unsuccessful search terminates at node R_i. Note that $u_i = 0$ for any node R_i which has both its left and right subtrees non-null, because a search can never terminate unsuccessfully at such a node. Then the expected search length is

$$p_s \sum_{i=1}^{n} s_i c_i + p_u \sum_{i=1}^{n} u_i c_i$$

where p_s is the probability of a successful search and p_u is the probability of an unsuccessful search, and

$$p_s + p_u = 1.$$

In some applications, the p_u may be much larger than p_s. For example, consider the use of a binary search tree to store numbers of stolen credit cards in an interactive credit-management system. Prior to making a sale, a store clerk keys in the number of the customer's credit card on a terminal and the system searches for that number in the tree. In nearly all cases, the search will be unsuccessful. The expected search length can be minimized by making these unsuccessful searches terminate with as few comparisons as possible. This implies that the tree should be as bushy as possible. The expected search length here is minimized when the maximum path length in the tree is minimized. Note that here too there is the problem of handling unpredictable insertions into the tree in such a way that search performances do not deteriorate.

INSERTING NODES

The operations of inserting nodes into binary trees and removing nodes from binary trees are fairly straightforward. For example, consider the insertion of a node labeled GNU which is to become the root of the right subtree of some node X of a binary tree. There are two cases: either GNU will be a leaf or GNU will not be a leaf, depending upon whether or not X's right subtree is initially empty. The possible results of inserting GNU are shown in Fig. 8–21(a).

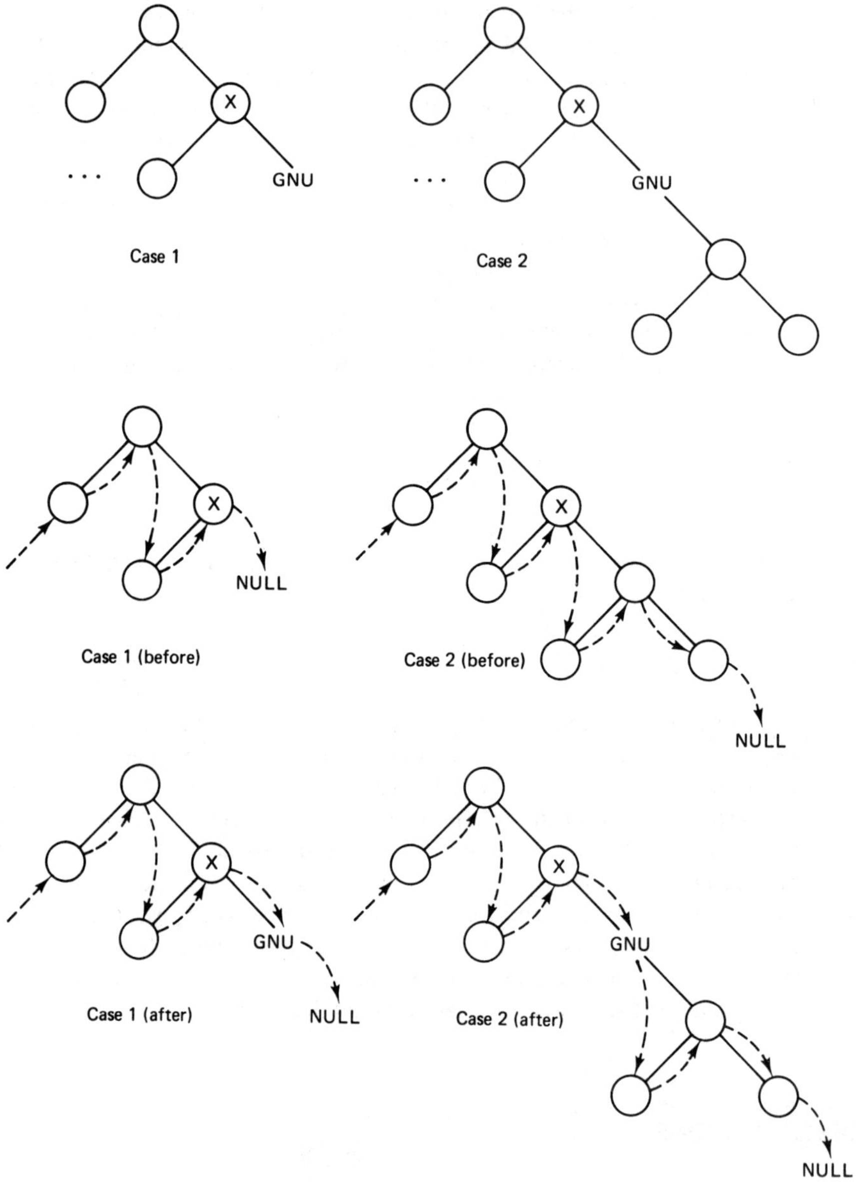

Figure 8–21   Inserting a node.

Unthreaded Insertion

A Pascal procedure to make these insertions in an unthreaded tree is as follows.

```
procedure insert(x:nodeptr;var gnu:nodeptr);
begin new(gnu);
      gnu ↑ .left : = nil;
      gnu ↑ .right : = x ↑ .right;
      x ↑ .right : = gnu
end;
```

The more difficult aspect of inserting nodes in trees is the determination of where they should go.

Threaded Insertion

If the tree is threaded, then the insertion procedure is a bit more complex. Fig. 8–21(b) shows the tree of Fig. 8–21(a) before and after insertion of GNU when the tree is threaded in in-order.

Figure 8–21(b)   Threaded insertion for the tree of Fig. 8–21(a).

The insertion procedure then becomes

```
procedure insert(x:nodeptr;var gnu:nodeptr);
begin new(gnu);
      gnu ↑ .left : = nil;
      gnu ↑ .right : = x ↑ .right;
      gnu ↑ .leftthread : = x;
      gnu ↑ .rightthread : = x ↑ .rightthread;
      x ↑ .right : = gnu;
      x ↑ .rightthread : = gnu
end;
```

You should develop the insertion algorithm for binary trees threaded in pre-order and post-order. For the pre-order case, determine what differences (if any) are necessary when a threadflag is used to note that left is either a left subtree pointer or a rightthread.

INSERTING NODES IN A BINARY SEARCH TREE

A new node in a binary search tree always is placed in the position of a leaf; the structure of the tree is dictated completely by the properties of a binary search tree and by the node insertion order. The insertion algorithm is very similar to the direct search algorithm. To insert a new node with key k in the binary search tree rooted at R_i, the following steps are taken.

1. If the tree is empty, the node with key k becomes the root.
2. If $k = K_i$, the insertion terminates unsuccessfully; the key is already in the tree.
3. If $k < K_i$, the left subtree of R_i is searched until the appropriate position for the new node is found.
4. If $k > K_i$, the right subtree of R_i is searched until the appropriate position for the new node is found.

This algorithm is programmed quite easily by using the same logic structure as did the previously written procedure to search a binary search tree. Let newptr be a pointer to a node which is to be inserted in the binary search tree at r. In Pascal—

```
procedure insert(newptr,var r:nodeptr);
begin if (r=nil)
        then r := newptr
        else if (newptr ↑ .key = r ↑ .key)
                then DUPLICATE-ENTRY
                else if (newptr ↑ .key < r ↑ .key)
                        then insert(newptr,r ↑ .left)
                        else {newptr ↑ .key > r ↑ .key}
                                insert(newptr,r ↑ .right)
end;
```

The condition that causes the search procedure to terminate unsuccessfully is the condition that causes the insertion procedure to terminate successfully; the condition that causes the search to terminate successfully is the condition that causes the insertion to terminate unsuccessfully.

Note that inserting keys into a binary search tree in order results in a long tree with no branching (see tree (b) of Fig. 8–17).

DELETING NODES

Threaded Removal

The removal of nodes from a binary tree is similar to insertion in that it involves "fixing up" the subtree pointers and the threads. Your experience with linked lists should make it clear that it is somewhat easier to remove nodes when the subtree linkages are bidirectional. To implement bidirectional subtree linkages requires just one additional pointer field per node: to the node's parent. In Pascal—

```
type nodeptr = ↑ nodetype;
     nodetype = record
                    left : nodeptr;
                    info : integer;
                    right : nodeptr;
                    leftthread : nodeptr;
                    rightthread : nodeptr;
                    parent : nodeptr
               end;
```

Removal of a node (call it X) from a binary tree is more complex if that node is not a leaf. A decision must be made about the disposition of the removed node's children. It may be the case that these offspring nodes should also be removed from the tree. The difficulty in implementing this policy is in fixing up the threads. Another alternative is to move the root of X's left subtree or right subtree into X's position. This is easy (except for the threads) when only one of these nodes is non-null. If both are non-null, a choice between them must be made. If the one selected has both its left and right subtrees non-null, further difficulties arise. (Try it!) A reasonable alternative in some situations is to avoid these problems by not allowing a node to be removed unless it is a leaf.

DELETING NODES FROM A BINARY SEARCH TREE

The operation of deleting a node from a binary search tree can be complex. If the node to be deleted is a leaf, then the process is simple; the leaf is pruned neatly from the tree. If the node to be deleted is not a leaf, then the process must do something to preserve that node's subtrees.

Consider first the deletion of the PGMR node from the binary search tree of Fig. 8–22. Removing the PGMR does not imply also removing the PILOT, rather PILOT can simply be moved into PGMR's vacated position, becoming the left subtree of SECY. Similarly, if instead SECY had been deleted, then PGMR could be moved into the vacated position; the tree rooted at PGMR would become the left subtree of SWEEPER. It appears that deleting a node with one null subtree implies moving the root of the node's non-null subtree into the node's vacated position.

Consider now the deletion of the node with key CLERK. Which of its two subtree roots should occupy its vacated position? Either can be moved in and not violate the rules of the binary search tree.

Deletion of a node like MNGR is more difficult. If FIREMAN takes MNGR's position, how are its subtrees, rooted at CLERK and HELPER, handled? You should develop an algorithm that will handle deletion of a node from any position in a binary search tree; first be sure that you understand the complexity of the problem.

Another approach to deletion is to avoid (at least temporarily) the complexity of the problem simply by marking the subject nodes as inactive. A later search or insertion needs to use a marked node's key to find its path through the tree. If the key looked for

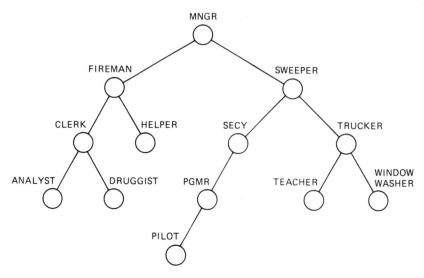

Figure 8–22   A binary search tree.

by the search or insertion procedure matches the key of a marked node, then the procedure must take different action than it normally would. You should modify the search and insert routines to accommodate marked nodes.

For more information about handling deletions, see J. Cohen's "Garbage collection of linked data structures," in *ACM Computing Surveys*, 13(3): 341–367, September 1981.

Collections of keyed data to which both rapid (direct) access to particular records and sequential access through the collection of records are required commonly are structured as binary search trees.

BALANCING BINARY SEARCH TREES

We have seen that the performance of a binary search tree is determined by the structure of the tree and the probabilities of access to the nodes. The structure is affected by the sequence of modifications to the tree; insertions and deletions both change the tree's shape.

Actually achieving the *optimal* binary search tree structure may require more work than it is worth; in fact it may be impossible because of lack of sufficient knowledge of access probabilities. Investigation has shown, however, that performance of binary search trees that are constructed by reasonable heuristic algorithms is competitive with that of optimal trees, while incurring much lower design costs. The two most obvious heuristics are those we have already introduced:

1. Put the nodes with frequently accessed keys near the root of the tree.
2. Keep the tree *balanced*; that is, for each node, the left and right subtrees should have as nearly as possible an equal number of nodes, thereby minimizing the maximum path length.

If the access probabilities were known and no insertions were to be made in the tree, the binary search tree that yields optimal performance could be constructed (with some work) and would do better than a tree resulting from one of those heuristics. However, the heuristics are quite good and require considerably less effort to apply. It has been shown that, in general, binary search trees constructed from the second heuristic—balancing—give nearly optimal expected search lengths; balanced trees perform better in general than do trees constructed from the first heuristic. This result is somewhat comforting in that the access probabilities required by the first heuristic are commonly unavailable.

For details of analysis of various heuristic algorithms for constructing binary search trees, you are urged to consult the references at the end of the chapter.

Keeping a binary search tree in balance when there are node insertions and deletions is hard work. The difficulty is due to having to preserve the proper relationships between keys in nodes and keys in their subtrees. For example, consider the binary search tree of Fig. 8–23.

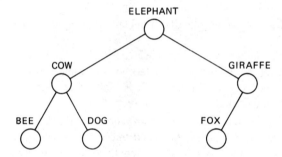

Figure 8–23   A binary search tree.

Inserting ZEBRA would be easy; it would be the right subtree of GIRAFFE and the tree would still be in balance. Instead, however, try to insert APE. The position of APE will be as the left subtree of BEE, which pulls the tree out of balance. The tree when balanced would be as shown in Fig. 8–24. *All* of the nodes of the original tree had to be moved! A similar problem may occur upon deletion of a node from the tree.

In order to reduce the amount of work required to maintain a binary search tree

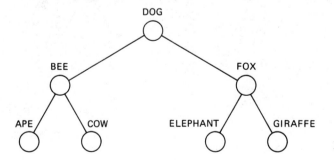

Figure 8–24   Balanced binary search tree.

while providing good search performance, we commonly relax the constraint and allow
the trees to deviate from being balanced. However, the allowed deviation is small enough
that the expected average search length is only slightly longer than that of completely
balanced trees. In the next two sections we introduce two classes of binary search trees
that allow relatively easy modification.

HEIGHT-BALANCED (AVL) TREES

One type of "almost completely" balanced trees is known as the *height-balanced tree*,
or the *AVL tree*, after its Russian discoverers G.M. Adelson-Velskii and E. M. Landis
(1962). A tree is height-balanced if its nodes are arranged such that for each node R_i, the
following property holds:

> The height of the left subtree of R_i and the height of the right subtree of R_i differ by at
> most 1.

Recall that the height of a tree is one plus the number of the highest level on which it
has nodes.

The binary search trees shown in Fig. 8–25 are all height-balanced. Note that although
it is height-balanced, tree (c) is not completely balanced. The binary search trees of Fig.
8–26 are *not* height-balanced. The height constraint is violated at node APE in tree (a),
at node COW in tree (b), and at node FOX in tree (c).

AVL trees provide good direct search performance. Although they tend to look
somewhat more sparse than do completely balanced trees, the searches they require are
only moderately longer. The worst possible search length for a completely balanced tree
of n nodes is $\log_2 (n + 1)$, while the worst possible search length for an AVL tree of n

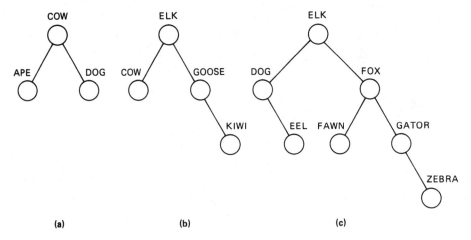

Figure 8–25   Height-balanced trees.

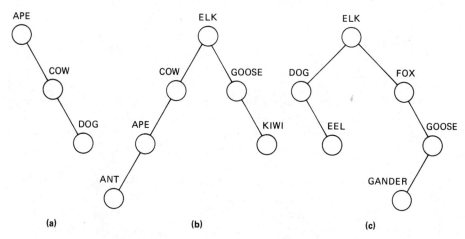

Figure 8–26   Binary trees that are not height-balanced.

nodes is 1.44 $\log_2 (n + 1)$. The expected average search length for a completely balanced tree of n nodes is $\log_2 (n + 1) - 2$, and the expected average search length for an AVL tree of n nodes is $\log_2 (n + 1) + \alpha$, where α is a constant which depends on the characteristics of the name distribution. (Consult Knuth [1973, pp. 453–454] for details of this analysis.) Thus AVL trees are nearly as good as completely balanced trees. The height constraint prevents an AVL tree from becoming too distant a cousin of a completely balanced tree.

If an insertion or deletion causes an AVL tree to become unbalanced, then the tree must be restructured to return to a balanced state. This restructuring process commonly is referred to as *rotation* and is not discussed further here. The interested reader could start investigation of tree-balancing techniques with perusal of Knuth (1973, pp. 453–463).

BOUNDED-BALANCED (BB) TREES

Another class of "almost completely" balanced trees is known as the *bounded-balanced trees*. These trees are also referred to as *BB trees* or *weight-balanced trees*. The basic idea of a bounded-balanced tree is to place a constraint on how far the tree can deviate from being completely balanced. This bound constrains the difference between the number of nodes in a left subtree and a right subtree. Although based on constraining subtree sizes rather than subtree heights, bounded-balance trees are similar in their properties to height-balanced trees. Both aim to reach a compromise between short search lengths and balancing requirements.

A bounded-balance tree carries a parameter β which controls this compromise. In a bounded-balance tree of balance β, where $0 < \beta \leq \frac{1}{2}$, for each node of the tree the fraction of the nodes in the node's left subtree lies between β and $1 - \beta$. More formally, if SIZE(N) is the number of nodes in the tree rooted at node N, then the constraint is

$$\beta \leqslant \frac{\text{SIZE}(\text{LEFT}(N)) + 1}{\text{SIZE}(N) + 1} \leqslant 1 - \beta$$

If $\beta = \frac{1}{2}$, then the left subtree and right subtree would have the same number of nodes, i.e., the tree would be completely balanced. If $\beta = \frac{1}{4}$, then one subtree could have up to three times as many nodes as the other. As the value of β approaches $\frac{1}{2}$, the bounding constraint becomes tighter. A tree designer selects the appropriate β value for the application.

The expected average search length for a bounded-balance tree is $O(\log_2 n)$, where n is the number of nodes in the tree. If insertion or deletion causes a tree of this class to become unbalanced relative to its bound β, then the same types of rotations as are applied to the class of height-balanced trees are applied to return the tree to a balanced state.

The work required to keep an AVL or BB tree in conformance with its height- or size-ratio is considerably less than the work required to keep a tree *completely* balanced. If a transformation is required to keep a tree completely balanced after an insertion or deletion, that transformation requires movement of $O(n)$ nodes, where n is the number of nodes in the tree. By contrast, if a transformation is needed to maintain height- or size-ratio conformance in an AVL or BB tree after an insertion or deletion, movement of $O(\log_2 n)$ nodes is required. The reduction in work is accomplished by localizing movement to nodes along a single path from root to leaf in the AVL or BB tree, while movement in the completely balanced tree affects the entire tree.

SUMMARY

This chapter introduced the special class of *graph* data structure called the *general tree*, an acyclic, connected, simple graph. Terminology pertaining to trees was introduced; then a special case of general tree, the *binary tree*, became the focus of attention. In a binary tree, each node has a maximum of two subtrees, which can be distinguished as a left and right subtree. Because it is easier to manage binary trees than general trees, it is useful to represent a general tree (or forest of general trees) by a binary tree form. An algorithm for this conversion was presented.

An important class of binary trees are those that are *almost complete*. Structuring a collection of nodes as an almost complete binary tree minimizes the maximum path length in the tree, thereby minimizing the longest search path through the tree to a particular node.

Sometimes instead of searching for a particular node, it is necessary to traverse a binary tree, that is, to visit all the tree's nodes. Several algorithms were presented for binary tree traversal: pre-order, in-order, and post-order. These algorithms differ in the order in which the root, left subtree, and right subtree are traversed. Each ordering is appropriate for a different type of application. To facilitate traversal, a tree may be threaded according to one of the traversal algorithms. Each node then points to its successor in the traversal path. Threads are commonly bidirectional, which makes node insertion and removal somewhat easier. Traversal of a general tree is accomplished by first converting the tree to its binary form.

The *binary search tree* is applicable to organizing large collections of data records with identifying keys, where access directly to a particular record and sequential access to the entire set of records are both required. Algorithms were presented to perform the basic operations on binary search trees: direct search, sequential search, node insertion, and node deletion.

Understanding the nature of a binary search tree makes it obvious that some structures yield better search performance than do other structures. Two reasonable heuristics for building binary search trees were discussed; one of these heuristics—keeping the tree balanced—gives very nearly optimal search lengths without the work of actually constructing an optimal tree.

The difficulty of keeping a binary search tree completely balanced when there are node insertions and deletions was discussed, and two classes of "almost balanced" binary search trees were introduced that give good search performance yet require considerably less maintenance work than do completely balanced trees. *AVL-trees* (also known as *height-balanced trees*) constrain the height difference between each node's left and right subtrees to be at most 1. *Bounded-balance trees* (also known as *BB trees* or *weight-balanced trees*) constrain the difference between the size (i.e., number of nodes) of each node's left and right subtrees. The tree designer here specifies the parameter used in establishing the constraint.

Insertions and deletions of nodes in a balanced binary search tree may take that tree out of balance; the height or size constraint may be violated. In order to return the tree to a balanced condition, rotation may be applied to the tree.

The expected average search length for a balanced binary search tree is $O(\log_2 n)$.

TERMS

almost complete binary tree

AVL tree

binary tree

binary search tree

bounded-balance tree

complete binary tree

equivalent trees

forest

height-balanced tree

in-order traversal

leaf node

left thread

level

node

path length

post-order traversal

pre-order traversal

right thread

rooted tree

rotation

similar trees

threaded tree

tree

tree height

tree traversal

tree weight

weight-balanced tree

SELECTED REFERENCES

ALLEN, B. and I. MUNRO. "Self-organizing binary search trees," *Jour. ACM*, 25(4): 526–535, Oct. 1978.

BAER, J.-L. and B. SCHWAB. "A comparison of tree-balancing algorithms," *Comm. ACM*, 20(5): 322–330, May 1977.

BALLARD, D. H. "Strip trees: a hierarchical representation for curves," *Comm. ACM*, 24(5): 310–321, May 1981.

BECKLEY, D. A., M. W. EVANS, and V. K. RAMAN. "Multikey retrieval from K-d trees and quad-trees," *Proc. ACM-SIGMOD 1985 Internat. Conf. on Management of Data, May 28–31, 1985, Austin TX*, pp. 291–301.

BRUNO, J., and E. G. COFFMAN. "Nearly optimal binary search trees," *Proc. IFIP Congress 1971*, North-Holland, pp. 99–103.

BURGE, W. H. "An analysis of binary search trees formed from sequences of nondistinct keys," *Jour. ACM*, 23(3): 451–454, July 1976.

CHANG, H. and S. S. IYENGAR. "Efficient algorithms to globally balance a binary search tree," *Comm. ACM*, 27(7): 695–702, July 1984.

DEJONGE, W., A. S. TANENBAUM, and R. P. VAN DE RIET. "Two access methods using compact binary trees," *IEEE Trans. on Software Engineering*, SE-13(7): 799–810, July 1987.

DRISCOLL, J. R. and Y. E. LIEN. "A selective traversal algorithm for binary search trees," *Comm. ACM*, 21(6): 445–447, June 1978.

DYER, C. R., A. ROZENFELD, and H. SAMET. "Region representation: boundary codes from quadtrees," *Comm. ACM*, 23(3): 171–179, March 1980.

EPPINGER, J. L. "An empirical study of insertion and deletion in binary search trees," *Comm. ACM*, 26(9): 663–669, Sept. 1983.

FOSTER, C. C. "Information storage and retrieval using AVL trees," *Proc. ACM 20th Natl. Conf.*, pp. 192–205, 1965.

GARGANTINI, I. "An effective way to represent quadtrees," *Comm. ACM*, 25(12); 905–910, Dec. 1982.

GONNET, G. H. "Balancing binary trees by internal path reduction," *Comm. ACM*, 26(12): 1074–1081, Dec. 1983.

HIBBARD, T. "Some combinatorial properties of certain trees with applications to searching and sorting," *Jour. ACM*, 9(1): 13–28, January 1962.

HIRSCHBERG, D. S. "An insertion technique for one-sided height-balanced trees," *Comm. ACM*, 19(8): 471–473, Aug. 1976.

HUANG, S-H. S. "Height-balanced trees of order (b,g,d)," *ACM Trans. on Database Syst.*, 10(2) 261–284, June 1985.

KARLTON, P. L., S. H. FULLER, R. E. SCROGGS, and E. B. KAEHLER. "Performance of height-balanced trees," *Comm. ACM*, 19(1): 23–28, Jan. 1976.

KESSELS, J. L. W. "On-the-fly optimization of data structures," *Comm. ACM*, 26(11): 895–901, Nov. 1983.

KNOTT, G. D. "A numbering system for binary trees," *Comm. ACM*, 20(2): 113–115, Feb. 1977.

KNUTH, D. E. *The Art of Computer Programming*: *Vol. 3, Sorting and Searching*. Reading, MA: Addison-Wesley Publishing Co., 1973, pp. 422–471.

KOSARAJU, S. R. "Insertions and deletions in one-sided height-balanced trees," *Comm. ACM*, 21(3): 226–227, March 1978.

KUNG, H. T. and P. L. LEHMAN. "Concurrent manipulation of binary search trees," *ACM Trans. on Database Syst.*, 5(3): 354–382, Sept. 1980.

LEE, K. P. "A linear algorithm for copying binary trees using bounded workspace," *Comm. ACM*, 23(3): 159–162, March 1980.

LUCCIO, F. and L. PAGLI. "Comment on generalized AVL trees," *Comm. ACM*, 23(7): 394–395, July 1980.

LUCCIO, F. and L. PAGLI. "Power trees," *Comm. ACM*, 21(11): 941–947, Nov. 1978.

LUCE, R. D. and H. RAIFFA. *Games and Decisions*. New York: John Wiley & Sons, Inc., 1958.

MANBER, U. "Concurrent maintenance of binary search trees," *IEEE Trans. on Software Engineering*, SE-10(6): 777–784, Nov. 1984.

MOITRA, A. and S. S. IYENGAR. "Derivation of a parallel algorithm for balancing binary trees," *IEEE Trans. on Software Engineering*, SE-12(3): 442–449, March 1986.

NEWBORN, M. *Computer Chess*. New York: Academic Press, 1975.

NIEVERGELT, J. "Binary search trees and file organization," *ACM Computing Surveys*, 6(3): 195–207, Sept. 1974.

NIEVERGELT, J. and C. K. WONG. "Upper bounds for the total path length of binary trees," *Jour. ACM*, 20(1): 1–6, Jan. 1973.

OTTMANN, T., H. W. SIX, and D. WOOD. "Right brother trees," *Comm. ACM*, 21(9): 769–776, Sept. 1978.

PFALTZ, J. L. "Representing graphs by Knuth trees," *Jour. ACM*, 22(3): 361–366, July 1975.

PROSKUROWSKI, A. "On the generation of binary trees," *Jour. ACM*, 27(1): 1–2, Jan. 1980.

RAIHA, K-J. and S. H. ZWEBEN. "An optimal insertion algorithm for one-sided height-balanced binary search trees," *Comm. ACM*, 22(9): 508–512, Sept. 1979.

ROTEM, D. and Y. L. VAROL. "Generation of binary trees from ballot sequences," *Jour. ACM*, 25(3): 369–404, July 1978.

SAMET, H. "Data structures for quadtree approximation and compression," *Comm. ACM*, 28(9): 973–993, Sept. 1985.

SAMET, H. "The quadtree and related hierarchical data structures," *ACM Computing Surveys*, 16(2): 187–260, June 1984.

SAMET, H. "A quadtree medial axis transform," *Comm. ACM*, 26(9): 680–693, Sept. 1983.

SAMET, H. "Deletion in two-dimensional quad trees," *Comm. ACM*, 23(12): 703–710, Dec. 1980.

SAMET, H. "Region representation: quadtrees from boundary codes," *Comm. ACM*, 23(3): 163–170, March 1980.

SARNAK, N. and R. E. TARJAN. "Planar point location using persistent search trees," *Comm. ACM*, 29(7): 669–679, July 1986.

SCOTT, D. S. and S. S. IYENGAR. "TIF—a translation invariant data structure for storing images," *Comm. ACM*, 29(5): 418–429, May 1986.

SEVERANCE, D. G. "Identifier search mechanisms: a survey and generalized model," *ACM Computing Surveys*, 6(3): 175–194, Sept. 1974.

SOLOMON, M. N. and R. A. FINKEL. "A note on enumerating binary trees," *Jour. ACM*, 27(1): 3–5, Jan. 1980.

STANDISH, T. A. "Trees," Chapter 3 in *Data Structure Techniques*. Reading, MA: Addison-Wesley Publishing Co., 1980, pp. 44–129.

STASKO, J. T. and J. S. VITTER. "Pairing heaps: experiments and analysis," *Comm. ACM*, 30(3): 234–249, March 1987.

STOUT, Q. F. and B. L. WARREN. "Tree rebalancing in optimal time and space." *Comm. ACM*, 29(9): 902–908, Sept. 1986.

TOMPA, F. W., J. GECSEI, and G. V. BOCHMANN. "Data structuring facilities for interactive videotex systems," *Computer*, 14(8): pp. 72–81, Aug. 1981.

YAU, M-M. and S. N. SRIHARI. "A hierarchical data structure for multidimensional digital images," *Comm. ACM*, 26(7): 504–515, July 1983.

ZWEBEN, S. H. and M. A. MCDONALD. "An optimal method for deletions in one-sided height-balanced trees," *Comm. ACM*, 21(6): 441–445, June 1978.

REVIEW EXERCISES

1. Draw two binary trees that are similar.
2. Draw two binary trees that are equivalent.
3. Can there be two binary trees that are equivalent but not similar? If so, give an example. If not, why not?
4. Can there be a cycle in a tree? If so, give an example. If not, why not?
5. What is the number of nodes on the Ith level of a complete binary tree with height K, where $I < K$?
6. What is the number of nodes on the Ith level of an almost complete binary tree with height K, where $I < K$?
7. Draw a complete binary tree with 10 nodes. Draw an almost complete binary tree with 10 nodes. What is the minimum maximum path length for a binary tree with 10 nodes? What is the maximum maximum path length for a binary tree with 10 nodes?
8. Why is it easier to represent binary trees in programs than it is to represent general trees?
9. Consider the following binary tree:

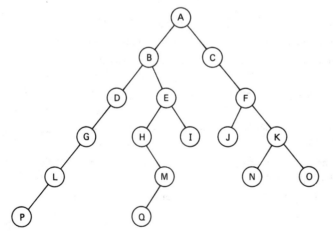

Figure P8–9

List the nodes of the tree in (a) pre-order, (b) post-order, (c) in-order. Draw the tree as threaded in (d) pre-order, (e) post-order, (f) in-order, representing threads by dashed lines.

10. Is the following statement true or false? "The leaves of a binary tree occur in the same relative position in pre-order, post-order, and in-order."

11. Draw the binary tree corresponding to the forest in Fig. P8–11.

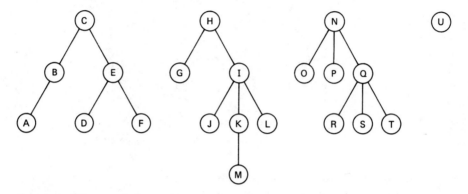

Figure P8–11

12. Transform the following general tree to a binary tree.

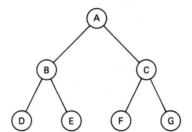

Figure P8–12

13. The following binary tree resulted from the transformation of a forest to a binary form. What was the forest?

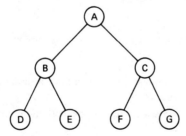

Figure P8–13

14. Represent the expression $((A + B)*C)/(D - E)$ as a binary tree. Traverse the tree in pre-order, post-order, and in-order. Why do you think post-order was chosen as the traversal order for expression evaluation, i.e., what can you see about the post-order traversal which makes computation easier than with the other orders?

15. Show the binary tree representation for the string ICDFEHABC produced (a) using pre-order, where the tree has structure

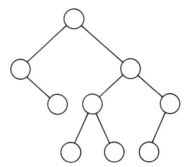

Figure P8–15

(b) using in-order, (c) using post-order.

16. Given a collection of keys $K_1, K_2, \ldots, K_n$, in what sequence should those keys be inserted to form a balanced binary search tree?

17. Do all of the compilers available at your installation use the same collating sequence? If not, how do they differ?

18. Show the in-order threads in the following tree.

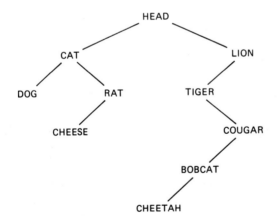

Figure P8–18

19. What type of threads should a binary search tree have in order to facilitate visitation of the nodes in sequence by their names?

20. Construct two additional binary search trees for the collection of keys structured in Fig. 8–17. Using the access probabilities

APE	.2
BEE	.4

COW   .3
DOG   .1

calculate the expected search lengths for your trees.

21. Give an example where post-order traversal is the most appropriate way to visit a tree. Do the same for in-order traversal and pre-order traversal.

22. Give the node structure for a binary tree that is threaded in both in-order and post-order.

23. Is it likely that a real binary tree would ever be threaded for more than one traversal type? Why or why not?

24. Consider a binary tree T with n nodes, $n \geq 0$. If T is not empty, the maximum level that any node of T can reach is n. If T is nonempty, then at least one node achieves some maximum level for that tree. What is the *minimum* value that this maximum level can be? For example, for $n = 1$ the answer is 1, while for $n = 2$ the answer is 2, and for $n = 3$ it is also 2. Express your answer as a formula in terms of n, $\log_2$ (logarithm to the base 2), and the ceiling function $\lceil \ \rceil$. Prove that your result is true.

25. Three basic orders for traversing a binary tree have been identified. Another alternative would be to
    (a) visit the root,
    (b) traverse the right subtree,
    (c) traverse the left subtree,
    using the same rule recursively on all nonempty subtrees. Does this new order bear any simple relation to the three orders already discussed? What kind of threads should be defined to make traversal in this order easier?

26. Describe what happens when the general-to-binary tree transformation is applied to a binary tree.

27. Write a procedure to reconstruct the original general tree from the binary tree that results from the transformation algorithm presented in this chapter.

28. Write a program that takes general trees as input and produces the corresponding binary trees as output.

29. Write iterative procedures to perform in-order traversal on a binary tree that is threaded in in-order; to perform pre-order traversal on a binary tree that is threaded in pre-order; to perform post-order traversal on a binary tree that is threaded in post-order. Write programs to implement the procedures.

30. Write recursive procedures to implement in-order, pre-order, and post-order traversal for un-threaded trees. Write a program to implement the procedures.

31. Write nonrecursive (i.e., iterative) procedures to implement in-order, pre-order, and post-order traversal for unthreaded trees. Write a program to implement the procedures.

32. What trade-offs are to be considered in deciding whether tree traversal should be implemented by a recursive or an iterative routine?

33. Write procedures to insert a new node in a binary tree that is threaded in in-order; in pre-order; in post-order.

34. Write procedures to remove a node from a binary tree; from a threaded binary tree.

35. What is the difference between a balanced tree and a height-balanced tree?

36. Write nonrecursive (i.e., iterative) procedures to search a binary search tree and to insert a new node in a binary search tree.

37. Modify the procedures that search a binary search tree and insert a new node in a binary search tree so that they will recognize nodes that have been marked as deleted but that have not yet been removed from the tree.

38. Write a procedure to delete a given node from a binary search tree. Be sure to accommodate situations where the node to be deleted has 0, 1, or 2 non-null subtrees.

39. Read about techniques for keeping a tree in balance. Write a program to implement one of the techniques.

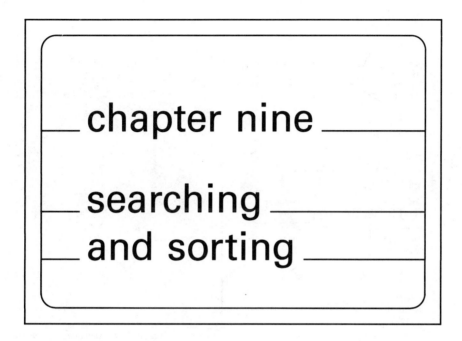

chapter nine

searching

and sorting

In this chapter we take a breather from learning about new data structures and instead study techniques for finding particular data values in structures and for sorting data values. Searching and sorting are quite closely related processes, as we shall see.

   Consider a collection of records, each of which has a *key* that can be used to identify it. A key is composed of one or more fields. Key values may be unique identifiers of records, or there may be duplicate values allowed. If duplicate key values are allowed, it may be desirable to differentiate between record occurrences with the same key value by their order of appearance in the collection. The concept of keys will extend throughout much of the rest of this book. *Searching* is the process of locating a record with a particular key value. *Sorting* is the process of arranging records so that they are in order by key value.

SEQUENTIAL SEARCHES

A search algorithm is a technique for finding a record that has some key value. We will call the key value, say k, the *argument* of the search. The search terminates either successfully when a record containing k is found or unsuccessfully when it is determined that there is no record containing k.

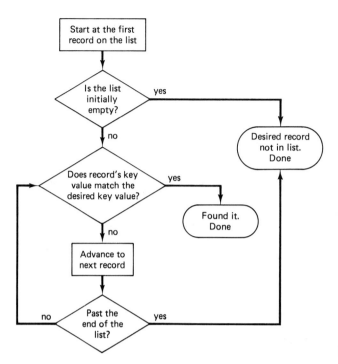

Figure 9-1 Sequential search algorithm.

There are many search algorithms. In this section we cover *sequential searches*, also known as *linear searches*. Later in the chapter we will consider nonlinear searches, which tend to perform considerably better than the sequential techniques. However, sequential searches are quite simple and provide a good place to start our investigation of searching and sorting.

Assume that the collection of records that we are searching through has been organized as a linear list. We have seen that a linear list may be represented by an array or by a linked list. We will use the array representation here; you should determine how the use of linked representation would alter the algorithms.

Let key(i) be the key value in the *i*th record of the list. The basic sequential search algorithm is to start at the beginning of the list and go through each record until one with the desired key value (k) is found or the end of the list is reached. A flowchart of the algorithm is in Fig. 9-1. The algorithm can be implemented in Pascal as follows. Assume there are n records in the list and that key, k, and n are global variables.

```
procedure findk;
var foundit: boolean;i:1 . . n;
begin
    foundit := false;
    i := 1;
    while(not foundit) and i ⩽ n
```

```
      do if k = key[i]
          then foundit := true
          else i := i + 1;
      if(foundit)
      then writeln ('record with key', k, 'found at position', i)
      else writeln ('record with key', k, 'not found')
end;
```

If the algorithm terminates with foundit = true, then a record with key value k is the ith one in the list. If the algorithm terminates with foundit = false, then the key value k does not appear in the list.

How efficient is this procedure? Let prob(i) be the probability that the ith record is the one being sought. Then

$$\sum_{i=1}^{n} \text{prob}(i) + Q = 1, \qquad \text{where } Q = \text{probability that the key is not present.}$$

The optimal situation is for the record sought to be the first one looked at. The worst case is when keys of all n records are compared with k and either key[n] = k or the sought record is not in the list.

The average, or expected, number of comparisons is

$$\sum_{i=1}^{n} i*\text{prob}(i) + Q*n$$

With probability prob(1), 1 comparison is required; with probability prob(2), 2 comparisons are required; . . .; with probability prob(n) + Q, n comparisons are required. If all records are equally likely to be retrieved and every key sought is in the list, then

$$\text{prob}(i) = \frac{1}{n} \text{ for all } i$$

and

$$\sum_{i=1}^{n} i*\text{prob}(i) = \sum_{i=1}^{n} \frac{i}{n}, \text{ which is } \frac{n+1}{2.}$$

That is, on the average, about half of the keys will be compared with the argument k.

In some situations, key values are not unique. To find all the records with a particular key value then requires scanning the full list. All of the key values must be compared with the search argument.

A sequential search algorithm is said to require "on the order of N" comparisons. That is, the expected number of comparisons is a linear function of the number of records in the collection. "On the order of N" is commonly denoted $O(N)$. Doubling the number of keys means that the process will take twice as long.

This is not a particularly good method of searching! For example, you probably have never used this technique to look up a name in the telephone directory, which is really just a linear list. How might we improve the situation?

IMPROVING SEQUENTIAL SEARCH PERFORMANCE

Consider again the expression for the expected number of comparisons with a sequential search.

$$\sum_{i=1}^{n} i*\text{prob}(i) + Q*n$$

If we have the freedom to arrange the records in the linear list in any order we choose, then the above expression is minimized when

$$\text{prob}(1) \geq \text{prob}(2) \geq \ .\ . \geq \text{prob}(n)$$

That is

$$\text{prob}(I) \geq \text{prob}(J) \text{ for } I < J.$$

By arranging the records by descending frequency of access, we improve the probability that fewer comparisons will be made. It may still be the case that n comparisons are needed (say we are looking for a key that is not in the list), but the *expected* number of comparisons will be minimized.

Sampled Accesses

Consider now the more typical situation in which the relative frequency of access to the records is not known. There are several schemes to handle this problem. One is to observe requests to the list over a period of time, keeping count of the number of accesses to each record. When a representative sample of activity has been gathered, the records can be reordered according to the detected probabilities of access.

Move to the Front

A second scheme is to let the list of records dynamically reorganize itself. With the *move-to-the-front* method, whenever there is a successful search for a key value, the corresponding record is moved to first position in the list. The record that was number one becomes number two, and so forth. A flowchart of the move-to-the-front algorithm is given in Fig. 9–2. The algorithm can be implemented in Pascal as follows, assuming that there are n records in the list and that rec (which contains key), k, and n are globally known.

```
procedure movetofront;
var foundit:boolean;
    i:1 . . n;
    j:0 . . n;
    temprec:rectype;
```

```
begin
    foundit := false;
    i := 1;
    while (not foundit) and i ≤ n
    do if k = key[i]
        then foundit := true
        else i := i + 1;
    if(foundit)
    then begin writeln ('record with key', k, 'found');
                temprec := rec[i];
                j := i − 1;
                while j > 0
```

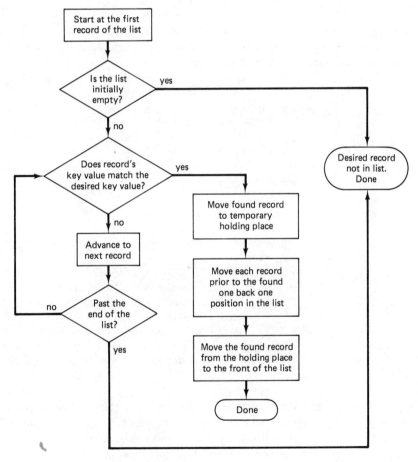

Figure 9–2 "Move-to-the-front" sequential search algorithm.

```
                        do begin rec[j + 1] : = rec [j];
                                  j : = j − 1
                            end;
                        rec[1] : = temprec
                end;
             else writeln ('record with key', k, 'not found')
         end;
```

This method would perform better on a linear list represented by a linked list than by an array. Why?

Transposition

Another dynamic reorganization scheme is the *transposition* method. Whenever there is a successful search for a key value, the corresponding record is interchanged with the immediately preceding one. In Pascal, making the same assumptions about variable declarations as in the *movetofront* procedure:

```
           procedure transpose;
           var foundit:boolean;
               i:1 . . n;
               temprec:rectype;
           begin
               foundit : = false;
               i: = 1;
               while (not foundit) and i ⩽ n
               do if(k = key[i])
                  then foundit : = true
                  else i : = i + 1;
               if(foundit and i > 1)
               then begin writeln ('record with key', k, 'found');
                          temprec : = rec[i];{transpose adjacent records}
                          rec[i] : = rec [i − 1];
                          rec[i − 1] : = temprec
                     end;
               else writeln ('record with key', k, 'not found')
           end;
```

The more frequently a record is retrieved, the more quickly it percolates to the number one position. Compared with the move-to-the-front method, the transposition method requires a longer period of activity to reorganize the collection of records. An advantage of the transposition method is that it does not allow an isolated request for a record to shift the entire collection of records. In effect, a record must earn its right to the top through a history of demand.

Sorting

One way to reduce the expected number of comparisons when there is a significant frequency of unsuccessful searches is to order the records by key value. That is:

$$\text{key}(I) \leqslant \text{key}(J)$$
$$\text{for} \quad I < J$$

(or key(I) $\geqslant$ key(J) for $I < J$ in descending order.) This technique is useful when the list is a list of exceptions, such as bad credit card numbers, to be compared against. Most of the lookups are unsuccessful. Now an unsuccessful search terminates when the first key value greater than the argument is found, rather than at the end of the list, as shown in the flowchart of Fig. 9–3. The algorithm can be implemented in Pascal as follows.

```
foundit := false;
i := 1;
while (not foundit) and (key [i] ≤ k)          and (i ≤ n)
do if(k = key[i])                                          ←——— bug.
    then foundit := true
    else i := i + 1;
```

Later in the chapter we will consider techniques for sorting the list entries.

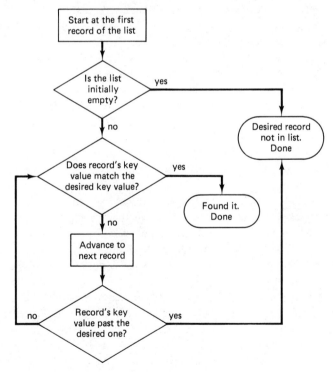

Figure 9–3   Sequential search algorithm for a sorted list.

THE BINARY SEARCH

All the sequential search techniques require $O(n)$ comparisons. The performance of the basic sequential search can be improved by smart positioning of the records (by knowing access probabilities, by moving target records immediately or more slowly to the front of the list, or by keeping the records in sorted order), but the $O(n)$ behavior will persist. Really improving performance requires using a different approach to searching—nonlinear techniques.

In Chapters 7 and 8 we began our study of nonlinear data structures. We discovered that by structuring data in a binary tree, the search time to a particular record of the collection could be reduced significantly over structuring that data in a linear data structure. For a collection of n records, the expected average search length of a balanced binary tree is $O(\log_2 n)$, whereas the average search length of a linear list is $O(n/2)$. For large n, the binary tree exhibits much better performance. Just as the branching structure of nonlinear data structures helps to reduce search lengths, so also can nonlinear searching and sorting techniques improve performance over sequential methods.

We already covered a nonlinear tree-based search strategy in our discussion of binary search trees. When we were looking for the node with a particular key value, the comparison at each intermediate node directed us down the proper branch of the tree toward our destination. In a completely balanced tree, each comparison removes from further consideration one-half of the nodes remaining on the tree. Thus the expected average search length in a balanced binary search tree is $O(\log_2 n)$. This is good performance compared with sequential searching methods.

The binary search technique can be applied to data in a linear list as well as to data in a binary search tree. The major prerequisites are that records in the list must be in sorted order by the search key value and the number of records must be known. The binary search technique cannot be applied unless these prerequisites are met.

The search proceeds by successive probes into the list. The first probe compares the value of the key in the middle of the sorted list with the value sought. If the sought value is less, then the half of the list following the middle can be removed from further consideration. On the other hand, if the sought value is greater, then the half of the list preceding the middle need not be considered further. The second probe is to the key in the middle of the retained half of the original list. Again, if the sought value is less than this probed key's value, then the half of the (half-) list following the probe can be removed from further consideration. If the sought value is greater than this probed key's value, then the half of the (half-) list preceding the probe need not be considered further. And so the probing process continues until the sought key value is located or is determined not to reside in the list.

For example, Fig. 9–4 shows the sequence of probing activity involved in a binary search for the key value 72 in a sample linear list. Initially there are 16 keys to consider. The first probe is to the 8th (16/2) key: 68. Because $68 < 72$, further search needs only look at the second half of the list. The second probe is to the 12th ((8 + 16)/2) key: 81. Because $81 > 72$, we now can discard the last quarter of the list. The third probe is to the 10th ((8 + 12)/2) key: 72, which is exactly the sought key value. Three probes were

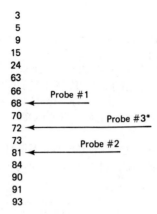

Figure 9–4   Binary search probes.

required here; a linear search would have required ten comparisons. For large lists, the performance improvement is even more dramatic.

The list is cut in half over and over again until either the middle key value is the desired value or the size of the remaining list is zero, implying that the sought key value is not in the list.

The binary search technique can be programmed as either an iterative algorithm or a recursive algorithm. An iterative binary search procedure written in COBOL follows. The linear list of N keys is housed in array KEYLIST; the sought key value is SKEY. FOUNDIT is set equal to the subscript of the array element with value SKEY if it exists or to 0 if SKEY is not found.

```
01   KEYLIST.
     02   KEYVALUE   OCCURS N TIMES      PICTURE S9(5).
01   AUX-VARIABLES.
     02   LOW         PICTURE 9(4).
     02   HIGH        PICTURE 9(4).
     02   MID         PICTURE 9(4).
     02   SKEY        PICTURE S9(5).
     02   FOUNDIT     PICTURE 9(4).

BINARY-SEARCH.
     COMPUTE FOUNDIT = 0.
     COMPUTE LOW = 1.
     COMPUTE HIGH = N.
     PERFORM PROBE UNTIL LOW > HIGH
                        OR FOUNDIT > 0.
```

where

PROBE.
            COMPUTE MID = (LOW + HIGH)/2.
        IF SKEY = KEYVALUE(MID)
                COMPUTE FOUNDIT = MID
        ELSE IF SKEY < KEYVALUE (MID)
                COMPUTE HIGH = MID − 1
            ELSE COMPUTE LOW = MID + 1.

In this routine, the subscripts LOW, MID, and HIGH are prevented from taking on fractional values because they are declared to be integers.

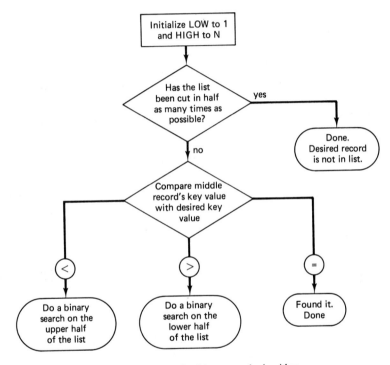

Figure 9–5 Recursive binary search algorithm.

A flowchart for a recursive binary search algorithm is given in Fig. 9–5. The algorithm can be written in Pascal as follows, assuming that the variable names are the same as for the above COBOL procedure, the array keylist and the sought variable skey are global variables, and the subscript range for key is from 1 to n.

```
procedure binsrch (var low,high,foundit : integer)
var mid : integer;
begin if (low > high) then foundit := 0
```

```
                          else begin {probe}
                                  mid := (low + high) div 2;
                                  if (skey = key[mid])
                                  then foundit := mid
                                  else if (skey < key[mid])
                                          then binsrch(low, mid − 1,foundit)
                                          else binsrch(mid + 1,high,foundit)
                          end {probe}
                  end {binsrch};
```

This procedure would be invoked by a statement such as binsrch(1,n,foundit); the variable foundit would attain the value of the subscript of the entry with value skey, or would become zero if skey does not exist in the array.

The maximum number of comparisons required for a binary search of a sorted linear list of n elements is $\log_2 n$; the minimum number of comparisons required is 1. The expected number of comparisons is $1/2 \log_2 n$. Thus the binary search is said to be $O(\log_2 n)$.

A binary search should nearly always be used rather than a sequential search on a large collection of items ordered by the search key. In fact, commonly it is advantageous to build lists in sorted order to start with for purposes of being able to use the binary search technique. Actually, this dictate of always using a binary search should be modified somewhat to indicate its applicability to searching collections of data entirely resident in main memory. The binary search is an internal search method. The concept of nonlinear searching also can be applied to data collections resident on secondary storage; we consider such data organizations later in this book.

INTRODUCTION TO SORTING

Let's look now at techniques for keeping records in sorted order, which we have seen can be important for improving search performance.

There are two basic categories of sorting techniques: internal sorts and external sorts. *Internal sorting* methods are applied when the entire collection of data to be sorted is small enough that the sorting can take place within main memory. The time required to read or write records is not considered to be significant in evaluating the performance of internal sorting techniques. Several internal sorting methods are introduced in this chapter. *External sorting* methods are applied to larger collections of data where some (frequently most) of the collection resides on an auxiliary memory device such as a magnetic tape or disk. Here read and write access times are major concerns in determining sort performance. We will study external sorting methods in the file processing part of this book.

Even though we are interested in obtaining sorted lists of records, we will routinely ignore the records and appear to be interested only in obtaining sorted lists of keys. Do not be confused by this short-cut. If you prefer, when we indicate that "a key" should be inserted in a list or that "a key" should be selected from a list or that "two keys" in a list should exchange positions, interpret "a key" to mean "a key and its accompanying record" or "a key and the pointer to its corresponding record."

Throughout, we assume that the result of sorting is to be the keys in ascending order. You should be able to make whatever changes to the algorithms are necessary to result in a descending ordering of keys.

We will not require that key values be unique identifiers of records. A sorting algorithm is said to be *stable* if the original ordering of records with equal keys is preserved in the sorted ordering of those records. It is important to use a stable sort method if that original record ordering is meaningful. For example, that ordering may have been established by time of entry of the records in the original list. Not all sort methods are stable. As in our discussion of linear search techniques, we assume here that the linear list to be sorted is represented by an array. You should determine how the use of linked list representation would alter the algorithms.

A SELECTION SORT

One family of internal sorting algorithms is the group of *selection sorts*. The basic idea of a selection sort is to repeatedly select the smallest key remaining in the unsorted list of data as the next key in a growing sorted list of data (Fig. 9–6).

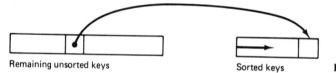

Remaining unsorted keys   Sorted keys   **Figure 9–6**   Selection sort.

The entire list of unsorted keys must be available for us to be able to select the minimum key value in that list. The sorted list, however, can be output as we go along.

For example, consider the following unsorted list of keys.

            14   3   22   9   10   14   2   7   25   6

The first selection pass identifies 2 as the minimum element and removes it from the unsorted list.

            <u>14   3   22   9   10   14   7   25   6</u>   <u>2</u>
            remaining unsorted keys   sorted list

The second selection pass identifies 3 as the minimum element and removes it from the unsorted list.

            <u>14   22   9   10   14   7   25   6</u>   <u>2   3</u>
            remaining unsorted keys   sorted list

After the sixth pass, we have the following.

| 14 | 22 | 14 | 25 | | 2 | 3 | 6 | 7 | 9 | 10 |

remaining unsorted keys   sorted list

In COBOL, the *straight selection sort* is

```
01  UNSORTED-TABLE.
    02  UNSORTED-ENTRY      OCCURS N TIMES      PIC S99.
01  SORTED-TABLE.
    02  SORTED-ENTRY        OCCURS N TIMES      PIC S99.
01  AUX-ITEMS.
    02  CURR-MIN-KEY        PIC S99   VALUE HIGH-VALUES.
    02  NEXT-IN-SORT        PIC 9(3)  VALUE 1.
    02  I                   PIC 9(3).
    02  MIN-POS             PIC 9(3).


PERFORM SELECT-NEXT N TIMES.
```

where

```
SELECT-NEXT.
    PERFORM PICK-MIN VARYING I FROM 1 BY 1
            UNTIL I > N.
    MOVE UNSORTED-ENTRY (MIN-POS) TO
        SORTED-ENTRY (NEXT-IN-SORT).
    MOVE HIGH-VALUES TO UNSORTED-ENTRY (MIN-POS).
    MOVE HIGH-VALUES TO CURR-MIN-KEY.
```

and

```
PICK-MIN.
    IF UNSORTED-ENTRY (I) < CURR-MIN-KEY
        MOVE I TO MIN-POS
        MOVE UNSORTED-ENTRY (I) TO CURR-MIN-KEY.
```

For a list of n records, this algorithm requires n passes over the unsorted list. In the ith pass, $n - i$ comparisons of key values are made. The total number of comparisons then is:

$$\sum_{i=1}^{n} (n - i)$$

which is $n(n - 1)/2$. This sort is said to require $O(n^2)$ comparisons, because the n^2 term dominates the expression. The number of comparisons is proportional to the square of the number of keys in the collection. Doubling the number of keys means that the process will take four times as long.

AN EXCHANGE SELECTION SORT

The above program uses nearly twice as much space as necessary. A modification of the straight selection sort is the *exchange selection sort,* in which the selected key value is moved into its final position by being exchanged with the key initially occupying that position. Consider again the unsorted list.

14   3   22   9   10   14   2   7   25   6

After the first pass, 2 is selected,

2 | 3 22 9 10 14 14 7 25 6
sorted   unsorted

After the second pass,

2   3 | 22 9 10 14 14 7 25 6
sorted   unsorted

After the sixth pass,

2   3   6   7   9   10 | 14 14 25 22
sorted   unsorted

Note that this is not a stable sort. For example, here the first pass placed the first 14 after the second 14; in the seventh and eighth passes, the 14s will be appended to the sorted list in that reversed order.

In COBOL, the exchange selection sort is

```
01   KEY-TABLE.
     02   KEY-ENTRY        OCCURS N TIMES     PIC S99.
01   AUX-ITEMS.
     02   CURR-MIN-KEY     PIC S99      VALUE HIGH-VALUES.
     02   NEXT-IN-SORT     PIC 9(3)     VALUE 1.
     02   I                PIC 9(3).
     02   MIN-POS          PIC 9(3).
     02   TEMP-KEY         PIC S99.

EXCHANGE-DRIVER.
     PERFORM SELECT-NEXT VARYING NEXT-IN-SORT FROM
               1 BY 1 UNTIL NEXT-IN-SORT = N.
```

where

```
SELECT-NEXT.
     PERFORM PICK-MIN VARYING I FROM
               NEXT-IN-SORT BY 1 UNTIL
               I > N.
```

```
        MOVE KEY-ENTRY (NEXT-IN-SORT)
            TO TEMP-KEY.
        MOVE KEY-ENTRY (MIN-POS)
            TO KEY-ENTRY (NEXT-IN-SORT).
        MOVE TEMP-KEY
            TO KEY-ENTRY (MIN-POS).
        MOVE HIGH-VALUES
            TO CURR-MIN-KEY.
```

and

```
    PICK-MIN.
        IF KEY-ENTRY (I) < CURR-MIN-KEY
            MOVE I TO MIN-POS
            MOVE KEY-ENTRY (I) TO CURR-MIN-KEY.
```

The exchange selection sort has essentially the same comparison requirements as does the straight selection sort; it is $O(N^2)$. Later we will consider other members of the family of selection sorts that perform better than this.

AN INSERTION SORT

Another family of internal sorting algorithms is the group of *insertion sorts*. The basic idea of an insertion sort is to take the next key of the unsorted list and insert it in its proper relative position in a growing sorted list of data (Fig. 9–7).

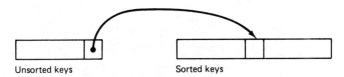

Unsorted keys   Sorted keys

Figure 9–7   Insertion sort.

The entire list of sorted keys must be available throughout the process in order to be able to insert a key in its proper relative position. The unsorted list, however, can be input as we go along.

Compare this sorting technique with the selection sort method of the preceding section. When you sort a hand of playing cards, if you pick each card up as it is dealt to you and place it in its appropriate "slot" relative to the cards you already have, then you are using an insertion sort. On the other hand, if you wait until the entire hand is dealt, then pick out the card that should be leftmost and put it there, then pick out the card that should be second and put it there, and so forth, then you are using a selection sort.

Both are relatively poor techniques, as each is O(N^2), but each is relatively easy to understand and to program. Both are widely used.

Consider again our example unsorted list of keys.

14   3   22   9   10   14   2   7   25   6

The first pass considers the first key, which is 14, and results in

3 22 9 10 14 2 7 25 6	14
unsorted list	sorted list

After the second pass,

22 9 10 14 2 7 25 9	3 14
unsorted list	sorted list

After the sixth pass,

2 7 25 6	3 9 10 14 14 22
unsorted list	sorted list

Like the exchange selection sort, the insertion sort can be programmed to sort in place. In Pascal—

```
procedure insertsort;
var key : array [1 . . n] of integer;
    tempkey : integer;
    i, j, jj : 1 . . n;
    foundpos : boolean;
begin
    for i := 2 to n
    do begin j := 1;
            foundpos := false;
            while (not foundpos) and j < i
            do if(key [i] < key [j])
                then foundpos := true
                else j := j + 1;
            if (foundpos)
            then begin tempkey := key [i];
                    jj := i - 1;
                    while (jj > j - 1)
                    do begin key [jj + 1] :=  key [jj];
                            jj := jj - 1
                        end;
                    key[j] := tempkey;
                end;
        end;
end.
```

This sort as programmed here is stable. Why? What change to the code would make it an unstable sort?

A variation on the straight insertion sort is based on using prior knowledge of the distribution of key values represented in the list. In an attempt to reduce the extent of data movement, keys are inserted in their relative sorted positions leaving some empty slots between keys to accommodate keys to be inserted in following passes.

Later we will consider other members of the family of insertion sorts that exhibit better than $O(N^2)$ behavior.

AN EXCHANGE SORT: THE BUBBLE SORT

A third family of internal sorting algorithms is the group of *exchange sorts*. The basic idea of an exchange sort is to compare pairs of key values and exchange them if they are not in the proper relative positions (Fig. 9–8).

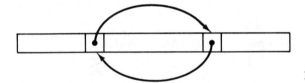

Figure 9–8   Exchange sort.

Very good sorting behavior can result from clever identification of the pairs to be compared. In this section, however, we first consider a not-so-clever exchange sort: the *bubble sort*. Like the selection and insertion sorts presented in this chapter, the bubble sort requires $O(N^2)$ comparisons. Nevertheless, the bubble sort is quite commonly used. We will investigate the better exchange sorts later.

The basic idea of the bubble sort is to allow each key to float to its proper position through a series of pairwise comparisons and exchanges with adjacent keys values. Each pass results in bubbling one key to its final position in the sorted list.

Consider again our example unsorted list of keys.

```
 6
25
 7
 2
14
10
 9
22
 3
14
```

Bubbles rise; so we arrange the list vertically with the first key at the bottom. Each key is compared with the key above it and exchanged if the above key is smaller. When a key larger than the subject key is found, the subject key becomes the top one of the pair, and the process continues. After the pass, all keys above the last one to be exchanged must be in their final positions. They need not be examined in later passes.

The activity of the first pass bubbles up 14, 22, and 25.

```
 6      25                                              25
25 °°°   6  _____        6
 7                              22                      22
 2                    22 °°°  7          resulting in    7
14          22 °°°  2                                     2
10     22 °°° 14                                         14
 9  22 °°° 10                                            10
22 °°°  9  _____                                        9
 3     14                                               14
14 °°°  3                                                3
```

We know 25 is in its final position.

The activity of the second pass bubbles up 14, 14, and 22.

```
                                                    ┌────┐
                                                    │ 25 │
 6      22                                           └────┘
22 °°°   6  _____                                     22
 7           14                                          6
 2    14 °°°  7          resulting in                   14
14 °°°  2  _____                                        7
10           14                                           2
 9    14 °°° 10                                          14
14 °°°  9                                               10
 3                                                       9
                                                         3
```

We know 22 is in its final position.

The activity of the third pass bubbles up 14 and 14.

```
                                                    ┌────┐
                                                    │ 25 │
                                                    │ 22 │
 6      14                                           └────┘
14 °°°   6  _____                                     14
 7           14                                          6
 2    14 °°°  7          resulting in                   14
14 °°°  2                                                7
10                                                       2
 9                                                      10
 3                                                       9
                                                         3
```

We know that 14 is in its final position.

The activity of the fourth pass bubbles up 10 and 14.

```
                                                              25
                                                              22
                                                              14
      6̸  ₀₀₀ 14                                                14
     14 ₀₀₀  6                                                 6
     ─────────────              resulting in                   10
      7̸         10                                             7
      2̸   10 ₀₀₀ 7                                             2
     10 ₀₀₀ 2                                                  9
      9                                                        3
      3
```

and so forth.

The bubble sort really has very little to recommend it except that it is well known (probably because of its name) and unfortunately often used (probably because it is relatively easy to implement). It behaves a bit like the exchange selection sort, in which the small keys sink to the bottom of the list.

THE PARTITION-EXCHANGE SORT (QUICKSORT)

Let's consider now a much better exchange sort: the *partition-exchange sort*, also known as *Hoare's quicksort*, or simply the *quicksort*. This method is attributed to C. A. R. Hoare (1962).

The basic idea behind the quicksort is to use the results of each comparison pass to guide the next comparison pass. During a comparison pass, keys are exchanged in such a manner that when the pass completes, the list has been partitioned so that key values in one partition (though unordered) are all less than a particular key value and key values in the other partition (though unordered) are all greater than that particular key value. The next comparison pass can then proceed with the two resultant partitions treated independently of each other. The comparison passes are localized successively to smaller and smaller partitions.

This sort technique is explained best perhaps by example. Consider again our example unsorted list of keys.

```
      6
     25
      7
      2
     14
     10
```

9
22
3
14

The first comparison pass has as its objectives

1. Identification of the final position of the first subject key (here 6) in the sorted list.
2. Partitioning of the list into two pieces, one of which contains only key values less than the first subject key, the other of which contains only key values greater than the first subject key.

To achieve these objectives, the subject key value first is compared with the last element (here 14) of the list, then the next-to-last element (here 3) until a key value is found that should precede rather than follow the subject key value; such a key then exchanges positions with the subject key value (Fig. 9–9(a)). The comparison then proceeds *with the same subject* key value from the other direction; 6 is here compared with 25. Because the two are not in proper relative position, an exchange occurs (Fig. 9–9(b)). Now the comparison switches direction again to bottom up. 6 is compared with 22, with 9, with 10, with 14, then with 2, which is on the "wrong" side of 6. An exchange occurs (Fig. 9–9(c)).

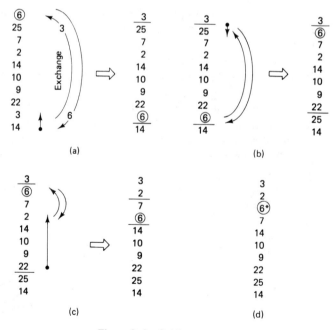

Figure 9–9   Quicksort passes.

Comparison again switches direction to top down. 6 is compared with 7, which is on the wrong side of 6. An exchange occurs, resulting in a completed pass (Fig. 9–9(d)). At this point 6 is in its final position; everything before 6 is less than 6; everything after 6 is greater than 6. The two resultant partitions can now be sorted independently. Let's consider the second partition.

```
   7
  14
  10
   9
  22
  25
  14
```

The comparison pass over this partition shows that 7 is already in proper position. The next partition to consider is

```
  14
  10
   9
  22
  25
  14
```

The pass proceeds with 14 the subject key (Fig. 9–10).

As the sizes of the sublist partitions shrink, a simpler sort algorithm, e.g., straight insertion or selection, can be applied to reduce overhead.

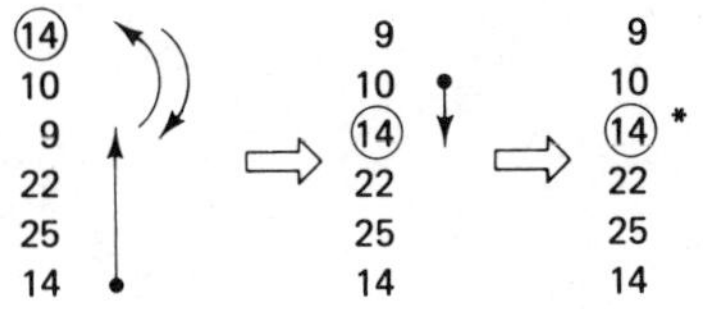

Figure 9–10 Final quicksort pass.

Performance

Analysis of the quicksort algorithm is rather straightforward. Consider first the average case. Assume that the proper final position for the first element K_i is in the middle of the unsorted list (Fig. 9–11).

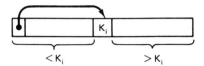

Figure 9–11 Quicksort pass.

The first pass results in partitioning of the list into two sublists, each of approximately $n/2$ keys. Define a "superpass" to be one processing of the entire list. The first superpass requires $n - 1$ compares.

The second superpass involves processing both sublists (Fig. 9–12).

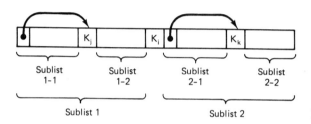

Figure 9–12 Second quicksort superpass.

Processing of sublist 1 requires approximately $\frac{1}{2}(n - 3)$ compares, as does processing of sublist 2. In fact, processing of each superpass requires $O(n)$ compares.

On the average, $\log_2 n$ superpasses are required to sort the list completely. Thus the quicksort requires an average of $O(n\log_2 n)$ comparisons. This is the best performance we have found so far in a sort technique; recall that the linear methods all required $O(n^2)$ comparisons.

In some cases, the quicksort requires more than $\log_2 n$ superpasses. In fact in the worst case, n superpasses are required. The worst case is when the initial list is already sorted. Rather than tending to reduce by half the number of comparisons needed at each superpass, sorting an initially sorted list results in a reduction of merely one comparison at each superpass. The worst case behavior of $O(n^2)$ is as bad as the linear sort algorithms' performances. However, it is possible to arrange that a quicksort never gets near its worst-case behavior. It is a very good sort.

THE HEAPSORT

The quicksort on the average improves performance over linear sort algorithms. In this section we consider another important nonlinear sort, the *heapsort*, which performs as well as the quicksort on the average *and* performs better than the quicksort in the worst cases. The heapsort has better all-around performance than any other internal sort that we present; however it is rather complex to program. (Nothing is free!) A properly engineered quicksort is sometimes faster than a well-engineered heapsort and is somewhat less complex to program. The heapsort was developed in 1964 by J. W. J. Williams.

The heapsort is based upon use of a special type of binary tree (called a *heap*) to structure the sorting process. The branching structure of the tree keeps the number of comparisons required at $O(n\log_2 n)$.

There are two phases to a heapsort:

1. Creation of the heap.
2. Processing of the heap.

In the first phase, the unsorted keys are placed into a binary tree in such a way that they form a heap.

Heap Structure

A heap of size n is a binary tree of n nodes that adheres to the following two constraints:

1. The binary tree is *almost complete*, i.e., there is an integer k such that:
   (a) every leaf of the tree is at level k or level $k + 1$, and
   (b) if a node has a right descendant at level $k + 1$, then that node also has a left descendant at level $k + 1$.
2. The keys in the nodes are arranged such that for each node i

   $$K_i \leq K_j$$

   where node j is the father of node i.

The first constraint means that levels of the heap are filled left to right and that a node is not placed on a new level until the preceding level is full. The binary trees of Fig. 9–13 all qualify as heaps. Note that these trees do not qualify as binary search trees, because in-order traversal does not sequence the nodes by ascending key values.

The binary trees of Fig. 9–14 are *not* heaps. The key-placement constraint is violated at nodes 2–13 and 56–72 in tree (a); the almost-complete constraint is violated on level 2 of tree (b); the key-placement constraint and the almost-complete constraint both are violated in tree (c).

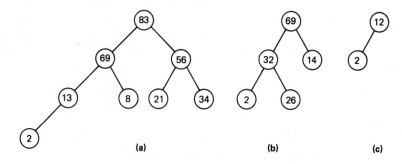

(a)   (b)   (c)

Figure 9–13 Example heaps.

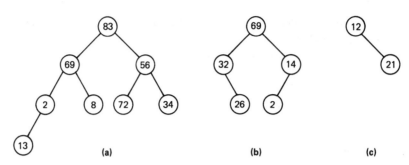

Figure 9-14   Binary trees that are not heaps.

Creating a Heap

Let us consider first the heap-creation phase of the heapsort. In this phase we pass sequentially through the unsorted keys, placing them into a heap. The size of the heap grows as each new key is added. To create a heap of size i, the ith key (K_i) is placed into an existing heap of size $i - 1$. The node first is positioned such that the almost-complete constraint is satisfied. Then the value of K_i is compared with the key value of the node's father. If K_i is greater, then the contents of that new node and the father node are interchanged. This comparison-interchange process is repeated until either the father's key value is not less than K_i or K_i is at the root of the tree. The tree will then qualify to be a heap of size i. More formally, in Pascal, to create a heap of size i by adding a key (here named newkey) to a heap (here globally known, named key and housed in an array) of size $i - 1$ (where $i \geqslant 1$):

```
procedure crheapi (i, newkey:integer);
var father, temp, next : integer;
begin next : = i;
        father : = next div 2;
        key[next] : = newkey;
        while (next <> 1 and key[father] < = key[next])
        do begin {interchange father and son}
                temp : = key[father];
                key[father] : = key[next];
                key[next] : = temp;
                {advance up tree}
                next : = father;
                father : = next div 2
        end;
end;
```

This procedure is called for each addition to the heap.

Fig. 9-15 illustrates the building of a heap to contain the following list of unsorted

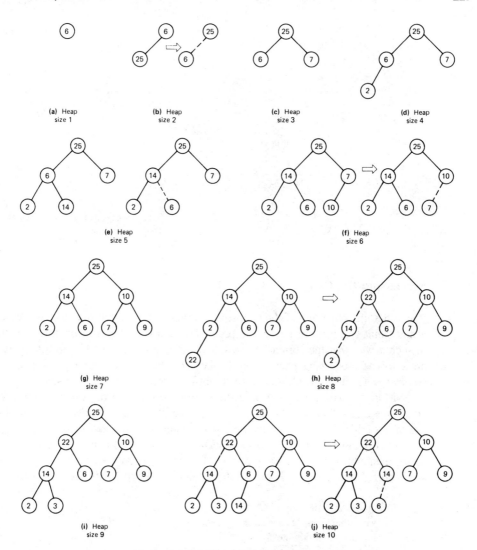

Figure 9–15 Steps in building an example heap.

keys: 6, 25, 7, 2, 14, 10, 9, 22, 3, 14. A dashed line in the figure indicates that the nodes on the ends of the edge have been interchanged.

This heap would be represented in an array as shown in Fig. 9–16. Note that node i is the father of nodes $2i$ and $2i + 1$. Thus, because the tree is a heap, key $(i) \leq$ key $(i/2)$, where use of integer division is assumed.

If the keys were initially in a different order in the unsorted list, then the resulting heap would be different. For example, the unsorted list 9, 14, 10, 22, 7, 25, 3, 14, 6, 2 results in the heap shown in Fig. 9–17.

Subscript	1	2	3	4	5	6	7	8	9	10
Key	25	22	10	14	14	7	9	2	3	6

Figure 9–16   Array representation of the heap in Fig. 9–15(j).

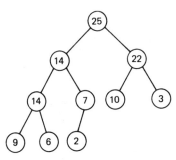

Figure 9–17   Another heap for the same set of keys as Fig. 9–15, presented in a different order.

Processing the Heap

Recall that the objective of the heapsort is to generate a sorted list of keys. All we have at this point is a heap of keys. The processing phase of the heapsort traverses the heap in such a way that the sorted keys result. Note that the largest key in a heap is always on top. The processing phase is built upon this fact. After creating the heap, the top element is again removed, and so forth until the resulting heap is of size 0.

More formally, a Pascal procedure to process a heap of size n follows. We take advantage of the fact that the heap is still housed in an array called key (resulting from use of our crheapi procedure); the largest key value is at the top of the heap: key[1]. We successively move that value to the end of the array (key[n] the first time through the loop), then adjust the array to be a heap of size $n - 1$. At the end, the keys in the array are in sorted order; key[1] is the smallest value and key[n] is the largest value.

```
procedure prheapn;
var father, son, last, waslastkey : integer;
for last := n downto 2
do begin {move root key down to last place}
          waslastkey := key[last];
          key[last] := key[1];
          {adjust tree to heap of size last − 1}
          father := 1;
          {find larger of root's sons}
          if(last − 1 >= 3) and (key[3] > key[2])
          then son := 3
          else son := 2;
          {move keys upward until find place}
          {for saved waslastkey}
          while (son <= last − 1 and key[son] > waslastkey)
```

```
do begin key[father] : = key[son];
         father : = son;
         son : = father * 2;
         {find larger of father's sons}
         if(son + 1 <= last − 1) and (key[son + 1] > key[son])
         then son : = son + 1
    end;
    key[father] : = waslastkey
end;
```

Fig. 9–18 illustrates processing of the heap built in Fig. 9–15. The doubly circled nodes are nodes that have been moved to their final positions in the array and are no longer part of the heap. A dashed line indicates that the nodes at the ends of the edge have been interchanged while adjusting the tree to be a heap again. After the *n*-1st (here 9th) pass, the keys can be read sequentially (1 to *n*) from the array housing the heap and will be in properly sorted order.

As with the quicksort algorithm, analysis of the heapsort algorithm is rather straightforward. During the heap-creation phase, insertion of the ith key requires $O(\log_2 i)$ comparisons and interchanges even in the worst case, where the keys arrive in already sorted

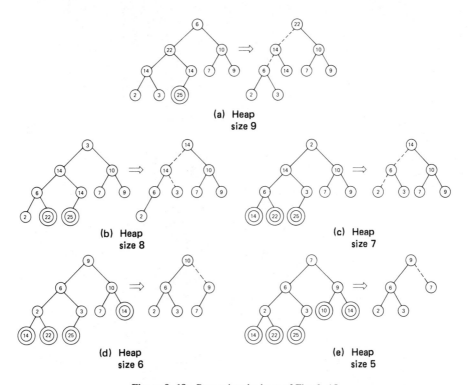

(a) Heap
size 9

(b) Heap
size 8

(c) Heap
size 7

(d) Heap
size 6

(e) Heap
size 5

Figure 9–18   Processing the heap of Fig. 9–15.

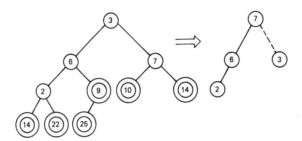

(f) Heap
size 4

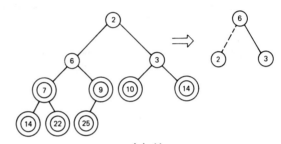

(g) Heap
size 3

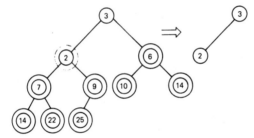

(h) Heap
size 2

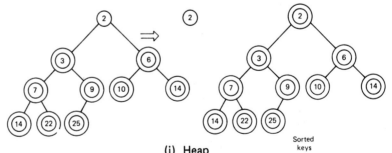

(i) Heap
size 1

Figure 9–18   *(Cont.)*

order. Insertion of a key on the kth level can force comparison and interchange with a maximum of k other keys along the branch to the root of the heap. Similarly, during the heap-processing phase, treatment of a heap of size i requires $O(\log_2 i)$ comparisons and interchanges even in the worst case. Movement can be made only along one of the heap's branches.

Thus on the average, the required number of comparisons and interchanges is

$$\frac{1}{2} \sum_{i=2}^{n} \log_2 i \quad + \quad \frac{1}{2} \sum_{i=2}^{n} \log_2 i$$

which is $(n - 1)\log_2 n$. In the worst case, the required number of comparisons and interchanges is

$$\sum_{i=2}^{n} \log_2 i \quad + \quad \sum_{i=2}^{n} \log_2 i$$

which is $2(n - 1)\log_2 n$. The worst case is not much worse than the average case. The heapsort therefore is *guaranteed* to be $O(n\log_2 n)$. For large n, the complexity of the algorithm is outweighed by the sort's efficiency.

THE TOURNAMENT SORT

Another important tree-based sort is the *tournament sort*. This sort is sometimes called the *tree-selection sort* and is attributed to E. H. Friend (1956). The tournament sort process looks like the knock-out or elimination tournament trees typically used to organize sporting (especially tennis, ping-pong, squash) matches. Pair-wise competitions among players proceed until a final winner is established.

The tournament sort is used perhaps more frequently than any other internal sort. Many software vendors incorporate it in their file-sorting packages. We will discuss the workings of the tournament sort here, then consider its incorporation in file sorts in Chapter 12.

Consider again the unsorted list of keys that we have been using in examples: 6, 25, 7, 2, 14, 10, 9, 22, 3, 14, augmented by 8, 12, 1, 30, 13. For expository purposes, assume that space constraints limit us to having only four of these keys in memory at once. The tournament sort pairs these four into two matches.

Assuming that we are performing an ascending sort, the winners of those matches are 6 and 2, which can then be paired for the finals.

```
  6⌐6
25⌐
     ⌐
  7⌐2
  2⌐
```

2 wins and is the first key output from the sort.

```
  6⌐6
25⌐
       2  ==>2
  7⌐2
  2⌐
```

The next pass of the tournament sort will identify the second key of the sorted list. 2 cannot participate in this second pass. We could just play with 7, who would win the first match by default, then would play against 6.

```
  6⌐6
25⌐
       6  ==> 2, 6
  7⌐7
  *⌐
```

This would result in a pure tree-selection sort. Instead, however, let us bring another candidate into the tournament from our remaining unsorted list: 14, 10, 9, 22, 3, 14. Then we can play the second pass of the tournament.

```
  6⌐6
25⌐
       6  ==> 2, 6
  7⌐7
 14⌐
```

This replacement policy will enable the sort to generate longer sorted strings than if we did not bring in new players. Our sort now more properly is named a *tree replacement-selection sort*.

The third pass then is

```
 10⌐10
 24⌐
        7  ==> 2, 6, 7
  7⌐7
 14⌐
```

The fourth pass is

<pre>
10┐
25┘10
        9 ==> 2, 6, 7, 9
 9┐
14┘9
</pre>

and the fifth pass is

<pre>
10┐
25┘10
        10 ==> 2, 6, 7, 9, 10
22┐
14┘14
</pre>

The sixth pass bring 3 into the tree.

<pre>
 3┐
25┘
22┐
14┘14
</pre>

If 3 is allowed to play, the sorted sequence of the output list will be broken. To prevent this, the tree replacement-selection sort invokes the following rule:

$$\text{If } Key_{new} < Key_{lastout}$$
then Key_{new} is placed into the tree but is temporarily disqualified.

We mark disqualified entrants by asterisks. Thus the sixth pass results in

<pre>
*3┐
25┘25
        14 ==> 2, 6, 7, 9, 10, 14
22┐
14┘14
</pre>

The next key of the unsorted list (14) is brought in, and can play since it is not less than 14.

<pre>
*3┐
25┘25
        14 ==> 2, 6, 7, 9, 10, 14, 14
22┐
14┘14
</pre>

Pass 8 brings in key value 8, which must be disqualified because it is less than 14, but the other entrants can play.

```
*3┐
25┘ 25
        22  ══> 2, 6, 7, 9, 10, 14, 14, 22
22┐
*8┘ 22
```

Pass 9 results in

```
*3┐
25┘ 25
        25  ══> 2, 6, 7, 9, 10, 14, 14, 22, 25
*12┐
*8 ┘ *
```

Pass 10 bring in 1.

```
*3┐
*1┘
*12┐
*8 ┘
```

Now all entries are disqualified. Note that even though we allowed only four players into the tournament at any given time, the resultant sorted string contains nine keys! We now remove the disqualifications and start again. This time we will generate a *second* sorted string. Pass 10, then, is

```
3┐
1┘ 1
       1  ══> 1        2, 6, 7, 9, 10, 14, 14, 22, 25;
12┐
8 ┘ 8
```

Pass 11 brings in 30.

```
3 ┐
30┘ 3
       3  ══> 1, 3     2, 6, 7, 9, 10, 14, 14, 22, 25;
12┐
8 ┘ 8
```

Pass 12 is

$$
\begin{array}{l}
13 \\
30
\end{array}\Big]13 \\
\qquad\qquad 8 \implies \begin{array}{l} 2, 6, 7, 9, 10, 14, 14, 22, 25; \\ 1, 3, 8 \end{array}\\
\begin{array}{l}
12 \\
8
\end{array}\Big]8
$$

Now the input list is empty, so we must enter placeholders into the tree and allow the tournament to be played to completion. Pass 13 results in

$$
\begin{array}{l}
13 \\
30
\end{array}\Big]13 \\
\qquad\qquad 12 \implies \begin{array}{l} 2, 6, 7, 9, 10, 14, 14, 22, 25; \\ 1, 3, 8, 12 \end{array}\\
\begin{array}{l}
12 \\
*
\end{array}\Big]12
$$

Passes 14 and 15 empty the tree.

This example has resulted in two sorted lists:

   2, 6, 7, 9, 10, 14, 14, 22, 25;

   1, 3, 8, 12, 13, 30

These two strings can now be merged to form a single sorted output string. The first elements of each string are compared and the one with the lower value is output and removed from further consideration. This simple *two-way merge* is shown in the flowchart of Fig. 9–19. It can be programmed in Pascal as follows. Arrays key1 and key2 hold the initally sorted lists; array merged holds the resultant merged list. n1 and n2 are subscripts of the next element to be considered in key1 and key2 respectively. Size1 and size2 are the number of elements in key1 and key2 respectively. Next is the subscript showing the place for the next element in the merged list.

```
begin
    next := 1;
    n1 := 1;
    n2 := 1;
    while (n1 <= size1) and (n2 <= size2)
    do begin if (key1[n1] <= key2[n2])
            then begin merged[next] := key1[n1];
                        n1 := n1 + 1
                 end;
            else begin merged[next] := key2[n2];
                        n2 := n2 + 1
                 end;
            next := next + 1
    end;
```

```
            while (n1 <= size1) {fill with remaining list 1}
            do begin merged[next] := key1[n1];
                       n1 := n1 + 1;
                       next := next + 1
            end;
            while (n2 <= size2) {fill with remaining list 2}
            do begin merged[next] := key2[n2];
                       n2 := n2 + 1;
                       next := next + 1
            end;
    end;
```

The example was arranged such that two sorted lists conveniently resulted. In reality, many sorted lists may result. These can be merged by a sequence of two-way merges or by higher order merges, say three or four lists at a time.

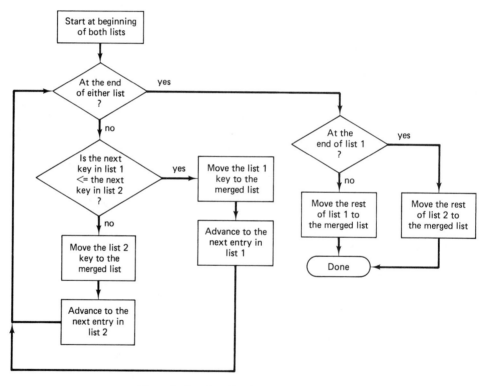

Figure 9-19   Algorithm for a two-way merge.

Performance

How well does the tournament sort perform? Consider first the case in which the tournament tree is spacious enough to hold all n keys to be sorted. To identify the first winner,

$$\frac{n}{2} + \frac{n}{4} + \ldots + \frac{n}{2^k} = n\sum_{i=1}^{k} \frac{1}{2^i}$$

comparisons must be made, where k is the number of levels in the tournament tree, $k = \log_2 n$. This expression is $O(n)$. After this initial setup of the tree, k comparisons are required to adjust the tree and identify the next winner. Thus the number of comparisons required to process the entire tree is $O(n\log_2 n)$. Note that only one string results when the entire field of players fits into the tournament tree.

Consider now the case in which the tournament tree can hold only p keys at any given time, $p << n$. Each pass through the tree now requires $\log_2 p$ comparisons to identify the next winner. Thus $n\log_2 p$ comparisons are required to generate the ordered sublists.

These sublists then must be merged. It can be shown that the expected length of each of the sorted lists resulting from the tournament sort with replacement of entries is $2*p$. (The interested reader should see Knuth's snowplow explanation of this fact in *The Art of Computer Programming, Vol. 3, Sorting and Searching*, from Addison-Wesley, 1973.) The n keys are thus allocated to $n/2p$ lists. Use of a two-way merge requires $\log_2 (n/2p)$ passes. For example, if $n = 256$ and $p = 8$, then the expected number of sublists is 16. Merging 16 lists, 2 at a time, requires $\log_2 16$, i.e., 4, passes (Fig. 9–20). Each pass requires n compares. Thus

$$n \log_2 (n/2p)$$

compares are required in the merge phase. Overall, then, on the average, the required number of comparisons is

$$n \log_2 p + n \log_2 (n/2p)$$

which is $O(n \log_2 n)$ for $n >> p$. We will return to use of the tournament sort for very large n and relatively small p in the later chapter on file-sorting techniques.

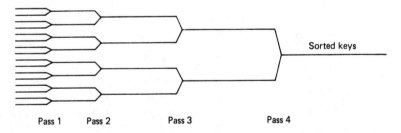

Pass 1   Pass 2   Pass 3   Pass 4

Figure 9–20   Example passes for a merge of 16 sublists.

SUMMARY

This chapter started with a discussion of linear search techniques. We showed that a basic sequential search can be improved by ordering the keys in the list of decreasing frequency of access. A linear list may reorganize itself dynamically by (1) moving a key to the front of the list when it is requested, or by (2) exchanging a key with its front neighbor when it is requested, thus gradually moving it toward the front. The number of comparisons required for unsuccessful searches can be reduced by having the list sorted by key value. All sequential searches are $O(n)$.

The *binary search* technique then was discussed as a method of obtaining $O(\log_2 n)$ search performance from a linear list. The prerequisite for applying the binary search technique is that the records in the list must be in sorted order by the search key value. The search proceeds by successive probes into the list; each probe eliminates one-half the remaining entries from further consideration. The binary search technique was presented in both recursive and iterative versions.

The rest of the chapter focused on techniques for sorting lists of records. The sorts are commonly done to prepare lists for later searches.

First, several basic internal sort methods were introduced. All required a number of comparisons approximately proportional to the square of the number of keys in the list; that is, all required $O(n^2)$ comparisons. The straight selection sort repeatedly selected the smallest key remaining in the unsorted list as the next key in the sorted list. The exchange selection sort sorted the list in place. The straight insertion sort took the next key of the unsorted list and inserted it in its proper relative position in a growing sorted list. The bubble sort (an exchange sort) repeatedly compared neighboring pairs of key values and exchanged them if they were not in proper relative order.

The *partition-exchange sort*, also known as *Hoare's quicksort*, was then presented as a method of obtaining good performance in a sort. During each comparison pass of the quicksort, keys are exchanged in such a way that when the pass completes, the list has been partitioned and the two sublists thereafter can be treated independently of each other. The quicksort requires an average of $O(n \log_2 n)$ comparisons, but in the worst case requires $O(n^2)$ comparisons.

The *heapsort* improves performance over the quicksort; it guarantees $O(n \log_2 n)$ comparisons, even in the worst case. The heapsort has two phases. In the first phase, the subject keys are structured into a heap, which is a special case of binary tree. In the second phase, the heap is processed and linearized in such a way that a sorted list of keys results.

The *tournament sort* (also known as *tree-selection sort*), and a variation, the *tree replacement-selection sort*, were presented as important techniques for sorting large collections of data. Keys are entered into a tournament tree and are compared in a pairwise manner to generate a sorted string. If the tree is not large enough to contain the entire collection of keys, then the sort generates several sorted strings. The strings then must be merged to produce the final sorted list. With replacement-selection, the sort of p keys generates an expected sorted-string length of $2*p$. This property makes the tournament sort a popular selection for the internal phase of external file sorts. The tournament sort, like the other tree-oriented sorts, requires $O(n \log_2 n)$ comparisons on the average.

Searching and sorting are exceedingly important data processing activities. The techniques used can be major factors in determining the performance of an information system.

TERMS

binary search
bubble sort
exchange selection sort
exchange sort
external sort
heap
insertion sort
internal sort
key
linear search
$O(n)$
$O(n^2)$

$O(n\log_2 n)$
partition-exchange sort
quicksort
search argument
searching
selection sort
sequential search
sorting
stable sort
tournament sort
tree-selection sort

SELECTED REFERENCES

ALANKO, T. O., H. H. A. ERKIO, and I. J. HAIKALA. "Virtual memory behavior of some sorting algorithms," *IEEE Trans. on Software Engineering*, SE-10(4):422–431, July 1984.

BITTON, D., D. J. DEWITT, D. K. HSAIO, and J. MENON. "A taxonomy of parallel sorting," *ACM Computing Surveys*, 16(3):297–318, Sept. 1984.

BLASGEN, M. W., R. G. CASEY, and K. P. ESWAREN. "An encoding method for multifield sorting and indexing," *Comm. ACM*, 20(11):874–878, Nov. 1977.

CASEY, R. G. "Design of tree structures for efficient querying," *Comm. ACM*, 16(9):549–560, Sept. 1973.

COOK, C. R. and D. J. KIM. "Best sorting algorithm for nearly sorted lists," *Comm. ACM*, 23(11):620–624, Nov. 1980.

GILL, A. "Hierarchical binary search," *Comm. ACM*, 23(5): 294–300, May 1980.

HERSTER, J. H. and D. S. HIRSCHBERG. "Self-organizing linear search," *ACM Computing Surveys*, 17(3):295–311, Sept. 1985.

HIRSCHBERG, D. S. "Fast parallel sorting algorithms," *Comm. ACM*, 21(8):657–661, Aug. 1978.

HORVATH, E. C. "Stable sorting in asymptotically optimal time and extra space," *Jour. ACM*, 25(2):177–199, April 1978.

KNUTH, D. E. *The Art of Computer Programming, Vol. 3, Sorting and Searching.* Reading, MA: Addison-Wesley Publishing Co., 1973.

LOESER, R. "Some performance tests of 'quicksort' and descendants," *Comm. ACM*, 17(3):143–152, March 1974.

LORIN, H. *Sorting and Sort Systems.* Reading, MA: Addison-Wesley Publishing Co., 1975.

MANACHER, G. K. "The Ford-Johnson sorting algorithm is not optimal," *Jour. ACM*, 26(3):441–456, July 1979.

PERL Y., A. ITAI, and H. AVNI. "Interpolation search: a log log n search," *Comm. ACM*, 21(7):550–553, July 1978.

SCHNEIDERMAN, B. "Jump searching: a fast sequential search technique," *Comm. ACM*, 21(10):831–834, Oct. 1978.

SEDGEWICK, R. "Implementing quicksort programs," *Comm. ACM*, 21(10):847–857, Oct. 1978.

SHIH, Z-C., G-H. CHEN, and R. C. T. LEE. "Systolic algorithms to examine all pairs of elements," *Comm. ACM*, 30(2):161–167, Feb. 1987.

STASKO, J. T. and J. S. VITTER. "Pairing heaps: experiments and analysis," *Comm. ACM*, 30(3):234–249, March 1987.

TENENBAUM, A. "Simulations of dynamic sequential search algorithms," *Comm. ACM*, 21(9):790–791, Sept. 1978.

THOMPSON, C. D. and H. T. KUNG. "Sorting on a mesh-connected parallel computer," *Comm. ACM*, 20(4):263–271, April 1977.

YAO, A. C-C. "Should tables be sorted?" *Jour. ACM*, 28(3):615–628, July 1981.

REVIEW EXERCISES

1. Show by example the distinction between a stable sort and an unstable sort.
2. Consider the following probabilities of being search arguments.

key(i)	prob(i)
8	.05
2	.26
10	.21
4	.15
12	.32

(a) What is the probability of an unsuccessful search?
(b) If the keys are ordered as shown above, what is the expected number of comparisons for a sequential search?
(c) Rearrange the keys to minimize the expected number of comparisons for a sequential search.
(d) What is the expected number of comparisons for a sequential search for your answer to (c)?

3. Describe two techniques for dynamically rearranging a linear list to improve expected search times.
4. Compare use of the "move-to-the-front" method on a linear list housed in an array and housed in a linked list.
5. Compare use of the "transposition" method on a linear list housed in an array and housed in a linked list.
6. Why is it desirable to have a sort perform "in place"?
7. Using playing cards or other cards bearing key values, demonstrate the difference between an insertion sort, a selection sort, and an exchange sort.

8. Write a program to implement the bubble sort.

9. Write an algorithm to search sequentially for all the records with a particular key value in a linked list.

10. The text discussed the binary search technique for application to sorted linear lists. Develop and analyze a ternary search technique.

11. The text algorithms for the binary search assumed that the linear list was housed in an array with subscript range from 1 to n. Modify the algorithms to cope with subscript range a to b, where a and b need not be positive integers.

12. The text algorithms for the binary search assumed that the linear list was housed in an array. What are the relative advantages and disadvantages of applying the binary search technique to a linear list housed in a linked list?

13. Explain the procedural improvements that distinguish sorts that require $O(n\log_2 n)$ operations from those that require $O(n^2)$ operations.

14. Graph n^2 and $n\log_2 n$ (or n and $\log_2 n$) versus n and convince yourself of the extent of improvement achieved in nonlinear sorting.

15. Rewrite the algorithms given in this chapter for descending rather than ascending sorts.

16. Write a program to perform a tree-selection sort.

17. Write a program to perform a tree replacement-selection sort.

18. Write a program to perform the quicksort. Run it with a variety of sets of input data and compare the expected and worst-case performance.

19. Write a program to perform the heapsort. Run it with the same sets of input data used in exercise 18 and compare the expected and worst-case performance.

20. Develop a sort algorithm that guarantees $O(n\log_3 n)$ performance. Characterize a sort algorithm that would guarantee $O(n\log_k n)$ performance.

21. Are there any sort algorithms that produce $O(\log_2 n^2)$ performance?

22. Develop guidelines for the effects of various relative values of n and p on tree replacement-selection sort performance. How should p be selected? What happens if $p = n$? What happens if p is nearly n? What happens if $p = 1$?

23. Consider a bidirectional linked list of data elements which has been implemented using pointer variables. When would you use a sequential search technique to find a particular element?

24. Analyze each of the sort algorithms presented in this chapter for stability. If a sort algorithm is not stable, how can it be modified to make it stable?

25. Explain how you would select the kind of sorting to use on a particular set of records. What factors need to be considered?

26. Explain how you would select the kind of searching to use on a particular set of records. What factors need to be considered?

27. Read Knuth's excellent work on sorting and searching.

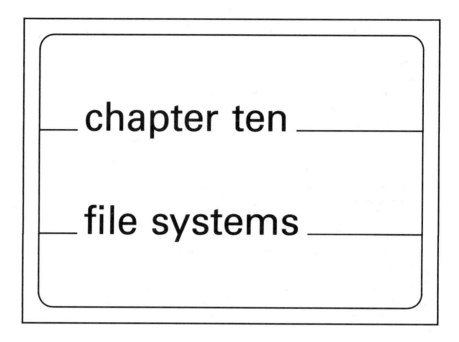

chapter ten

file systems

In the first part of this book we assumed that the entire data structure resided in main memory; generally the data structures were housed in arrays or used main-memory pointers. When evaluating the performance of a program that accessed a data structure, we assumed that there was essentially equal time required to access any element of the structure given its address or a pointer to it. In general, however, not all of the data to be processed by a program can reside simultaneously in that program's main memory space. Instead, large collections of data commonly are stored on auxiliary memory devices. The various techniques that have been developed for structuring these collections of data are the topic of the rest of this book.

This chapter should give you an understanding of what files are, of their roles in information systems, and of the basic problems in their organization and management. It then introduces file systems and their basic responsibilities for directory management, buffer management, and input/output (I/O) control. The chapter closes by introducing the role of file systems in database environments.

FILES

A *file* is a collection of logically related records. Recall from Chapter 3 that a record is a structure of logically related fields, or elements, of information. Usually all of the record occurrences on a file are of a single format, although we will study some examples of files with multiple record formats. Generally the records on a file are stored together for some common purpose; for example, they support payroll processing or employee benefit record-keeping, or they contain inventory information or data gathered in a scientific experiment or a model developed using a Computer-Aided Design (CAD) system.

There are at least three good reasons for structuring a collection of data as a file. The primary reason is to store data independently of the execution of a particular program. When a program run-unit ends, its working memory space is reallocated to another run-unit; any data in the temporary memory of the first program are gone. By contrast, a file provides for permanent data storage. The second reason for a file is to store a data collection that is too large to fit in the program's working memory. Thirdly, data may be stored as a file because only a small portion of the collection is accessed by a program at any given time, making it unreasonable to store the entire collection in main memory simultaneously. Tape and disk files can be shelved in archives and later made accessible to the appropriate programs and users on demand.

Classifying Files by Function

There are six basic kinds of files, classified by the functions they perform in an information system:

1. Master file
2. Transaction file
3. Report file
4. Work file
5. Program file
6. Text file

A file only rarely has more than one of these functions. A *master file* represents a static view of some aspect of an organization's business at a point in time. For example, a manufacturing organization might have a payroll master file, a customer master file, a personnel master file, an inventory master file, a material requirements master file, and others. A record on a master file keeps track of the status of something, for example, an employee, a customer, a product, an account. Depending upon how recently the contents of a master file were brought up to date and how much the pertinent status has changed since that time, the master file is a more or less accurate snapshot of some aspect of the "real world." A master file contains relatively permanent data or historical status data. A special kind of master file is a dictionary file, which contains descriptions of data rather than the data themselves.

Changes that are going to be applied to a master file are collected on a *transaction file*. As we discuss later in this chapter, a *transaction* may contain data to add a new record or to remove or modify an existing record on a master file. Each record on a transaction file represents an event or change in something whose status is tracked on a master file.

A *report file* contains data that are formatted for presentation to a user. The file may be spooled to a printer to produce a hard-copy report or may be displayed on a terminal screen. A report file may be produced by a report-writer package or by an application program.

A *work file* is a temporary file in a system. It has neither the long-term character of a master file nor the input or output character of a transaction or report file. One common use of a work file is to pass data created by one program to another.

A *program file* contains instructions for the processing of data which may be stored in other files or resident in main memory. The instructions may be written in a high-level language (e.g., COBOL, Pascal), an assembler language, machine language, or a job

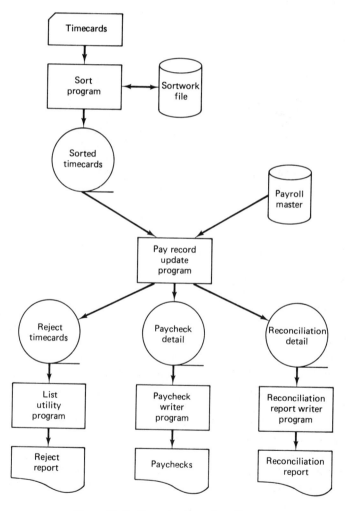

Figure 10–1 Example system flow diagram.

control language. The instructions may be in the form of source code or may be the result of compilation, linking, interpretation, or other processing.

A *text file* contains alphanumeric and graphic data input using a text editor program. A text file may be processible only by that text editor, or may be stored in such a way that it can be processed by several editors.

Consider the example system flow diagram given in Fig. 10–1. This system is a rudimentary payroll system that eventually produces paychecks from employee timecard and payroll information. The following table lists the name of each file and its function in the information system. The actual execution of this system generally would involve the use of other files, containing for example, system audit data, diagnostics, user accounting data, executable program code, and job control instructions.

FILE	FUNCTION
timecards	transaction
sort program	program
sort-work file	work
sorted-timecards	transaction
payroll master	master
pay record update program	program
reject timecards	work
paycheck detail	work
reconciliation detail	work
list utility program	program
reject report	report
paycheck writer program	program
paychecks	report
reconciliation report writer program	program
reconciliation report	report

Modes of Accessing Files

Another approach to classifying the use of a file in an information system is by the way that a particular program accesses the file. There are three possible modes of access to a file by a program:

1. Input
2. Output
3. Input/output

An *input* file is only read by the program. For example, a file of tax rates and tables would be an input file for the program that computes income taxes. A transaction file is generally an input file to an update program. A program file of source code is an input file to a compiler program.

An *output* file is only written to by a program; it is created by the program. For example, a report file may be the output of a program that updates a master file. A program file of object code is an output file from a compiler program.

An *input/output* file is both read from and written to during a program's execution. For example, the payroll master file might be used by the payroll program both as a source of data about employee pay rates and as a repository of month-to-date and year-to-date pay totals. An input/output file could be created by one phase of a program, then either modified or read by another phase of the same program. A master file commonly is an input/output file, as are the work files of sort programs. The chapter on file sorting techniques will illustrate the extensive use of the temporary input/output files that are used as work files by sort programs.

The following table indicates the mode of access for the files in the system shown in Fig. 10–1.

program file	input file	output file	input/output file
1. sort	timecards	sorted timecards	sort-work file
2. pay record update	sorted timecards	reject timecards paycheck detail reconciliation detail	payroll master
3. paycheck writer	paycheck detail	paychecks	
4. reconciliation report writer	reconciliation detail	reconciliation report	
5. list utility	reject timecards	reject report	

Note that a file may have more than one function if it is used by more than one program. A common example of this is the output of a file by one program that is input to another.

FILE ORGANIZATIONS

The technique used to represent and store the records on a file is called the *file organization*. The four fundamental file organization techniques that we will discuss are the following:

1. Sequential
2. Relative
3. Indexed sequential
4. Multi-key

Precise definitions of each of these techniques will be presented in later chapters.

There are two basic ways that the file organization techniques differ. First, the organization determines the file's *record sequencing*, which is the physical ordering of the records in storage.

Second, the file organization determines the set of operations necessary to find particular records. Individual records are typically identified by having particular values in search-key fields. This data field may or may not have duplicate values in the file; the field can be a group or elementary item. Some file organization techniques provide rapid accessibility on a variety of search keys; other techniques support direct access only on the value of a single one.

The organization most appropriate for a particular file is determined by the operational characteristics of the storage medium used and the nature of the operations to be performed on the data. The most important characteristic of a storage device that influences selection of a file organization technique (or, to turn the argument around, that influences selection of a storage device once the appropriate file organization technique has been determined) is whether the device allows *direct access* to particular record occurrences without accessing all physically prior record occurrences that are stored on the device, or allows only *sequential access* to record occurrences. Magnetic disks are examples of direct access storage devices (abbreviated DASD's); magnetic tapes are examples of sequential storage devices.

FILE OPERATIONS

The way that a file is going to be used is an important factor in determining how the file should be organized. Two major aspects of a file's use are its mode of use and the nature of the operations on the file.

A file can be accessed by a program that executes in *batch* mode or by a program that executes *interactively*. With batch mode access, transactions generally can be sorted to improve master file access, whereas with interactive access the transactions are processed as they arrive. With batch mode access, performance is typically measured by *throughput*, which is the number of transactions processed in a time period. With interactive access, performance is also measured by *response times* to individual transactions. Some file organizations are better suited to support interactive access than are others.

The fundamental operations that are performed on files are the following:

1. Creation
2. Update, including:
   record insertion
   record modification
   record deletion
3. Retrieval, including:
   inquiry
   report generation

4. Maintenance, including:
   restructuring
   reorganization

Creating a File

The initial *creation* of a file also is referred to as the *loading* of the file. The bulk of the work in creating transaction and master files involves data collection and validation. In some implementations, space is first allocated to the file, then the data are loaded into that skeleton. In other implementations, the file is constructed a record at a time. We will see examples of both approaches. In many cases, data are loaded into a transaction or master file in batch mode, even if the file actually is built one record at a time. Loading a master file interactively can be excessively time-consuming and labor-intensive if large volumes of data are involved.

The contents of a master file represent a snapshot in time of the part of the real world that the master file represents. For example, the payroll master file represents the present state of the company's payroll situation: month-to-date and year-to-date fields indicate appropriately accumulated figures for amounts paid, vacation taken, vacation due, etc., for each employee.

Updating a File

Changing the contents of a master file to make it reflect a more current snapshot of the real world is known as *updating* the file. These changes may include (1) the insertion of new record occurrences, e.g., adding a record for a newly hired employee, (2) the modification of existing record occurrences, e.g., changing the pay rate for an employee who has received a raise, and (3) the deletion of existing record occurrences, e.g., removing the record of an employee who has left the company. The updated file then represents a more current picture of reality.

In some implementations, the records of a file can be modified in place, new records can be inserted in available free space, and records can be deleted to make space available for reuse. If a file is updated in place by a program, then the file usually is an input/output file for that program.

Some implementations are more restrictive and a file cannot be updated in place. In these cases the old file is input to an update program and a new version of the file is output. The file is essentially recreated with current information. However, not all of the records need to have been modified; some (maybe even most) of the records may have been copied directly from the old version to the updated version of the file. We will consider this situation further in the chapter on sequential file organization.

Retrieving from a File

The access of a file for purposes of extracting meaningful information is called *retrieval*. There are two basic classes of file retrieval: inquiry and report generation. These two classes can be distinguished by the volume of data that they produce. An inquiry results in a relatively low-volume response, whereas a report may create many pages of output. However, some installations prefer to distinguish between inquiry and report generation by their modes of processing. If a retrieval is processed interactively, these installations would call the retrieval an inquiry or query. If a retrieval is processed in batch mode, the retrieval would be called report generation. This terminology tends to make report generation more of a planned, scheduled process and inquiry more of an *ad hoc*, spontaneous process. Both kinds of retrieval are required by most information systems.

An inquiry generally is formulated in a *query language*, which ideally is a natural-language-like structure that is easy for a "non-computer-expert" to learn and to use. A *query processor* is a program that translates the user's inquiries into instructions that are used directly for file access. Most installations that have query processors have acquired them from vendors rather than designing and implementing them inhouse.

A file retrieval request can be comprehensive or selective. *Comprehensive* retrieval reports information from all the records on a file, whereas *selective* retrieval applies some qualification criteria to choose which records will supply information for output. Examples of selective retrieval requests formulated in a typical but fictitious query language are the following:

- FIND EMP-NAME OF EMP-PAY-RECORD WHERE
  EMP-NO = 12751
- FIND ALL EMP-NAME, EMP-NO OF EMP-PAY-RECORD
  WHERE EMP-DEPT-NAME = "MIS"
- FIND ALL EMP-NAME, EMP-NO OF EMP-PAY-RECORD
  WHERE 20,000 < EMP-SAL < 40,000
- FIND ALL EMP-NAME, EMP-AGE, EMP-PHONE OF
  EMP-PAY-RECORD WHERE EMP-AGE < 40 AND
  EMP-SEX = "M" AND EMP-SAL > 50,000
- COUNT EMP-PAY-RECORDS WHERE EMP-AGE < 40
- FIND AVERAGE EMP-SAL OF EMP-PAY-RECORD
  WHERE DEPT-NAME = "MIS"

In each case the WHERE clause gives the qualification criteria. Note that the last two queries apply aggregate functions COUNT and AVERAGE to the qualifying set of records. Some file organizations are better suited to selective retrievals and others are more suited to comprehensive retrievals. We will study examples of both types.

Maintaining a File

Changes that are made to files to improve the performance of the programs that access them are known as *maintenance* activities. There are two basic classes of maintenance operations: restructuring and reorganization. *Restructuring* a file implies that structural changes are made to the file within the context of the same file organization technique. For example, field widths could be changed, new fields could be added to records, more space might be allocated to the file, the index tree of the file might be balanced, or the records of the file might be resequenced, but the file organization method would remain the same. File *reorganization* implies a change from one file organization to another.

The various file organizations differ in their maintenance requirements. These maintenance requirements are also very dependent upon the nature of activity on the file contents and how quickly that activity changes. Some implementations have file restructuring utilities that are automatically invoked by the operating system; others require that data processing personnel notice when file activity has changed sufficiently or program performance has degraded enough to warrant restructuring or reorganization of a file. Some installations perform file maintenance on a routine basis. For example, a utility might be run weekly to collect free space from deleted records, to balance index trees, and to expand or contract space allocations.

In general, master files and program files are created, updated, retrieved from, and maintained. Work files are created, updated, and retrieved from, but are not maintained. Report files generally are not updated, retrieved from, or maintained. Transaction files are generally created and used for one-time processing.

FILE SYSTEMS

Accessing (reading and writing) data in files requires a great deal of activity that is transparent to the application programmer. Programming languages enable programmers to define rather complex file organization techniques with quite simple statements. A *file system* provides support to enable programmers to access files without being concerned about details of storage characteristics and device timings. The file system converts the programmer's relatively simple file access statements to low-level I/O instructions. A programmer's simple request to READ or WRITE a record on a file typically invokes a complex sequence of supporting device management operations. The programmer's job would be considerably more difficult if it involved contending with these detailed I/O control operations.

The responsibilities of a file system are many and varied. They include

1. Maintaining a directory of file identification and location information.
2. Establishing pathways for data flow between main memory and secondary storage devices.
3. Coordinating communication between the central processing unit (CPU) and secondary storage devices and vice versa, including
   (a) Handling the imbalance in speeds of the computer's CPU and of storage devices in such a way that the CPU does not spend an inordinate amount of time waiting idly for I/O operations to be completed.
   (b) Handling data in such a way that they can be held if the sender (CPU or secondary storage device) and the receiver (secondary storage device or CPU) are not ready at the same time.
4. Preparing files for input or output use.
5. Handling files when their input or output use has terminated.

We now consider these tasks in more detail.

FILE DIRECTORIES

Before a file can be accessed by a program, the file system must know where the file is located. Nearly all file systems use some sort of directory structure to manage the identification and location information about files.

Figure 10–2 illustrates the basic concepts of a directory structure typically used to keep track of files. The directory shown is for one unit (e.g., disk pack or tape reel) of secondary storage. The label includes identifying information, access control information, and a pointer to a table of contents, which contains a control block for each file on the unit. A control block contains information about the name of a file, its attributes (such as record length, block size, organization), and its boundaries on the storage medium. A control block points to the start of the corresponding file. When a file is requested, the table of contents of the appropriate unit is consulted for information required to locate the file in storage.

Different systems use different structures for their file control blocks. One representative system constructs two tables to describe each file. The first contains information on file organization and processing mode, descriptions of record sizes and types, blocking sizes, error counts and flags, information used to determine file status and position, and the file's logical (external) name. It also contains a pointer to the file's second descriptive table, which is associated with a particular storage device and contains information about its physical characteristics and current status. Device controller routines use this table to interface requests to the file and to monitor the status of I/O activities on the file. Control

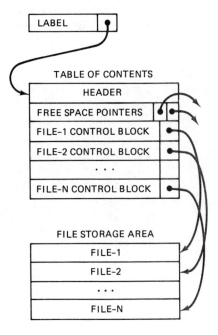

Figure 10–2   Basic file directory structure.

information in this system is modularized between the tables to improve the efficiency of I/O processing.

DEVICE CONTROL

I/O activities basically involve the movement of data between main memory and secondary storage devices or devices such as printers and terminals. While they may appear to be simple to programmers, these operations actually require detailed device control support. For example, assume that the file directory has already been consulted and the requested file's location on a secondary storage device has been determined. In order to be able to write to that device or read from that device, the following tasks must first be accomplished: A pathway between main memory and the device must be established, and it must be determined that the necessary components of the pathway (including the target device) are available and ready for use. The I/O operation itself requires that appropriate signals be transmitted to the device to cause it to react correctly: disk arms may be moved and read/write heads activated; a cursor on a terminal screen may be positioned; a page eject command may be sent to a printer. If errors occur during I/O activity, they must be handled. At the end of the I/O operation, the requestor must be notified that activities have terminated successfully or unsuccessfully, as the case may be.

Channels

In many operating systems the CPU is not burdened with handling these I/O-related tasks. Rather, responsibility for device control is delegated to I/O processors, which are also known as I/O *channels*. An I/O channel is itself a programmable processor; the programs that it executes are called *channel programs*. These programs specify the operations required for device accesses and control the data pathways. The file system has routines that are used to drive the I/O channels.

Figure 10–3 illustrates some of the components involved in I/O activity. The channel interfaces with one or more device control units to drive the storage devices. This arrangement simplifies channel programs significantly, as it is a control unit's responsibility

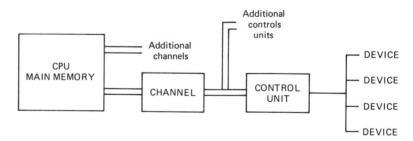

Figure 10–3 Computer system components involved in I/O processing.

to interpret I/O signals appropriately for the particular types of devices under its control and to control the devices accordingly.

Before an I/O operation can begin, a path between main memory and the device must be established. If the channel, the control unit, or the addressed device is busy, then the pathway construction must wait. In order to avoid such waits, a computer system may have several channels and control units. Usually the devices managed by a particular control unit must be of the same type, for example all disk drives, or all tape drives, or all line printers.

Kinds of Channels

There are several kinds of channels. A *selector channel* can manage data flow between main memory and only one device at a time. Since channels are fast processors, selector channels are usually used only with high-speed devices such as disks. Putting a relatively slow device such as a terminal on a selector channel could waste the channel's processing power.

A *multiplexor channel* can manage data flow between main memory and several devices. Multiplexor channels are more effective with slow-speed devices than are selector channels. With a multiplexor channel, several devices can be active simultaneously, but the channel must complete the channel program for one device before it starts the program for another. A channel program controls a single read or write to the device; so no device needs to wait very long.

A *block multiplexor channel* further interleaves the data flow to multiple devices. A block multiplexor channel can execute one instruction of the channel program for one device, then can switch to perform an instruction of the channel program for another device. Each channel program may contain several instructions. The entire channel program for one device does not have to be completed before another is serviced.

Kinds of Devices

There are two basic kinds of I/O devices: *dedicated* devices, which are suitable for access by only one user at a time, and *shared* devices, which allow concurrent access by multiple users. A terminal is an example of a dedicated device, while a disk is an example of a shared device.

The control activities for shared devices are more complex than they are for dedicated devices. Two of the important control functions required for shared devices are space allocation and the granting of access rights. The latter activity may include ordering requests to the shared device in an attempt to improve performance. For example, shared disk requests could be ordered to minimize arm-movement time.

A third kind of device is a unit that users would like to share but that is not really suitable for concurrent use. For example, multiple programs might want to address a printer concurrently, but the resultant output of interleaved lines from several sources would be quite useless. *Virtual* devices are used to address this need. A program that is using a virtual printer has the impression that it is writing to a printer, but in reality it is writing to disk. When that ouput file is completed by the program, it is then queued and written in its entirety to the printer. Support of virtual I/O devices sometimes is called *spooling*, after *S*imultaneous *P*eripheral *O*peration *On-Line*. The purpose of a spooling system is to permit the apparent concurrent sharing of devices that are really only sequentially sharable. Nearly all multi-user computer systems support spooling.

Channel Activities

We have seen that a channel is an intermediary between the CPU-main memory and the control unit-storage devices. The CPU communicates with a channel via some simple commands. A representative channel would respond to instructions such as

1. Test I/O, to determine whether or not the pathway to the addressed device is busy.
2. Start I/O, on a particular device.
3. Halt I/O, on a particular device.

A channel commonly communicates with the CPU through interrupts. An interrupt would be issued when an error is detected, e.g., invalid CPU command, or when an I/O activity is completed. When an interrupt occurs, control branches to an interrupt-handler routine, which determines what caused the interrupt, performs appropriate actions, then returns control to the caller.

Processing a Read

When a program requests a READ from a file, the following sequence of events typically occurs (see Fig. 10-4).

1. The program issues a READ, which interrupts the I/O controller.
2. The I/O controller builds a channel program in main memory.

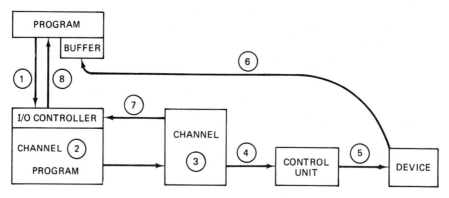

Figure 10-4   Sequence of events in processing a file READ.

3. The channel program is executed by the addressed channel.
4. Appropriate signals are transmitted to the addressed control unit.
5. These signals are interpreted by the control unit and used to control device operations to read the requested data.
6. The requested data flows from the device along the pathway to the file's buffer area in the program's memory space.
7. An interrupt is issued by the channel to signal continuation of the program's execution.
8. Control returns to the program.

Note that the data are read into a buffer, which is an area of main memory reserved to hold data for this file. When the buffer is full, the program can begin to use the data.

An analogous sequence of events occurs when a program requests a WRITE to a file. Thus the expense of device accesses! These events must occur for *every* READ and WRITE command that is issued to a device.

Blocking Records

The most commonly used technique to reduce a program's device accesses is to block records such that multiple records are read/written in a single device access. If there are *n* records per block, then only every *n*th READ by the program causes a device access. Commonly, a program's READ command is translated to a GET instruction by the file system. The channel program then converts the GET to a device READ if the buffer is empty, causing the buffer to be filled. The program's GET procures the next record from the buffer (Fig. 10–5).

The buffer provides the holding area required to interface relatively slow storage devices with the much faster CPU. It also provides the holding area that makes blocking of records feasible. Large blocking factors can be important to the performance of files that are accessed sequentially. Every record on the file will be accessed, so as many

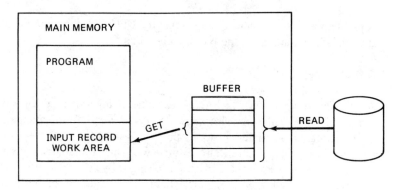

Figure 10–5   Device access with blocked records.

records as possible should be procured at once. The cost of a large block size is, of course, the cost of the additional main memory required.

MANAGING BUFFERS

We consider now several important but relatively simple approaches to managing file buffers. We start with single buffering, then consider multiple buffers.

Single Buffering, On Demand

Figure 10–6 shows the data structure of a buffer in a simple system in which there is one record per block and one buffer per file, and where the buffer is filled *on demand* from a program. The buffer structure includes a pointer to the starting address of the channel program for this file's current operation.

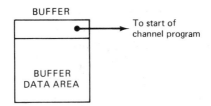

Figure 10–6   Buffer structure with one buffer for the file, fetched on demand.

The basic structure of the channel program to fill this buffer is

- Wait for READ request from the program.
- Issue start-I/O command to control unit.
- Wait while buffer is being filled.
- Issue interrupt to program so that it may start reading from the buffer.

A problem with this simple system is that the CPU (and therefore the user program also) sits idle while waiting for the buffer to be filled.

Anticipatory Buffering

An alternative approach which removes some of this potential for a waiting CPU is to use *anticipatory buffering*, also known as *prefetching*. With anticipatory buffering, the file system attempts to anticipate the program's need for data. It tries to keep the buffer always full, so that the data are already there when the program issues its READ instruction. The objective is to keep the CPU from having to wait.

Anticipatory buffering requires slight modification of the buffer's data structure to include a flag that indicates whether or not the buffer is full (Fig. 10–7). The channel

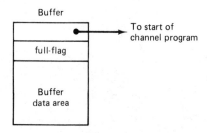

where full-flag = 0 if the buffer is empty,
= 1 if the buffer is full.

Figure 10–7 Buffer structure with one buffer per file and prefetching.

keeps testing this flag. If the buffer becomes empty because the user program has read its contents, the flag is reset and the channel program initiates refill of the buffer.

The basic structure of the channel program to fill a buffer with anticipatory buffering is

> loop: if full-flag = 1 go to loop.
>   issue start-I/O command to control unit.
>   wait while buffer is being filled.
>   full-flag: = 1.
>   go to loop.

A complementary routine to empty the buffer into the program's record work area is also required.

Our buffer filling and emptying routines come in pairs: one of the pair represents a producer and one a consumer. For an input file, the producer is the channel program and the consumer is the user program. For an output file, the producer is the user program and the consumer is the channel program.

The consumer routine that accompanies the above producer routine is

> wait: if full-flag = 0 go to wait.
>   read the buffer contents into the
>   record work area.
>   full-flag : = 0.
>   go to wait.

Initially, full-flag = 0, causing the channel program to fill the buffer.

Buffering with Blocks

Let us now use a blocking factor of n records per block. The producer/consumer routines must be changed to reflect the fact that only every nth READ by the user program causes a device access. The buffer structure needs to be modified slightly to include a counter or pointer that keeps track of which record of the n records in the buffer should be next read into the user program's record work areas (Fig. 10–8).

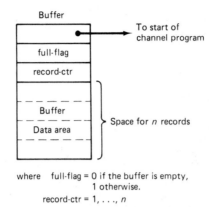

where   full-flag = 0 if the buffer is empty,
                     1 otherwise.
        record-ctr = 1, . . ., *n*

Figure 10-8   Buffer structure with *n* records per block.

The producer routine is modified only slightly.

> loop: if full-flag = 1 go to loop.
>   issue start-I/O command to control
>   unit.
>   wait while buffer is being filled.
>   record-ctr : = 1.
>   full-flag : = 1.
>   go to loop.

The consumer routine is changed a bit more.

> wait: if full-flag = 0 go to wait.
>   read record (record-ctr) into the
>   record work area.
>   record-ctr : = record-ctr + 1.
>   if record-ctr > n
>   full-flag : = 0.
>   go to wait.

Initially, full-flag = 0. The program's consumer routine is in the wait state between READs, but the program itself can be executing other instructions. Does the program ever have to really wait because the buffer is empty? Yes—it waits for every *n*th record. While the buffer is in the state of being emptied by a consumer, it cannot also be being filled by a producer.

Double Buffering

In order to reduce the probability of program waiting, double buffering is commonly used. Two buffer areas instead of just one are assigned to the file. The basic idea of double buffering is that while the consumer is emptying one of the buffers, the producer can be

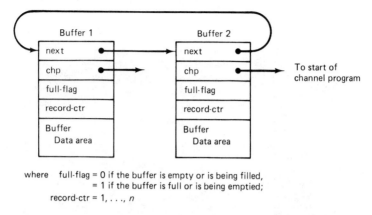

Figure 10–9 refers to the where clause below:

where   full-flag = 0 if the buffer is empty or is being filled,
         = 1 if the buffer is full or is being emptied;
      record-ctr = 1, . . ., n

Figure 10–9   Buffer structures for double buffering.

filling the other one. By the time the first buffer is emptied, the second should be full. The consumer can then empty the second while the producer fills the first, and so forth.

The buffer structure for double buffering now includes a pointer to the next buffer (Fig. 10–9). We now are ready for the anticipatory producer and consumer routines for the case of n records per block. Two auxiliary pointers are required:

- pfill, which points to the next buffer to be filled or being filled,
- pempty, which points to the next buffer to be emptied or being emptied.

The producer fills the buffer that is pointed to by pfill, which initially should point to buffer 1. Initially the full-flags of both buffers should be 0, since they are both empty. For an input file, the channel is the producer and executes the following channel program.

```
loop: if pfill ↑ .full-flag = 1 go to loop.
      issue start-I/O command to control unit.
      wait while pfill ↑ .buffer is being filled.
      pfill ↑ .record-ctr : = 1
      pfill ↑ .full-flag : = 1
      pfill : = pfill ↑ .next
      go to loop.
```

The channel program loops at loop only when one buffer is full and the other, which pfill points to, contains a record-ctr value less than n, indicating that it is either full or being emptied but is not yet empty.

The consumer empties the buffer that is pointed to by pempty, which initially should point to buffer 1. For an input file, the user program is the consumer and executes the following input routine.

```
wait:  if pempty ↑ .full-flag = 0 go to wait.
       read record (pempty ↑ .record-ctr) into the
           record work area.
       pempty ↑ .record-ctr : = pempty ↑ .record-ctr + 1
       if pempty ↑ .record-ctr > n
         begin;
           pempty ↑ .full-flag = 0
           pempty : = pempty ↑ .next
         end;
       go to wait.
```

This routine loops at wait only when one buffer is empty and the other, which pempty points to, contains a record-ctr value greater than n, indicating that it is either empty or being filled but is not yet full.

If the producer is filling the buffers at a faster rate than the consumer is emptying them, then the producer (the channel program for input files) will spend time looping at loop. It is usually more desirable to have the channel program loop than to have the CPU wait, which happens if the buffers are being emptied at a faster rate than they are being filled. One approach to reducing this problem is to chain together more than two buffers for the file.

Three Buffers

Figure 10–10 illustrates a three-buffer system. The situation that is illustrated is the following:

- Buffer 1 is full.
- Buffer 2 is being filled.
- Buffer 3 is being emptied; the mth record in the buffer will be read into the record work area next.
- The next buffer that will be emptied is buffer 1.
- The next buffer that will be filled is buffer 3.

This approach assumes that if any buffer is empty, the producer can act to fill it. For example, if, after buffer 3 is filled in the above situation, the consumer is still emptying buffer 1, then the producer should fill buffer 2; otherwise the consumer will have to wait.

If the producer consistently fills the buffers at a slower rate than the rate at which the consumer empties them, the consumer *will* have to wait. Multiple buffering can be effective in smoothing the results of uneven data requirements by the user program.

Thus the advantage of having more than one buffer is the potential to overlap the filling and emptying operations, thereby reducing CPU wait time. The cost of multiple

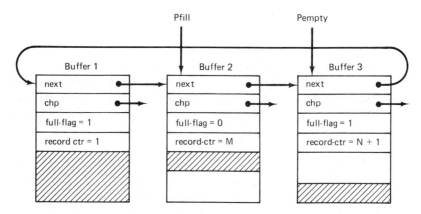

Figure 10–10 Three chained buffers.

buffering is the increase in complexity and processing time of the producer and consumer routines and the increased main memory requirements.

OPENING AND CLOSING FILES

We have now considered a few aspects of a file system's responsibilities in some detail. We have glimpsed the complexity of activity that occurs when a program issues a simple READ statement. (Description of activities ensuing from a WRITE is left as an exercise.) Let us now see what happens when a file is opened and when it is closed.

Before a program can access a file for input or output, that file must be opened. This processing may be initiated by an OPEN statement (required in COBOL) or in conjunction with the first READ or WRITE issued to the file. In either case, essentially the same activities result. These activities include the following:

- If necessary, a request is issued to an operator to mount the requested volume (e.g., tape reel or removable disk).
- The required channel program skeletons are constructed.
- Labels are checked if the file is opened for input; labels are written if the file is opened for output.
- The user's authorization to access the file is verified.
- The file's buffer area(s) are constructed and flags are properly initiated.
- If anticipatory buffering is in effect for an input file, then the first buffer is filled.
- The file's control block in the system's file directory is completed.

The information that is used to complete the file's control block can be extracted from several sources, including the program (using, for example, the FILE-CONTROL and FILE SECTION entries in COBOL), job control statements external to the program, and the file's labels (for an input file). File systems impose priorities on these sources for purposes of resolving conflicts that arise should they contain contradictory descriptions for a file.

After a program has completed its use of a file, the file needs to be closed. This processing may be initiated by a CLOSE statement or by default at program termination. Closing a file prepares it for later use by another program execution. The activities involved in closing a file include the following:

- The buffer area(s) for an output file are emptied.
- The buffer area(s) and channel program spaces are released.
- End-of-file marks and trailer labels are written for an output file.
- The volume's disposition (e.g., rewind, dismount) is handled.

In a large program that uses several files, space requirements can be reduced by having files open only while they are active, rather than opening all files at the beginning of the program and postponing their closure until program termination.

DATABASE SYSTEMS

Just as a file system relieves the application programmer from dealing with directories, devices, channels, and buffers, a *database management system* (DBMS) further raises the level of interface provided for the programmer. A file-oriented information system is depicted in Fig. 10–11. Each application program, represented by a box, "owns" its own files, and files are controlled by particular programs. The programs use file-system services to access their data.

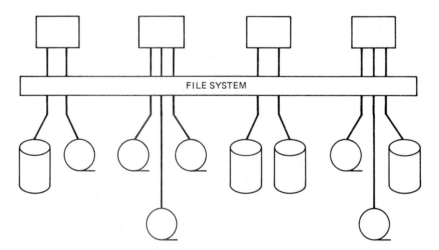

Figure 10–11   Application programs using the file system directly.

Very commonly, the data that are required to support one program are also required by another program. Sometimes both programs expect the same format and organization, but sometimes they do not. The result is replication of data across multiple files, for use by different programs. Data duplication is not attractive. It causes update inconsistency problems and it wastes storage space. Additionally, it can be difficult to correlate and integrate data *across* application programs. Consider a sales manager's request for a ''graph that correlates salespersons' salaries versus their revenue-generated-to-date figures.'' Presumably sales-persons' salaries are stored in a payroll master file, and revenue data are buried in an accounts-receivable master file. Although the data exist, it may be quite a difficult task to overcome data format, coding, and organization incompatibilities to be able to respond to the request.

A *database* is a collection of logically related data that supports shared access by multiple users and applications (Fig. 10–12). Whereas a file typically contains data about one type of entity (say personnel, orders, customers, sales), a database contains data about multiple types of entities *and* information about how the entities are logically related to each other. The data are integrated, and there are multiple access paths provided through the data.

A DBMS provides the services necessary for controlling shared access to the files that comprise the database. Application programs use DBMS services; the DBMS uses file system services. A database typically is structured physically using the file organization techniques we discuss in Chapters 13 through 16. A DBMS also provides services for

- *Defining*, *representing*, and *storing* data so that they can be accessed later.
- *Organizing* data so that they can be selectively and efficiently accessed.

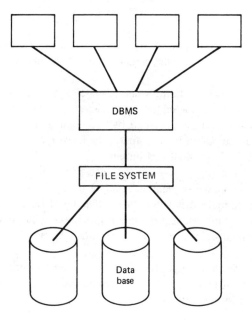

Figure 10–12 Application programs using DBMS services.

- *Interfacing* with users in ways that effectively support the users' decision-making environments.
- *Protecting* the data, including security, recovery, shared access control, and integrity protection mechanisms.

The DBMS maintains a stored description of the database structure and its contents; an application programmer need not recode these descriptions. The DBMS manages the internal implementation of the data; an application programmer need not maintain indexes and access paths. The DBMS provides appropriate interface facilities for users: natural, easy-to-learn query languages and report writers for noncomputer users and procedural languages for programmers. The DBMS provides access control, backup, concurrency, and data integrity protection; the application programmer need not build this functionality into each new program constructed. Most of today's DBMS functions are implemented in software. In the future these functions will increasingly be provided in hardware or firmware (micro-code).

The market for DBMS products is well established, especially for supporting Decision Support Systems and On-line Transaction Processing (like banking, airline reservations, and shop floor control). The file system on a computer is nearly always provided as part of the operating system. The DBMS may be provided by that same vendor, or may be acquired from a third party.

We will not go into more details of DBMS functionality here, as that is the subject of many other texts and courses.

SUMMARY

Files and databases are the cornerstones of information systems. They provide permanent storage for collections of related data, independent of the execution of any particular program run-unit.

Files have various basic functions in information systems; a file may contain master data, transaction data, data that are formatted for reports, temporary working data, program instructions, or text. Files also can be classified by the manner in which a particular program accesses them: input, output, or input/output. A database typically contains master data and is commonly used for both input and output.

The four fundamental file organization techniques that will be discussed in the remaining chapters of this text are the sequential, relative, indexed sequential, and multi-key organizations. These techniques differ in their sequencing of records and the accessibility of the records. Some organizations provide for direct access based upon data-item value; others support sequential access to series of records. All are used in the implementation of databases.

The selection of the appropriate organization for a file in an information system is important to the performance of that system. The fundamental factors that influence the selection process include the following:

1. Nature of operations to be performed
2. Characteristics of storage media to be used
3. Volume and frequency of transactions to be processed
4. Response time requirements

File management consumes a significant portion of many computer systems' resources. File systems are responsible for managing directories, controlling device accesses, and managing buffers. Nearly all file systems use some sort of directory structure to manage the identification and location of information about files. This information describes both a file's organization and characteristics of the physical storage device upon which it resides.

Responsibility for device control is commonly delegated to I/O processors, or channels. These programmable processors execute channel programs that instruct device control units to perform the operations required to fulfill a program's request to a file. Selector, multiplexor, and block multiplexor channels were introduced. The concepts of spooling and virtual devices were briefly discussed.

Understanding of the basic sequence of events required to perform a single device access shows the benefits of blocking records. Single and double buffering were introduced, and sample producer and consumer routines for buffer management were given.

The remainder of this book is dedicated to giving an understanding of the fundamental file organization techniques and the trade-offs between them.

TERMS

anticipatory buffering
auxiliary memory
batch mode
block
block multiplexor channel
blocking factor
buffer
channel
channel program
database
database management system
dedicated device
demand buffering
direct access
directory
double buffering
file
file organization

file system
indexed sequential file
    organization
input file
input/output file
interactive mode
interrupt
main memory
master file
multi-key file organization
multiplexor channel
output file
prefetching
primary storage
program file
query language
query processor
record

relative file organization

report file

report-writer package

response time

secondary storage

selector channel

sequential file organization

serial access

shared device

spooling

text file

throughput

transaction

transaction file

virtual device

work file

SELECTED REFERENCES

CENFETELLI, A. R., "Data management concepts for DOS/360 and TOS/360," *IBM Syst. Jour.*, 6(1):23–37, 1967.

KERNIGHAN, B. W. AND R. PIKE. *The UNIX Programming Environment*. Englewood Cliffs, NJ: Prentice-Hall, 1984.

LOOMIS, M. E. S. *The Database Book*. New York: Macmillan, 1987.

REVIEW EXERCISES

1. For what reasons might a collection of records be structured as a file on secondary storage rather than as a data structure in main memory?

2. Why do most computer systems support several file organization techniques?

3. What file organization techniques are supported by the various compilers available at your installation?

4. Who at your installation selects the type of organization that a file will have?

5. What, if any, general-purpose report-writer programs are available at your installation? What types of file organizations do the programs accommodate for their input files?

6. Obtain access to a system flow diagram for a production system at your installation. Identify the master files, transaction files, report files, work files, and program files. Can you identify any additional types of files?

7. For several of the major programs of the system studied for question 6, identify the input files, output files, and input/output files. Complete the following table by filling in the names of files in each function-access mode classification. Are there any boxes with no entries? Which boxes would you expect to be empty and why?

	Input	Output	Input/Output
Master files			
Transaction files			
Report files			
Work files			

8. How much of a programmer's time in your installation is expended in activities related to each of the following: file creation, file update, file retrieval, and file maintenance?

9. What kinds of operations are typically required to maintain files?

10. What are the typical responsibilities of a file system?

11. What kinds of information are typically found in a file system's directories?

12. What is a channel and what does it do?

13. Describe the major kinds of channels.

14. What is a virtual device and why is it useful?

15. Why is blocking of records an important concept?

16. What is the major benefit of anticipatory buffering?

17. Is multiple buffering always anticipatory buffering? If yes, why? If not, why not?

18. Following are two incomplete buffer management routines.

Channel program	Application program
Loop: If flag = 0 go to Loop.	Wait: If flag = **(b)** _____ Go to Wait.
Empty the buffer.	Counter : = Counter + 1
Counter : = 0	Move record work area into record
Flag : = **(a)** _____	[counter]
Go to Loop.	If counter : = **(c)** _____
	then flag : = **(d)** _____ .
	Go to Wait.

    Assume that there are n records per block. Fill in the four blanks in the two routines.

(e) Does the application program have the file opened for input or for output?

(f) Explain the meanings of the possible values of flag.

(g) How many buffers are in use?

19. What benefits might there be in requiring a programmer to open a file explicitly rather than implicitly in the first access to the file?

20. What benefits might there be in closing a file explicitly rather than implicitly at the end of a run unit?

21. What arrangement of devices on channels is used at your installation?

22. Write consumer and producer routines for double buffering for an output file. Who is the producer? Who is the consumer? Assume n records per block.

23. Obtain and try to understand the listing for a channel program in use at your installation.

24. Find out what directory structure is used to manage files at your installation.

25. Describe the major differences between a file system and a database management system.

26. What DBMS packages are available for use at your installation?

27. Talk to a programmer who has worked both with a DBMS and without one. Find out what the differences are from the programmer's point of view.

28. Look through a current issue of *Datamation*, *Computerworld*, *MIS Week*, or some other data processing business publication. Identify the DBMS products advertised or mentioned and their vendors.

29. Look through classified advertisements for data processing personnel. Identify the positions that are available for people with database knowledge and experience.

chapter eleven

sequential file organization

Sequentially organized files have been the workhorses of many data processing organizations for years. In this chapter we first discuss the characteristics of sequential files, then introduce the basic operations on sequential files: their creation, retrieval of their contents, and updating of their records. We also consider factors that affect the performance of sequential files.

DEFINITIONS

The most basic way to organize the collection of records that form a file is to use *sequential organization*. In a sequentially organized file, the records are written consecutively when the file is created and must be accessed consecutively when the file is later used for input (Fig. 11–1).

In many cases the records of a sequential file are ordered by the value of some field in each record. Such a file is said to be a *sorted* file; the field(s) whose value is used to determine the ordering is known as the *sort key*. If a file is sorted by the value of a field named KEY, ascending, then, record *I* precedes record *J* if and only if the value of KEY in record *I* is less than or equal to the value of KEY in record *J*. A file may be sorted in ascending or descending order by a sort key comprised of one or more fields. In Chapter

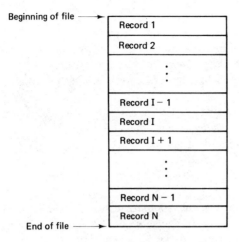

Beginning of file

| Record 1 |
| Record 2 |
| ⋮ |
| Record I − 1 |
| Record I |
| Record I + 1 |
| ⋮ |
| Record N − 1 |
| Record N |

End of file

Figure 11–1   Structure of a sequential file.

12 we will discuss several techniques that are commonly used for sorting sequential files.

A sequentially organized file may be composed of one record type or records of several different kinds. Multiple record types would be grouped together to form a file if they had a common functional purpose and were closely related logically.

Example

In an integrated personnel-payroll system, the employee file might contain two types of records. An employee may have one personnel record (Fig. 11–2(a)) and one or more payroll records (Fig. 11–2(b)), one for each account from which his or her salary is paid. The records on the file need not have the same format and need not be of the same size.

PERSONNEL

REC TYPE	EMPNO	NAME	PHONE	ADDRESS	MARITAL STATUS	SEX	HOME LOC	MIL CODE	EDUC		SO
									YR	DEG	
1											

(a)

PAYROLL

REC TYPE	EMPNO	FUND TYPE	ACCOUNT		BASE SALRATE	% TIME	RESP DEPT	DATE START	DATE CHANGE	...
			CODE	NO						
2										

(b)

Figure 11–2   Example record layouts.

However, there does need to be a way to determine the type of any given record occurrence. Here the first field of the record is used for that purpose. This example file might be sorted by EMP-NO,REC-TYPE. An employee's records would be consecutive; the employee's personnel record would precede the related payroll records. The value of the REC-TYPE field could be used by a program to determine the format of a particular record.

Variable length and/or format records are not supported directly by all file systems. It may be necessary in these systems to make the records appear to be nonvariable, e.g., by padding short records with trailing blanks to provide consistent record lengths.

Ordering Records

Processing requirements determine the appropriate order for sorting the records of a sequential file. For example, the records of a sequential file used to generate the white pages of a telephone directory would be sorted by subscriber last name and first name, because that is the required ordering for the report.

There are some cases, however, when it *is* useful to have a telephone directory with records sorted by subscriber address, or by zip code, or type of business. For example, a telephone poll of opinions based on particular areas of a city or a follow-up campaign for census data might use such a directory. If the directory data are stored as a sequential file, they can be in only one sorted order. One sequential file of records cannot be in sorted order by last name, first name and *also* be in sorted order by address. To satisfy both of these sort requirements, there would have to be two sequential files. They would contain the same data but be sequenced differently.

Information systems that are built around sequential files tend to replicate records across files that are in different sort orders. Usually not all of these files are retained; many are considered to be temporary and are deleted after they have been input to a following program or their contents have been printed. For example, a payroll system might generate a variety of reports; some would order the same pay data by employee social security number, some by source account code, some by check number, some by deposit account number, and so on.

Processing

Because the records of a sequentially organized file must be accessed consecutively, sequential files are used more commonly in batch processing than in interactive processing. For example, a sequential file of customer data (names, addresses, credit ratings, and the like) could be accessed in batch mode to print mailing labels to advertise a special sale; each customer record would be accessed. A sequential file of employee payroll data could be accessed in batch mode to generate paychecks; nearly all employee records would have activity. Changes to employee benefit information could be gathered over a period (say a week or month), then batched together to update the employee file. Monthly processing (such as customer billings), quarterly processing (such as tax reporting), semiannual processing (such as inventory reporting), and annual processing are examples of types of applications in which transactions are collected and then applied as a batch to be processed together. Later in this chapter we will discuss more fully the processing of sequential files.

Advantages and Disadvantages

The major advantage of the sequential technique of organizing files is the ability to access the "next" record quickly. As long as the pattern of access to a sequential file matches the ordering of records on the file, access times are very good. However, if a program's patterns of access do not match the record ordering pattern, then performance of the program can be terrible.

Consider, for example, a sequential file of employee information sorted by EMP-NO. Accessing employee records sequentially by EMP-NO (or by requesting "next" through the entire file) matches the file organization. Accessing employee records by EMP-NAME does not match the file organization, nor does accessing records in the order EMP-NO = 12751, EMP-NO = 98103, EMP-NO = 54216. Actually, we have turned the design process around here. The pattern of access should be determined and *then* the file should be organized to suit that pattern, not vice versa.

Another advantage of sequential file organization is its simplicity.

STORING SEQUENTIAL FILES

There are two basic classes of secondary storage devices: *serial-access* and *direct-access* devices. On a serial-access storage device, the time required to access two records is a function of the space between their locations (addresses) on the device. It takes longer to access them if they are far apart than if they are closer together. By contrast, on a direct-access storage device, the time required to access two records is not necessarily dependent on their relative locations. In some cases it may be faster to access a record that is farther on the device from the starting point than to access a relatively close record. The physical arrangement of data on either kind of device can affect the performance of a program that accesses the data.

Sequential files can be stored on either serial- or direct-access devices. Typically the serial-access devices are considerably less expensive than the direct-access devices on a computer system. For example, in a mainframe system, the choice is commonly between magnetic tape (a serial device) and a rotating magnetic disk (a direct-access device). Tape drives are less expensive than these disk drives, and a tape reel is less expensive than a disk pack. Of course, a disk pack can store so much more data than a tape reel that the cost per bit is only slightly more on disk. In a workstation or personal computer system, the choice is typically between floppy disk or diskette (a serial device) and hard disk (a smaller version of a mainframe magnetic disk). The cost and capacity trade-offs are the same. A floppy disk drive is less expensive than a hard-disk drive, and a diskette is much less expensive than a hard disk. The hard disk can store many floppies-worth of data.

The direct-access storage devices on a computer system nearly always provide larger capacities and faster data access than do the serial devices on the machine. Some of the other reasons to store a sequential file on a direct-access storage device are the following.

1. The computer may be configured with fewer serial-access drives than are required for a particular application. For example, if three sequential files are used in a program, say an old master file, a transaction file, and an updated master file, and there are only two tape drives, then one of the files could be stored on disk.
2. The system may be configured such that certain types of files are always written on disk. For example, the printer controller may expect that all files that are to be printed will be spooled to disk. Thus if a report file is created by a program, it will be assigned to a disk device.
3. The characteristics of channel traffic and channel capacities in a system may make it advantageous to split files across devices. For example, a system might be configured with two tape drives on one channel and two disk drives on another channel. If large volumes of data are generated by a program for two sequential files, it can be advantageous to put them on separate channels (and here therefore on different types of devices) rather than to have them assigned to devices that share a channel.

In some installations it is the programmer's responsibility to assign files to devices. In other installations the system will supply a default assignment if the programmer does not select a device. In many systems the programmer assigns a file to a *type* of device (such as magnetic disk or magnetic tape) rather than to a *particular* device. For example, if a sequential file is being written on tape, the programmer may not know (or care) which specific reel of tape is used; it suffices that the reel number be known *after* the file is created, so that the file can be used as input to another program execution.

If a sequential file is used as input to a program and the programmer is specifying that file's device assignment, the device type must match the actual type of device on which the file is stored. A reel of magnetic tape cannot be mounted easily on a disk drive!

Because sequential files are most commonly stored on magnetic tape, we shall now consider that medium more thoroughly. We'll discuss some of the details of disk storage in Chapter 13, where we introduce direct-access files.

MAGNETIC TAPE

Magnetic tape storage has roots in a voice recorder (called a Telegraphone) that was patented in 1898 by Denmark's Valdemar Poulsen. This particular device apparently was never commercially built but served as a source of ideas for development of related voice-recording devices that were used widely in the 1930s. By the late 1940s magnetic tape storage was used with computers and their utility for data storage was recognized. Substantial improvements in both the storage medium and tape access mechanisms have resulted in the highly reliable, low-cost, high-capacity tape devices that we use today.

We can expect these improvements to continue to produce new generations of magnetic tape devices.

There is a variety of magnetic tape media available today; we will describe here a representative example of the most commonly used choices. The tape medium is a strip of thin (about 2 mils thick), flexible plastic called Mylar, with a coating of ferric-oxide film. The tape is generally 2400 feet (732 meters) long and $\frac{1}{2}$ inch (1.27 centimeters) wide, although shorter and narrower tapes also are common, especially for use with microcomputers. The tape is kept on a reel, which is mounted on a *tape drive* (the access mechanism) for read/write access. A single tape drive can be used to access any number of tape reels, one at a time.

The records on the tape are stored in physically sequential order. The time required to access two records is a function of how far apart they are on the tape. The best case is that the second record would appear immediately following the first; the worst case is that the second record would be at the other end of the tape. It is possible to read the records on a tape file in other-than-sequential order, but such access requires rewinds and advances and can be quite time-consuming. In nearly all cases, tape files are read sequentially; they are usually written sequentially. Once a tape file has been written, a record in the middle usually cannot be updated. Some tape drives allow new records to be appended to the end of an existing tape file, but this is the only type of change allowed.

Data Representation and Density

Data are recorded digitally on the tape medium as magnetized spots in the ferric-oxide film coating. Positive magnetization represents a 1-bit, while negative magnetization represents a 0-bit, or vice versa. These areas of magnetization are induced when the tape is moved (at a typical speed of 200 inches per second—about 5 meters per second) past an appropriately charged coil in a tape drive's write-head mechanism. The ferric-oxide film retains the resultant magnetization; thus the medium is nonvolatile. The data representation is retained even without power to the machine. To read the recorded data, the tape is moved past a tape drive's read-head mechanism. The magnetization induces current in the coil, and the represented data can be sensed.

The magnetized areas are not randomly located on the medium; rather they are

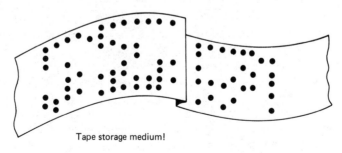

Tape storage medium!

Figure 11–3 Recording on a tape.

arranged in tracks, which run parallel to the edge of the tape. There are usually nine tracks on a tape. Eight of them record data and the ninth records error-control bits. Figure 11–3 diagrams a section of a tape; the bits of a single character appear essentially perpendicular to the edge of the tape.

One important characteristic of a tape is the density at which data are recorded. Density is a function of both the tape medium and the drive used to record onto the medium. Some devices can accommodate multiple densities. Density is measured in units of bits per inch (bpi), which is equivalent to a measure of characters per inch. The most common densities are 1600 bpi and 6250 bpi.

Parity and Error Control

In order to interpret correctly the data that are stored on a tape, the encoding scheme that was used when the data were written must be known. For example, the data might be represented in EBCDIC, or ASCII, or some other code. Additionally, the technique used to record error-control bits has to be known in order for that information to be used. One common technique for error control on magnetic tapes is *parity*. If data on a tape are recorded using *odd parity*, there must be an odd (as opposed to even) number of 1-bits represented for each character. If the bits making up a character's binary representation already have an odd number of 1-bits, then the parity bit (in the ninth track of a 9-track tape) is a 0-bit; if there is an even number of 1-bits, the parity bit for that character is a 1-bit, making the total number of 1-bits for that character's representation odd. Similarly, parity bits on a tape with *even parity* are recorded so that there is an even number of 1-bits represented for each character.

Parity bits are written when data on the tape are written, then are checked when the tape is read to verify that an error has not occurred. For example, a speck of dust or ash on the tape surface might interfere with the read head and cause a 0-bit to be sensed incorrectly as a 1-bit. A parity discrepancy can be used to detect the error. This simple technique of even/odd parity can detect single-bit (or 3-bit or 5-bit or 7-bit) errors in a character's representation, but can not detect 2-bit, 4-bit, 6-bit, or 8-bit errors. Furthermore, the technique does not indicate which of the bits is wrong.

When a parity error is detected, the read may be retried automatically, then if the error persists, the computer operator is notified. The error can be overridden or access to the file may be terminated. Some operating systems allow the person who sets up a program's job control specifications to request that parity errors be ignored for a tape. The result, of course, may be missing or incorrect interpretation of data on the tape. Such a request may be quite useful, however, for salvaging data from a "bad" tape.

Errors may appear on a magnetic tape because of dirt deposits, bends or wrinkles, areas where the ferric-oxide coating is missing, worn edges, stretched areas, too low a level of magnetization, errors in recording the data in the first place, and so on. A good quality tape generally can be read or written several thousand times before the medium deteriorates. This assumes however that the tape is kept in a dust-free, controlled-humidity environment. The faulty-write problem commonly is approached by positioning the read and write heads of the access mechanism so that the tape passes by the read head after passing by the write head. This configuration allows a read to be attempted immediately after a write, for a self-check on parity.

Blocking

Data are read from or written to a tape in groups of characters called *blocks*. A block is the smallest amount of data that can be transferred between secondary memory and primary memory in one access. A block may contain one or more records. A block is sometimes referred to as a *physical record*. In order to read or write data properly, the tape medium must be moving at a constant speed when it passes by the head mechanism. Because requests to read or write blocks do not arrive at a tape drive at a constant rate, there must be a gap (sometimes called an *interblock gap*) between each pair of blocks, forming a space to be passed over as the tape slows from read/write speed and as the tape accelerates to read/write speed. The medium is not strong enough to withstand the stress that it would sustain with instantaneous starts and stops. If you have seen a magnetic tape drive in operation, you may have noticed the jerky nature of the movement of the reel. Because the tape is not moving at a constant speed while the read/write head is positioned at a gap, a gap can not contain user data. Figure 11–4 diagrams a section of tape, showing the gaps and the user records.

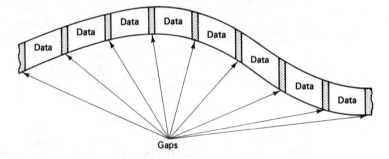

Figure 11–4 Tape section showing data blocks and interblock gaps.

Each gap typically is 0.6 inches (1.5 centimeters) long. The block size can significantly affect the amount of data that can be stored on a tape. Contrast, for example, the case of one 100-character record per block with the case of twenty 100-character records per block. Assume that the medium is 2400 feet in length and that data are recorded at a density of 6250 bpi. With one record per block, the tape can contain

$$\frac{\dfrac{2400 \text{ ft}}{\text{tape}} * \dfrac{12 \text{ in}}{\text{ft}}}{\dfrac{1 \text{ rec}}{\text{block}} * \dfrac{100 \text{ char}}{\dfrac{6250 \text{ char}}{\text{in}}} + \dfrac{.6 \text{ in}}{\text{gap}} * \dfrac{1 \text{ gap}}{\text{block}}} = \frac{46,753 \text{ blocks}}{\text{tape}}$$

which is 46,753 records, while with twenty records per block, the tape can contain

$$\frac{\dfrac{2400\ \text{ft}}{\text{tape}} * \dfrac{12\ \text{in}}{\text{ft}}}{\dfrac{20\ \text{rec}}{\text{block}} * \dfrac{\text{rec}}{\dfrac{6250\ \text{char}}{\text{in}}} + \dfrac{.6\ \text{in}}{\text{gap}} * \dfrac{1\ \text{gap}}{\text{block}}} = \frac{31{,}304\ \text{blocks}}{\text{tape}}$$

which is 626,086 records. In the first case, 97.5% (28,052 inches) of the tape is occupied by gaps; with twenty records per block, the gaps occupy 65.2% of the tape. Increasing the number of records per block (also known as the *blocking factor*) would improve further the use of the tape space.

Perhaps more important is the effect of the blocking factor on the time required to access the tape. Assume that the required tape speed for read/write access is 200 inches per second and that 4 milliseconds are required to stop and restart through a gap. The time required to access our example full tape with 1 record per block and a delay in each gap is

$$\frac{\dfrac{46{,}753\ \text{blocks}}{\text{tape}} * \dfrac{.016\ \text{in}}{\text{block}}}{\dfrac{200\ \text{in}}{\text{sec}}} + \frac{46{,}753\ \text{blocks}}{\text{tape}} * \frac{.004\ \text{sec}}{\text{gap}} * \frac{1\ \text{gap}}{\text{block}} = \frac{190.75\ \text{sec}}{\text{tape}}$$

whereas the time required to access the same collection of records with 20 records per block is

$$\frac{2338\ \text{blocks} * \dfrac{.32\ \text{in}}{\text{block}}}{\dfrac{200\ \text{in}}{\text{sec}}} + 2338\ \text{blocks} * \frac{.004\ \text{sec}}{\text{gap}} * \frac{1\ \text{gap}}{\text{block}} = 10.55\ \text{sec}.$$

A program that accesses a file of data stored on a tape can execute no faster than that file can be accessed. Selection of the appropriate blocking factor of a tape file thus is significant to the performance of a program that accesses that file. The blocking factor used when a file is written must be known when that file is later read.

Why not just have one block include all of the records of the file? This approach certainly would minimize the number of blocks, and also minimize the number of gaps and the time required to access the file. The problem with this approach is that regardless of the block size, there must be space allocated in main memory to hold the contents of a block prior to writing the block onto the tape (for an output file) or prior to reading the block into a program (for an input file). This space in main memory is called a *buffer* and is shown in Fig. 11–5, which should be compared with Fig. 10–5, which represents the same concept.

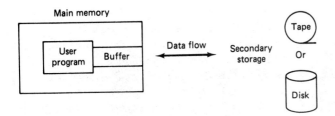

Figure 11–5 Buffering and secondary storage.

The size of a buffer for a file is the same as that file's block size. Main memory is relatively much more expensive than is tape storage. Furthermore, main memory is commonly a scarce resource, especially in smaller computer systems. Not only do the charging algorithms used in many computing facilities reflect the expense and scarcity of main memory, but in many cases tasks are prioritized by the amount of main memory they require to execute: small tasks generally get higher priority than do the large tasks.

When a program requests a record from a tape file with a blocking factor of one record per block, the tape is accessed, one block is moved into the buffer, and the record is available. The next read of the file causes the same sequence of events to occur. What happens when there is more than one record per block? A program still requests a read of *one* record at a time, but an entire block must be brought into the buffer at once. As we saw in Chapter 10, the file system makes the data available to the program one record at a time, keeping track of which records have been released to the program. When the buffer is empty (i.e., when all records have been accessed by the program), the file system initiates another access to the tape, another block is moved into the buffer, and the first record of the new block is made available to the program.

Charging algorithms in many computing facilities include the number of access requests to secondary storage in their calculations of costs. This is another reason why it may be beneficial to use a large blocking factor. Selection of the appropriate blocking factor for a tape file thus involves trade-offs between the time required to access the tape, the cost of main memory buffer space, and the number of accesses to secondary storage.

Tape Marks and Labels

Now let us consider several other characteristics of the tape medium. The beginning (after a leader section) and end (before a trailer section) of the tape reel are each marked by an aluminum, reflective strip that can be sensed by a photoelectric sensor in the tape drive. The tape mark at the beginning of the tape reel is known as the *load point*. When the tape reel is mounted on the drive, the tape is threaded through the access mechanism and positioned at the load point. Data can be written on the tape after this point, and up until the point where the other tape mark, which is known as the *end-of-tape mark*, is encountered. A primary function of the end-of-tape mark is to prevent the unthreading of the tape and consequent destruction of part of the reel.

A tape reel generally has an *external label*, which is a piece of adhesive affixed to the reel's plastic casing. This label bears a number and is used by the operator and tape librarian to identify the reel.

A tape may also have an *internal label*, which is recorded electronically on the tape. A tape with an internal label is called a *labeled tape*. Standards have been developed for formatting internal labels; some computer facilities instead use their own home-grown formats. An internal label contains information such as tape number (which is usually the same as the external number), retention period, password, creation date, and similar information. Some tapes also have trailer labels, which follow the user data.

It may be important to ensure that a program does not write on a tape file that already contains data, thus obliterating that data. To allow write access to a tape, a plastic ring can be inserted in the tape casing, thus activating the write head. The ring also can be removed easily by an operator should it be necessary to prevent writing to the tape.

Tape Usage

Magnetic tape has evolved to be an important medium for the storage of large master files, backup files, and archive-history files. The medium is portable and provides low-cost storage for relatively large quantities of data. Its serial-access nature seriously impacts the design and processing of files stored on tape. In fact, the serial access nature of the tape medium also has impacted many experienced programmers' and analysts' approaches to designing data systems; they have continued to impose unnecessarily the limitations of the tape medium on files stored on direct-access media. Direct-access files will be discussed later. For now we shall continue studying sequential files.

DECLARING SEQUENTIAL FILES

Nearly all programming languages have facilities for declaring sequentially organized files, and nearly all programming languages provide this capability differently. In this section we introduce the basic concepts required to be able to declare sequential files in COBOL and Pascal. For details of declaration requirements you should consult local language manuals and inquire about installation standards and procedures.

COBOL

The COBOL programmer provides file declaration information in both the ENVIRON-MENT DIVISION and the DATA DIVISION of a program. The entries in the ENVI-RONMENT DIVISION identify the storage devices to be used for files; the entries in the DATA DIVISION describe the organization, physical characteristics, and format of records in files. Let us look first at pertinent ENVIRONMENT DIVISION entries.

File-oriented information is provided in the INPUT-OUTPUT SECTION of the ENVIRONMENT DIVISION. The SELECT clause of the FILE-CONTROL paragraph associates each file used in the program with a storage device. The format of the SELECT clause is*

---

* See the appendix for explanation of the syntax notation used here.

SELECT [OPTIONAL] filename ASSIGN TO [implementor-name]...

[RESERVE integer $\begin{bmatrix} \text{AREAS} \\ \text{AREA} \end{bmatrix}$]
[ORGANIZATION is SEQUENTIAL]
[ACCESS MODE is SEQUENTIAL]
[FILE STATUS is data-name].

The filename is the name by which the file is known in this program. The implementor-name is the name of the device upon which the file resides. Depending upon the compiler and the computer installation, the implementor-name may refer to 1) a particular device (e.g., card reader #1, tape reel #9T4311, disk unit #DA2), 2) a class of devices (e.g., card reader, tape reel, disk unit), or 3) a logical device (e.g., PRSNMSTR, TRANS) which will be assigned to a physical device by commands external to the program. The third approach provides greatest flexibility, because device assignments can be changed without recompilation.

The OPTIONAL phrase indicates that this particular file need not be present when the program is executed. For example, a program might expect a variable number of transaction files.

The RESERVE phrase is used to specify the number of input-output areas (buffers) to be allocated to the file.

The ORGANIZATION and ACCESS MODE phrases specify the file organization technique and the manner in which records in a file are accessed, respectively. (A sequentially organized file can support only sequential access.) In most installations, both ORGANIZATION and ACCESS default to SEQUENTIAL unless otherwise specified.

The FILE STATUS phrase is used to declare a variable whose value will indicate the status of each I/O operation performed on the file, e.g., successful completion, permanent I/O error, at end-of-file.

Typical SELECT clauses for sequential files are

```
SELECT TRANS-FILE       ASSIGN TO INPUT.
SELECT EXCP-RPT-FILE    ASSIGN TO OUTPUT.
SELECT MSTR-FILE        ASSIGN TO SYS024-UT-2400-S-
                            MSTRIN.
SELECT SUM-RPT-FILE     ASSIGN TO SYS001-UR-1403-S.
```

The MULTIPLE FILE clause of the I-O-CONTROL paragraph of the INPUT-OUTPUT SECTION is used to specify the location of files when more than one share the same physical reel of tape. The format of the clause is

MULTIPLE FILE TAPE CONTAINS {file name-1
        [POSITION integer-1]} . . . .

Only the files on the reel that are used in the program need to be specified.

MULTIPLE FILE TAPE CONTAINS
TRANS-WEST-DIV POSITION 1
TRANS-EAST-DIV POSITION 4.

A program can have only one multiple-file tape open at any time.

File-oriented information is also provided in the FILE SECTION of the DATA DIVISION. Each file used in the program must have an associated FD (file description) entry. An FD contains clauses that give information about the physical structure, identification, and record names of a given file. The basic clauses have the following format:

$$
\begin{aligned}
&\underline{\text{FD}} \text{ filename} \\
&\quad [\underline{\text{BLOCK}} \text{ CONTAINS } [\text{integer 1 } \underline{\text{TO}}] \\
&\qquad\qquad\qquad \text{integer 2} \left\{ \begin{array}{l} \text{RECORDS} \\ \text{CHARACTERS} \end{array} \right\}] \\
&\quad [\underline{\text{RECORD}} \text{ CONTAINS } [\text{integer 3 } \underline{\text{TO}}] \\
&\qquad\qquad\qquad \text{integer 4 CHARACTERS}] \\
&\quad \text{LABEL} \left\{ \begin{array}{l} \underline{\text{RECORD}} \text{ IS} \\ \underline{\text{RECORDS}} \text{ ARE} \end{array} \right\} \left\{ \begin{array}{l} \underline{\text{STANDARD}} \\ \underline{\text{OMITTED}} \end{array} \right\} \\
&\quad [\underline{\text{DATA}} \left\{ \begin{array}{l} \underline{\text{RECORD}} \text{ IS} \\ \underline{\text{RECORDS}} \text{ ARE} \end{array} \right\} \quad [\text{dataname 1}] \dots].
\end{aligned}
$$

The filename in the FD is the same as the filename in the SELECT clause for the file. The BLOCK CONTAINS and RECORD CONTAINS clauses indicate minimum and maximum block and record sizes on the file. The LABEL RECORDS clause is the only mandatory clause in an FD; it indicates the presence or absence of internal labels. The DATA RECORDS clause names the record type(s) to be found on this file. Other clauses are sometimes available to specify the character code set used externally to represent the file's data, to specify the logical page size for print/display files, to give a value to an item in the file's label record, and to name the reports in a report file.

One or more record description entries follow a file's FD. Each describes the format of a record type (see Chapter 3).

The following program excerpts illustrate a COBOL declaration of four sequential files: RPT-FILE, TRANS-FILE, MSTR-FILE-IN, and MSTR-FILE-OUT.

```
        .
        .
        .

    ENVIRONMENT DIVISION.
    INPUT-OUTPUT SECTION.
    FILE-CONTROL.
        SELECT RPT-FILE   ASSIGN TO OUTPUT.
        SELECT TRANS-FILE   ASSIGN TO TAPE1.
```

```
SELECT MSTR-FILE-IN   ASSIGN TO TAPE3.
SELECT MSTR-FILE-OUT   ASSIGN TO TAPE2.
I-O-CONTROL.
    MULTIPLE FILE TRANS-FILE POSITION 2.

 . . .

DATA DIVISION.
FILE SECTION.
FD RPT-FILE
    LABEL RECORDS OMITTED.
01  RPT-REC              PICTURE X(132).
FD  TRANS-FILE
    RECORD CONTAINS 13 TO 82 CHARACTERS
    LABEL RECORDS STANDARD
    DATA RECORDS TRANS-REC-ADD, TRANS-REC-DELETE.
01  TRANS-REC-ADD.
    02  TRANS-REC-CODE      PICTURE X.
    02  TRANS-REC-ADD-DETAIL        PICTURE X(81).
01  TRANS-REC-DELETE.
    02  TRANS-REC-CODE      PICTURE X.
    02  TRANS-REC-DELETE-DETAIL          PICTURE X(12).
FD  MSTR-FILE-IN
    BLOCK CONTAINS 40 RECORDS
    LABEL RECORDS STANDARD.
01  MSTR-REC-IN          PICTURE X(87).
FD  MSTR-FILE-OUT
    BLOCK CONTAINS 40 RECORDS
    LABEL RECORDS STANDARD.
01  MSTR-REC-OUT         PICTURE X(87).

 . . .
```

Pascal

The input/output facilities of the Pascal language have not been standardized. You will find considerable variation in file declaration requirements from compiler to compiler. We use a representative example of Pascal here, but be sure to verify the particular requirements of the Pascal compiler that you use.

The names of the files that are used in a Pascal program are given in its <u>program</u> statement. For example,

program mstrupdt (outfil,trans,mstrin,mstrout);

Some compilers require that the names of files that are used as input be distinguished from the names of output files. For example,

program mstrupdt (outfil,trans*,mstrin*,mstrout);

Files are assigned to storage devices by statements external to the Pascal program. However, use of some file names (such as input or output) may imply use of a particular storage device or class of storage devices.

The format of the records on a file is declared using either type or var statements, as discussed in Chapter 3. Each file (except input and output if they are system defaults) is declared of type file.

The following program excerpts illustrate a Pascal declaration of four sequential files: outfil, trans, mstrin, and mstrout.

```
program mstrupdt(outfil,trans,mstrin,mstrout);
type mstrrec = record
                   empno : 1 . . 99999;
                   empname : packed array [1 . . 25] of char;
                   dept : packed array [1 . . 5] of char;
                   . . .
               end;
     transrec = record
                   transcode : A,D;
                   detail : packed array [1 . . 81] of char
               end;
var outfil : text;
    trans : file of transrec;
    mstrin,mstrout : file of mstrrec;
```

In many cases the Pascal programmer cannot specify the same level of detail about the physical characteristics of a file as can a COBOL programmer. However, because the input/output facilities of a Pascal compiler are implementor-defined, the level of file specification capability given the programmer varies.

CREATING A SEQUENTIAL FILE

The creation of a sequential file involves writing records in the desired sequence onto a storage medium. The creation of a sequential transaction file involves the tasks of collecting data, converting the data to a machine-readable form, editing the data, correcting rejected transactions, and sorting the edited data (Fig. 11–6).

Data entry devices include key-to-card, key-to-tape, key-to-disk, optical scanners, and devices that respond to voice input. The input process often includes a verification procedure to check that the data values entered were actually the same as the data values written or marked on the transaction documents.

Editing Transactions

The edits performed on transaction data might include the following types of checks.

1. Proper ranges of values, e.g., hours worked must be less than 60; sex must be M or F.

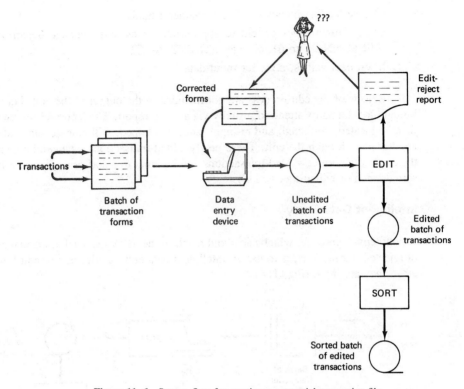

Figure 11–6 System flow for creating a sequential transaction file.

2. Presence of required fields, e.g., must have employee number.

3. Proper types of values, e.g., numeric in numeric field.

4. Accuracy of self-checking field values, e.g., low-order digit of the sum of the first 8 digits of account-code must equal the 9th digit of account-code.

5. Presence of related fields, e.g., if transaction is of type add, then transaction fields empno, department, and start-date must not be blank.

6. Control totals, e.g., sum of dollar amounts for all transactions in batch must equal an input total.

7. Counts, e.g., count of transactions must equal an input count.

8. Check sums, e.g., total of employee-numbers for all transactions (a non-sensical quantity) must equal an input total.

These checks help to find incorrect transactions, incorrectly input but correct transactions, and cases where transactions were lost or re-input during the input process.

The edits also might include checks and changes that are not related directly to finding bad data. For example, the edit might

9. Change leading blanks to zeros in numeric fields.
10. Change mnemonics or text to appropriate codes, e.g., change department value 'PERSONNEL' to 61; change 'STREET' to 'ST'.
11. Insert data values, e.g., for input-data.

Rejects of the edit process are not included in the output of the edit, but rather are brought to a human's attention, usually via a reject report. The incorrect transactions can then be located, corrected, and re-input, and, it is hoped, will emerge successfully from another pass through the edit. These newly edited transactions then can be merged with the originally correct, edited transactions and be input to a sort procedure to produce the sorted batch of edited transactions.

Intelligent Data Entry

An attractive approach, which can avoid much of the delay incurred in manual correction of rejected transactions, is to use an intelligent data-entry device and to edit transactions when they are input (Fig. 11–7).

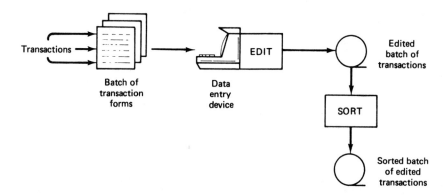

Figure 11–7   Combining transaction editing with transaction input.

If the operator of the data-entry device cannot correct an error, the transaction will have to be corrected and re-input later.

Batched transactions generally are sorted to put them in the same sequence as the master file that they are destined to update. We will discuss the update of sequential files later in this chapter and the sorting of sequential files in Chapter 12.

Writing Records

Records are written on a sequential file using the following kinds of statements.
    In COBOL—

WRITE record-name [FROM identifier]

where the record-name is defined in the file's FD and the optional identifier of the FROM clause is defined in WORKING-STORAGE.

In Pascal—

writeln (filename, recordname);
or write (filename, recordname);

depending upon whether or not a new line is to be started after this one, where the filename appears in the program statement and the recordname variable contains the data to be written. The records will appear on the file in the same order as they are written.

All sequential files are created in about the same way. However, we shall consider report files in more detail.

Report Files

Creating a sequential report file involves gathering the data to be reported, formatting the data, and calculating appropriate summary information. The records on such a file are of several kinds:

1. *Heading* records, including report headings, page headings, and group headings—identifying information.
2. *Detail* records—the "meat" of the report, generally arranged in columns.
3. *Foot* records, including group, page and report foot lines—summary information.

Summary data are generally calculated in *control breaks*, which are changes in the value of some identified field. For example, the data records for a sales report might be in sorted order by REGION, DEPARTMENT, SALESMAN-ID.

REGION major,
DEPARTMENT,
SALESMAN-ID minor.

Control breaks might be specified upon change of SALESMAN-ID (giving totals for each salesperson), upon change of DEPARTMENT (giving totals for all sales-people within each department), and upon change in REGION (giving totals for all departments within each region). Report totals might also appear.

Commonly, a report file is created in a separate program from the routine that actually creates the data to be reported (Fig. 11–8).

The editing, sorting, and report writing processes may be implemented either as applications programs with code written specifically for the particular files and applications involved, or as more general-purpose utility routines. Very common utilities include software that can do the following:

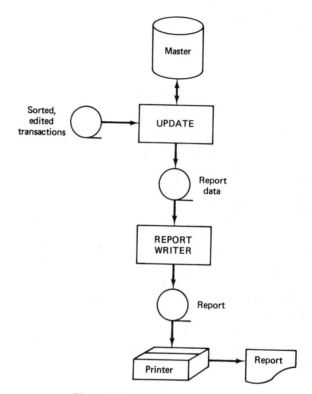

Figure 11–8 Creating a report file.

1. Copy a sequential file from one storage medium to another, e.g., card to tape, card to disk, tape to disk, disk to tape, tape to print, disk to print.
2. Copy a sequential file to another sequential file on the same storage medium, e.g., tape to tape, disk to disk.
3. Perform simple edits on records, e.g., value type, sequence checking.
4. Perform simple reformatting of records, e.g., rearranging fields, simple calculations.
5. Sort a file on given fields, ascending or descending.
6. Merge multiple sorted files to form a single sorted file, based on the value of given fields, ascending or descending.
7. Prepare reports, including formatting and a variety of control-break summaries.

Some programming languages include features that are designed to simplify the creation of report files. For example, the full syntax for the COBOL WRITE statement for sequential files is

WRITE recordname   [FROM identifier-1]

$$\left[\left\{ \begin{matrix} \underline{BEFORE} \\ \underline{AFTER} \end{matrix} \right\} ADVANCING \left\{ \begin{matrix} \left\{ \begin{matrix} identifier\text{-}2 \\ integer \end{matrix} \right\} \left[\begin{matrix} LINE \\ LINES \end{matrix} \right] \\ \left\{ \begin{matrix} mnemonic\text{-}name \\ \underline{PAGE} \end{matrix} \right\} \end{matrix} \right\} \right]$$

$$\left[AT \left\{ \begin{matrix} \underline{END\text{-}OF\text{-}PAGE} \\ \underline{EOP} \end{matrix} \right\} \quad imperative\text{-}statement \right]$$

The programmer can thus control line spacing (single, double, triple . . .) and activities to be executed in conjunction with page ejection. The FD for a report file can include a specification of the number of lines per page so the programmer can control page ejection.

COBOL also includes a report-writer facility. The format of a report file is defined in an RD (report description) rather than in an FD. Features enable the declaration of control break levels and of various kinds of field editing and print formatting. Rather than using WRITE for records to these files, the programmer uses GENERATE statements. After being OPENed, the report file is readied using an INITIATE statement. The final control break is caused by a TERMINATE statement.

RETRIEVING FROM SEQUENTIAL FILES

Records must be retrieved from a sequential file in consecutive order. The order in which records were written to the file when the file was created determines the order in which records can be retrieved from the file. In fact, it is really the other way around: the desired order of record retrieval should dictate the order in which records should be written.

Retrieval from a file can be classified as either report generation or inquiry, depending on the volume of output produced. Sequential files are very commonly accessed in report-generation mode. Because the records must be accessed consecutively, it is quite efficient to access every record on the file. Report generation from a sequential file is the same as creating a sequential report file, where the input to the process is a sequential file (for example, see Fig. 11–8).

Using the terminology that was introduced in the previous section, each record of the input file produces a detail line on the report. The basic logic flow of report generation is shown in Fig. 11–9. The control levels might be

1. salesman-id,
2. department,
3. region.

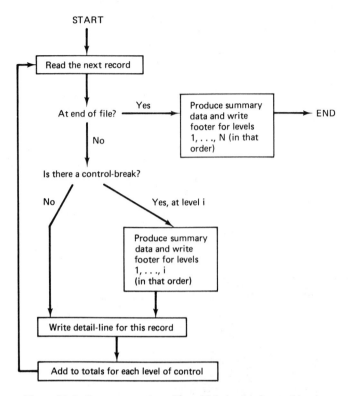

Figure 11–9 Report generation with multiple levels of control breaks.

Here there are three control breaks unless there is an overall report footing defined, in which case there would be four. The logic would be somewhat different if multiple records were combined to form a single detail-line.

Records are read from a sequential file using the following types of statements. In COBOL—

> READ filename INTO identifier
> AT END imperative-statement.

where the filename is defined in an FD, the optional INTO clause specifies an identifier in WORKING-STORAGE that will receive the contents of the record (which will also be received by any records defined with the file's FD), and the AT END clause is required to specify what is to happen when the input file is exhausted.

In Pascal—

> read (filename,recordname);
> or readln (filename,recordname);

depending on the disposition of any "leftover" characters in the input record, where the filename appears in the program statement and the recordname variable will receive the data.

Inquiry from a sequential file is constrained by the consecutive-retrieval requirement. (Many so-called inquiries are really report generators.) However, the following types of inquiries might be serviced satisfactorily by a sequential employee file, since each requires access to all the records of the file.

- What are the mean and standard deviation for employee salaries?
- How many employees are enrolled in each of our four medical-benefit plans?
- Which employee has the maximum number of years with the company?
- Which employee has the lowest ratio of salary to years of service with the company?

The *hit ratio* for an inquiry of a file is the number of records that must be accessed to respond to the inquiry divided by the number of records on the file. The lower the hit ratio, the more inappropriate is sequential organization; the higher the hit ratio, the more satisfactory is sequential organization.

UPDATING SEQUENTIAL FILES

A master file represents a static view of some aspect of an organization's business. However, most aspects of an organization's business are not static; rather, changes occur continuously: employees are hired and fired, product prices change, job asssignments change, and so forth. In order for a master file to reflect accurately the state of an organization, these changes must be incorporated into the data on the master file; the master file must be updated.

How Often to Do It?

Because we are discussing sequential files, we confine our attention now to batch updating. Transactions are collected and are periodically applied to update a master file. The frequency at which a master file should be updated depends on several factors, including the following:

- Rate of change of the data
- Size of the master file
- Urgency of need for current data on master file
- File activity ratio

The *file activity ratio* is the number of master file records affected by a batch of transactions divided by the number of records on the master file. The number of records affected does not necessarily equal the number of transactions in the batch; several transactions may affect a single master record. (Rarely does one transaction affect more than one master record We postpone discussion of transactions such as "Give each employee a 7% raise" and require that a transaction specify only one master record.) In general, the greater the length of time between master file updates, the greater will be the file activity ratio.

Between updates, the average age of data on the master file increases. If the master file is accessed for retrieval between updates, then some of the reported data will no longer be current. The greater the need to have current data on the master file, the more frequently it should be updated.

However, the more frequently that the master file is updated, the higher is the processing cost, especially with a large file. Thus the fundamental trade-off: the more current the data, the higher the processing cost.

Interactive transaction processing of a sequential file can be very expensive. The records must be accessed sequentially; transactions applied interactively usually are not in the appropriate order for a sequential file update.

Additionally, most sequential files cannot be updated in place; rather they must be rewritten. Thus the general system flow diagram for update of a sequential file is as shown in Fig. 11–10. The old master and new master are two separate files. The lower the file activity ratio, the greater the number of records that are merely copied from the old file to the new one: expensive busy-work for the computer.

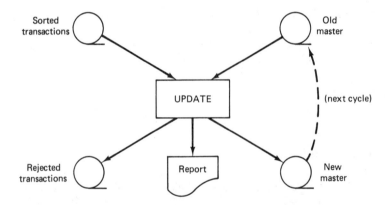

Figure 11–10   Updating a sequential master file, forming a new generation.

Generation Files

During the next cycle of updating, today's new master will be the old master file. These multiple versions of a master file are commonly known as *generation files*.The files have the same name; they differ only in their generation numbers. If today's old master were generation 1, then today's new master would be generation 2; the new master in the next cycle would be generation 3, and so forth. If absolute generation numbers like these are used then the actual generation number needs to be known in order for one to refer to a particular version of the file. Relative generation numbers can also be used. For example, if today's old master were relative generation 0, then today's new master would be relative generation $+1$, next cycle's new master would be $+2$ (relative to today's old master) or $+1$ (relative to today's new master), last cycle's old master would be -1 relative to today's old master or -2 relative to today's new master or -3 relative to the next cycle's new master, and so forth. Both conventions are used. In most systems, omission of an absolute or relative generation number results in a reference to the most current version of the file.

An organization might retain several generations of a file for purposes of facilitating recovery or for historic reporting needs.

Kinds of Updates

There are three basic kinds of updates that can be applied to a master file:

1. Insert a new record.
2. Delete an existing record.
3. Modify an existing record.

Each transaction contains a code that indicates its type and the value of the key of the corresponding master record. If the transaction is an insertion, it generally specifies not only the key for the new master record, but also values for other fields in the new master; an example is given in Fig. 11–11.

TRANS -CODE	EMPNO	NAME	ADDRESS	DEPT	PHONE
I	12751	SMITH, IGOR	EASY STREET	TOY	

Figure 11–11   Example transaction record.

The transaction code and key value are required here; the other fields could be left blank (to be updated later). If the transaction were a deletion it commonly would be enough to specify just the key value of the corresponding master record. If the transaction were a modification, the key value and values of fields to be modified would be required. Usually those fields that are not to be changed are left blank. (Note that program logic must not interpret those blanks as "change to spaces.")

Changes to a master file result either from real changes (such as hiring or terminating an employee or changing an office assignment) or as attempts to correct errors that have gotten into the file in previous runs. Commonly no real distinction in processing is made between these two types of transactions.

Handling Errors

There are many kinds of errors that must be accounted for in a file update, including trying to

1. Insert a record that already exists.
2. Delete a record that does not exist.
3. Modify a record that does not exist.

The proper action to take when these errors occur is application-dependent, but errors should not be allowed to pollute the file. Generally an update program produces an error report that identifies each transaction that was not processed and the reason it was not processed.

Update Logic

The logic required to process a batch of transactions that update a sequential file is classic. The same basic logic is used over and over in many different programs. The idea is to merge the keys of the transaction records and the keys of master file records. We assume that the transaction file and the master file have matching sort orders. Consider first the case of only one transaction record per master file record. A flowchart of the logic is given in Fig. 11–12. We use TRANS-KEY, OLD-MSTR-KEY, and NEW-MSTR-KEY to refer to the key fields of records on the transaction file, old master file, and new master file, respectively. The meat of the logic is comparing the next TRANS-KEY and the next OLD-MSTR-KEY. There are three possible cases. (1) The TRANS-KEY is lower. There can be no old master record that matches this transaction record. The transaction must be either an insertion or an error. Once the transaction is processed, another must be read from the transaction file to be matched with the pending old master record. (2) The TRANS-KEY is greater. There can be no transaction record that matches this old master record. The old master record must be copied directly to the new master file. Another record must be read from the old master file to be matched with the pending transaction. (3) The keys match. If the transaction is a MODIFY, the changes are made and a record is written on the new master. If the transaction is a DELETE, the old master record is ignored. Other transaction types are errors. In any case, the next transaction record must be read. If there was not an error (that is, if the old master record was processed), then a record must also be read from the old master file. It is likely that one file will be exhausted before the other; the records from the remaining one must be processed.

The logic is somewhat more complex when multiple transactions can affect a single old master record. In this case, a break in TRANS-KEY must occur (to indicate that all transactions for a given old master record have been handled) before writing (or not writing) the modified record to the new master file. With multiple transactions, it is usually important to apply them in the order in which they appear in the transaction file. However,

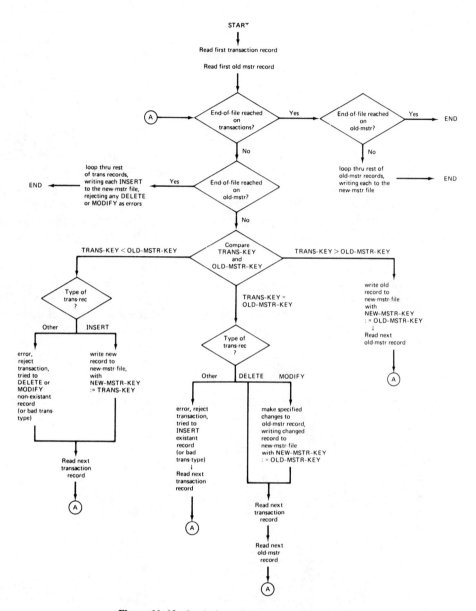

Figure 11–12 Logic for updating sequential master file.

in some applications, the programmer needs to table all the transactions with a given TRANS-KEY value, then apply them according to some rules of precedence established by the application, even though the transactions may have been entered in some other sequence. We leave specification of the multiple-transaction update logic as an interesting exercise.

PERFORMANCE OF SEQUENTIAL FILES

The performance of a sequential file is determined by three major factors: blocking factor, file length, and key selection.

Blocking Factor

In this chapter we have already discussed the importance of the blocking factor on the performance of a sequential file stored on tape. In fact, blocking factor is typically the single most important factor influencing sequential file performance.

When a sequential file is stored on a serial-access storage device, it is generally desirable to make the blocks as large as possible. The limiting factors become main memory buffer space availability, operating system parameters (which may limit block size), and the local charging algorithm (which trades off main memory use and secondary storage accesses).

When a sequential file is stored on a direct-access storage device, it is generally desirable to make the block size as close as possible to the sector size (if sector addressing is used) or to the track size (if cylinder-track addressing is used), since an entire sector or track will be passed over to access anything on that sector or track anyway. Sector and track layout on direct-access storage will be discussed in Chapter 13.

File Length

File length is determined by data volumes and record design, which is the problem of determining which fields are in which records in which files.

One guideline is to segment fields into records according to how frequently they are accessed together. For example consider an application that needs a file of employee personnel information. Some information about employees may be used more frequently than other information about the same employees. If so, it may be advantageous to split the employee data into two record types and to place them in separate files. For example, a primary employee personnel file might contain records of the format shown in Fig. 11–13.

EMPNO	DEPT	JOBCODE	PROJECT	HEALTH PLAN	COVERAGE CODE	INS. PLAN	HIRE DATE

Figure 11–13   Example record layout.

A secondary employee personnel file might contain records of the format shown in Fig. 11–14.

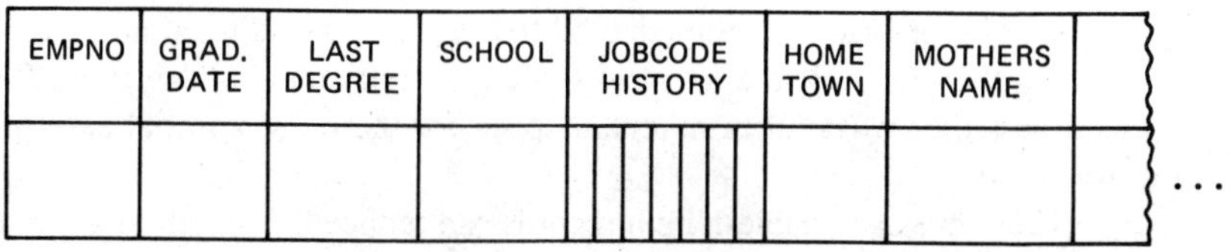

EMPNO	GRAD. DATE	LAST DEGREE	SCHOOL	JOBCODE HISTORY	HOME TOWN	MOTHERS NAME	

Figure 11-14   A second example record layout.

Splitting the employee data into an active file and a relatively inactive file reduces the size of the active file and therefore reduces processing time on that file. The split does complicate processing procedures, however, since it must be possible to recognize when there is activity on the relatively inactive file.

Sometimes a sequential file is split into an active file and an inactive file by record occurrences rather than by field types. For example, an organization might have one file of mailing label information for its frequent customers and another file of the same type of information for customers who are contacted semiannually instead of weekly. Again, the activity ratio is a reasonable indicator of how active a file is.

Records can be fixed length, in which case all records have the same length, or they can be variable length, in which case some records are longer than others. Consider, for example, the following student record, declared in COBOL.

```
                  01   STUDENT.
                       02   MATRIC-NO          PIC 9(5).
                       02   NAME.
                            03   LAST           PIC X(10).
                            03   INIT1          PIC X.
      assume                03   INIT2          PIC X.
       104           02   ADDRESS.
     characters            03   STREET         PIC X(25).
                            03   CITY           PIC X(10).
                            03   STATE          PIC X(2).
                            03   ZIP            PIC 9(5).
                       . . .
                       02   NO-OF-COURSES      PIC 9(2).
                       02   COURSE OCCURS 0 TO 50 TIMES
                                 DEPENDING ON NO-OF-COURSES.
                            03   DEPT           PIC X(4).
       each                03   ID             PIC X(4).
        17                 03   SEQUENCE-NO    PIC 9(5).
     characters            03   SEMESTER       PIC 9.
                            03   YR             PIC 9(2).
                            03   GRADE          PIC X.
```

This record type has minimum size of 104 characters and maximum size of 954 (104 + 50 * 17) characters. If the average student record contains data for 15 courses, then it would be rather wasteful to maintain space for the more unusual case of 50 courses for every student.

Thus, use of variable-length records can reduce the length of a file, making it faster to access. Some compilers, however, do not support variable-length records. Variable-length records are stored with some control information that specifies the length of each individual record. This control information generally appears in a system-used field that precedes each record on the file. The programmer cannot access the control field but needs to account for its presence when specifying record lengths (but not in the record descriptions).

Selecting the Key

The key of a sequential file determines the order in which its records are accessed.

The appropriate field(s) to form the key of a sequential file are determined by the application requirements. If the file is a transaction file, then it should have the same key as does the master file that it updates. If the file is a report file, then the ordering of records is determined by the desired form of the output. If the file is a master file, the key usually is some obvious identifier. If the wrong fields are chosen as the key, excessive searching, rewinding, and rereading may be necessary. If a sequential file is not sorted on a particular field, records will simply appear in the order they were written.

SUMMARY

A sequentially organized file is a collection of logically related records whose access sequence is determined by their ordering. The records must be written consecutively when the file is created, and they must be read consecutively when the file is later used for input. A sequential file operates in the same way as does a large queue: the first physical record is the first record written. Because the records must be accessed consecutively, sequentially organized files are used more commonly in batch processing than in interactive processing. The major advantage of sequential organization is the ability to quickly access the "next" record.

A sequentially organized file may be stored on either a serial-access or a direct-access storage medium. Some aspects of the declaration of a file appear in programs; other aspects are specified external to programs. The basic concepts required for declaring sequential files in COBOL and Pascal were covered and illustrated with examples.

The fundamental process of creating a sequential file was discussed and illustrated. The differences between creating transaction files, master files, and report files were introduced. Some programming languages, such as COBOL, have special features for defining and creating report files.

Retrieval from a sequential file is usually high-volume report generation but sometimes can be the result of low-volume inquiry. Examples of statements used to retrieve from sequential files in COBOL and Pascal programs were given. The concept of hit ratio was introduced.

The process of updating a sequential master file is important. The frequency at which a master file should be updated depends on several factors, including volatility of the data, size of the file, urgency of need for current data, and the file activity ratio. The concept of generation files was introduced, and absolute and relative generation numbers were discussed. The basic kinds of updates to a master file are insertion of new records, deletion of old records, and modification of existing records. The logic required to apply these updates was introduced.

The fundamental determinants of sequential file performance are blocking factor, file length (affected by record design), and key designation. Sequentially organized files have been used for a great many years; they are simple and can be stored on inexpensive media. They are very suitable for applications that require only sequential access to the contained data. They are not suitable for applications that require direct access to only particular records of the collection. They do not provide adequate support for interactive applications. Nonetheless, they will continue to be important.

TERMS

access mechanism
block
blocking factor
buffer
channel
direct-access storage device
disk drive
diskette
end-of-tape mark
even parity
external label
file activity ratio
floppy disk
generation file
hit ratio
interblock gap
internal label
labeled tape
load point

magnetic disk storage
magnetic tape storage
main memory
nonvolatile storage
odd parity
parity
physical record
primary storage
secondary storage
sector
sequential file organization
serial-access device
sorted file
sort key
spooling
storage medium
tape drive
track

SELECTED REFERENCES

DWYER, B. "One more time: how to update a master file," *Comm. ACM*, 24(1): 3–8, Jan. 1981.

GAUSS, E. J. "Built-in checklist reduces file destruction," *Comm. ACM*, 24(2): 73, Feb. 1981.

INGLIS, J. "Updating a master file: yet one more time," *Comm. ACM*, 24(5): 299, May 1981.

LEVY, M. R. "Modularity and the sequential file update problem," *Comm. ACM*, 25(6): 362–367, June 1982.

MARCH, S. T. and D. G. SEVERANCE. "The determination of efficient record segmentations and blocking factors for shared data files," *ACM Trans. on Database Systems*, 2(3): 279–296, Sept. 1977.

MENDELSON, H., J. S. PLISKIN, and U. YECHIALI. "Optimal storage allocation for serial files," *Comm. ACM*, 22(3): 124–130, Feb. 1979.

PECHURA, M. "File archival techniques using data compression," *Comm. ACM*, 25(9): 605–609, Sept. 1982.

SCHNEIDERMAN, B. and V. GOODMAN. "Batched searching of sequential and tree structured files," *ACM Trans. on Database Systems*, 1(3): 268–275, Sept. 1976.

SMITH, A. J. "Long term file migration: development and evaluation of algorithms," *Comm. ACM*, 24(8): 521–532, Aug. 1981.

WILLARD, D. E. "Good worst-case algorithms for inserting and deleting records in dense sequential files," *Proc. ACM-SIGMOD 1986 Internat. Conf. on Management of Data, May 28–30, 1986*, Washington DC, *SIGMOD Record*, 15(2): 251–260, June 1986.

REVIEW EXERCISES

1. Figs. 11–6 and 11–7 show a sort following the edit program. Why might this be preferable to sorting before editing?

2. An installation has two tape drives and one disk drive. An application program requires access to three sequential files: an old master file, a transaction file, and an updated master file. Which file should be stored on the disk?

3. Consider a miniscule master file containing 10 records. Assume that the following batch of transactions is to be processed:

Rec-Id	Trans-Type
111	2
111	1
96	3
400	1
96	1
111	2
400	3
342	3
96	2

What is the file activity ratio for this batch of transactions?

4. What factors should be considered when deciding how frequently a sequential master file should be updated?

5. What factors should be considered in determining how many generations of a file should be retained?

6. What kinds of information can a COBOL programmer declare about a file?

7. Describe a process for updating a sequential master file from a sequential file of transactions, where the two files do not have matching sort orders.

8. What is the typical retention period for sequential master files at your installation? How many generations of a sequential master file are retained?

9. Find out who designs record layouts for files at your installation. Determine whether or not any formal design guidelines are used in the design process.

10. Find out whether your installation has any files that are split into active and inactive portions. What is the criterion used for deciding when a record occurrence is inactive? How is a record from the inactive file reactivated?

11. Write a program to create a sequential file.

12. Write a program to print or display the contents of a sequential file.

13. Write a program to update a sequential file, creating a new version of the file. Accommodate record insertions, deletions, and modifications. Assume that there will be a maximum of one transaction applied to a master file record.

14. Do exercise 13 with the assumption that there may be up to five transactions per master file record. These transactions are to be processed in the order in which they are received.

15. Do exercise 13 with the assumption that there may be up to five transactions per master file record. Assume there are three types of modify transactions. Type 1 must be applied before type 2, which must be applied before type 3. *Do not assume* that transactions are always sorted by type.

16. Write the basic logic for report generation when two records are combined to form each detail line.

17. Write the basic logic for report generation when there are no detail lines but only summary (foot) lines.

18. Write the basic logic for a master file update in which multiple transaction records can affect a single old master record. Be sure to consider all possible conditions.

19. Consider a short section of tape that contains the following codes:

track 1:	1	1	1	1	1	1
	1	1	1	1	1	1
	0	0	0	0	1	1
.	1	0	1	0	0	0
.	0	0	1	1	0	1
.	1	0	0	0	0	0
	1	0	0	0	1	0
track 8:	1	1	1	1	1	0

What does track 9 contain if the data are recorded using (a) even parity, (b) odd parity?

20. Why does a computer installation nearly always have a variety of storage devices available?

21. Consider a magnetic tape with 1600 bpi and 0.6 inch interblock gaps. Assume that 80-byte records are to be stored on a 2400-foot tape. (a) How many records could be stored on the tape if a blocking factor of 5 records per block were used? (b) How many records could be stored on the tape if a blocking factor of 15 were used?

22. Assume that the transport speed for the tape of exercise 21 is 200 inch/sec when reading or writing and that it takes .004 seconds to start or stop the tape between blocks. (a) How long would it take to read the tape with a blocking factor of 5 records per block? (b) How long would it take to read the tape with a blocking factor of 15 records per block?

23. For what reasons might a collection of records be structured as a file on secondary storage rather than as a data structure in main memory?

24. Why do most computer systems support several file organization techniques?

25. What file organization techniques are supported by the various compilers available at your installation?

26. Who at your installation selects the type of organization that a file will have?

27. What, if any, general-purpose report-writer programs are available at your installation? What types of file organizations do the programs accommodate for their input files?

28. Obtain access to a system flowchart for a production system at your installation. Identify the master files, transaction files, report files, work files, and program files. Can you identify any additional types of files?

29. For several of the major programs of the system studied for question 28, identify the input files, output files, and input/output files. Complete the following table by filling in the names of files in each function-access mode classification. Are there any boxes with no entries? Which boxes would you expect to be empty and why?

	Input	Output	Input/Output
Master files			
Transaction files			
Report files			
Work files			

30. How much of a programmer's time in your installation is expended in activities related to each of the following: file creation, file update, file retrieval, and file maintenance?

chapter twelve

sorting and merging files

A common requirement of an information system is file sorting. Transaction files must be ordered for efficient updating of sequential master files; output data must be ordered to support proper formatting of sequential report files. Use of efficient sorting methods can be important to the overall performance of a computer installation and of an information system.

The sort methods that we discussed in Chapter 9 were internal sorting techniques. Each requires that the complete collection of items to be sorted resides simultaneously in main memory. These methods are inappropriate for sorting large collections of records. Thus a variety of *file sorting*, or *external sorting* techniques have been developed; these techniques are the subject of this chapter.

INTRODUCTION TO FILE SORTING AND MERGING

Consider a file of 2000 records that must be sorted, and assume that only 1000 of these records will fit in the main memory at once. One approach to the problem is to apply any internal sort method to sort separately two subsets of the file: records 1–1000 and records 1001–2000. (See Chapter 9 for a discussion of the relative performance characteristics of the better internal sorting methods.) The output from each internal sort is a

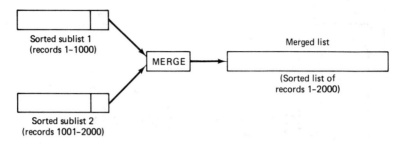

Figure 12–1   Natural merge of two sorted lists.

sequentially organized file containing the sorted sublist. The two sorted sublists then can be merged (Fig. 12–1). The merge involves pairwise comparison of the "next" record key in each of the two sorted sublists. Whichever record has the lower key value (for an ascending sort) is the next record to be written to the merged file.

Merge Logic

The basic logic for the merge is given in Fig. 12–2, which should be compared with Fig. 11–12, which is the basic logic for updating a sequential file. Key1, key2, and keyM are used to refer to the record keys on sublist 1, sublist 2, and the resultant merged list, respectively. This logic relies upon having the incoming sublists in sorted order by the key that guides the merge. Note that the incoming lists need not be the same length; when one list is depleted, the remainder of the other list is copied (in order) to the resultant merge file.

Phases

A file sort has three phases:

1. Internal sort phase, which sorts the records into several runs distributed on two or more storage devices.
2. Merge phase, which combines the sorted subfiles into a single run.
3. Output phase, which copies the sorted file onto its final storage medium.

Nearly all of the file sorting techniques operate in essentially this way. The collection of records to be sorted is divided into a number of sublists, each of which is sorted by application of an internal sort method. Each sorted sublist is written as a sequential file. These sorted files are then merged to form the final sorted file. Thus file sorting techniques commonly are called *sort/merges*.

The file sort/merge techniques differ from each other in the following ways:

1. The internal sort method applied.
2. The amount of main memory space allocated to the internal sort.

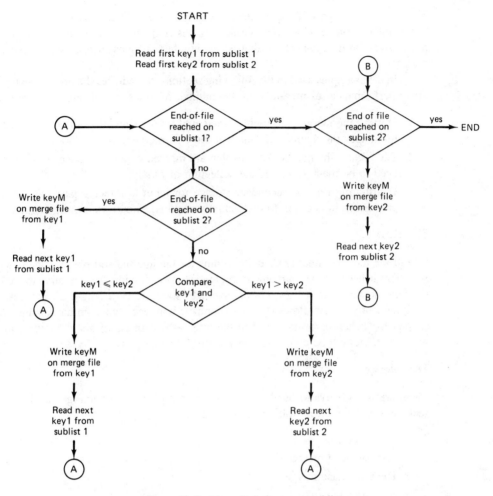

Figure 12–2 Merge logic for two sorted lists.

3. The distribution of sorted sublists on secondary storage.
4. The number of sorted sublists that are merged together in one merge pass.

Given a file to be sorted, these parameters then determine the number of sorted sublists generated by the internal sort phase and the number of merge passes.

Sort/Merge Performance

We evaluated internal sort methods in Chapter 9 by the number of comparisons each required to sort a collection of N keys. This is an inappropriate measure for the evaluation of file sort methods, because the CPU time required for key comparisons is negligible relative to the I/O time required to access secondary storage in reading and writing files.

Thus file sort/merge techniques are compared by their relative frequencies of reference to secondary storage. One good measure of this frequency of reference is the number of passes over the data collection, that is, the number of times each record is involved in a merge.

In the examples used in the following sections, we will see that the following factors affect performance, as measured by the number of times records are read/written.

1. Starting the merge phase with sorted subfiles (or *runs*) that are as long as possible minimizes the number of runs that must be merged.
2. The greater the number of runs that are merged together at once, the fewer passes need to be made to merge the collection of runs.
3. Distributing runs on secondary storage for input to a merge pass may require I/O processing in addition to that actually required in performing the merge.

The Sort

One of the most commonly used algorithms for the internal sort phase is the *tournament sort*. This is because the tournament sort tends to generate long runs relative to the amount of main memory that it uses. On the average, sorted runs of length $2P$ will result from a tournament sort that allows P keys to compete with each other. In the remainder of this chapter the actual algorithm used in the internal sort phase of a sort/merge will not be of interest; we will be concerned only with the merge phase.

The Merge

There are many ways to handle the merge phase of a file sort/merge. In the following sections we consider the following approaches:

- The natural merge
- The balanced merge
- The polyphase merge
- The cascade merge

NATURAL MERGES

A merge that handles two input files at once is called a two-way merge; a merge that handles M input files at once is called an M-way merge. M is referred to as the *degree* of the merge. An M-way *natural merge* is defined as a merge with M input files and just one output file.

Example

Consider the problem of sorting a file of 6000 records. Figures 12–3, 4, 5, and 6 illustrate several natural merges applied to this collection of data. The number of sorted runs input to the merge phase and the degrees of the merges are major factors determining the

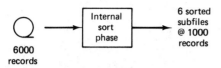

2-way merge: Assume 2 input files and 1 output file

(1) Distribute sorted runs onto 2 files (may be done in conjunction with internal sort phase)

(2) Merge pass 1:

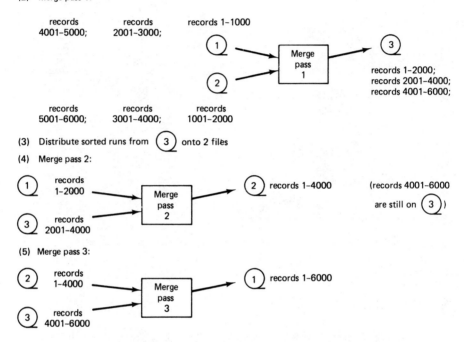

(3) Distribute sorted runs from ③ onto 2 files

(4) Merge pass 2:

(5) Merge pass 3:

Figure 12–3   2-way natural merge example.

performance of each sort/merge. The storage medium depicted in the figures is tape; actually it could be a direct-access storage device or any serial storage device. We use "tape" here generically as a device that stores sequentially organized files. Note that between merges, the sorted runs generated by the prior pass must be redistributed from the one output file onto the appropriate number (M) of input files for the next pass.

Performance

A natural sort/merge can require a significant amount of copying of data back and forth, causing high I/O activity. The greater the number of initial runs and the lower the degree of the natural merge, the greater are the resultant I/O requirements, and the slower the process is.

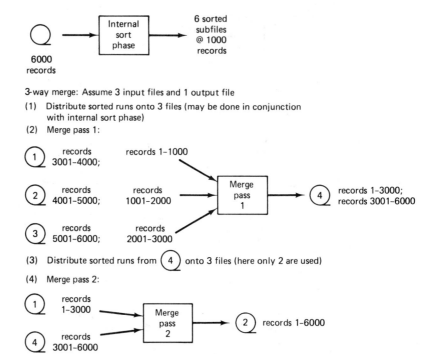

Figure 12-4   3-way natural merge example.

✗ BALANCED MERGES

Nearly half the I/O activity of a natural merge is devoted to redistributing newly merged runs output from one pass onto multiple files in preparation for input to the next pass. The I/O requirements of a natural merge can be reduced by using a *balanced merge*.

A balanced merge avoids much of this copying of records back and forth by distributing the results of a merge pass directly onto the appropriate number of files for input to the next merge pass. By contrast, a natural merge distributes all its output merge runs onto a single file. An M-way natural merge uses M+1 files, while an M-way balanced merge uses 2M files. In a balanced merge, the data are moved back and forth between an equal number of input and output files.

Example

Consider for example a computer installation with four tape drives. The output sequences from the internal sort phase could be written onto two tapes. By alternating tapes, approximately half of the sorted runs would appear on each tape. The remaining two tape drives would be used to receive the results of the first merge pass. Initially, one run from

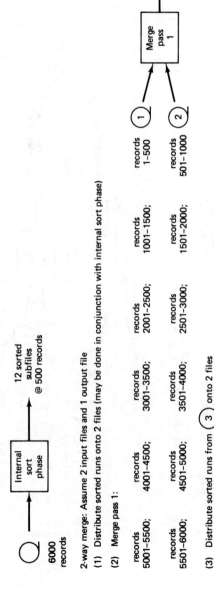

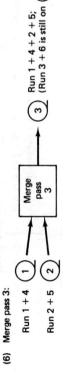

6000 records → Internal sort phase → 12 sorted subfiles @ 500 records

2-way merge: Assume 2 input files and 1 output file

(1) Distribute sorted runs onto 2 files (may be done in conjunction with internal sort phase)

(2) Merge pass 1:

records 5001–5500; records 4001–4500; records 3001–3500; records 2001–2500; records 1001–1500; records 1–1000; (Run 1)
records 5501–6000; records 4501–5000; records 3501–4000; records 2501–3000; records 1501–2000; records 1001–2000; (Run 2)
records 2001–3000; (Run 3)
records 3001–4000; (Run 4)
records 4001–5000; (Run 5)
records 5001–6000. (Run 6)

records 1–500 (1)
records 501–1000 (2)

Merge pass 1 → (3)

(3) Distribute sorted runs from (3) onto 2 files

(4) Merge pass 2:

Run 3; Run 2; Run 1 (1)
Run 6; Run 5; Run 4 (3)

Merge pass 2 →
Run 1 + 4; *
Run 2 + 5;
Run 3 + 6; (2)

*Note that "Run 1 + 4" denotes the result of merging (not concatenating) Runs 1 and 4.

(5) Distribute sorted runs from (2) onto 2 files

(6) Merge pass 3:

Run 1 + 4 (1)
Run 2 + 5 (2)

Merge pass 3 →
Run 1 + 4 + 2 + 5;
(Run 3 + 6 is still on (2)) (3)

(7) Merge pass 4:

Run 1 + 4 + 2 + 5 (3)
Run 3 + 6 (2)

Merge pass 4 →
Run 1 + 4 + 2 + 5 + 3 + 6 =
sorted file. (1)

Note that Record 1 is read and written 7 times

Figure 12–5 2-way natural merge example.

307

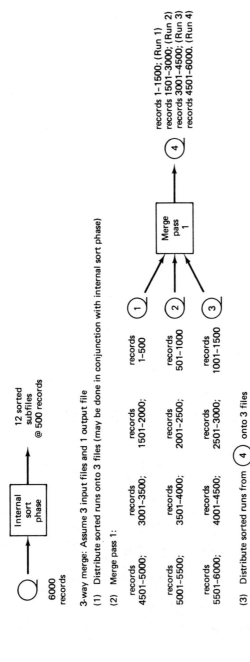

Figure 12-6 3-way natural merge example.

6000 records → Internal sort phase → 12 sorted subfiles @ 500 records

3-way merge: Assume 3 input files and 1 output file

(1) Distribute sorted runs onto 3 files (may be done in conjunction with internal sort phase)

(2) Merge pass 1:

records 4501–5000; records 3001–3500; records 1501–2000; records 1–500 (1)

records 5001–5500; records 3501–4000; records 2001–2500; records 501–1000 (2)

records 5501–6000; records 4001–4500; records 2501–3000; records 1001–1500 (3)

Merge pass 1

records 1–1500; (Run 1)
records 1501–3000; (Run 2)
records 3001–4500; (Run 3)
records 4501–6000. (Run 4)
(4)

(3) Distribute sorted runs from (4) onto 3 files

(4) Merge pass 2:

Run 1 (1)
Run 2 (2)
Run 3 (4)

Merge pass 2

Run 1 + 2 + 3 (3)
(Run 4 is still on (4))

(5) Merge pass 3:

Run 1 + 2 + 3 (3)
Run 4 (4)

Merge pass 3

Run 1 + 2 + 3 + 4 (1)
= sorted file

Note that Record 1 is read and written 5 times.

308

6000 records

Internal sort phase → 12 sorted subfiles @ 500 records

2-way balanced merge: Assume 4 files

(1) Distribute sorted runs onto 2 files (may be done in conjunction with internal sort phase)

(2) Merge pass 1:

records 5001-5500; records 4001-4500; records 3001-3500; records 2001-2500; records 1001-1500; records 1-500
records 5501-6000; records 4501-5000; records 3501-4000; records 2501-3000; records 1501-2000; records 501-1000

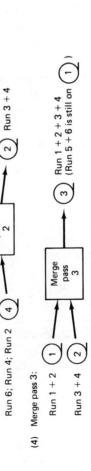

records 1-1000; (Run 1)
records 2001-3000; (Run 3)
records 4001-5000; (Run 5)

records 1001-2000; (Run 2)
records 3001-4000; (Run 4)
records 5001-6000. (Run 6)

(3) Merge pass 2:

Run 5; Run 3; Run 1
Run 6; Run 4; Run 2

Merge pass 2 →
① Run 1 + 2; Run 5 + 6
② Run 3 + 4

(4) Merge pass 3:

① Run 1 + 2
② Run 3 + 4

Merge pass 3 →
③ Run 1 + 2 + 3 + 4
(Run 5 + 6 is still on ①)

(5) Merge pass 4:

① Run 5 + 6
③ Run 1 + 2 + 3 + 4

Merge pass 4 →
② Run 1 + 2 + 3 + 4 + 5 + 6 = sorted file

Note that Record 1 is read and written 5 times.

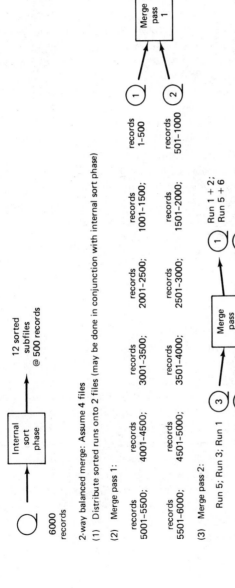

Figure 12-7 Example 2-way balanced merge.

each input tape is merged into a longer run and written on one output tape. The second run from each input tape then is merged into a longer run and written on the second output tape. The third runs are merged onto the first output tape, and so forth, alternating output tapes until the input tapes are exhausted. The two output tapes now become the input tapes for the second merge pass. (See Fig. 12–7.)

Performance

During each merge pass, the total number of runs is divided by the degree of the merge, while each run is lengthened by a factor equal to the degree of the merge. In Fig. 12–7 the number of runs output from each merge pass is half the number of runs input to the pass. Each output run is approximately twice as long as each input run. If the internal sort phase results in R sorted subfiles to be merged, then an M-way balanced merge will require $O(\log_M R)$ merge passes.

POLYPHASE MERGES

We have just seen that an M-way balanced merge uses $2M$ files. At any given time, runs are being read from M files and being written on one file. Thus $M - 1$ files are always idle. "Unbalancing" the merge can result in better file use. These unbalanced merges attempt to achieve a merge power greater than M by reading from more than M files at a time, using up to $2M - 1$ input files and a single output file.

One type of unbalanced merge is the *polyphase merge*, in which a constant number of input files is used. An M-way polyphase merge uses $2M - 1$ input files. (We will discuss another type of unbalanced merge in the next section.)

Example

The internal sort phase of an M-way polyphase merge must distribute its sorted runs onto $2M - 1$ files in a manner that facilitates the later merge. Let us assume that the internal sort phase results in 17 sorted runs. As shown in Fig. 12–8, these runs should be distributed (for a two-way polyphase merge) onto three files such that file 1 contains 7 runs, file 2 contains 6 runs, and file 3 contains 4 runs. This distribution was determined by the sequence shown in Table 12–1. First one run is written on each file. Then in cycle 2 the number of runs on file 1 is written on files 2 and 3. In cycle 3 the number of runs on file 2 is written on files 1 and 3. And in cycle 4 the number of runs on file 3 is written on files 1 and 2. If there were more runs, then the number of runs on file 1 would be written on files 2 and 3, and so forth through the successive cycles.

Each pass then merges the runs from the input files until *one* of the input files is empty; the others still contain runs. That empty input file becomes the output file for the next merge pass. This approach reduces the amount of copying of records, because the next merge pass is still working with runs that were on the input files to the last pass. In fact, in this example, run 1 on file 1 is not copied to output until merge pass 3. Note that

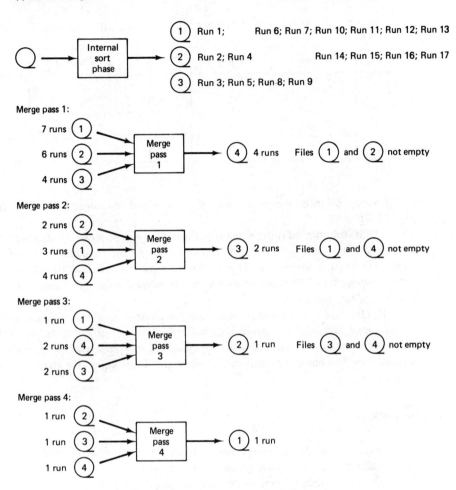

Figure 12–8 Example polyphase merge.

TABLE 12–1 DETERMINING RUN DISTRIBUTIONS FOR A POLYPHASE MERGE

runs/file

	Cycle 1	Cycle 2	Cycle 3	Cycle 4
file 1	1	1	3	7
2	1	2	2	6
3	1	2	4	4
Total	3	5	9	17

TABLE 12–2   RUN DISTRIBUTIONS DURING PASSES OF A POLYPHASE MERGE

	Start pass 1	End pass 1	End pass 2	End pass 3	End pass 4
File 1	7	3	1	0	1
2	6	2	0	1	0
3	4	0	2	1	0
4	0	4	2	1	0
Total	17	9	5	3	1

if this were a balanced merge, records of run 1 would have been copied five times (see Fig. 12–7).

The distribution of runs on the files during the merge passes is shown in Table 12–2. Compare this table with Table 12–1, which shows the sequence of distributing runs during the internal sort phase. The similarity is more than coincidental! Actually, our initial assumption of 17 sorted runs was not accidental either; 17 happens to be a good number for this situation.

Padding the data collection with dummy records may be necessary to obtain the proper initial layout. For a given data collection, it is nearly impossible to determine exactly how many runs will result from the internal sort phase without actually doing the internal sort. The number of runs can be estimated if one knows the characteristics of the internal sort.

CASCADE MERGES

Another type of unbalanced merge that attempts to reduce the copying of records is called the *cascade merge*. A cascade merge of degree M uses $2M - 1$, then $2M - 2$, then $2M - 3, \ldots$, then two input files during the various phases of a merge pass. Like a polyphase merge, a cascade merge relies on a clever initial distribution of the runs by the internal sort phase.

Each merge pass begins with a merge from $2M - 1$ input files to one output file. When the first input file is emptied, it becomes the output file and the prior output file is set aside. Now $2M - 2$ input files are merged onto the new output file. As an input file is emptied, it becomes the output file and the prior output file is retired temporarily. Eventually all input files will be emptied. At the end of the merge pass, each record has been processed once.

Then the next merge pass starts. $2M - 1$ inputs are merged, then $2M - 2$, and so forth until the cycles of merge phases have been completed.

Example

A cascade merge of degree 2 for 17 initial runs, distributed as they were in Fig. 12–8, is shown in Fig. 12–9. The cascade merge here achieves the same amount of run copying as did the polyphase merge, using the same number of files, but using a different method.

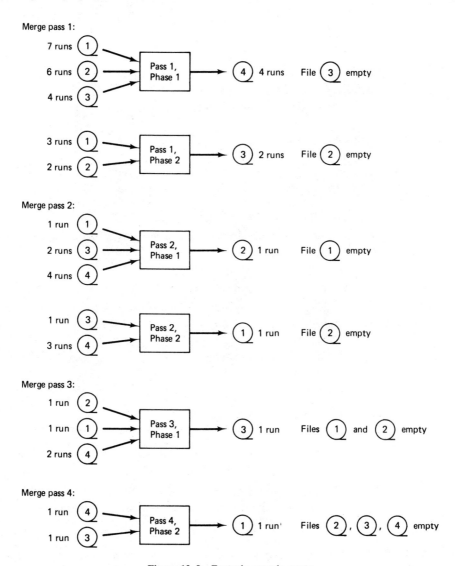

Figure 12–9 Example cascade merge.

SORTING/MERGING WITH UTILITIES

We have already stated that file sort/merging is a very common operation in information systems. Rather than reprogramming these sort/merges time after time, many installations make extensive use of acquired sort/merge packages (or utilities). The vendors of these packages are both independent software firms and hardware/software companies.

A sort/merge utility by definition provides general-purpose file sort/merge support.

The details of the utilities vary from vendor to vendor, but in general they appear to be quite similar. Their capabilities generally are three:

1. Sort (one or more files),
2. Merge (two or more sorted files),
3. Sort and merge (two or more files).

Specifying the Process

The user of the sort/merge package must supply various directives to guide the process. These directives include the following types of specifications:

1. Names of files to be sorted/merged.
2. Identifications, locations, lengths, and data types of fields to be used as the sort/merge key.
3. Ordering (major to minor) of key fields.
4. Sequencing (ascending or descending) to be applied to each key field.
5. Collating sequence to be applied to each key field. The collating sequence determines the ordering of characters. For example, does blank precede A? Does a precede A? Does 0 precede A?
6. Name of the output file to contain the results of the sort/merge.

Additionally, some packages allow the user to specify other parameters, such as

7. A user-defined collating sequence.
8. The algorithm to be used in the internal sort phase (e.g., tournament, heap).
9. The algorithm to be used in the merge phase (e.g., balanced, polyphase, cascade).
10. The action to be taken before/after using files (e.g., rewind, unload).
11. Verification that input records to the merge phase are actually in correct sequence.
12. Period to be used to checkpoint/dump records for recovery purposes.
13. Estimated number of input records.

As part of its output, a sort/merge utility usually lists the number of records that were input to the internal sort phase and the number of records that were written to the final output file. In most cases these figures should balance.

Example

For example, use of a hypothetical but representative sort/merge might require the following stream of job control commands.

```
/ / SORTNOW    EXEC    SORTMRG
/ / SORTIN     DD      DSN = name of input file, . . . ,
```

```
/ /                                        DISP = (OLD,KEEP)
/ / SORTOUT     DD          DSN = name of output file, . . . ,
/ /                                        DISP = (NEW,KEEP)
/ / SYSIN       DD              *
     SORT FIELDS = (1,4,CH,A,20,10,CH,D),FILEZ = E2000
/ *
```

Here the sort key is comprised of two fields: the major field starts in byte 1, for a length of 4 bytes, is character data, and is to be arranged in ascending order; the minor field starts in byte 20, for a length of 10 bytes, is character data, and is to be arranged in descending order. The input file contains an estimated 2000 records.

Another Example

The following commands give another example of use of a sort/merge utility.

```
SORTMRG(inputfilename,outputfilename)
. . .
SORT,VAR = POLY
FILE,INPUT = name(CU),OUTPUT = name(R)
FIELD,DEPT(1,4,ASCII6),SALEDATE(20,10,ASCII6)
KEY,DEPT(A,ASCII6),SALEDATE(D,ASCII6)
```

Here the merge phase is to be a polyphase merge; the input file is to be closed and unloaded (CU) when the sort terminates; the output file is to be rewound (R). The sort keys are DEPT (major) in positions 1–4, of type ASCII6, and SALEDATE (minor) in positions 20–29, also of type ASCII6. Records are to be sorted in ascending DEPT order and descending SALEDATE order.

Customizing the Process

Some sort/merge packages have the provision that a user may specify "own-code" or "sort exit" procedures that are to be executed in the context of the sort/merge activities. These procedures commonly are written in an assembler language and can be used to manipulate records at the following times:

1. After a record is read from the input file but before it enters the internal sort phase.
2. After a record leaves the internal sort phase but before it is written onto a file output from the internal sort phase.
3. When multiple records with matching values are encountered during the internal sort phase.
4. When multiple records with matching key values are encountered during the merge phase.

These procedures might eliminate records with certain characteristics (for example, DEPT-TYPE = 'ABOLISHED') from further consideration, or might select just one record when there are multiple records with matching key values, and so forth. In these cases the numbers of input and output records very well might not balance.

SORTING/MERGING IN COBOL PROGRAMS

Much file sorting/merging is conducted by use of utilities rather than through programming languages. However, COBOL does have a built-in feature that allows a sort/merge utility to be invoked from *within* a COBOL program.

The SORT verb creates a sorted file from one or more input files and has the following syntax.

$$\underline{\text{SORT}} \text{ filename-1} \left(\text{ON} \left\{ \begin{array}{l} \underline{\text{ASCENDING}} \\ \underline{\text{DESCENDING}} \end{array} \right\} \text{KEY dataname1[,dataname2]}. . . \right) . . .$$

[COLLATING SEQUENCE IS alphabet-name]

$$\left\{ \begin{array}{l} \underline{\text{INPUT PROCEDURE}} \text{ IS section-name-1} \left[\left\{ \begin{array}{l} \underline{\text{THROUGH}} \\ \underline{\text{THRU}} \end{array} \right\} \text{section-name-2} \right] \\ \underline{\text{USING}} \text{ [filename-2] . . .} \end{array} \right\}$$

$$\left\{ \begin{array}{l} \underline{\text{OUTPUT PROCEDURE}} \text{ IS section-name-3} \left[\left\{ \begin{array}{l} \underline{\text{THROUGH}} \\ \underline{\text{THRU}} \end{array} \right\} \text{section-name-4} \right] \\ \underline{\text{GIVING}} \text{ [filename-3]} \end{array} \right\}$$

The simplest form of the SORT verb for one input file is (for example)

```
        SORT SORTWORK ON ASCENDING KEY DEPT
                      ON DESCENDING KEY SALE-DATE
              USING INPUTFILENAME
              GIVING OUTPUTFILENAME.
```

SORTWORK here is a temporary file used during the sort/merge (Fig. 12–10). It must be declared in an SD entry (as opposed to FD entry) in the FILE SECTION of the DATA DIVISION. The input and output files must both be sequentially organized.

The INPUT PROCEDURE option allows the programmer to manipulate records prior to their release to the internal sort; the OUTPUT PROCEDURE option allows the programmer to manipulate records after their return from the sort but before they are

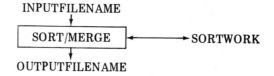

Figure 12–10   Files used in a COBOL sort.

written to the output file. These procedures are like the sort exits that were mentioned previously. Two examples of their use follow. Both procedures use the following DATA DIVISION:

```
DATA DIVISION.
FILE SECTION.
FD IN-FILE LABEL RECORD IS STANDARD.
01   IN-REC.
     02   IN-DEPT          PIC X(4).
     02   FILLER           PIC X(15).
     02   IN-SALE-DATE     PIC X(10).
     02   DEPT-TYPE        PIC X(9).
     02   FILLER           PIC X(500).
FD OUT-FILE LABEL RECORD IS STANDARD.
01   OUT-REC.
     02   OUT-DEPT         PIC X(4).
     02   FILLER           PIC X(15).
     02   OUT-SALE-DATE    PIC X(10).
     02   DEPT-TYPE        PIC X(9).
     02   FILLER           PIC X(500).
SD SORT-FILE.
01   SORT-REC.
     02   DEPT             PIC X(4).
     02   FILLER           PIC X(15).
     02   SALE-DATE        PIC X(10).
     02   DEPT-TYPE        PIC X(9).
     02   FILLER           PIC X(500).
```

The results of both examples are the same.

First Example

This one uses an INPUT PROCEDURE to eliminate records. Assume that a switch

```
01   EOF-IN-FILE-SW PIC X VALUE "N".
     88   EOF-IN-FILE VALUE "Y".
```

has been defined in WORKING-STORAGE.

```
PROCEDURE DIVISION.
MAIN-LINE SECTION.
     . . .
     SORT SORT-FILE ON ASCENDING KEY DEPT
                    ON DESCENDING KEY SALE-DATE
```

```
        INPUT PROCEDURE IS READ-IN-REC
        GIVING OUT-FILE.

        . . .
    READ-IN-REC SECTION.
    DRIVER.
        OPEN INPUT IN-FILE.
        READ IN-FILE AT END MOVE "Y" TO EOF-IN-FILE-SW.
        PERFORM READ-REC UNTIL EOF-IN-FILE.
        CLOSE IN-FILE.
        EXIT.
    READ-REC.
        IF DEPT-TYPE OF IN-REC NOT = "ABOLISHED"
        THEN MOVE IN-REC TO SORT-REC
            RELEASE SORT-REC.
        READ IN-FILE AT END MOVE "Y" TO EOF-IN-FILE.
```

Second Example

This next example uses an OUTPUT PROCEDURE to eliminate records. Assume that a switch

```
    01   EOF-SORT-FILE-SW      PIC X    VALUE "N".
         88   EOF-SORT-FILE    VALUE "Y".
```

has been defined in WORKING-STORAGE.

```
    PROCEDURE DIVISION.
    MAIN-LINE SECTION.

        . . .
        SORT SORT-FILE ON ASCENDING KEY DEPT
                        ON DESCENDING KEY SALE-DATE
        USING IN-FILE
        OUTPUT PROCEDURE IS WRITE-OUT-REC.

        . . .
    WRITE-OUT-REC SECTION.
    DRIVER.
        OPEN OUTPUT OUT-FILE.
        RETURN SORT-FILE RECORD
            AT END MOVE "Y" TO EOF-SORT-FILE-SW.
        PERFORM WRITE-REC UNTIL EOF-SORT-FILE.
        CLOSE OUT-FILE.
        EXIT.
```

WRITE-REC.
 IF DEPT-TYPE OF SORT-REC NOT = ''ABOLISHED''
 THEN MOVE SORT-REC TO OUT-REC
  WRITE OUT-REC.
 RETURN SORT-FILE RECORD
  AT END MOVE ''Y'' TO EOF-SORT-FILE-SW.

The first of these two examples would be the more efficient, since it reduces the number of records handled by the sort/merge.

Merging Sorted Files

The COBOL MERGE verb is used to merge already-sorted input files. The syntax is as follows.

$$\underline{\text{MERGE}}\text{ filename1}\left(\text{ON}\left\{\frac{\underline{\text{ASCENDING}}}{\underline{\text{DESCENDING}}}\right\}\text{KEY dataname1[,dataname2]}\ldots\right)\ldots$$

[COLLATING $\underline{\text{SEQUENCE}}$ IS alphabet-name]
$\underline{\text{USING}}$ filename2 [filename3] . . .

$$\left\{\begin{array}{l}\underline{\text{OUTPUT}}\text{ PROCEDURE IS sectionname1}\left[\left\{\frac{\underline{\text{THROUGH}}}{\underline{\text{THRU}}}\right\}\text{sectionname2}\right]\\ \underline{\text{GIVING}}\text{ filename-4}\end{array}\right\}$$

Note that no INPUT PROCEDURE can be specified and that at least two input files must be named.

SORT/MERGE PERFORMANCE

There are many factors that interact to determine how well a particular file sort/merge technique performs. With a given technique, performance is dependent upon

1. The number of records to be sorted/merged.
2. The size of the records.
3. The number of storage devices used.
4. The distribution of those devices on available I/O channels.
5. The distribution of key values in the input file(s).

In most cases it takes about as long to sort 100,000 records, each with 10 characters, as to sort 10,000 records, each with 100 characters. It is the total volume of data rather than the volume of records which tends to be the more important factor. The actual key field size is usually an inconsequential factor. In fact, it is usually preferable to sort records with their keys rather than to sort detached keys and then later have to access and rearrange the records.

A practical factor which has not really entered the discussion of this chapter until now is the importance of being able to recover from a sort that terminates early and abnormally, because of either I/O errors or other system problems. One important axiom is never to destroy the files input to a sort/merge until the entire process has been completed successfully.

In general, it is quite difficult to determine which merge pattern is the best one to use for a particular situation. The strategy employed in the initial allocation of sorted runs to files and the order in which they subsequently are merged also have significant impact on the performance of the file sort. In general, however, a natural merge performs worse than the other types of merges. A polyphase merge generally is better than a balanced merge when there are fewer than ten I/O-units available. A polyphase merge tends to be better than a cascade merge. There are other variations on "unbalanced" merging that perform better than the polyphase merge in particular situations, especially if there are more than ten I/O-units available.

SUMMARY

Nearly all techniques for file sorting use the following sequence of phases: (1) an internal sort phase that sorts the file into a number of sorted sublists (or runs) using an internal sort method; these runs are distributed to two or more files in some more or less clever manner; (2) a merge phase that combines the sorted runs into a single sorted run; and (3) an output phase that copies the sorted run to its final storage medium.

A tournament sort commonly is used for the internal sort phase because it tends to generate long runs relative to the amount of main memory that it uses.

There are many possible algorithms that can be used to implement the merge phase. An M-way natural merge uses M input files and one output file. Much of the consequent copying of records can be avoided by using a balanced merge. An M-way balanced merge uses M input files and M output files. At any given time, $M - 1$ of the output files are idle. Utilization can be improved by using an unbalanced merge, which attempts to achieve a merge power greater than M by reading from up to $2M - 1$ input files and using a single output file. An M-way polyphase merge uses a constant number of input files ($2M - 1$). By clever distribution of runs on those files, the output file can be recycled as an input file and the amount of record copying can be reduced significantly. A cascade merge of degree M uses $2M - 1$, then $2M - 2$, then $2M - 3$, . . . , then 2 input files through the various phases of a merge pass; the output files are not recycled into the merge.

Many vendors provide software that implements one or more sort/merge approaches. These packages, which fall into the category of utilities, can be invoked either by job control commands or from within COBOL programs by use of the SORT and MERGE verbs. The user supplies descriptions of the input and output files and of the keys to guide the sort/merge.

The most popular sort/merge technique is probably the polyphase merge used in conjunction with an internal tournament sort. For a particular situation, however, another technique may give better performance.

TERMS

balanced merge	merge degree
cascade merge	merge phase
collating sequence	natural merge
external sort	polyphase merge
file sort	run
internal sort phase	sort/merge
merge	tournament sort

SELECTED REFERENCES

BITTON, D., D. J. DeWITT, D. K. HSAIO, AND J. MENON. "A taxonomy of parallel sorting," *ACM Computing Surveys*, 16(3): 297–318, Sept. 1984.

BITTON, D. AND D. J. DeWITT. "Duplicate record elimination in large data files," *ACM Trans. on Database Systems*, 8(2): 255–265, June 1983.

BROWN, M. R. AND R. E. TARJAN. "A fast merging algorithm," *Jour. ACM*, 26(2): 211–226, April 1979.

EVEN, S. "Parallelism in tape-sorting," *Comm. ACM*, 17(4): 202–204, April 1974.

HOLLAAR, L. A. "Specialized merge processor networks for combining sorted lists," *ACM Trans. on Database Systems*, 3(3): 272–284, Sept. 1978.

HWANG, F. K. AND D. N. DEUTSCH. "A class of merging algorithms," *Jour. ACM*, 20(1): 148–159, Jan. 1973.

KNUTH, D. E. "External Sorting," chapter 4 in *The Art of Computer Porgramming, Vol. 3, Sorting and Searching*. Reading, MA: Addison-Wesley, 1973.

LORIN, H. *Sorting and Sort Systems*. Reading, MA: Addison-Wesley, 1975.

MANACHER, G. K. "Significant improvements to the Hwang-Lin merging algorithm," *Jour. ACM*, 26(3): 434–440, July 1979.

PALVIA, P. "Expressions for batched searching of sequential and hierarchical files," *ACM Trans. on Database Systems*, 10(1): 97–106, March 1985.

PIWOWARSKI, M. "Comments on batched searching of sequential and tree-structured files," *ACM Trans. on Database Systems*, 10(2): 285–287, June 1985.

RADKE, C. E. "Merge-sort analysis by matrix techniques," *IBM System Jour.*, 5(4): 226–247, 1966.

REVIEW EXERCISES

1. Why is a tournament sort usually a good sort to use for the internal sort phase of a file sort?

2. Why is the performance of an external sort usually evaluated by number of copies rather than by number of comparisons?

3. What kind of merge is used in the sort/merge utility available at your installation?

4. What kind of sort is used in the internal sort phase of the sort/merge utility available at your installation?

5. Compare the operation and performance of a balanced merge and an unbalanced merge.

6. Compare the operation and performance of a polyphase merge and a cascade merge.

7. Obtain a file of unsorted data. Sort the file in various ways, e.g., using the COBOL SORT verb, and using each of the merge-type options available in your local sort/merge utility. Compare the performance of the several methods.

8. Obtain a file of unsorted data. Sort the file in various ways, with each method allowing you either to extract or combine some records in addition to sorting the file—for example, using an INPUT PROCEDURE with the COBOL SORT verb, using an OUTPUT PROCEDURE with the COBOL SORT verb, and using data manipulation capabilities of the sort/merge utility. Compare the performance of the several methods.

chapter thirteen

relative file
organization

In this chapter we introduce another fundamental approach to organizing files: relative organization. The organization method is first defined, then its applicability in information systems is discussed. Many techniques have been developed for implementing the concept of relative file organization, and some of the commonly applied methods are covered here. We then discuss the declaration and use of relative files in programs, including creation of relative files, retrieval from relative files, and update of relative files. The chapter closes with a review of some of the factors that should be considered in the design of a file with relative organization.

DEFINITIONS

An effective way to organize a file when there is a need to access individual records directly is *relative organization*. In a relative file, there is a predictable relationship between the key used to identify a particular record and that record's location in the file. However, it is important to understand that the logical *ordering* of records need bear no relationship to their physical sequencing (Fig. 13–1). The records *do not* necessarily appear physically in sorted order by their key values.

How then is the Nth record found? When a relative file is established, the relationship

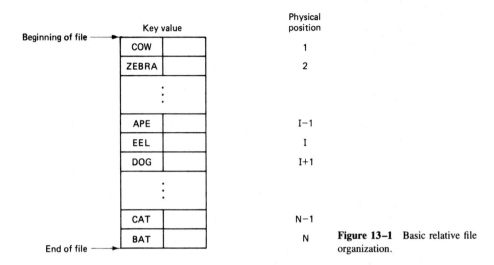

Figure 13–1   Basic relative file organization.

that will be used to translate between key values and physical addresses is designated. This relationship, call it R, is a mapping function

$$R \text{ (key value)} \longrightarrow \text{address}$$

from key values to addresses in the file.

Processing

When a record is to be written into a relative file, the mapping function R is used to translate the record's key value to an address, which indicates where the record is to be stored. When it is necessary to retrieve the record with a particular key value, the mapping function R is applied to that key value, translating it to the address where the record can be found. Thus the predictable relationship between record key values and record storage locations is used both when a record is stored and when it is retrieved.

Note that, in contrast to sequentially organized files, it is not necessary to access the records of a relative file in serial order. Rather, a particular record occurrence can be accessed directly. The direct-access character of relative file organization could not be taken advantage of if a relative file were stored on a serial-access medium such as magnetic tape. Therefore relative files are stored in main memory or on direct-access storage devices (DASD), such as magnetic disks.

It *is* possible to access the records of a relative file in physically consecutive order. However, it should be understood that the keys may not be in logical sequence. For example, serial access to the file depicted in Fig. 13–1 retrieves records in the order:

COW, ZEBRA, . . . , APE, EEL, DOG, . . . ,CAT, BAT.

A relative file might be accessed serially when input to a file sort/merge. Or, a relative file of customer records might be accessed serially by a program that generates a mailing label for each customer but that does not care about the order in which those mailing labels are generated.

Example

Because they can support rapid access directly to particular records, relative files are used commonly in interactive processing. For example, consider an on-line banking system in which tellers have terminals and direct access to customer account data. A simple master file might have records of the format shown in Fig. 13–2(a).

CUSTOMER–ACCOUNT

ACCOUNT NUMBER	ACCOUNT TYPE	BALANCE	DATE-LAST –CREDIT	DATE-LAST –DEBIT

Figure 13–2(a)   Example master file format.

Assume that the CUSTOMER-ACCOUNT file is a relative file, with key ACCOUNT-NUMBER. Teller inputs might be formatted into transactions with the format shown in Fig. 13–2(b).

TRANSACTION

ACCOUNT NUMBER	TRANS –TYPE	AMOUNT	DATE

Figure 13–2(b)   Example transaction file format.

When a teller keys in a transaction, the specified ACCOUNT-NUMBER would be used to determine the location of the corresponding CUSTOMER-ACCOUNT record. That record would be read and made available to the on-line transaction-processing program. If the TRANS-TYPE = 'I', the account's balance would be displayed to the teller. If the TRANS-TYPE = 'C' or 'D', the CUSTOMER-ACCOUNT record would be modified according to the AMOUNT and DATE information contained on the transaction, and the CUSTOMER-ACCOUNT record would be rewritten to the relative file, with the AC-COUNT-NUMBER again used to determine the record's location on that file.

First, note that it is not necessary to access master file records other than the target record. Compare this with the processing situation of a sequential master file! Second, note that records of the relative master file can be updated in place. Compare this with the way that a sequential master file is updated, by recreating the entire file.

Advantages and Disadvantages

Thus the major advantage of a relative file is the ability to access individual records directly. A record can be retrieved, inserted, modified, or even deleted without affecting the other records on the file. (Actually this last statement is a bit of a generalization. We will see later that the insertion or deletion of a record may affect other records, but the effects are slight and quite localized.)

Before considering relative file concepts in detail, I shall discuss direct-access storage devices and the characteristics that make them suitable for relative files.

MAGNETIC DISK STORAGE

The first direct-access storage device, the magnetic drum, was developed in the mid-1950s as a means to increase a computer's memory capacity and to provide direct-access capability to that capacity. Although magnetic tapes had been used for computer data storage for only a few years, the limitations of that serial-access device were readily apparent.

The RAMAC (*Random Access*) was the first direct-access storage device made available to the computer industry. This magnetic disk unit, developed by International Business Machines, Inc., was physically much larger than today's devices. It stood several feet tall and had fifty fixed disk platters, each about two feet in diameter. Like today's magnetic disks, the platters rotated at a high rate of speed on a spindle. Access arms with read/write heads were positioned between the platters and performed retrieval and storage of data representations on the surfaces of the platters. Data were recorded in concentric tracks, much as they are today. The RAMAC's capacity was about 5 million characters.

Continuous development since the RAMAC's appearance in 1955 has resulted in much faster, higher capacity, smaller magnetic disk devices. The ones available today come in a wide range of configurations that offer a choice of performance, capacity, and price to match the needs of various computer systems. Disks differ with respect to their number of recording surfaces, data transfer rates, read/write head movement times, access mechanism technologies, rotational delays, densities, and other features. We will describe here representative examples of the most commonly used devices. Development in technologies will continue to produce improved devices.

Physical Characteristics of Magnetic Disks

The typical magnetic disk storage device is a *disk pack* composed of several stacked, rigid aluminum platters mounted on a spindle. Commonly there are eleven platters in a pack. Each platter is 14 inches in diameter (8 inches in mini-disks) and resembles a phonograph record; its suface is coated with a metal-oxide film that retains magnetization in much the same way that the film on a magnetic tape does. In contrast to the way information is recorded on a phonograph record, data are recorded on a disk platter in concentric *tracks* rather than in a spiral groove. The number of tracks on a platter is determined by the recording characteristics of the surface coating and the capabilities of the disk drive and access mechanism. Today's disks have from 200 to 800 tracks per surface. (The number of tracks on a platter is fixed.) There are twenty recording surfaces in a disk pack of eleven platters; both sides of each platter are used except for the topmost and bottommost surfaces, which are more susceptible to contamination than are the inside surfaces. Also the arms for those outside surfaces would access only half as much data.

For access, a disk pack is mounted on a disk drive, which includes a controller, access arms, read/write heads, and a mechanism for rotating the pack. Some drives are manufactured with built-in disk packs, which are *nonremovable*. A drive that can support any number of disks (one at a time) uses *removable* disk packs. Disk drives are commonly combined in banks of two, six, or eight, sometimes with an additional spare drive; the combination of drives is referred to as a *unit*.

A *disk controller* handles decoding of record addresses, including selection of the appropriate drive of a unit and decoding of the position of the requested data on the disk pack of that drive. The controller also manages buffer storage for the unit, handles error detection and correction, and controls read/write activities.

The platters of a mounted disk pack spin continuously at a speed of about 3600 revolutions per minute. Unlike magnetic tape devices, a rotating disk device does not stop between block accesses.

The read/write heads of the disk drive are mounted on access arms that are positioned between the platters of the device. The heads float on a cushion of air less than 1-millionth of an inch above the surface of the platter. The unfortunate case of having a read/write head actually come into contact with a platter surface is called a *head crash*. Such contact can damage the head and the recording surface rather severely and take the disk out of commission.

Data Representation and Addressing

The data on a disk are blocked in the same way as are the data on a magnetic tape. Recall that a block is the amount of data that is accessed in one request to the storage device. As was discussed for tape storage, data from a disk device are moved to a buffer in the main storage of the computer for access by a program. The selection of the proper block size for a disk file is somewhat more difficult than for a tape file. The direct-access capability of the disk device implies that records will not always be accessed sequentially. Increasing the block size will not always reduce the number of accesses to the DASD.

There are two basic techniques for addressing the data records that are stored on a disk: the cylinder method and the sector method. With the *cylinder method*, a record's address is its cylinder number, surface number, and record number. All the tracks of a given diameter on the disk pack form a cylinder (see Fig. 13–3). Thus a disk pack with 200 tracks per surface has 200 cylinders. The surface number part of a record's address determines on which surface of the cylinder the record is stored. If there are eleven platters, then the surface numbers range from 0 to 19 (or 1 to 20). The record number part of an

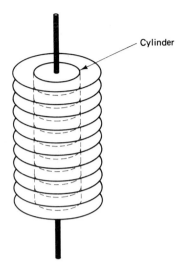

Cylinder

Figure 13-3 Disk pack cylinders.

address determines where the record resides on the particular track designated by the cylinder number, surface number. An index point can be sensed by the disk access mechanism at the start of each track.

With the *sector method*, each track of the pack is divided into sectors, as illustrated in Fig. 13-4. Each sector is a storage area for a fixed number of characters. A record's address is simply its sector number. Given a sector number, the disk controller can determine which track should be accessed and where on the track the addressed record resides.

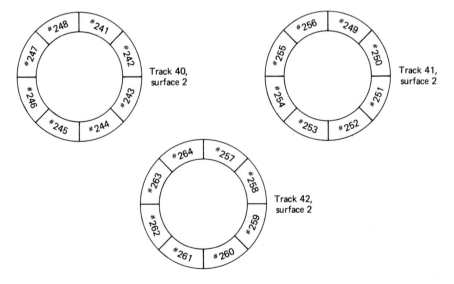

Figure 13-4 Example of sector addressing.

Each track on a platter has the same recording capacity, even though the tracks are of different diameters. The uniformity of capacity is achieved by appropriate adjustment of the density of data representation for each track's dimensions. A major benefit of this uniform-capacity approach is that files can be relocated on the disk without changing the number of sectors (or tracks or cylinders) allocated to the file. Some operating systems allow the person who sets up a program's job control specifications to request the number of sectors (or tracks or cylinders) that are to be allocated to a file.

Movable-head Disk Access

There are several types of access mechanisms available today for magnetic disk storage devices. A *movable-head disk drive* has one read/write-head for each recording surface. A mechanical system is used to position the set of access arms such that the read/write head of the addressed surface is at the desired track. All of the access arms of the device move in unison, but only the head for the desired surface is activated. The head-positioning system requires a high degree of accuracy in order to locate the heads precisely over the closely spaced tracks. Environmental factors, including temperature variations and usage, can affect the accuracy of positioning; movable-head disk drives require periodic maintenance to keep the positioning servomechanisms within tolerance limits.

The following sequence of events must occur to access a record stored on a disk pack. The disk controller decodes the desired record's address and determines on which track of the device the record resides. The access arms are moved so that the read/write heads are positioned at the appropriate cylinder. The read/write head for the desired track is activated. The disk then must rotate until the desired record is located at the read/write head. The data then can be read and transferred across the channel to the requesting program in the computer.

This sequence of events has the following time components:

$$\text{ACCESS TIME} = \text{SEEK TIME (move arms to cylinder)}$$
$$+ \text{HEAD-ACTIVATION TIME (select track)}$$
$$+ \text{ROTATIONAL DELAY (select record)}$$
$$+ \text{TRANSFER TIME.}$$

Of these factors, *seek time* is the most significant because it involves the mechanical movement of the access arms. A typical disk drive requires an average of 25 milliseconds to seek the desired cylinder. By contrast, head-activation time is essentially zero, since it is an electrical function. *Rotational delay* (sometimes called *latency*) times are determined by the revolution speed of the disk platters. At 3600 revolutions per minute, the worst case rotational delay is 16.6 milliseconds, when the desired record has just been passed over (Fig. 13–5(a)). The best case is when the read/write head is correctly positioned at the start. In the average case, rotational delay is 8.3 milliseconds (Fig. 13–5(b)). Transfer time is determined by the speed of revolution and the amount of data to be transferred. A typical data transfer rate is 1000 kilobytes per second.

If records of a file stored on disk are to be accessed sequentially, then access times

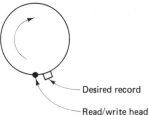

Figure 13–5(a) Worst case read situation.

Figure 13–5(b) Average case read situation.

can be minimized by properly allocating disk space to the file. Assume the file requires ten tracks of space. Rather than allocating ten tracks on one surface to the file, space should be allocated to tracks of one cylinder, thereby minimizing the arm movement required to access the records.

Actually, minimizing seek time can be very difficult in a multi-user environment in which different users' accesses to the same disk can be interleaved. Also difficult to optimize are the usual cases in which the direct-access capabilities of the disk are used. It may be impossible to predict the order of access to records.

Fixed-head Disk Access

A *fixed-head disk drive* sharply reduces access times by virtually eliminating the major delay component of movable-head systems: seek time. A fixed-head disk drive has one read/write head for each track of each recording surface. The time components of access time then reduce to

$$\text{ACCESS TIME} = \text{HEAD-ACTIVATION TIME}$$
$$+ \text{ROTATIONAL DELAY}$$
$$+ \text{TRANSFER TIME.}$$

In addition to the advantage of reduced access times, the mechanical simplicity of the fixed-head approach results in enhanced reliability over the movable-head approach. The mean time between failures is typically 1000 hours for a movable-head disk drive and 10,000 hours for a fixed-head disk drive. Fixed-head disk drives also tend to be easier to repair. The basic causes of disk failures are mechanical problems including head crashes, electronic malfunctions, and errors due to surface contamination.

The costs of the fixed-head approach are increased price and decreased capacity. The number of read/write heads causes the price of a fixed-head disk drive to exceed that of a movable-head disk drive. A drive to access disks with 200 tracks per surface has 200 times as many heads if the heads are fixed rather than movable. Disks for use with fixed-head drives tend to have slightly lower capacities than do disks for use with movable-head drives; they also have lower densities because of head spacing requirements.

Head-per-track Drives and Winchester Disks

One variation on the fixed-head disk drive is the *parallel head-per-track drive*, which can activate more than one head at the same time. Thus data can be read from multiple tracks in parallel. This type of device requires a controller that expects parallel streams of data. These drives are not used widely today, but they may come into greater use with the database machines of the 1990s.

Another variation on the direct-access storage devices we have introduced is the *Winchester disk*, supposedly named after Winchester Boulevard, Silicon Valley site of an early IBM facility. The recording surfaces, access mechanism, and read/write heads of a Winchester disk are manufactured together in a sealed cartridge, which can be either removable (i.e., multiple packs can be used on a single drive) or nonremovable (i.e., it is manufactured as an integral part of the disk drive). These devices provide for very high storage densities. For example, the IBM 3350 records more than 3 million bits of data per square inch of disk surface. The increased densities result from the Winchester head configuration, which governs the flow of air around the head so that it floats very close to the disk surface.

A typical Winchester disk has an average seek time of 40 milliseconds, an average rotational delay of 8.3 milliseconds, and an 800 kilobyte per second data transfer rate.

The cost of direct-access storage has been decreasing steadily. Today, $1 can buy storage space for over 16,000 characters, whereas in 1964, $1 could buy storage space for about 300 characters. Each magnetic disk is substantially more expensive than is a magnetic tape, but each disk has much higher capacity, as well as direct-access capability. Much of the cost improvement in disk storage has been the result of technologies that have increased recording densities. One surface of a modern disk pack typically can store more data than could the entire RAMAC device with fifty 2-foot-diameter platters.

Flexible Disk Storage

One of the most important developments in DASD's has been flexible disk storage devices, now familiar as *floppy disks*, or just *floppies*, or *diskettes*. The floppy was introduced in 1970 as a storage medium for a large IBM magnetic disk storage system. The flexible disks are now widely used as direct access storage devices for microcomputers and minicomputers, as auxiliary memory for intelligent terminals, and as a storage medium for key-data entry devices.

The medium of a floppy disk is essentially the same as that of a magnetic tape: mylar coated with a magnetic oxide film. A floppy is thicker than magnetic tape and is cut as a disk. Diameters vary, but dimensions are typically $3\frac{1}{2}$ or $5\frac{1}{4}$ inches. The "typical" floppy has 77 concentric tracks, each with 26 sectors, each with a user-addressable space of 128 characters. A floppy's track density is about 48 tracks per inch, while a Winchester disk has a track density of about 1000 per inch. Recording density on a floppy is typically 3200 bpi. The user-addressable capacity of the storage surface is approximately 242K bytes. (Three of the tracks are usually reserved for system usage.) Some floppies have just one recording surface; others can have data recorded on both sides. The flexible disk is enclosed in a square plastic or paper envelope, much like a dust-jacket for a phonograph record.

For access, the disk-and-envelope medium is inserted into a slot in the drive, and the disk is held against a rotating spindle by a clamp. The material used as the interior surface of the envelope allows the disk to rotate inside the envelope while the envelope is held stationary. Typical rotation speed is 360 rpm. Pressure pads hold the read/write head in physical contact with the disk surface. This contact causes some wear of the surface, but many vendors guarantee their floppies for 2 million passes per track.

Floppies provide inexpensive, direct-access secondary storage capability. Their usage, especially with microcomputers, undoubtedly will continue to grow.

ADDRESSING TECHNIQUES

Let us now delve into the problems of implementing relative files. There are three fundamental techniques used by mapping functions R, where R (key value)———→ address:

1. Direct mapping
2. Directory lookup
3. Calculation

DIRECT MAPPING TECHNIQUES

The simplest technique for translating a record key to a storage address is direct mapping. Direct mapping is not widely used. We discuss it here primarily because understanding of the disadvantages of the direct mapping techniques helps to build an understanding of the benefits of the other techniques.

Absolute Addressing

One simple approach to implementing

$$R \text{ (key value)} \longrightarrow \text{address}$$

is to have

$$\text{key value} = \text{address}.$$

This mapping function is called *absolute addressing*. The key value supplied by a human or program user is the same as the record's actual address. When the record is first stored on the file, the target location of the record ([cylinder-number, surface-number, record-number] if cylinder addressing is used, or [sector-number, record-number] if sector addressing is used) must be determined by the user. When the record is later to be retrieved, its absolute location again must be known and supplied by the user.

There are two advantages to this absolute addressing scheme:

1. The mapping function R is very simple.
2. Given a record's key value, no processing time is required to determine the record's location on secondary storage.

The disadvantages of the scheme nearly always outweigh the advantages.

1. Logical and physical considerations are not independent with absolute addressing; the user must know exactly how the records are stored physically.
2. Users generally do not supply the appropriate types of key values, e.g., use of the ACCOUNT-NUMBER key value in the earlier banking example. Use of ACCOUNT-NUMBER is a natural and logical way to identify CUSTOMER-ACCOUNT records; ACCOUNT-NUMBERs do not usually make reasonable physical storage addresses!
3. Absolute addresses are device-dependent. Should it be desirable to upgrade or change the device upon which the file resides, it is likely that key values would also need to be changed.
4. Absolute addresses are address-space-dependent. Should it be desirable to reorganize the relative file but to keep it on the same device, it is likely that key values would need to be changed. This reorganization might be for purposes of enlarging the address space, consolidating free space, collecting garbage space, or decreasing the address space.

Relative Addressing

Another simple approach to implementing

$$R \text{ (key value)} \longrightarrow \text{address}$$

which has essentially the same advantages as does direct addressing, but which removes some of the disadvantages of absolute addressing, is called *relative addressing*. Here

$$\text{key value} = \text{relative address.}$$

A relative address can be supplied to a channel program for translation to an absolute address.

The relative address of a record in a file is the record's ordinal number in the file. A file with space for N records has records with relative addresses from the set $\{1, 2, 3, \ldots, N - 1, N\}$ (or $\{0, 1, 2, \ldots, N - 2, N - 1\}$). The Ith record has relative address I (or $I - 1$ if we start counting at 0).

The advantages of the relative addressing scheme are two:

1. The mapping function R is very simple.
2. Given a record's key value, essentially no processing time is required to determine the record's location on secondary storage.

Relative addresses are not nearly so device-dependent as are absolute addresses, thereby eliminating one of the disadvantages listed for absolute addressing. However, like absolute addresses, relative addresses are address-space-dependent.

Some types of natural key values are not well-suited for use as relative addresses. For example, although it could be converted to a numeric equivalent, employee name values are not good relative addresses; nor are many natural, numeric key values. For example, social security numbers are poor relative addresses. Why? Consider an organization with 2000 employees. The organization needs a relative file of employee data and wants to use social security numbers for the key. Such a relative file would have to be implemented with space allocated for 999,999,999 employees, since key values of employees could range from 1 to 999,999,999. The file will be 99.99998% empty. Even use of a 4-digit employee number would here result in a file that is 80% empty. The size of the file (i.e., the size of the file's address space) is determined by the range of possible values for the relative address, which with relative addressing is equivalent to the range of *possible* values for the key, *not* by the actual number of key values used.

One approach to this key-space problem is to identify or invent a key whose range of values is highly populated. For instance, in a relative file of part inventory data, a 4-digit part number might be a very good relative address, if the inventory contains, say 8200 types of parts. But, requests to access data about a particular part would have to be phrased in terms of the part's 4-digit part number, not in terms of its name or type or some other field value.

DIRECTORY LOOKUP TECHNIQUES

After direct mapping, the next most simple approach to implementing

$$R \text{ (key value)} \longrightarrow \text{address}$$

is *directory lookup*. This very commonly used approach takes advantage of the benefits of direct mapping while eliminating its disadvantages. It does, however, introduce a couple of new costs.

The basic idea of the directory lookup approach is to keep a table or directory of key value:address pairs (or key value:relative address pairs). In order to find a record on a relative file, one locates its key value in the directory and then the indicated address is used to find the record on storage.

Directory Structure

In its simplest form, the directory is implemented as an array of key value:address records, as illustrated in Fig. 13–6. Here the directory entries are sorted by key value so that a binary rather than sequential search can be used to locate a target entry more rapidly. Note that the relative file entries are *not* in sorted order.

The directory alternatively could be organized as a binary search tree (see Fig. 13–7).

DIRECTORY

KEY	ADDRESS
APE	I−1
BAT	N
CAT	N−1
⋮	
COW	1
DOG	I+1
EEL	I
⋮	
ZEBRA	2

RELATIVE FILE	Relative address
COW	1
ZEBRA	2
⋮	
APE	I−1
EEL	I
DOG	I+1
⋮	
CAT	N−1
BAT	N

Figure 13−6 Relative file with directory structured as a table.

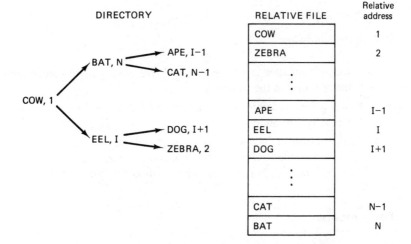

DIRECTORY

RELATIVE FILE	Relative address
COW	1
ZEBRA	2
⋮	
APE	I−1
EEL	I
DOG	I+1
⋮	
CAT	N−1
BAT	N

Figure 13−7 Relative file with directory structured as a tree.

Storing Records

It is a fairly straightforward process to retrieve a record using the directory lookup scheme, but how are records stored in the relative file using this approach? One approach is to assign an address to every possible key value, making the directory initially complete. Addresses could be assigned using any of a variety of techniques, many of which we will introduce later in this chapter. The advantage of this approach is clear: it is easy to determine where a new record should be stored. The disadvantages usually outweigh the advantage. If the directory is initially full, then it really is not necessary to store the directory at all—as we will see in our discussions of address calculation techniques.

A more usual approach is to determine where there is free space for a record at the time the record is stored. Perhaps the record is placed as near to the top as possible, or as near to the record with a similar key value as possible, or at random. That new key value: address pair then would be added to the directory. If the directory is to be a sorted table (as shown in Fig. 13–6), the new entry must be inserted in its proper position, with consequent movement of its successor entries. If the directory table is implemented as a sorted linked list, then insertion of the new entry is easier, but a binary search becomes impractical. If the directory is structured as a balanced binary search tree, then insertion of the new entry must include keeping the tree in balance. Directories are commonly implemented as B-trees, because of the need to insert and delete entries with relative ease and speed. We will discuss B-trees and tree balancing in some detail in Chapter 14.

Advantages

Thus the advantages of the directory lookup scheme to implement

$$R \text{ (key value)} \longrightarrow \text{address}$$

include the following:

1. A record's location can be determined with essentially no processing, once the key value is found in the directory.
2. Keys can be represented in intuitively understandable forms, since they are translated "internally" to addresses.
3. Logical-physical independence is achieved, because the key values are address-space-independent. If the relative file is reorganized, address entries in the directory must be changed, but the key values will not be affected.

Performance

The performance of the directory lookup scheme can be measured by the number of accesses to the directory that are required to find a desired key value. The technique used to implement the directory (e.g., unordered table versus B-tree) is an important determinant of search requirements. The organization of the directory is also an important determinant of the amount of processing required to maintain the directory.

We should note here that for very large relative files, the directory may also be large. In fact the directory usually is implemented as a separate file. If space permits, the entire directory file may be copied into main memory prior to execution of transactions that access the corresponding relative file. Commonly, space constraints do not permit this luxury.

ADDRESS CALCULATION TECHNIQUES

Another common approach to implementing

$$R \text{ (key value)} \longrightarrow \text{address}$$

is to perform a calculation on the key value such that the result is a relative address. This technique can be used alone or in conjunction with the directory lookup scheme that was introduced in the last section.

The basic idea of address calculation is to apply a function that translates a relatively large domain of possible key values to a relatively small range of relative address values. Recall that one of the disadvantages of relative addressing is that space must be allocated to accommodate the entire range of key values, regardless of how many are actually used. Consider again the company with 2000 employees that wants to use social security numbers for the record access key of an employee file with relative organization. A desirable address calculation function for this example would map the domain of values (1 through 999,999,999) onto approximately 2000 addresses.

One potential problem encountered in this process is that such a function may not be one-to-one; the calculated addresses may not all be unique. This situation, where

$$R (K_1) = R (K_2)$$

but

$$K_1 \neq K_2$$

is called a *collision*; two unequal keys have been calculated to have the same address. K_1 and K_2 here are called *synonyms*. Just as there are many possible address calculation techniques, there are a variety of collision resolution techniques. We will introduce the address calculation techniques in this section and discuss approaches to the collision resolution problem in the following section.

The concept of address calculation was first used to manage access to in-core symbol tables and later for addressing records in the early direct-access storage devices. A tremendous body of work since that time has contributed to the development of the many techniques for implementing the concept. Address calculation techniques are also referred to as

- Scatter storage techniques
- Randomizing techniques
- Key-to-address transformation methods
- Direct addressing techniques
- Hash table methods
- Hashing

We will use the term *hashing* here, primarily because of its prevalence elsewhere. The calculation applied to a key value to obtain an address is called a *hash function*.

The primary advantages of using hashing to implement

$$R \text{ (key value)} \longrightarrow \text{address}$$

are

1. Natural key values can be used, since they are translated "internally" to addresses.
2. Logical-physical independence is achieved, because the key values are address-space-independent. If the relative file is reorganized, the hash function may need to be changed, but the key values will not be affected.

The basic costs of using the hashing approach are

1. The processing time required to apply the hash function.
2. The processing time and I/O accesses required to resolve collisions.

Thus a primary objective of a hash function is to generate relatively few collisions. A set of synonyms is sometimes called an *equivalence class*. A good hash function has small equivalence classes and few of them. Additionally, a good hash function is not too complex computationally.

Hashing is important not only for addressing into a relative file, but also for addressing into main-memory tables. The hash function is applied to record keys to calculate the subscripts of corresponding records in the table. Thus, a record can be found with one probe (unless a collision occurs); no table search is needed.

Hashing can be used in conjunction with directory lookup, as shown in Fig. 13–8. The benefits of avoiding recalculation and collision resolution for old records are paid

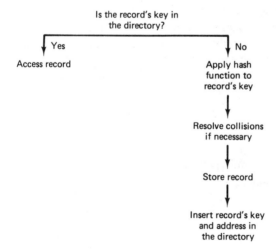

Figure 13–8 Fundamental logic for hashing with directory lookup.

for by the cost of storing and maintaining the directory. Also, depending upon directory organization and collision patterns, directory lookup and hashing together may yield longer search times than would hashing alone.

The performance of a hashing technique can be measured by its processing requirements and the I/O needed to store or retrieve a record. The performance of a particular hash function is dependent upon

1. The distribution of key values that are actually in use.
2. The number of key values that are actually in use relative to the size of the address space.
3. The number of records that can be stored at a given address without causing a collision (for now we assume 1).
4. The collision resolution technique used.

Let us now discuss some of the most common hash functions:

- Division-remainder
- Mid-square
- Folding

We then will compare these approaches.

Division-Remainder Hashing

Some of the earliest investigations in hashing yielded a hash function known as the *division-remainder method*, or simply the division method. The basic idea of this approach is to divide a key value by an appropriate number, then to use the remainder of the division as the relative address for the record.

For example, let div be the divisor, key be the key, and addr be the resultant address. In Pascal, the function

$$R \text{ (key)} \longrightarrow \text{address}$$

would be implemented as

$$\text{addr} := \text{key mod div};$$

and in COBOL as

DIVIDE KEY BY DIV GIVING TEMP REMAINDER ADDR.

The remainder (and result of the mod function) is defined as the result of subtracting the product of the quotient and divisor from the dividend. That is,

$$\text{ADDR} = \text{KEY} - \text{DIV*TEMP}.$$

In all cases here, ADDR should be declared to be an integer.

While the actual calculation of a relative address, given a key value and divisor, is straightforward, the choice of the *appropriate* divisor may not be quite so simple. There are several factors that should be considered in selecting the divisor. First, the range of values that result from the operation key $\underline{mod}$ div is 0 through div -1. Thus the value of div determines the size of the relative address space. If it is known that our relative file is going to contain at least n records, then we must, assuming that only one record can be stored at a given relative address, have div $> n$.

Second, the divisor should be selected such that the probability of collision is minimized. In fact, this is a difficult objective to achieve. We try to select a divisor that keeps the probability of collision relatively low, but we usually do not go to the effort of actually minimizing collisions. Investigations have shown that divisors that are even numbers tend to perform poorly, especially with the sets of key values that are predominantly odd.

Some research (e.g., W. Buchholz, "File organization and addressing," *IBM Systems Journal*, vol. 2, pp. 86–111, June 1963) has suggested that the divisor should be a prime number, thereby reducing skewed results. However, other work (e.g., V. Y. Lum, et al., "Key-to-address transform techniques: A fundamental performance study on large existing formatted files," *Communications of the ACM*, vol. 14, no. 4, pp. 228–239, April 1971) suggests that nonprime divisors work as well as prime divisors, as long as the nonprime divisors do not contain small prime numbers as factors. They suggest that selecting a number that does not contain any prime factor less than 20 is probably sufficient to ensure good performance.

It is not enough to pick a divisor that does not introduce skewed distribution of addresses. Additionally, it has been shown that regardless of how "good" the divisor is, when the address space of a relative file gets full enough, the probability of collision rises dramatically. Fullness of a relative file is measured by its *load factor*, which is defined as the ratio of the number of records in the file to the number of records that the file could hold if completely full:

$$\text{load factor} = \frac{\text{\# records in file}}{\text{max. \# of records file can contain}}$$

All hash functions begin to work quite poorly when the target file becomes almost full. As a general guideline, a load factor of 0.7 or 0.8 is about as great as can be tolerated with reasonable performance. When the file becomes greater than 70% or 80% full, it should be enlarged and reorganized. Thus, if it is known that our relative file is going to contain about n records, then the address space should have enough room for at least $1.25n$ records (for 80% loading).

For example, consider design of a relative file that will contain about 4000 records. The address space should accommodate at least 5000 records for 80% loading. A number that is approximately 5000 and that does not contain any prime factors less than 20 is 5003. Fig. 13–9 illustrates use of this divisor with a small set of key values.

key value	relative address	
123456789	2762	
987654321	2086	
123456790	2763	
555555555	2424	
000000472	0473 ←	
100064183	4184	
200120472	0473	**collision**
200120473	0474	
117400000	4606	
027000400	3613	

Figure 13-9 Example using divisor 5003.

Mid-square Hashing

In this hashing technique, the key is squared, then specified digits are extracted from the middle of the result to yield the relative address. If a relative address of n digits is desired, then digits are truncated at both ends of the squared key, leaving n digits from the middle. The same n digit positions must be extracted for each key. Fig. 13-10 illustrates use of the mid-square hashing technique for the same key values that were shown in Fig. 13-9. Digits in positions 7-10 (counting from the right) have been extracted to form a 4-digit relative address.

key value	key squared	relative address
123456789	15241578750190521	8750
987654321	975461055789971041	5789
123456790	15241578997104100	8997
555555555	308641974691358025	4691
000000472	00000000000222784	0000 ←
100064183	10012860719457489	0719
200120472	40048203313502784	3313
200120473	40048203713743729	3713
117400000	13782760000000000	0000 **collision**
027000400	02430021600160000	1600

Figure 13-10 Example using mid-square hashing.

Note that in order to accommodate 4000 records, 4-digit relative addresses are required. The resultant address space has room for 10,000 records, giving a load factor of 0.4. Using the mid-square hashing function, the size of the resultant file is 10^n, where n is the number of digits extracted from the squared key values.

Hashing by Folding

In this hashing technique the key value is partitioned into a number of parts, each of which (except the last one) has the same number of digits as does the target relative address. These partitions are then folded over each other and summed. The result, with its highest order digit truncated, if necessary, is the relative address.

For example, consider the key value 123456789 and assume that the target relative address will have 4 digits. The key value is partitioned into 4-digit chunks

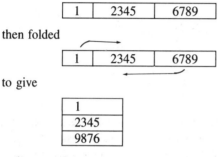

then folded

to give

and summed to

13221.

The high-order digit is truncated, giving relative address 3221.

Fig. 13–11 shows the relative addresses that result when folding is applied to our set of example key values.

key value	relative address
123456789	3221
987654321	8999
123456790	4321
555555555	6110
000000472	2740
100064183	4820
200120472	4752
200120473	5752
117400000	2740 **collision**
027000400	2740 **collision**

Figure 13–11   Example with hashing by folding.

As was true with the mid-square method, the size of the relative address space is an integral power of 10.

Comparison of Hash Functions

There are many possible hash functions; we have introduced just three of them here. Thorough analysis of the performance of various hash functions has been reported in a series of papers, including the paper by Lum et al. that was referenced earlier, V. Y. Lum and P. S. T. Yuen, "Additional results on key-to-address transform techniques," *Communications of the ACM*, vol. 15, pp. 996–997, November 1972; V. Y. Lum, "General performance analysis of key-to-address transformation methods using an abstract file concept," *Communications of the ACM*, vol. 16, pp. 603–612, October 1973; and S. P. Ghosh, and V. Y. Lum, "An analysis of collisions when hashing by division," IBM Research Report RJ1218, May 1973. We summarize those results here.

Although another technique may perform better in particular situations, the division-remainder technique gives the best overall performance. No hash function *always* performs better than all others. The mid-square method can be applied to files with fairly low loading factors to give generally good performance, but sometimes it can generate poor performance with many collisions. The folding method may be the easiest technique to compute, especially if bit patterns rather than decimal values are used, but it produces quite erratic results, unless the key length is approximately the same as the address length.

If the distribution of key values is not known, then the division-remainder method is the preferred hashing technique. Thus, it is very commonly used. Like any other address calculation technique, it can be used in conjunction with a directory lookup scheme. (See Fig. 13–8 again.)

Note that hashing can be applied to non-numeric keys as well as to numeric keys. The collating sequence positions of the characters in a key value can be used as their "numeric" equivalents. Alternatively, the hash algorithm acts upon the binary representations of the characters.

The introduced hash functions all have addressed a fixed-size space. Increasing the size of a relative file created using one of these functions implies changing the hash function to address the larger space and reloading the new file. Other hash techniques have been developed that allow the file to grow or shrink without forcing the relocation of old records. These schemes are known as dynamic hashing, extendible hashing, and virtual hashing. The allocated storage space is divided into buckets. When a record is to be inserted into a full bucket, it is split into two buckets among which the records are distributed. This approach will appear again later in our discussion of B-trees.

Dynamic hashing uses a binary-tree index structure to keep track of buckets and to guide access to records. *Extendible hashing* uses a tabular directory based on a degenerate trie structure to keep track of buckets and to guide access to records. *Virtual hashing* is a general name given to "any hashing which may dynamically change its hashing function" (W. Litwin, "Virtual hashing: A dynamically changing hashing," *Proc. 4th Conf. Very Large Databases*, W. Berlin, 1978, pp. 517–523). This term is quite broad and includes not only dynamic and extendible hashing but also techniques that do not use any indexes. For sources of further information about these approaches, you should consult the references listed at the end of this chapter.

APPROACHES TO THE PROBLEM OF COLLISIONS

Because a hashing function maps a relatively large key-value space to a relatively small address space, there are certain to be collisions; more than one key value will be mapped to a single relative address.

Consider two key values K_1 and K_2, which are synonyms with hash function R. Assume that the equivalence class that contains K_1 and K_2 contains no other key values; that is, K_1 and K_2 have no other synonyms. If K_1 is stored in the file first and its address is $R(K_1)$, then K_1 is said to be stored at its *home address*.

There are two basic approaches to deciding where K_2 should be located: (1) *open addressing*, in which some address other than the home address is found for K_2 in the relative file, and (2) *separate overflow*, in which some address is found for K_2 outside of the primary area of the relative file in a special overflow area that is used only for storage of records that cannot be located at their home addresses.

Numerous techniques have been developed to handle collisions. We now consider two of the most common approaches:

- Linear probing, which is an open addressing technique
- Double hashing, which can be applied as either an open addressing or separate overflow technique

We will compare the performance of these techniques and then introduce two methods of improving behavior:

- Synonym chaining
- Bucket addressing

Linear Probing

One way to find a location for a record when it cannot be stored at its home address is to use *linear probing*, which is a process of searching sequentially from the home address to find the next empty location. This technique is also referred to as the *consecutive spill* method. In order to implement linear probing, it must be possible to determine whether or not an address is empty. This may be done by setting a flag in each location as it is filled. The basic logic of storing a record by hashing with the linear probe technique is shown in Fig. 13–12.

Note first that linear probing can be used in conjunction with any hash technique. Note also that the application of linear probing must be done in such a way that ADDR does not fall off the end of the file. Rather than quitting when the bound of the address space is met, we cycle back to the beginning of the space and probe from there. It then becomes necessary to be able to detect when the home address (here HOMEADDR) has been encountered again, in which case the file is completely full and there is no room for KEY.

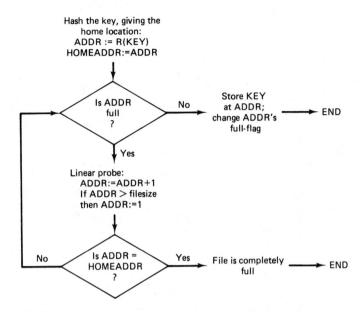

Figure 13-12   Logic for record storage by hashing with linear probing.

If linear probing is used to resolve collisions when records are stored, it must also be used when records are retrieved, unless a directory lookup scheme is used in conjunction with hashing. The basic logic for retrieving a record by hashing with linear probing is shown in Fig. 13-13. The key values of records encountered at the home address and at addresses reached by linear probe must be compared with the sought KEY value to determine whether or not the target record has been located. Many probes may be required to determine that the target record is not in the file or to find the target record if it was stored far from its HOMEADDR. A more efficient method for handling synonyms will be introduced in the section on synonym chaining.

Deletion of records makes things more difficult. Why? How would you modify the logic of Fig. 13-12 and 13-13 to accommodate deleted records?

Double Hashing

Another approach to finding a location for a record when it cannot be stored at its home address is to use *double hashing*, which applies a second hash function to a combination of the original key and the result of the first hash. The target address space of the rehash may be either the relative file itself or a separate overflow relative file. In the first case, where all records appear in a single file, the open addressing method is in use. In the second case, where only one record from each equivalence class appears in the primary file and synonyms appear in an overflow file, the separate overflow method is in use. In

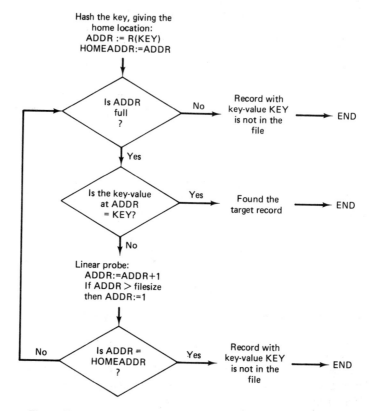

Figure 13-13 Logic for record retrieval by hashing with linear probing.

either case, some method for resolution is needed if collisions occur during the second hash.

The advantage of the separate overflow method is that it avoids the situation, which can occur in the open addressing method, whereby a record that is not stored in its home location displaces another record which later hashes to that home location. This problem can be avoided with open addressing simply by moving the offending foreign record to another location (by probing or rehashing or . . .) and storing the new record at the now-empty home address. If directory lookup is being used with hashing, the directory must be updated to reflect the changed address of the moved record.

The cost of the separate overflow method is the overhead of maintaining a separate file. The relative file really is implemented as two files: a primary area and an overflow area. Both have relative organization.

Comparison of Linear Probing and Double Hashing

Linear probing and double hashing result in different distributions of synonyms in a relative file. Let us consider first the case of a file with a low load factor, say less than 0.5. Linear probing tends to cluster synonyms, while double hashing tends to disperse synonyms more widely across the address space.

For example, consider a small example relative file with 224 records and a load factor of 0.7. Our data show an average of 1.31 probes per record required with linear probing and 1.20 probes per record required with double hashing. Thus both are about the same. However, the average distance that a displaced record is from its home location is 3.1 slots with linear probing and 122.1 slots with double hashing. In a paged environment, the clustering effects of linear probing may be quite desirable.

However, the clustering effects of linear probing can also be a disadvantage. For example, consider a very small file of 9 records in an address space for 19 records. Assume that records have been inserted in slots 2, 3, 5, 6, 12, 13, 14, 15, and 17, as shown in Fig. 13–14.

0	1	2	3	4	5	6	7	8	9	10	11	12	13	14	15	16	17	18
		X	X		X	X						X	X	X	X		X	

Figure 13–14 Example initial record distribution.

The next record to be added will go into one of the ten available spaces. However, there is not a 10% likelihood that the record will go into any one of the slots. For example, address 16 will be the location of the new record if it hashes to address 12, 13, 14, 15, or 16. Address 8 will be the location of the new record only if it hashes to address 8. The probabilities of each address receiving the next record are given in Fig. 13–15, which assumes that the hash function yields a uniform distribution of addresses. The result of this clustering effect is that long searches tend to get even longer. With even moderate file load factors, there is relatively high probability that a new record will extend a cluster rather than start a cluster.

Double hashing tends to perform about as well as does linear probing for small load factors (less than 0.5), but does somewhat better than linear probing for larger load factors. At loading greater than 80%, linear probing generally results in terrible performance,

Address	0	1	2	3	4	5	6	7	8	9
Probability of receiving next record	.05	.05	0	0	.16	0	0	.16	.05	.05

Address	10	11	12	13	14	15	16	17	18
Probability of receiving next record	.05	.05	0	0	0	0	.26	0	.11

Figure 13–15 Effects of a uniform hash function on the example of Fig. 13–14.

while double hashing is quite tolerable for successful searches but not so good for un-successful searches.

Synonym Chaining

One good way to improve the performance of a relative file that uses address calculation without an auxiliary directory to guide retrievals is to chain together synonyms. Maintaining a linked list of records with the same home address does not reduce the number of collisions, but it *does* reduce the access times to retrieve records that are not at their home locations. Synonym chaining can be used with any collision resolution technique. Fig. 13–16(a) and (b) illustrate chaining of synonyms when linear probing and double hashing, re-spectively, have been used to resolve collisions.

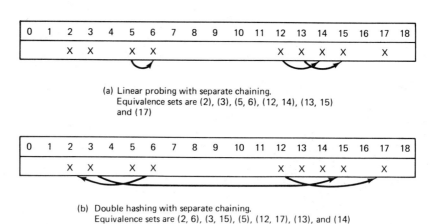

(a) Linear probing with separate chaining.
Equivalence sets are (2), (3), (5, 6), (12, 14), (13, 15)
and (17)

(b) Double hashing with separate chaining.
Equivalence sets are (2, 6), (3, 15), (5), (12, 17), (13), and (14)

Figure 13–16   Synonym chaining with two different collision-resolution techniques.

When a record is to be retrieved from the file, the basic logic illustrated in Fig. 13–17 is applied. Note that only synonyms of the target key are accessed. Without synonym chaining, nonsynonyms can also be accessed in pursuit of the target record. Note that this logic requires that a record not be displaced from its home location by a previously stored nonsynonym. If it were, then the linked list followed would not contain synonyms of the target record, and the target record would never be found.

Deletion of records also is handled gracefully by the chained synonym approach. When a record is deleted, it simply is removed from its linked list. Recall that the deletion of records without synonym chaining can be a problem: either the vacated space must be marked so as not to be confused with a never-filled space, which would cause synonym searches to terminate prematurely, or synonyms have to be moved around to fill the vacated space.

Synonym chaining can be used whether the open addressing method is used or the separate overflow method is used. That is, the linked list beginning at a home address may have its next node either in the same file or in a separate file.

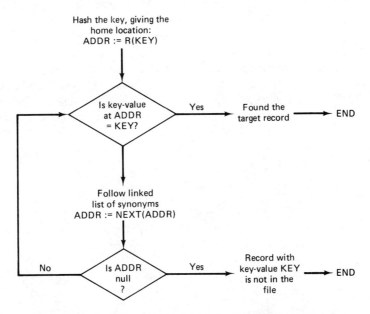

Figure 13–17   Logic for record retrieval by hashing with synonym chaining.

Synonym chaining nearly always works better than does collision resolution without synonym chaining, unless a directory lookup scheme is used to keep track of where records are actually stored. Synonym chaining and directory lookup both keep the number of accesses required to find records small, even with heavily loaded files.

Bucket Addressing

Another approach to handling the problem of collisions is to hash to blocks (or buckets) of space that can accommodate multiple record occurrences, rather than hashing to individual record slots. For example, consider a relative address space of 0 to M, and a bucket size of B records. The address space thus can contain $B(M + 1)$ records. If the file contains N records, then its load factor is

$$\frac{N}{B(M + 1)}.$$

B records can all hash to the same relative address without causing a problematic collision.

When a bucket does overflow, some new location must be found for the offending record. The approaches to the bucket overflow problem are basically the same as the approaches taken to handle collisions with record-slot addressing. If open addressing is used, available space is sought either in the next bucket (i.e., with linear probing) or in some other bucket (i.e., with double hashing). If the separate overflow area technique is used, the new record is placed in a specially designated set of buckets that are reserved for overflow usage. Each primary bucket generally would have a pointer to a chain of the records in the overflow area that should have been stored in the primary bucket but that ended up in overflow buckets instead. One overflow bucket could accommodate records that had hashed to several different primary buckets.

The records stored in a bucket may be managed in one of two ways: (1) They can be inserted in order by their arrival at the bucket. (2) They can be maintained in sorted order by their key values. The basic trade-off is ease of insertion versus ease of retrieval. When a record is retrieved from a relative file that uses bucket addressing, with bucket overflow handled by linear probing, the basic logic shown in Fig. 13–18 is followed.

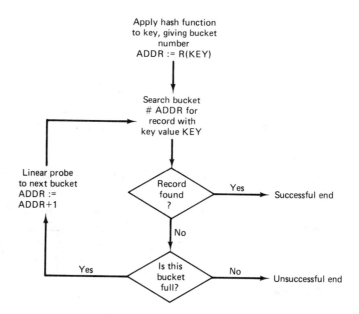

Figure 13–18 Logic for record retrieval by hashing with bucket addressing, with bucket overflow handled by linear probing.

When a record is retrieved from a relative file that uses bucket addressing, with bucket overflows placed in an overflow area and synonym chaining within the overflow buckets, the logic shown in Fig. 13–19 is followed.

Just as the records in the primary bucket area may be kept ordered by key value (*within* a bucket), so may the records on a synonym chain be maintained in order by key value. If so, adding a record to a full primary bucket may cause a record from that bucket to be moved into the overflow area, while the inserted record is stored in the primary area.

The use of bucket addressing is common. The size of a bucket may be determined by the size of a track or of a sector on a disk or by the system's natural page size. Bucket size generally should be the same as block size for the file. This match allows the search for a record in its home bucket to be conducted with just one access to secondary storage. Access to the next bucket or to an overflow bucket would require a second I/O access.

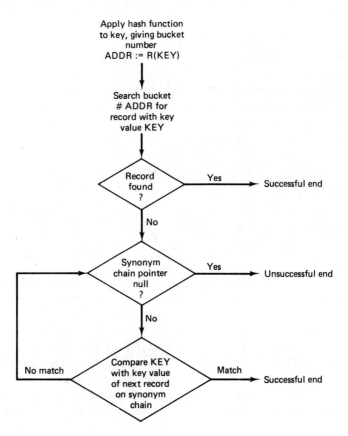

Figure 13-19 Logic for record retrieval by hashing with bucket addressing, with bucket overflow into overflow area and synonym chaining in the overflow area.

One important advantage of using buckets that can hold multiple records is that variable-length records can be accommodated. With bucket addressing and variable-length records, the process of finding available space in a bucket for a new record becomes more complex than just searching sequentially for the first open slot. The space found must be large enough to accommodate the new record. Commonly space is managed in such a situation by maintaining a linked list of holes in the bucket. Holes may be dispersed among actual records because of deletions. The hole chain is searched when free space is requested. Recall the discussion in Chapter 6 of the linked Avail stack of holes used when a linked list was housed in an array. It is convenient to order the list of holes of a bucket by increasing size. The search for a hole results in the selection of the hole whose size most closely meets (or exceeds) the required amount of space.

Figure 13–20 illustrates a bucket that contains a chain of holes. The bucket header includes information about where its smallest hole starts and how large its largest hole is. When a new record hashes to this bucket, the search for free space can proceed directly

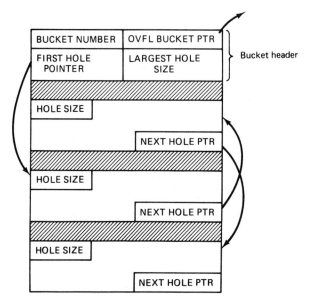

Figure 13–20 Bucket containing a hole chain.

to the next bucket, or to an overflow bucket if this home bucket does not have an adequately large hole. Otherwise the hole chain is searched. In the diagram, the hashed areas denote space where records a e stored; the blank areas are holes.

When a hole is used to store a record, there may not be an exact fit. Leftover space can be returned in the form of a new (smaller) hole to an appropriate position in the hole chain.

When a record is deleted, its freed space should be added as a hole to the hole chain. If this freed space is contiguous to previously existing holes, the spaces can be combined to make one larger hole. A few large holes are more desirable than many small holes, because the probability of having to route a new record out of its home bucket is higher with smaller maximum hole sizes.

When variable-length records and bucket addressing are used, it is usually the record manager system rather than the programmer who is responsible for bucket space management.

USING RELATIVE FILES

Relative files are used so commonly that many programming languages support their declaration, creation, retrieval, and update. Pascal is a notable exception, although some Pascal compilers do support language extensions for relative files.

In COBOL, FORTRAN, and PL/I, the programmer supplies to the system a record's relative address when the record is stored and when it is retrieved. It is the programmer's responsibility to perform the key-to-address transformation; this mapping is not done automatically by the system. Additionally the programmer must resolve any collisions that may occur. Thus the access methods that support relative files declared in these languages are quite efficient. They have very little overhead and do little processing. They are given relative addresses and convert these to absolute addresses for record access. The access methods do not do the hashing, directory lookups, or collision resolutions.

Declaring a Relative File

When a relative file is declared in a program, the information that is required includes the following:

- File name
- Specification of physical device upon which the file resides
- Organization relative (as opposed to sequential or other possibilities)
- Identification of the variable that contains relative addresses for records
- Record formats

along with other possible information about label records, and so forth. The techniques used to determine relative addresses and to resolve collisions are defined in the procedural code.

Creating a Relative File

A relative file may be created in either sequential or direct-access mode. When it is created sequentially, the records are written in consecutive order. Sequential creation of a relative file is commonly used in conjunction with a directory lookup scheme. If an address calculation technique is used to map keys to addresses, sequential creation is nearly impossible, unless the records have been stored in an auxiliary table to be dumped sequentially to the file.

When hashing is used, a relative file more commonly is created in direct-access mode. In some implementations, a skeleton file of dummy records is created first, then records are inserted in some random order.

Retrieving from Relative Files

Similarly, records can be retrieved from a relative file in either sequential or direct-access mode. Sequential access retrieves the records in physically consecutive order, which may not be in key-sequence order. Many compilers support direct positioning of a relative file at a point (based on relative address) and sequential read access from that point.

More commonly, a relative file is accessed in direct mode. The key identifying a record to a user is translated by an application program into a relative address. The program then reads the record at that address. If there is no record at that location, then the target record does not exist. If there is a record at that location, the program then checks to determine if it has the desired key value. If so, the record is delivered to the user. If not, then the sought record is not at its home address and the application program applies its collision-handling technique to find the desired record. It either finds the record or determines that the record does not exist.

Updating Relative Files

A relative file is nearly always updated in direct mode. The program uses a direct-retrieval algorithm to locate the desired record, makes specified modifications, then rewrites the record in place. In some languages (such as COBOL and PL/I) rewrite (modify) of an existing record is distinguished from write (insert) of a new record. In other languages (such as FORTRAN) the two actions use the same verb.

Programmer Responsibilities

In addition to doing the hashing, detecting and resolving collisions, and possibly maintaining directories, the programmer who uses a relative file must also continually check for unexpected conditions. Examples of the types of conditions that can be signaled are listed below.

1. Sequential read
   - at end-of-file
2. Direct read
   - no record exists at the specified relative address
   - specified relative address out-of-bounds for the file
3. Sequential write
   - space limits exceeded on device
4. Direct write
   - record already exists at the specified address (i.e., collision)
   - specified relative address out-of-bounds for the file
5. Direct rewrite
   - no record exists at the specified address
   - specified relative address out-of-bounds for the file.

When a record is delivered on a read, the program needs to verify that it has the desired user-key value. If not, the collision resolution technique used on the file must be applied to locate the desired synonym.

RELATIVE FILES IN COBOL

We now introduce the basic concepts required to declare and use relative files in COBOL programs. Other languages that support relative files use basically the same types of procedures for file creation and manipulation and ask the programmer to specify essentially the same information to define the file. For details of requirements, you should consult local language manuals and inquire about local installation standards and procedures. File I/O is commonly nonstandard.

Declaring a Relative File

As for sequential files, declaration information for relative files is supplied in both the ENVIRONMENT DIVISION and the DATA DIVISION of a COBOL program. The format of the SELECT clause of the FILE-CONTROL paragraph of the INPUT-OUTPUT SECTION of the ENVIRONMENT DIVISION for a relative file is

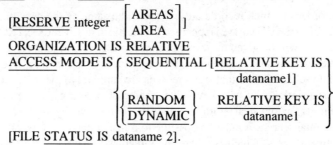

The filename is the name by which the file is known in this program. The implementor-name is the name of the device(s) upon which the file resides. (See Chapter 11 for more details of this clause, the RESERVE clause, and the FILE STATUS clause.)

The ORGANIZATION IS RELATIVE clause is required in the declaration of a relative file. If this clause were omitted, the file would default to having sequential organization.

The ACCESS MODE clause specifies the manner in which records in the file are going to be accessed. The field identified by dataname1 in the RELATIVE KEY phrase is the name of the field that contains the record's relative address, which in COBOL must be an integer *greater* than 0. Thus if the division-remainder hash method were used, 1 would be added to the resultant remainder. For example

DIVIDE USER-KEY BY DIV GIVING TEMP REMAINDER ADDR
ADD 1 TO ADDR

where ADDR is the specified RELATIVE KEY field. This variable (dataname1) does not appear within the file's records or in the file's record description entries.

SEQUENTIAL access is the default. Sequential access of a relative file means that records will be accessed (read/written) in order by ascending relative addresses. RANDOM access means that records will be accessed by value of dataname1, which will contain relative addresses. DYNAMIC access means that records will be accessed sometimes in SEQUENTIAL mode and sometimes in RANDOM mode by the program.

Each relative file used in a program must have an associated FD (file description) entry. An FD contains clauses that give information about block size, record size, label records, and data records in the file. The entry is essentially the same for relative files as for sequential files.

Creating a File

When a relative file is created in COBOL, it must be open for OUTPUT or I-O. Records then are written to the file either sequentially or not sequentially, using the WRITE verb.

If the file has ACCESS MODE SEQUENTIAL, the following verb form is used.

<u>WRITE</u> recordname [<u>FROM</u> identifier]

The order in which records are written is the same as their resultant physical order. If a RELATIVE KEY phrase is specified for the file in its FILE CONTROL entry, the associated data item will be given the value of the record's relative address in the file. These relative addresses might be loaded into a directory for later use in accessing the file by a directory-lookup scheme. Note that if the records are supplied to the file in some meaningful order, say sequentially by user-key value, then that ordering will be mirrored in the records' positions on physical storage. In order to retrieve by user-key value while avoiding sequential search, it must be possible to translate the user-key value to the corresponding relative address, which is where the directory-lookup scheme becomes useful.

If the file has ACCESS MODE RANDOM, then the following verb form is used.

<u>WRITE</u> recordname [<u>FROM</u> identifier]
<u>INVALID KEY</u> imperative-statement.

At the time that the WRITE for a record is executed, the data item specified in the RELATIVE KEY phrase for the file (in its SELECT clause) must contain the relative address for the record. If the INVALID KEY condition is raised, then a record with specified relative key value already exists in the file, i.e., collision. The program would then apply its collision-resolution technique and try to write again. An example of the basic logic for this process follows.

```
    . . .
    SELECT EMP-MSTR ASSIGN TO DISK
        ORGANIZATION IS RELATIVE
        ACCESS IS RANDOM
            RELATIVE KEY IS REL-ADDR.
    . . .
    FD EMP-MSTR
        LABEL RECORD IS STANDARD.
    01  EMP-REC.
        02  EMP-NO              PIC 9(8).
        02  FILLER              PIC X(316).
```

```
    . . .
    WORKING-STORAGE SECTION.
    01  FLAGS.
        02  COLLISION-FLAG        PIC X.
            88  NO-COLLISION      VALUE 'N'.
            88  COLLISION         VALUE 'Y'.
    . . .
    DRIVER.
        OPEN OUTPUT EMP-MSTR.
        ACCEPT EMP-REC.
        PERFORM PROCESS-EMP-REC UNTIL EMP-NO = ZEROS.
        CLOSE EMP-MSTR.
        STOP RUN.
    PROCESS-EMP-REC.
        PERFORM HASH-ON-EMP-NO.
        MOVE 'N' TO COLLISION-FLAG.
        WRITE EMP-REC
            INVALID KEY MOVE 'Y' TO COLLISION-FLAG.
        PERFORM RESOLVE-COLLISION UNTIL NO-COLLISION.
        . . .
        ACCEPT EMP-REC.
    RESOLVE-COLLISION.
        ADD 1 TO REL-ADDR.
        MOVE 'N' TO COLLISION-FLAG.
        WRITE EMP-REC
            INVALID KEY MOVE 'Y' TO COLLISION-FLAG.
    HASH-ON-EMP-NO.
        . . .
```

This example uses simple linear probing to resolve collisions. Foreign records may displace other records from their home addresses, and synonyms are not chained.

Retrieving Records

When records are retrieved from a COBOL relative file, the file must be open for INPUT, or for I-O if records are going to be both read and written. Records can be retrieved from the file either sequentially or not sequentially, using the READ verb. Sequential access may be positioned by the START verb.

  If the file has ACCESS MODE IS SEQUENTIAL, then the following verb form is used:

READ filename RECORD [INTO identifier]
AT END imperative-statement.

A loop through this statement will access the records in order by physical location. As with a sequential WRITE of a relative file, the associated RELATIVE KEY data item will be given the value of a record's relative address in the file as it is read. The AT END condition is raised when the end-of-file is encountered.

The START verb can be used to position subsequent sequential reads. The format of the START verb is

$$\underline{\text{START}} \text{ filename [KEY IS} \left\{ \begin{array}{l} \underline{\text{EQUAL}} \text{ TO} \\ = \\ \underline{\text{GREATER}} \text{ THAN} \\ > \\ \underline{\text{NOT LESS}} \text{ THAN} \\ \underline{\text{NOT}} < \end{array} \right\} \text{ dataname]}$$

[<u>INVALID</u> KEY imperative-statement].

Positioning is done such that the relative address (of the next record to be accessed by a READ) bears the specified relationship to the RELATIVE KEY data item for the file (given in its FILE CONTROL entry). The dataname specified in a START statement must be the same as the name of the RELATIVE KEY data item for the file. If the KEY phrase of the START verb is omitted, = is assumed. The INVALID KEY condition is raised if:

1. There is no record with this relative address (for =).
2. There is no record in any position higher than the one specified by the key (for >).
3. There is no record in the position specified by the key or in any higher position (for NOT <).

If the file has ACCESS MODE IS RANDOM, then the following verb form is used for retrieval:

<u>READ</u> filename RECORD [<u>INTO</u> identifier]
INVALID KEY imperative-statement.

This statement causes read of the record whose relative address is contained in the data item named in the RELATIVE KEY clause for the file. If there is no record at this address, then the INVALID KEY condition is raised. If the file was created using a hashing technique, the program would need to verify that the retrieved record is the actual target record and not one of its synonyms. An example of the basic logic for this process follows, where the same ENVIRONMENT and DATA DIVISION entries are used as in the preceding program segment, with the addition of flag

```
02  FOUND-FLAG          PIC X.
    88  LOOKING          VALUE 'L'.
```

```
          88  FOUND              VALUE 'Y'.
          88  NOT-FOUND          VALUE 'N'.
      DRIVER.
          OPEN INPUT EMP-MSTR.
          ACCEPT EMP-NO-TARGET.
          PERFORM FIND-EMP-REC UNTIL
              EMP-NO-TARGET = ZEROS.
          CLOSE EMP-MSTR.
          STOP RUN.
      FIND-EMP-REC.
          PERFORM HASH-ON-EMP-NO-TARGET.
          MOVE 'L' TO FOUND-FLAG.
          READ EMP-REC
              INVALID KEY MOVE 'N' TO FOUND-FLAG.
          PERFORM CHECK-REC UNTIL NOT-FOUND OR FOUND.
          IF NOT-FOUND
              DISPLAY 'EMP' EMP-NO-TARGET 'NOT IN FILE'
          ELSE DISPLAY EMP-REC.
          ACCEPT EMP-NO-TARGET.
      CHECK-REC.
          IF EMP-NO = EMP-NO-TARGET
              MOVE 'Y' TO FOUND-FLAG
          ELSE ADD 1 TO REL-ADDR
              READ EMP-REC
                  INVALID KEY MOVE 'N' TO FOUND-FLAG.
      HASH-ON-EMP-NO-TARGET.
          . . .
```

Again note that simple linear probing without synonym chaining is used.

If a relative file has ACCESS MODE IS DYNAMIC, then both sequential and direct (random) retrieval are supported.

Updating a File

When a COBOL relative file is updated, it must be open for I-O. New records then can be added using the WRITE verb; old records can be removed using the DELETE verb; records can be modified using the REWRITE verb.

If the file has ACCESS MODE IS SEQUENTIAL, then WRITE cannot be used. Records will be accessed in consecutive order. The sequential form of the DELETE verb is

<u>DELETE</u> filename RECORD

Execution of the DELETE must have been preceded by a successful READ for the file. The record that was read is deleted.

The sequential form of the REWRITE verb is

REWRITE recordname [<u>FROM</u> identifier]

As for the DELETE, execution of a sequential REWRITE must be preceded by a successful READ. The record that was read is replaced by the REWRITE.

If the file has ACCESS MODE IS RANDOM, then records can be accessed in any order. The random form of the DELETE is

<u>DELETE</u> filename RECORD
<u>INVALID</u> KEY imperative-statement.

The record identified by the RELATIVE KEY data item for the file is deleted. The INVALID KEY condition is raised if there is no record at the specified address.

The random form of the REWRITE is

REWRITE recordname [<u>FROM</u> identifier]
<u>INVALID</u> KEY imperative-statement.

The record identified by the RELATIVE KEY data item for the file is replaced. The INVALID KEY condition is raised if there is no record at the specified address. Note that neither the random REWRITE nor the random DELETE requires the target record to have been read previously.

Sequential and random update of a relative file can be intermingled in one program if the file has ACCESS MODE DYNAMIC.

PERFORMANCE OF RELATIVE FILES

The primary questions that need to be addressed in designing a relative file include the following:

1. What is the layout of fields in the records?
2. What is the key field(s) used to identify record occurrences?
3. What is an appropriate key-to-address mapping function?
4. What is the appropriate bucket size?
5. What is an appropriate collision resolution method?
6. What are the capabilities provided by the relative file facility of the programming language to be used?

The answers determine the performance of the file, which is quite application-dependent. Changing the characteristics of the way that the application uses the file can affect the appropriateness of a design decision.

As we indicated in the discussion of sequential file performance, the record layout problem was introduced in Chapter 3. Fixed-length records can be accommodated by relative files with bucket size = 1. The presence of variable-length records implies that buckets that can accommodate multiple records must be used.

The appropriate field(s) to form the user key of a relative file is determined by the application. Use of a relative file rather than a sequential file implies that there is a need to access individual records directly. The field whose value is specified by a user to identify individual records should be the key field. If multiple, different key fields seem appropriate, then one of the file organizations that will be introduced in Chapter 16 may be more appropriate than relative organization.

The appropriate key-to-address mapping function is determined by the following factors:

1. Characteristics of the user-key field, e.g., if non-numeric, then a direct mapping technique is inappropriate.
2. Density of population of the range of values of the user-key field. If it is sparse, then a calculation technique can be used to reduce the size of the address space.
3. Expected increase in size of the file, which affects the selection of address calculation method. File load factors greater than 0.8 tend to result in poor performance.
4. Need for rapid accessibility, which may be facilitated by a directory lookup scheme. Records can be stored using a calculation technique, then accessed later via a directory without having to recalculate addresses and deal with collisions.
5. Distribution of user-key values, which can be used (if known) to optimize an address calculation technique.

Appropriate bucket size is determined by characteristics of the storage device to be used (e.g., bucket size = track size), by the size of records to be stored, by whether or not variable-length records need to be accommodated, by installation standards, and by characteristics of user-key value and the key-to-address mapping function. Use of buckets that are large enough to hold more than one record can significantly reduce the effects of collisions.

The appropriate collision resolution method is determined by

1. The probability and patterns of collision.
2. The desirability of clustering synonyms physically.
3. The desirability of avoiding clusters of synonyms.
4. Bucket size.

If a directory lookup scheme is not being used for retrievals from a hashed file, then synonyms should nearly always be chained.

The capabilities of the programming language to be used also affect the design of the relative file. Many vendors supply nonstandard file organization techniques that implement relative files in a variety of ways. For example, one of the nonstandard COBOL compilers offers four distinct types of "relative" file organization: RELATIVE, DIRECT, STANDARD, and ACTUAL KEY.

SUMMARY

In a relative file organization there is a predictable relationship between the key used by a user (human or program) to identify a particular record and that record's storage location. The physical ordering of records need bear no logical relationship to their ordering by key value. The major advantage of relative organization is the ability to access quickly an individual record by its key value without accessing other records.

The fundamental techniques for determining a record's location, given its user-key value, were discussed. These techniques include direct mapping (absolute and relative addressing), directory lookup, and address calculation (division-remainder, mid-square, and folding). When address calculation is used, it becomes necessary to be able to resolve collisions which occur when multiple records hash to one address. Techniques to handle collisions include linear probing, double hashing, synonym chaining, and bucket addressing. The relative performance of these methods was compared.

A relative file must be stored either in main memory or on a direct-access device. The file can be created either sequentially by writing the records in their desired physical order, or directly by supplying individual records without regard to their resultant physical order. The file can be accessed either sequentially (in physically consecutive order) or by direct specification of particular records' key values. The file can be updated in place; new records can be written, old records can be deleted, and existing records can be replaced without access to unaffected records on the file. The basic concepts required for declaring and using a relative file in COBOL were introduced. The same types of procedures are used for creating and accessing relative files in other programming languages. Finally, several aspects of the design of relative files were reviewed.

Relative files are used extensively. They generally require little system overhead and they provide for rapid access to individual record occurrences. They are the fundamental method of supporting many interactive applications.

TERMS

absolute addressing	direct-access storage device
bucket addressing	disk drive
collision	diskette
collision resolution technique	disk pack
controller	division-remainder hashing
cylinder	double hashing
cylinder addressing	dynamic hashing
directory lookup addressing	equivalence class

extendible hashing
fixed-head disk
floppy disk
hash function
hashing
head crash
home address
latency
linear probing
load factor
movable head disk
open addressing
parallel head-per-track drive

relative addressing
relative file organization
rotational delay
secondary storage
sector
sector addressing
seek time
separate-overflow addressing
synonym chaining
synonyms
track
virtual hashing
Winchester disk

SELECTED REFERENCES

ACKERMAN, A. F. "Quadratic search for hash tables of size p n," *Comm. ACM*, 17(3): 164, March 1974.

ANDERSON, M. R. and M. G. ANDERSON. "Comments on perfect hashing functions: a single probe retrieving method for static sets," *Comm. ACM*, 22(2): 104, Feb. 1979.

BATAGELJ, V. "The quadratic hash method when the table size is not a prime number," *Comm. ACM*, 18(4): 216–217, April 1975.

BATORY, D. S. "Optimal file designs and reorganization points," *ACM Trans. on Database Systems*, 7(1): 60–81, March 1982.

BAYS, C. "The reallocation of hash-coded tables," *Comm. ACM*, 16(1): 11–14, Jan. 1973.

BELL, R. C. and B. FLOYD. "A Monte Carlo study of Cichelli hash-function solvability," *Comm. ACM*, 26(11): 924–925, Nov. 1983.

BELL, J. R. "The quadratic quotient method: a hash code eliminating secondary clustering," *Comm. ACM*, 13(2): 107–109, Feb. 1970.

BLAKE, I. F. and A. G. KONHEIM. "Big buckets are (are not) better!" *Jour. ACM*, 24(4): 591–606, Oct. 1977.

BOBROW, D. G. "A note on hash linking," *Comm. ACM*, 18(7): 413–415, July 1975.

BOLOUR, A. "Optimality properties of multiple-key hashing functions," *Jour. ACM*, 26(2): 196–210, April 1979.

BUCHHOLZ, W. "File organization and addressing," *IBM Systems Journal*, 2: 86–111, June 1963.

BURKHARD, W. A. "Partial-match hash coding: benefits of redundancy," *ACM Trans. on Database Systems*, 4(2): 228–239, June 1979.

BURKHARD, W. A. "Hashing and trie algorithms for partial match retrieval," *ACM Trans. on Database Systems*, 1(2): 175–187, June 1976.

CHANG, C. C., R. C. T. LEE, and M. W. DU. "Symbolic Gray code as a perfect multiattribute hashing scheme for partial match queries," *IEEE Trans. on Software Engineering*, SE-8 (3): 235–249, May 1982.

CHEN, W-C. and J. S. VITTER. "Analysis of new variants of coalesced hashing," *ACM Trans. on Database Systems*, 9(4): 616–645, Dec. 1984.

CICHELLI, R. J. "Minimal perfect hash functions made simple," *Comm. ACM*, 23(1): 17–19, Jan. 1980.

CLAPSON, P. "Improving the access time for random access files," *Comm. ACM*, 20(3): 127–135, March 1977.

DODDS, D. J. "Reducing dictionary size by using a hashing technique," *Comm. ACM*, 25(6): 368–370, June 1982.

DU, M. W., T. M. HSIEH, K. F. JEAN, and D. W. SHIEH. "The study of a new perfect hash scheme," *IEEE Trans. on Software Engineering*, SE-9 (3): 305–313, May 1983.

ELLIS, C. S. "Concurrency in linear hashing," *ACM Trans. on Database Systems*, 12(2): 195–217, June 1987.

FAGIN, R., J. NIEVERGELT, N. PIPPENGER, and H. R. STRONG. "Extendible hashing: a fast access method for dynamic files," *ACM Trans. on Database System*, 4(3): 315–344, Sept. 1979.

FALOUTSOS, C. "Multiattribute hashing using gray codes," *Proc. ACM-SIGMOD 1986 Internat. Conf. on Management of Data, May 28–30, 1986, Washington DC, SIGMOD Record*, 15(2): 227–238, June 1986.

GHOSH, S. P., and V. Y. LUM. "An analysis of collisions when hashing by division," IBM Research Rpt. RJ1218, May 1973.

GONNET, G. H. "Expected length of the longest probe sequence in hash code searching," *Jour. ACM*, 28(2): 289–304, April 1981.

GUIBAS, L. J. "The analysis of hashing techniques that exhibit k-ary clustering," *Jour. ACM*, 25(4): 544–555, Oct. 1978.

HALATSIS, C. and G. PHILOKYPROU. "Pseudochaining in hash tables," *Comm. ACM*, 21(7): 554–557, July 1978.

JAESCHKE, G. "Reciprocal hashing: a method for generating minimal perfect hashing functions," *Comm. ACM*, 24(12): 829–833, Dec. 1981.

KAWAGOE, K. "Modified dynamic hashing," *Proc. ACM-SIGMOD 1985 Internat. Conf. on Management of Data, May 28–31, 1985, Austin TX*, pp. 201–213.

KNOTT, G. D. "Hashing functions," *Computer Jour.*, 18(3): 265–278, August 1975.

LARSON, P-A. and M. V. RAMAKRISHNA. "External perfect hashing," *Proc. ACM-SIGMOD 1985 Internat. Conf. on Management of Data, May 28–31, 1985, Austin TX*, pp. 190–200.

LARSON, P-A. "Linear hashing with overflow-handling by linear probing," *ACM Trans. on Database Systems*, 10(1): 75–89, March 1985.

LARSON, P-A. and A. KAJLA. "File organization: implementation of a method guaranteeing retrieval in one access," *Comm. ACM*, 27(7): 670–677, July 1984.

LARSON, P-A. "Performance analysis of linear hashing with partial expansions," *ACM Trans. on Database Systems*, 7(4): 566–587, Dec. 1982.

LARSON, P-A. "A single-file version of linear hashing with partial expansions," *Proc. Eighth Internat. Conf. on Very Large Data Bases, Sept. 8–10, 1982, Mexico City*, pp. 300–309.

LIPTON, R. J., A. L. ROSENBERG, and A. C. YAO. "External hashing schemes for collections of data structures," *Jour. ACM*, 27(1): 81–95, Jan. 1980.

LITWIN, W. "Virtual hashing: A dynamically changing hashing," *Proc. 4th Conf. Very Large Data Bases*, W. Berlin, September 1978, pp. 517–523.

LOMET, D. B. "Bounded index exponential hashing," *ACM Trans. on Database Systems*, 8(1): 136–165, March 1983.

LUM, V. Y. "General performance analysis of key-to-address transformation methods using an abstract file concept," *Comm. ACM*, 16(10): 603–612, Oct. 1973.

————, et al. "Key-to-address transform techniques," *Comm. ACM*, 14(4): 228–239, April 1971.

————, and P. S. T. YUEN. "Additional results on key-to-address transform techniques," *Comm. ACM*, 15(11): 996–997, Nov. 1972.

LYON, G. "Packed scatter tables," *Comm. ACM*, 21(10): 857–865, Oct. 1978.

MAURER, W. D. and T. G. LEWIS. "Hash table methods," *ACM Computing Surveys*, 7(1): 5–19, March 1975.

MAURER, W. D. "An improved hash code for scatter storage," *Comm. ACM*, 11(1): 35–37, Jan. 1968.

MENDELSON, H. "Analysis of extendible hashing," *IEEE Trans. on Software Engineering*, SE-8 (6): 611–619, Nov. 1982.

MENDELSON, H. and U. YECHIALI. "A new approach to the analysis of linear probing schemes," *Jour. ACM*, 27(3): 474–483, July 1980.

MENDELSON, H. and U. YECHIALI. "Performance measures for ordered lists in random-access files," *Jour. ACM*, 26(4): 654–667, Oct. 1979.

MOR, M. and A. S. FRAENKEL. "A hash code method for detecting and correcting spelling errors," *Comm. ACM*, 25(12): 935–938, Dec. 1982.

NISHIHARA, S. and K. IKEDA. "Reducing the retrieval time of hashing method by using predictors," *Comm. ACM*, 26(12): 1082–1088, Dec. 1983.

OTOO, E. "A multidimensional digital hashing scheme for files with composite keys," *Proc. ACM-SIGMOD 1985 Internat. Conf. on Management of Data, May 28–31, 1985, Austin TX*, pp. 214–229.

QUITTNER, P., S. CSOKA, S. HALASZ, D. KOTSIS, and K. VARNAI. "Comparison of synonym handling and bucket organization methods," *Comm. ACM*, 24(9): 579–583, Sept. 1981.

RAMAMOHANARAO, K. and R. SACKS-DAVIS. "Recursive linear hashing," *ACM Trans. on Database Systems*, 9(3): 369–391, Sept. 1984.

RAMAMOHANARAO, K., J. W. LLOYD, and J. A. THOM. "Partial-match retrieval using hashing and descriptors," *ACM Trans. on Database Systems*, 8(4): 552–576, Dec. 1983.

RIVEST, R. L. "Optimal arrangement of keys in a hash table," *Jour. ACM*, 25(2): 200–209, April 1978.

ROSENBERG, A. L. and L. J. STOCKMEYER. "Hashing schemes for extendible arrays," *Jour. ACM*, 24(2): 199–221, April 1977.

SCHOLL, M. "New file organizations based on dynamic hashing," *ACM Trans. on Database Systems*, 6(1): 194–211, March 1981.

SPRUGNOLI, R. "Perfect hashing functions: a single probe retrieving method for static sets," *Comm. ACM*, 20(11): 841–850, Nov. 1977.

VALDURIEZ, P. and Y. VIEMONT. "A multikey hashing scheme using predicate trees," *ACM SIGMOD 1984 Proc. of Annual Meeting, SIGMOD Record*, 14(2): 107–114, June 1984.

VEKLEROV, E. "Analysis of dynamic hashing with deferred splitting," *ACM Trans. on Database Systems*, 10(1): 90–96, March 1985.

VITTER, J. S. "Implementations for coalesced hashing," *Comm. ACM*, 25(12): 911–926, Dec. 1982.

REVIEW EXERCISES

1. What is the difference between a fixed-head disk and a movable-head disk with respect to data access time?

2. Which of the following activities makes the greatest contribution to the access time of a block on a movable-head disk? (a) head activation, (b) cylinder selection, (c) rotational delay.

3. Which of the following activities makes the greatest contribution to the access time of a block on a fixed-head disk? (a) head activation, (b) cylinder selection, (c) rotational delay.

4. Compare the relative advantages and disadvantages of absolute addressing and relative addressing.

5. Discuss several alternative techniques for implementing a directory to be used for lookup of addresses into a relative file. Compare the techniques.

6. Compare the relative advantages and disadvantages of direct addressing, directory lookup, and address calculation (hashing). Consider both retrieval of records and storage of new records.

7. On what factors is the performance of a hash function dependent?

8. How is the performance of a hash function evaluated?

9. Compare the operations involved in the division-remainder, mid-square, and folding hash functions.

10. In the absence of information about the distribution of key values, which type of hash function in general performs the best?

11. At what load factor should a relative file generally be enlarged and reorganized?

12. Why does use of synonym chaining require that a record not be displaced from its home address by a record that is not its synonym?

13. Explain the clustering effect exhibited when linear probing is used.

14. What is the primary purpose of each of the following: (a) hash function, (b) linear probing, (c) double hashing, (d) synonym chaining?

15. Explain at least two techniques for handling bucket overflow.

16. Why can a bucket size > 1 record allow variable-length records to be accommodated?

17. How is free space managed when a bucket can hold multiple records? Consider both record insertion and deletion.

18. Discuss the differences in free-space management when a bucket can contain variable-length records instead of just fixed-length records.

19. Learn about virtual hashing techniques. Compare their performance with that of static hashing methods.

20. Modify the retrieval logic of Fig. 13–13 to accommodate possibly deleted records.

21. Write an algorithm to delete a record from the file created using the logic of Fig. 13–12.

22. Give examples of the kinds of application changes that could cause the performance of a relative file to change.

23. Give examples of the kinds of application changes that would be irrelevant to the performance of one of the application's relative files.

24. Obtain a listing of a production program that creates or maintains a relative file from your installation. Determine how addresses are determined and how collisions are resolved.

25. Write a program that creates a relative file using division-remainder hashing and linear probing. Write another version of the program that additionally chains synonyms. Compare the performance of the two program versions with record insertion and retrieval activity.

26. Modify your program versions to accommodate deletion activity. How are you handling deletions? Compare the performance of the two program versions.

chapter fourteen

index structures

In the last chapter, we discussed techniques for organizing data so that a key value could be used to locate a particular record relatively rapidly. The fundamental concept was to use the key value in calculating the record's physical location. In this chapter, we introduce additional techniques for providing rapid access to particular records in a file. These techniques supplement the data collection using a tree that guides access to the desired records.

Indexes support applications that selectively access individual records, rather than searching through the entire collection in sequence. One field (or a group of fields) is used as the index field. For example, in a banking application, there might be a file of records describing Branch Offices. It might be appropriate to index the file on Branch Name, providing access to Branch Office information to support interactive inquiries.

We shall start with a relatively simple tree-structured index and then progress to more complex structures.

BINARY SEARCH TREES AS INDEXES

Let us first reconsider the binary search tree, which was discussed in Chapter 8. Recall that the nodes of a binary search tree are arranged in such a way that a search for a particular key value proceeds down one branch of the tree. The sought key value is compared with the key value of the tree's root: if it is less than the root value, the search proceeds down the left subtree; if it is greater than the root value, the search proceeds down the right subtree. The same logic is applied at each node encountered until the search is satisfied or it is determined that the sought key is not included in the tree. See Figures 8–16, 17, 22, 23, and 24 to refresh your memory.

Typically, a key value does not stand alone. Rather, the key value is associated with information fields to form a record. In general, storing these information fields in the binary search tree would make for a very large tree. In order to speed searches and to reduce the tree size, the information fields of records commonly are stored separate from the key values. These records are organized into files and are stored on secondary storage devices such as rotating disks. The connection between a key value in the binary search tree and the corresponding record in the file is made by housing a pointer to the record with the key value. Thus, the node structure for a binary search tree may be defined as follows in Pascal.

$$\underline{type}\ nodeptr\ =\ \uparrow nodetype;$$
$$recptr\ =\ \uparrow rectype;$$
$$nodetype\ =\ \underline{record}$$
$$key: \underline{integer};$$
$$infoptr: recptr;$$
$$left: nodeptr;$$
$$right: nodeptr$$
$$\underline{end};$$

where rectype is defined appropriately for the application. Key is defined here as integer data type; it could be of other types.

Fig. 14–1 shows the binary search tree of Fig. 8–23 with pointers included to the

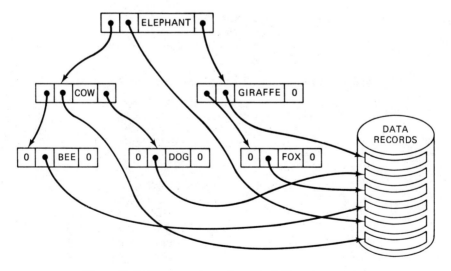

Figure 14–1 Binary search tree from Fig. 8–23 used as an index.

data records. This augmentation of the binary search tree to include pointers (i.e., addresses) to data records outside the structure qualifies the tree to be an index. An *index* is a structured collection of key value and address pairs; the primary purpose of an index is to facilitate access to a collection of records. An index is said to be a *dense index* if it contains a key value-address pair for each record in the collection. An index that is not dense is sometimes called a *sparse index*. There are many ways to organize an index; the augmented binary search tree is one approach.

At this time we will not concern ourselves with the actual location of those records on primary or secondary storage. Suffice it to say that in contrast to relative files where the physical locations of records are determined by a hash algorithm applied to key values, there is significantly more freedom in the physical placement of records in an indexed file.

Processing of this augmented binary search tree is the same as was presented in Chapter 8. When a search terminates successfully, the infoptr may be followed to find the data associated with the sought key.

Just as a binary search tree can be used as an index, so can an AVL tree or a BB tree (see Fig. 8–24). As shown in Chapter 8, the maximum path length through an AVL tree is $O(\log_2 n)$. Thus use of an AVL tree to house a dense index to n records would result in a maximum search path length of $O(\log_2 n)$ to locate the address of the sought record. Actually the maximum search length of an AVL tree is $1.40 \log_2 n$; the worst case to find a key when $n = 10$ then is about four comparisons through the tree.

M-WAY SEARCH TREES

The performance of an index can be enhanced significantly by increasing the branching factor of the tree. Rather than binary branching, m-way ($m > 2$) branching can be used. For expository purposes, we ignore for the moment pointers out of the structure to data records and consider only the internal structure of the tree. An *m-way search tree* is a tree in which each node has out-degree $<\, = m$. When an m-way search tree is not empty, it has the following properties.

1. Each node of the tree has the structure shown in Fig. 14–2.

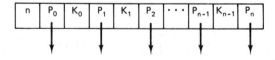

Figure 14–2 Fundamental structure of a node in an m-way search tree.

The $P_0, P_1, \ldots, P_n$ are pointers to the node's subtrees and the $K_0, \ldots, K_{n-1}$ are key values. The requirement that each node have out-degree $<\, = m$ forces $n <\, = m - 1$.

2. The key values in a node are in ascending order:

$$K_i < K_{i+1}$$

for $i = 0, \ldots n - 2$.

3. All key values in nodes of the subtree pointed to by P_i are less than the key value K_i for $i = 0, \ldots, n - 1$.

4. All key values in nodes of the subtree pointed to by P_n are greater than the key value K_{n-1}.

5. The subtrees pointed to by the P_i, $i = 0, \ldots, n$ are also m-way search trees.

Note that the arrangement of key values in nodes is analogous to their arrangement in binary search trees. A five-way search tree has a maximum of five pointers out of each node, i.e., $n < = 4$. Some nodes of the tree may contain fewer than five pointers.

Example

Fig. 14–3 illustrates a three-way search tree. Only the key values and the non-null subtree pointers are shown. In the figure, leaf nodes have been depicted as containing just key values. Each internal node of the search tree has the structure depicted in Fig. 14–2, here with a maximum of three subtree pointers.

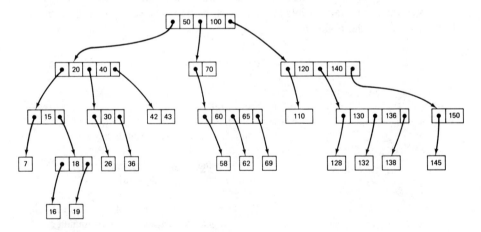

Figure 14–3   Example three-way search tree.

M-Way Search Trees as Indexes

When an m-way search tree is used as an index, each key-pointer pair (K_i, P_i) becomes a triplet P_i, K_i, A_i where A_i is the address of the data record associated with key value K_i. Thus, each tree node not only points to its child nodes in the tree, but also points into the collection of data records. If the index is dense, every record in the collection will be pointed to by some node in the index.

We can define the node type for an *m*-way search tree index as follows in Pascal.

```
type nodeptr = ↑ nodetype;
     recptr = ↑ rectype;
     n1, keytype = integer;
     nodetype = record
                    n: integer
                    keyptrs: array [0..n1] of record
                                ptr: nodeptr;
                                key: keytype;
                                addr: recptr
                             end;
                    keyptrn: nodeptr
                 end;
```

Again key's type need not be *integer*; $n \leq m - 1$ and $n1 = n - 1$.

Searching an M-Way Search Tree

The process of searching for a key value in an *m*-way search tree is a relatively straight-forward extension of the process of searching for a key value in a binary search tree. A recursive version of the search algorithm follows. The variable skey contains the sought key value; r initially points to the root of the tree. The search tree is assumed to be global, with var node: nodetype.

```
procedure search(skey: keytype; var r: nodeptr, foundrec: recptr);
var i: 0..n;
begin if (r = nil)
      then foundrec: = nil
      else begin i: = 0;
              while (i < n and skey > node.key[i])
              do i : = i + 1;
              if (i < n and skey = node.key[i])
              then foundrec : = node.addr[i]
              else if i < n
                   then search (skey, node.ptr[i], foundrec)
                   else search(skey, node.keyptrn, foundrec)
           end;
end;
```

Compare this logic with that presented in Chapter 8 for direct searches of a binary search tree. The primary difference is that the array of keys in each node of the *m*-way tree must be scanned to find the appropriate pointer to follow either down to a child node or directly to the data record.

Performance

The maximum search length is the height of the tree. No more than one node is ever visited on any given level of the tree. To minimize this height for a tree containing n keys, the tree should be as bushy as possible. A three-way tree can provide shorter path lengths than can a two-way tree for the same set of keys. In general, the higher the order of branching of the tree, the shorter is the maximum search length. Each node visitation causes a selection from among a greater number of possible branches.

Consider an m-way tree with height h. The maximum number of nodes in this tree is

$$\sum_{i=0}^{h-1} m^i$$

which is $\dfrac{m^h - 1}{m - 1}$. Each node carries a maximum of $m - 1$ key values. Thus the maximum number of keys in the tree is $m^h - 1$.

Turning the argument around, an m-way tree of n keys has a minimum height of

$$\lceil \log_m(n + 1) \rceil.$$

The maximum search length of an optimal m-way tree of n keys, then, is $O(\log_m n)$. Setting $m = 2$ gives the expected results for optimal binary search trees.

In order to have an m-way search tree of n keys have a maximum height of h, m must be at least $(n + 1)^{1/h}$. For example, to ensure a maximum path length of 4 with 255 keys, the tree must have at least four-way branching; to ensure a maximum path length of 4 with 65,535 keys, the tree must have at least 16-way branching.

The extent of branching is not the only factor that determines the performance of an m-way search tree. As we discussed for binary search trees, performance can be improved by keeping the tree balanced. Note that the definition of an m-way search tree does not ensure that each interior node of the tree will have m non-null pointers to subtrees. The tree of Fig. 14–3 could have improved search performance if it were balanced. As we discovered for binary search trees, keeping an m-way search tree completely balanced may not be worth the effort. Rather, it may be sufficient to constrain the extent to which we allow the tree to deviate from complete balance. Just as AVL trees enjoy more widely spread use than do their completely balanced binary search tree counterparts, so are almost-balanced m-way search trees called B-trees more popular than completely balanced m-way search trees.

B-TREES

The basic B-tree structure was discovered by R. Bayer and E. McCreight (1970) of Boeing Scientific Research Labs and has grown to become one of the most popular techniques for organizing an index structure. Many variations on the basic B-tree have been developed; we cover the basic structure first and then introduce some of the variations.

A *B-tree of order m* is an *m*-way search tree with the following properties.

1. Each node of the tree, except for the root and the leaves, has at least ⌈½*m*⌉ subtrees and no more than *m* subtrees.
2. The root of the tree has at least two subtrees, unless it is itself a leaf.
3. All leaves of the tree are on the same level.

The first constraint ensures that each node of the tree is at least half full. The second constraint forces the tree to branch early. The third constraint keeps the tree nearly balanced.

The size of a B-tree of order *m* and its search path lengths may be larger than for the optimal *m*-way search tree for the same collection of keys. However, as we will see in the next section, maintaining a B-tree is significantly easier than maintaining an optimal *m*-way search tree. The reasons for using a B-tree of order *m* rather than an optimal *m*-way search tree are the same as the reasons for using an AVL (or BB) tree instead of a completely balanced binary search tree. Less overhead is required to maintain the B-tree structure when key values are inserted or deleted; yet maximum search lengths are nearly as good as those of an optimally structured, balanced *m*-way search tree of the same order.

It should be noted that some authors use a different notation than we do. You may see a B-tree of order *m* defined as a *d*-way search tree in which each node bears a minimum of *m* keys and *m* + 1 pointers and a maximum of 2*m* keys and 2*m* + 1 pointers; here *d* = 2*m* + 1. We will *not* use this notation.

Example

Fig. 14–4 illustrates a B-tree of order 3 that contains the keys of the three-way search tree of Fig. 14–3. Each node has been marked with a letter to facilitate later references to this example tree. Not shown for each node is an indicator of the number of non-null subtree pointers that it contains. The leaves need not have space for those pointers. B-trees of higher order are certainly more interesting but become difficult to draw. Each node of a B-tree of order *m* has the same structure as a node of an *m*-way search tree. When a B-tree is used as an index, its nodes contain pointers to the records corresponding to each of the key values.

Searching a B-tree

The search for a particular key value in a B-tree follows the same procedure as does the direct search of an *m*-way search tree. How well does a B-tree search perform? Consider first the question of the minimum number of keys in a B-tree of order *m* with height *h*. By definition, the root of a B-tree has at least two children. Each of these nodes has at least ⌈½*m*⌉ children, and so forth down the tree to level *h*-2 (the leaves are on level *h*-1). Thus the tree must contain at least

$$1 + 2 + \sum_{i=3}^{h-2} 2 * \lceil \tfrac{1}{2}m \rceil^{i-2}$$

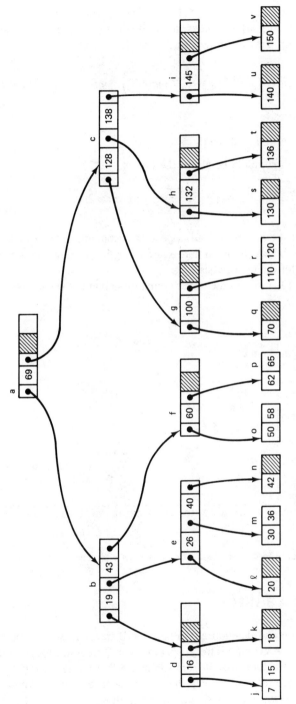

Figure 14-4 Example B-tree of order 3 containing keys of the three-way search tree of Fig. 14-3.

interior nodes and at least $2*\lceil\tfrac{1}{2}m\rceil^{h-2}$ leaves. Each interior node except the root must contain at least $\lceil\tfrac{1}{2}m\rceil - 1$ keys; the root and each leaf must contain at least 1 key. Thus the minimum number of keys in the tree is

$$n \geq 1 + \left(2 + \sum_{i=3}^{h-2} 2*\lceil\tfrac{1}{2}m\rceil^{i-2}\right)(\lceil\tfrac{1}{2}m\rceil - 1) + 2*\lceil\tfrac{1}{2}m\rceil^{h-2}$$

which reduces to

$$n + 1 \geq 2*\lceil\tfrac{1}{2}m\rceil^{h-2}$$

That is, the maximum height of the tree is

$$h \leq 2 + \log\lceil\tfrac{1}{2}m\rceil\left(\frac{n+1}{2}\right) \text{ for } m > 2$$

Recall that the leaves will all appear on a maximum level of $h - 1$. Since the tree's height determines the maximum search length, we now know that the B-tree performs very well for direct searches.

Fig. 14–5 graphs the upper bound on height (h) versus the order of the tree (m) for $n = 2*10^{7}$.

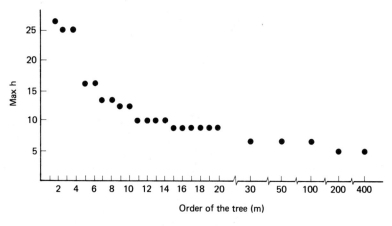

Figure 14–5   B-tree worst-case performance for direct search.

INSERTING INTO A B-TREE

The insertion and deletion algorithms for B-trees are somewhat more interesting. Like operations on AVL and BB trees, operations on B-trees must preserve the balanced character of the data structure. Recall from Chapter 8 that insertion or deletion in an AVL or BB tree may force rotation to keep the tree in balance. The algorithms for keeping a B-tree balanced are conceptually simpler than are those rather complex rotation algorithms.

Fig. 14–6 outlines the logic for inserting a key value into a B-tree. First, a B-tree

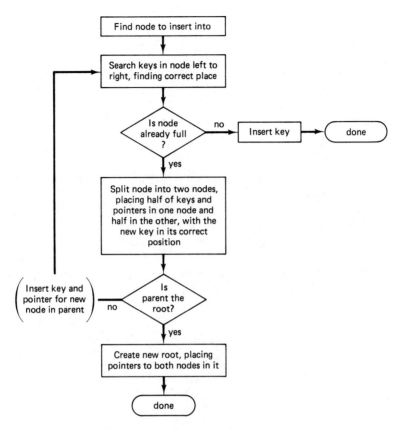

Figure 14–6 Flowchart for insertion in a B-tree.

search (which is the same as an *m*-way tree search) must be done to find the correct location for the key value in the tree. Then the key is inserted. Usually, especially with higher-order trees, the node has space available for another key value and pointer. Sometimes, however, the node is already full and cannot accommodate another key value. The node must be split into two, with half the key values and pointers going into one node and half into the other. These ''twin'' nodes have the same parent, which must be modified for the additional key value and pointer. In the worst case, the splitting procedure must be carried all the way up the tree to the root. The tree then increases in height by one level, lengthening the expected search length by one. B-tree insertion is commonly programmed recursively, since the splitting process is the same, regardless of tree level.

Example

Consider first insertions of several new keys—say 22, 41, 59, 57, 54, 33, 75, 124, 122, 123—into the B-tree of Fig. 14–4. The key value 22 should reside in node 1; that node has space enough for another key, so it simply is inserted (Fig. 14–7(a)).

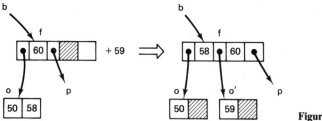

Figure 14–7(a)

Similarly, key value 41, which should reside in node n, may be inserted there because space is available (Fig. 14–7(b)).

Figure 14–7(b)

Note that the proper sequence of key values must be maintained; key value 42 is shifted right to make room for key value 41.

Key value 59 should reside in node o. However, node o already contains the maximum allowable number of key values for a B-tree of order 3. Whenever a key needs to be inserted in a node that is already full, a *split* occurs. The one node becomes two nodes; half of its keys go in one of the two nodes and half in the other. The remaining value is moved up to the parent node. The parent node also be must adjusted to include a pointer to the spawned node. Here, nodes f and o are both modified (Fig. 14–7(c)).

Figure 14–7(c)

Now, insertion of 57, the next key value, proceeds by simply placing 57 in node o (Fig. 14–7(d)).

Figure 14–7(d)

Key value 54 also should be placed in node o, but node o is again full. The same splitting algorithm is applied (Fig. 14–7(e)).

Figure 14–7(e)

However, the parent node f is also full and cannot accommodate another key value and a pointer to node o″. The splitting algorithm is again applied, this time to node f (Fig. 14–7(f)).

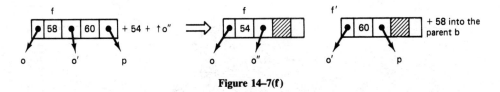

Figure 14–7(f)

Again, the parent node b happens to be full and cannot accommodate another key value and a pointer to f′. The splitting procedure is now applied to node b (Fig. 14–7(g)).

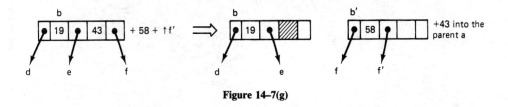

Figure 14–7(g)

The parent node a does have space available for another key value and a pointer to b′ (Fig. 14–7(h)).

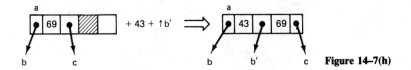

Figure 14–7(h)

Insertion of the next four keys in our example sequence—33, 75, 124, and 122—can be accommodated easily. Insertion of 123, however, causes the B-tree to grow one level in height. The resultant tree is shown in Fig. 14–8. You should work through these insertions to verify your understanding of node splitting. Note that the tree can now accommodate numerous insertions without node splitting, since each prior split opened space for insertions.

Performance

How frequently does node splitting occur? In the worst case, inserting a new node causes splitting to percolate up the entire tree, splitting $h - 1$ nodes, where h is the tree's height before the insertion. We shall start with a B-tree containing just a root node and see how the tree grows. The first split adds two new nodes; all other splits produce one new node apiece. A tree with f nodes is the result of $p - 2$ splits. It contains at least

$$1 + (p - 1) (\lceil \tfrac{1}{2}m \rceil - 1)$$

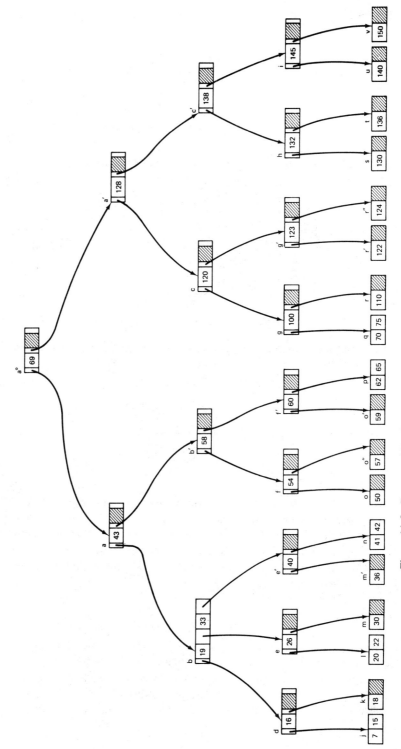

Figure 14-8 B-tree resulting from sequence of insertions into the B-tree of Fig. 14-4.

keys because each node has a minimum of $\lceil \frac{1}{2}m \rceil - 1$ keys, except the root, which must have at least one key.

The probability that an additional split is required upon insertion of a key value is less than the ratio of splits to keys:

$$\frac{p - 2}{1 + (p - 1)(\lceil \frac{1}{2}m \rceil - 1)}$$

which is less than 1 split per $\lceil \frac{1}{2}m \rceil - 1$ key insertions (since $1/(p - 2)$ approaches 0 for large p and $(p - 1)/(p - 2)$ is approximately 1).

For $m = 10$, the split probability is .25; for $m = 100$, the split probability is .0204; for $m = 200$, the split probability is .0101. The higher the order of the B-tree, the lower the probability that key insertion will cause a node to split.

DELETING FROM A B-TREE

Deletion of a key from a B-tree is only slightly more complicated than is insertion. In order to keep the B-tree a B-tree, two nodes need to be merged when one node would have fewer than the minimum required keys and pointers.

Fig. 14–9 outlines the logic for deleting a key value from a B-tree. As with an insertion, a B-tree search must first be done to find the node containing the victim key. If the key to be deleted is in an interior node, the tree is transformed to move this key into a leaf because it is easier to delete a leaf. Once the deletion is made, other keys may need to be shifted or leaves be combined to meet the minimum-key and minimum-pointer requirements for a B-tree. These node combinations may be needed for several levels.

If a merge percolates all the way to the highest level, a new root is formed and the height of the B-tree is decreased by 1. As with splitting, the probability of node merging decreases as the order of the B-tree increases.

Example

Consider deletion of the following sequence of keys from the B-tree of Fig. 14–8: 65, 7, 40, 16.

Removal of key value 65 from node p is easy (Fig. 14–10(a)). Removal of key value 7 from node j is also easy (Fig. 14–10(b)). Note that 15 has been shifted left to maintain proper key sequencing.

Removal of key value 40 leaves node e' with two pointers but no keys. Some key must be found to place in e' so that the minimum key requirement is met. A proper key value is the leftmost key of the subtree pointed to by the pointer after the deleted key; here that key value is 41 in node n (Fig. 14–10(c)).

Sometimes keys are distributed in such a way that nodes must be merged to maintain compliance with B-tree constraints. Deletion of 16 from node d gives us such a case. Not only are d and e merged, but j and k are also merged and ancestor node b is also affected (Fig. 14–10(d)).

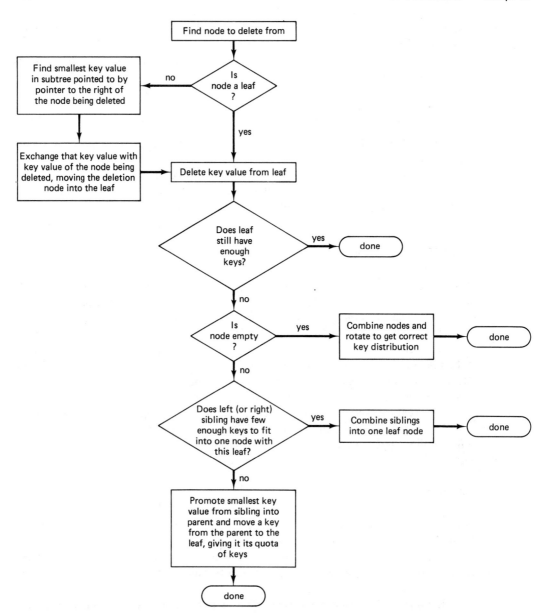

Figure 14–9 Outline of logic to delete a key from a B-tree.

Understanding the insertion and deletion operations on B-trees will increase your comprehension of why B-trees are defined as they are. Splitting of a full node results in two nodes that both meet the requirement for a minimum number of keys and pointers. A subminimal and a minimally loaded node fit together nicely without violating the constraint on maximum number of keys and pointers when two nodes must be merged.

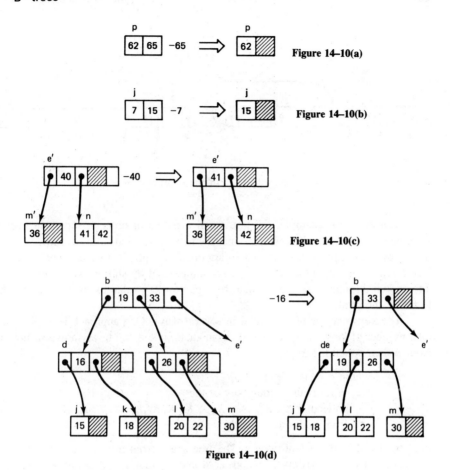

Figure 14–10(a)

Figure 14–10(b)

Figure 14–10(c)

Figure 14–10(d)

The key arrangement makes it easy to find the prior or next key from any key in the tree. Tree maintenance actions will become clearer if you play "tree-manager" and perform various insertions and deletions yourself.

B*-TREES

The B*-tree data structure was identified by Knuth in his tome on searching and sorting (1973) as one of several possible variations on the basic B-tree. One motivation for the multitude of B-tree variations that have been proposed has been to reduce the overhead required to accommodate insertions and deletions. The other primary motivation has been to improve the direct search performance.

A *B*-tree* is a B-tree in which each node is at least two-thirds full instead of at least half full. A basic idea of the B*-tree is to reduce the frequency of node splitting. When a node becomes full, rather than its being split, a redistribution scheme takes keys and pointers from the full node and places them into a brother node.

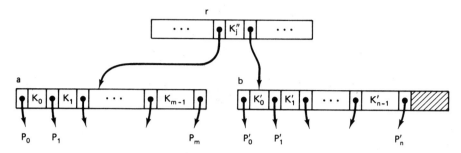

Figure 14–11 Part of a B-tree of order m.

Consider, for example, the portion of a B-tree of order m shown in Fig. 14–11. Assume that insertion of a key value into the tree causes node a to overflow with one too many key-pointer pairs. For the sake of argument, assume that the extra pair is K_m, P_{m+1}, where $K_m < K_j''$. This insertion can be accommodated by shifting key values from node a to node b through node r. Note that the separator key value in node r must be changed to reflect the rotation.

The keys may be redistributed in several ways. One approach is to place half the total number of keys, here $m + 1 + n$, in each node a and b, as shown in Fig. 14–12. Node a then contains c keys,

where $c = \lceil (m + 1 + n)/2 \rceil$.

Key K_{c+1} is the middle key of the
collection $K_0, K_1, \ldots K_{m-1}, K_m, K_j'', K_0', K_1', \ldots, K_{n-1}'$
from nodes a, r, and b.

K_{c+1} is placed in the parent node r. The free space from brother node b has been used to accommodate the overflow from node a. Moreover, that free space has been redistributed between nodes a and b such that each now has about half of it.

Inserting into a B*-tree

Consider the situation shown in Fig. 14–13. Adding a key value 24 to node a will cause overflow; node a is already full. However, the insertion can be done by shifting key values from node a to node b through node r. The total number of keys involved is seven (18, 20, 22, 24, 26, 33, 35). About half (i.e., $\lceil 7/2 \rceil$) of the keys (18, 20, 22) would be placed in node a; the middle key (24) would become the separator key in node r; the remaining $\lceil 7/2 \rceil$ keys (26, 33, 35) would be placed in node b, as shown in Fig. 14–14. Free space from node b has been used to accommodate the overflow from node a. Moreover, the remaining free space has been redistributed between nodes a and b such that each now has half of it.

What if node b were also full and did not have free space to accommodate node a's overflow? In a B*-tree, *two* nodes are split to form *three* nodes, each of which is about two-thirds full. The total number of keys involved is $2m + 2$ (m from each a and

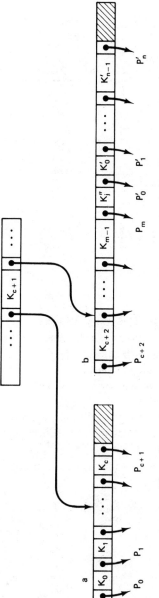

Figure 14–12 Redistribution of keys and pointers in nodes a and b from Fig. 14–11.

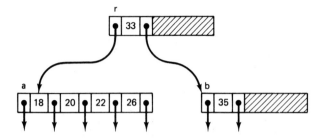

Figure 14–13   Example part of B*-tree.

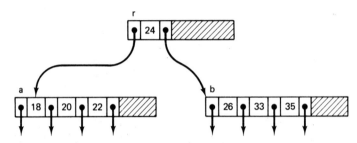

Figure 14–14   Redistribution of keys and pointers of nodes a and b of Fig. 14–13, to accommodate insertion of key value 24.

b, 1 in r, 1 to be added). The resultant three nodes should contain each about $(2m)/3$ keys; two keys are placed into the parent node to act as separators. A diagram illustrating the result of the split is shown in Fig. 14–15.

Returning to our example, consider the situation shown in Fig. 14–16. Now insertion of 24 cannot be accommodated by shifting key values from node a to node b, because node b is already full. Instead we split nodes a and b into three nodes, each of which is about two-thirds full. The total number of keys involved is 10. About one-third of the keys that are not separators are placed in each node a, a', and b as shown in Fig. 14–17.

As another example, consider a B*-tree of order $m = 90$. Assume that nodes a and b are both full. Say

> node a:key values $K_{100}, \ldots, K_{189}$
> node b:key values $K_{191}, \ldots, K_{280}$
> node r:key values $\ldots, K_{99}, K_{190}, K_{281} \ldots$

We wish to insert key value K'_{189} where $K_{189} < K'_{189} < K_{190}$. K'_{189} cannot fit in node a, and node b has no free space to share. A new node—call it node a'—is allocated and keys are shifted such that

> node a :key values $K_{100}, \ldots, K_{159}$
> node a':key values $K_{161}, \ldots, K_{219}$
> node b :key values $K_{221}, \ldots, K_{280}$
> node r :key values $\ldots, K_{99}, K_{160}, K_{220}, K_{281}, \ldots$

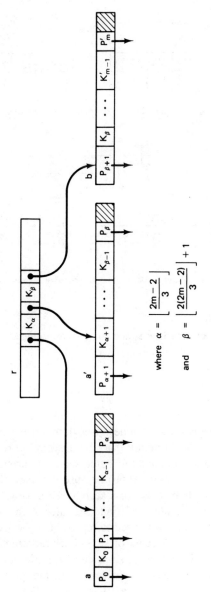

Figure 14-15 Result of splitting nodes a and b from B*-tree.

where $\alpha = \left\lfloor \dfrac{2m-2}{3} \right\rfloor$

and $\beta = \left\lfloor \dfrac{2(2m-2)}{3} \right\rfloor + 1$

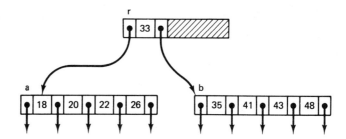

Figure 14–16   Example part of B*-tree.

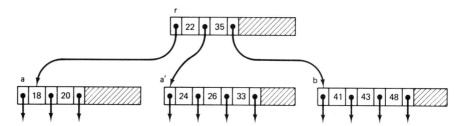

Figure 14–17   Result of splitting nodes a and b of B*-tree of Fig. 14–16, to accommodate insertion of key value 24.

Nodes a, a', and b each has free space for 29 key values. The new key K'_{189} resides in node a'.

TRIES

To this point we have based our searches through tree structures on comparisons between key values. A trie is a data structure that uses instead the representations of key values as sequences of characters or digits to guide searches through the structure. The name *trie* was suggested by E. Fredkin (1960) because it is part of information re*trie*val.

A trie is an *m*-ary tree. It is *not* a search tree of order *m*; that is, the ordering of key values in the nodes does not conform to the rules of an *m*-way search tree. The order of a trie is determined by the radix used to represent key values. The *radix* of key values represented by digits is 10; the radix of key values represented by alphabetic characters is 26 (or 27 if the space is included). Each node of a trie of order *m* is essentially a one-dimensional array of *m* pointers. Each element in the array corresponds to one of the elements of the radix set. A node in a 10-ary trie is shown in Fig. 14–18.

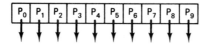

Figure 14–18   Node structure for a 10-ary trie.

Note that the node is composed entirely of pointers. The position of a pointer in the node determines the value to which it corresponds.

The height of a trie is determined by the length of the key field. For a node on the jth level of a 10-ary trie, P_i points to a subtree representing all key values whose j^{th} digit is i. For example, P_4 on the sixth level of a 10-ary trie points to a subtree representing all key values whose sixth digit is 4.

Example

Fig. 14–19 illustrates part of a trie for structuring a collection of 4-digit key values. This example trie represents the following collection of key values:

```
2302,  2303,  2305,  2306,  2307,  2308
2350,  2352,  2353,  2355,  2356,  2358,  2359
2581,  2582,  2584,  2585,  2586,  2588,  2589
2590,  2591,  2593,  2594,  2596,  2597,  2599
2900,  2901,  2903,  2904,  2905,  2906,  2907,  2908,  2909
32xx . . .
35xx . . .
52xx . . .
59xx . . .
7312,  7313,  7315,  7316
7390,  7391,  7393,  7395,  7397,  7399
7490,  7492,  7494,  7496,  7498.
```

When a trie is used as an index, the leaf nodes contain addresses of data records with the corresponding key values. A trie can also be used to represent a collection of values, without a file of associated data. In that case, the leaf nodes would simply contain placeholders indicating the presence or absence of a corresponding value.

A node in a trie used to represent alphabetic key values contains 26 pointers. For a node on the jth level of such a trie, P_i points to a subtree whose j^{th} character is the ith letter of the alphabet. For example P_{10} on the third level of the trie points to a subtree containing all key values whose third character is J.

Searching a Trie

Successful direct searches in a basic trie must terminate at leaf nodes. To find the pointer to a particular record requires visiting all levels of the tree. At each level, the next branch to follow is determined by the pertinent digit of the key value. Thus the length of a successful search is determined by the height of the trie, which is determined by the length of the key field. For contrast, recall that the length of a search in an m-way search tree is determined by the number of key values represented. In the trie of Fig. 14–19, a

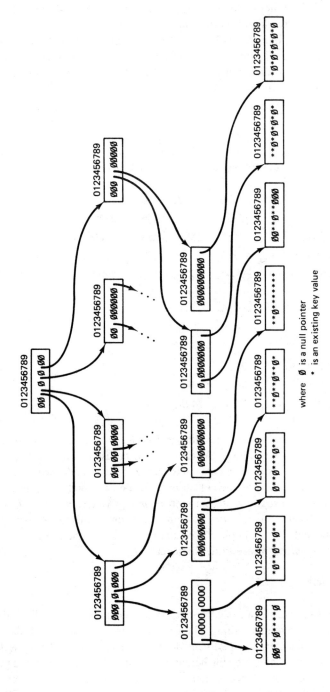

Figure 14-19 Example trie for a collection of 4-digit key values.

where **Ø** is a null pointer
    * is an existing key value

successful search requires visiting four nodes regardless of whether there are three key values represented or 10^4.

On the other hand, an unsuccessful search terminates when it is determined that a sought key value does not reside in the structure. In a trie, an unsuccessful search may terminate on any level of the structure. For example, visiting only the root node of the trie of Fig. 14–19 is enough to determine that there are no key values in the trie with high-order digit from the set $\{0, 1, 4, 6, 8, 9\}$. This good performance for unsuccessful searches is a major attractive feature for use of the trie in some applications.

Maintaining a Trie

Inserting a new key value in a trie is relatively easy. The correct leaf to represent the new value is located using a direct search. It may be that the correct leaf does not exist. In this case, nodes must be added properly to the index part of the structure to direct a search to the new leaf node. The correct element of that leaf is found and changed from non-null to a place-holder value or, if the trie is used as an index, to the address of the related data record.

Note that even though the maximum structure of the trie is fixed by the key set's radix and the key field's length, the basic trie shown in Fig. 14–19 does not include all possible nodes. With radix r and key length k, there could be k levels, with r^{i-1} nodes on each level i. The nodes that contain only null pointers are not shown. These empty nodes have the potential to exist and can be inserted into the tree when key value insertion makes them nonempty.

Not storing empty nodes makes better use of memory when the distribution of key values is such that there are many null nodes. This very well may be the case, especially when the key range is sparsely used. For example, consider a company with 250 employees. Assume that the 9-digit social security number is used as the key field to identify employee payroll records. A basic trie built upon this key field would have nine levels and potentially space for 10^9 employee record pointers on the leaf level. Only 250 of these elements (.000025%) would be occupied.

Deletion of a key value also requires locating and modifying the proper elements to have null values. Note that there is no node splitting or merging, although nodes may need to be added when a new value appears the first time in a particular position of the key.

Trie Variations

There are several variations possible on the basic trie. For example, the trie can be modified slightly to accommodate more efficiently a variable-length key field. Consider an alphabetic key field with values that are people's last names. Some of these names are very short, others are quite long. Building a 26-way trie to structure names of up to, say, 30 characters would mean that even searches for short names would require 30 node visitations.

Assume that 80% of the names to be represented are no more than eight characters in length. The trie can be built with the following node structure. Each internal node can

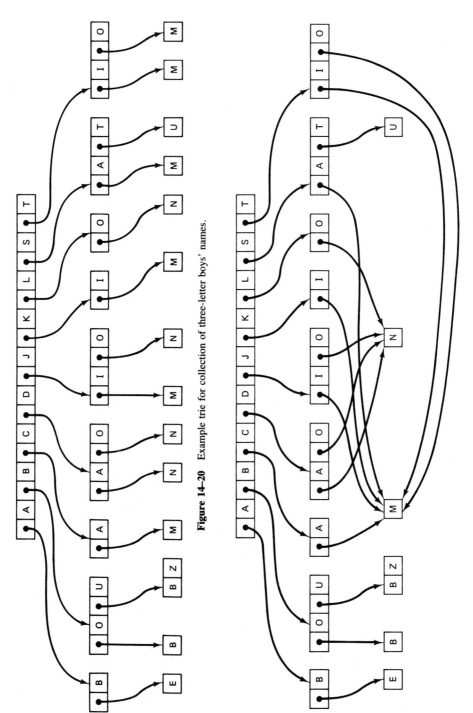

Figure 14-20 Example trie for collection of three-letter boys' names.

Figure 14-21 Variation on the trie of Fig. 14-20, with sharing of some leaf nodes.

392

contain 27 elements; 26 are for the letters of the alphabet, and one (say ξ) is to represent key values that terminate at the represented length. Each name is represented as if its low-order character were ξ. For example, IGOR is represented as IGORξ. A name that terminates with a ξ on level j would be a name with j characters. For example, the name IGOR would be represented with an I on level 0, pointing to a G on level 1, pointing to an O on level 2, pointing to an R on level 3, pointing to ξ on level 4.

The trie itself could be constructed with eight levels because 80% of the names have a maximum of eight characters. Each leaf node could contain the 27 usual elements, plus pointers to auxiliary indexes (for example binary search trees) containing the remaining parts of the names with more than eight characters. Thus 80% of the searches would require a maximum of eight node visitations; 20% of the searches would travel completely through the trie and into another index.

Another alternative for improving the space requirements of a trie is to reduce node sizes by not making provision for all possible values of the radix in each node. Instead, only those values that are actually in use might be represented. Fig. 14–20 shows an example trie that uses this variation in storing a small set of three-letter boys' names. Each internal node of the trie contains both pointers and the radix value corresponding to each pointer; each leaf of the trie contains one or more radix values. Each leaf could contain pointers indexing into a file of data records about the boys.

Prior knowledge of distributions of key values can be used to further reduce memory needs. For example, if the trie of Fig. 14–20 were used only to store names (not an index to corresponding data records), we could take advantage of the fact that N and M appear frequently in leaves. There could be a single N node shared as a leaf by multiple parents. Similarly, a single M node could be shared, as shown in Fig. 14–21. This structure is not a tree according to our original definition in Chapter 8, which requires each node to have only one parent.

SUMMARY

This chapter began with a discussion of the use of binary search trees as indexes into larger collections of data. The performance of an index can be enhanced significantly by increasing the branching factor of an index tree. Rather than using binary branching, m-way ($m > 2$) branching can be used. This discussion motivated our introduction of the data type *m-way search tree*, which is a generalization of the binary search tree. In general, the higher the order of branching of a search tree, the shorter is the maximum search length. Visiting each node forces a selection from among a greater number of possible branches.

A special case of m-way search tree, the *B-tree of order m* was introduced as a data type that approximates a completely balanced m-way search tree. The basic operations on B-trees—direct search, insertion, and deletion—were covered. The worst case direct search length in a B-tree of order m containing n keys was shown to be $O\left(\log_{\lceil \frac{1}{2}m \rceil} \frac{n+1}{2} \right)$. Insertion and deletion algorithms require procedures to keep the

B-tree in conformance with B-tree constraints. Insertion of a new key may require splitting of a node into two nodes. In the worst case, this splitting percolates all the way to the root of the tree, causing the tree to grow one level in height. The probability that a key insertion will cause a split in a B-tree of order m is less than 1 in $\lceil \frac{1}{2}m \rceil - 1$. Deletion of a key may require shifting of other key values within the tree and merging of nodes. If a merge percolates all the way to the tree's root, the height of the tree is decreased by one. As with node splitting, the probability of node merging decreases linearly as the order of the B-tree increases.

B-trees have been the subject of much interest, both to practitioners and researchers. They are the most widely used data structure for organizing indexes. Numerous variations on the basic B-tree have been developed. One variation introduced in this chapter is the B*-tree. A *B*-tree* is a B-tree in which each node is at least two-thirds full instead of at least half full. This variation tends to make better use of memory and to decrease the maximum direct search length through the tree.

A *trie* uses the representation of key values as sequences of characters or digits to guide searches. The order of the basic trie is determined by the radix used to represent key values. The height of the basic trie is determined by the length of the key field. The actual shape of a trie is determined by the distribution of key values; uniform distribution of key values results in a relatively balanced trie.

These tree structures all can be used to build indexed files. Two extensions to indexed files are covered in the next two chapters: (1) indexed sequential files, which provide both access directly to data records with particular key values as well as access sequentially to the entire data collection, and (2) multi-key files, which are supported by more than one index and provide several direct access paths based on the values of the pertinent indexed fields. Relative files cannot easily be extended to provide indexed sequential access. We will see, however, that they are sometimes used in conjunction with index structures to implement multi-key files.

TERMS

AVL tree	index
BB tree	*m*-way search tree
binary search tree	path length
bounded balance tree	radix
B-tree	sparse index
B*-tree	trie
dense index	

SELECTED REFERENCES

AL-SUWAIYEL, M. and E. HOROWITZ. "Algorithms for trie compaction," *ACM Trans. on Database Systems*, 9(2):243–263, June 1984.

BAYER, R. and K. UNTERAUER. "Prefix B-trees," *ACM Trans. on Database Systems*, 2(1):11–284, March 1977.

BAYER, R., and E. McCREIGHT. "Organization and maintenance of large ordered indexes," *Acta Informatica*, 1:290–306, 1972.

BAYER, R. and J. K. METZGER. "On the encipherment of search trees and random access files," *ACM Trans. on Database Systems*, 1(1):37–52, March 1976.

BENTLEY, J. L. "Multidimensional binary search trees used for associative searching," *Comm. ACM*, 18(9):509–517, Sept. 1975.

BURKHARD, W. A. "Hashing and trie algorithms for partial match retrieval," *ACM Trans. on Database Systems*, 1(2):175–187, June 1976.

COMER, D. "Analysis of a heuristic for full trie minimization," *ACM Trans. on Database Systems*, 6(3):513–537, Sept. 1981.

COMER, D. "The ubiquitous B-tree," *ACM Computing Surveys*, 11(2):121–137, June 1979.

COMER, D. "Heuristics for trie index minimization," *ACM Trans. on Database Systems*, 4(3):383–395, Sept. 1979.

COMER, D. and R. SETHI. "The complexity of trie index construction," *Jour. ACM*, 24(3):428–440, July 1977.

CULIK, K., T. OTTMANN, and D. WOOD. "Dense multiway trees," *ACM Trans. on Database Systems*, 6(3):486–512, Sept. 1981.

FOSTER, C. C. "A generalization of AVL trees," *Comm. ACM*, 16(8):513–517, Aug. 1973.

GUDES, E. and S. TSUR. "Experiments with B-tree reorganization," *Proc. ACM-SIGMOD 1980 Intl. Conf. on Management of Data, May 14–16, 1980, Santa Monica CA*, pp. 200–206.

GUTTMAN, A. "R-trees: a dynamic index structure for spatial searching," *ACM SIGMOD '84 Proc. of Annual Meeting, SIGMOD Record, Vol. 14, no. 2, June 1984*, pp. 47–57.

HELD, G. and M. STONEBRAKER. "B-trees re-examined," *Comm. ACM*, 21(2):139–143, Feb. 1978.

HUANG, J. C. "A note on information organization and storage," *Comm. ACM*, 16(7):406–410, July 1973.

HWANG, K. and S. B. YAO. "Optimal batched searching of tree structured files in multiprocessor computer systems," *Jour. ACM*, 24(3):441–440, July 1977.

KNUTH, D. E. *The Art of Computer Programming, Vol. 3, Sorting and Searching*. Reading, MA: Addison-Wesley Publishing Co., 1973, pp. 471–505.

KWONG, Y. S. and D. WOOD. "A new method for concurrency in B-trees," *IEEE Trans. on Software Engineering*, SE-8(3):211–222, May 1982.

KWONG, Y. S. and D. WOOD. "On B-trees: routing schemes and concurrency," *Proc. ACM-SIGMOD 1980 Internat. Conf. on Management of Data, May 14–16, 1980, Santa Monica CA*, pp. 207–213.

LEHMAN, P. L. and S. B. YAO. "Efficient locking for concurrent operations on B-trees," *ACM Trans. on Database Systems*, 6(4):650–670, Dec. 1981.

LEE, D. T. and C. K. WONG. "Quintary trees: a file structure for multidimensional database systems," *ACM Trans. on Database Systems*, 5(3):339–353, Sept. 1980.

LITWIN, W. "Trie hashing," *Proc. ACM-SIGMOD 1981 Intl. Conf. on Management of Data*, Sept. 1981, Ann Arbor MI, pp. 19–29.

LOMET, D. B. "Partial expansions for file organizations with an index," *ACM Trans. on Database Systems*, 12(1):65–84, March 1987.

LOMET, D. B. "Multi-table search for B-tree files," *Proc. ACM-SIGMOD 1979 Intl. Conf. on Management of Data, May 30–June 1, 1979, Boston MA*, pp. 35–42.

MALY, K. "A note on virtual memory addresses," *Comm. ACM*, 21(9):786–787, Sept. 1978.

MARUYAMA, K. and S. E. SMITH. "Analysis of design alternatives for virtual memory indexes," *Comm. ACM*, 20(4):245–254, April 1977.

McCREIGHT, E. M. "Pagination of B*-trees with variable-length records," *Comm. ACM*, 20(9):670–674, Sept. 1977.

ROSENBERG, A. L. and L. SNYDER. "Time- and space-optimality in B-trees," *ACM Trans. on Database Systems*, 6(1):174–193, March 1981.

ROSENBERG, A. L. and L. SNYDER. "Compact B-trees," *Proc. ACM-SIGMOD 1980 Intl. Conf. on Management of Data, May 14–16, 1980, Santa Monica CA*, pp. 43–51.

ROUSSOPOULOS, N. and D. LEIFKER. "Direct spatial search on pictorial databases using packed R-trees," *Proc. ACM-SIGMOD 1985 Intl. Conf. on Management of Data, May 28–31, 1985, Austin TX*, pp. 17–31.

SHEIL, B. A. "Median split trees: a fast lookup technique for frequently occurring keys," *Comm. ACM*, 21(11):947–958, Nov. 1978.

STRONG, H. R., G. MARKOWSKY, and A. K. CHANDRA. "Search within a page," *Jour. ACM*, 26(3):457–482, July 1979.

REVIEW EXERCISES

1. What is the difference between a binary search tree and an *m*-way search tree?

2. A binary search tree is a two-way search tree. True or false?

3. An AVL tree is to a binary search tree as a _____ is to an *m*-way search tree. (Fill in the blank.)

4. A full node in a 16-way search tree contains how many key values? How many pointers?

5. A node in a 16-way search tree contains a minimum of how many key values? How many pointers?

6. What is the maximum number of nodes in a three-way tree with height 5? What is the maximum number of key values in this tree?

7. What is the maximum number of nodes in a four-way tree with height 5? What is the maximum number of key values in this tree? (Compare with exercise 6.)

8. What is the minimum height of a three-way tree with 242 key values? With 1023 key values?

9. What is the minimum height of a four-way tree with 242 key values? With 1023 key values? (Compare with exercise 8.)

10. A full node in a B-tree of order 16 contains how many key values? How many pointers? (Compare with exercise 4.)

11. A node in a B-tree of order 16 contains a minimum of how many key values? How many pointers? (Compare with exercise 5.)

12. What is the probability that a key insertion will cause a split in a B-tree of order 16?

13. What is the number of nodes that need to be visited in the worst case to find a key in a B-tree of order 3 with 242 keys? With 1023 keys?

14. What is the number of nodes that need to be visited in the worst case to find a key in a B-tree of order 16 with n keys?

15. Write an algorithm for traversing a B-tree of order m in in-order.

16. Perform a sequence of key insertions and deletions on the B-tree of Fig. 14–4.

17. Write a program that builds a B-tree of order 3 from an input sequence of key values.

18. Write a program to traverse a B-tree of order 3 in sequence by key value.

19. Write a program to locate a given key value in a B-tree of order 3.

20. Fill out the details of the B-tree insertion logic given in Fig. 14–6.

21. Fill out the details of the B-tree deletion logic given in Fig. 14–8.

22. Write a program to maintain a B-tree of order 3. Be able to accommodate key insertions and deletions.

23. Propose refinements to the B-tree structure and algorithms to accommodate records with duplicate key values.

24. What is the difference between a B-tree and a B*-tree?

25. What is the difference between a B-tree and a trie?

26. What determines the shape of a trie? When is a trie short and bushy? When is a trie tall and slender?

27. When would you want to balance a trie?

28. What is the node structure of a trie used to represent the employee numbers 0001 to 9999, where 70% of the available numbers are used? How many levels does the trie have?

29. Draw a trie to represent all two-letter English words. What is the node structure? How many levels does the trie have?

30. Modify the trie from exercise 29 to represent all one- and two-letter English words. What is the node structure? How many levels does the trie have?

31. Draw a trie to represent the set of key values shown in the B-tree of Fig. 14–8.

32. Write an algorithm to insert into a trie.

33. Write an algorithm to delete from a trie.

34. Write an algorithm to list the entries in a trie in alphabetic order.

```
┌─────────────────────────────────────────────┐
│  ╭─────────────────────────────────────────╮ │
│  │                                         │ │
│  │                                         │ │
│  │   ──chapter fifteen──────               │ │
│  │                                         │ │
│  │   ──indexed sequential──                │ │
│  │   ──file organization──                 │ │
│  │                                         │ │
│  │                                         │ │
│  ╰─────────────────────────────────────────╯ │
└─────────────────────────────────────────────┘
```

chapter fifteen

indexed sequential file organization

In this chapter we introduce another major approach to organizing data on secondary storage: indexed sequential file organization. The organization method is first defined and then its utility in information systems is discussed. Two approaches to implementing the concept of indexed sequential organization are covered. We then discuss the declaration and use of indexed sequential files in programs. The chapter closes with a review of some of the factors that should be considered in the design of a file with indexed sequential organization.

DEFINITIONS

An effective way to organize a collection of records when there is the need both to access the records sequentially by some key value and also to access the records individually by that same key is *indexed sequential file organization*. An indexed sequential file provides the combination of access types that are supported by a sequential file and a relative file.

There are several approaches to structuring both the index and the sequential data portions of an indexed sequential file. The most common approach is to build the index as a tree of key values. The tree is typically a variation on the B-tree introduced in Chapter 14. The other common approach is to build the index based on the physical layout of the data in storage. This chapter will discuss both approaches.

Examples

One way to think of the structure of an indexed sequential file is as an index with pointers to a sequential data file (Fig. 15–1). In the pictured example, the index has been structured as a binary search tree. The index is used to service a request for access to a particular record; the sequential data file is used to support sequential access to the entire collection of records.

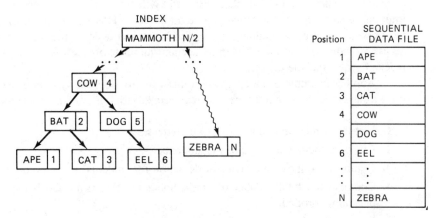

Figure 15–1   Use of a binary search tree and a sequential file to provide indexed sequential access.

You are already familiar with this approach to structuring a collection of information to facilitate both sequential and direct access. For example, consider a dictionary: the thumb tabs provide an index into the sequentially organized collection of words. In order to find a particular word, say "syzygy," you usually do not scan the dictionary sequentially. Rather, you select the appropriate thumb tab, S, the first letter of the word, and use that tab to direct your search into the approximate location of the word in the data collection. Again, you probably would not proceed with a sequential search from the beginning of the S's to find your target word, "syzygy." Instead, you would use the column headings on each page which indicate the first and last elements on that page. Once you have located the proper page, your search might proceed sequentially to find the sought word.

It is important to note from the dictionary example that the key that is used to sequentialize entries is the same as the key that is used to search directly for an individual entry. The thumb tab and column-heading index structure does not work *unless* this point is true.

APPLICATIONS

Because of its capability to support both sequential and direct access, indexed sequential organization is used frequently to support files that are used for both batch and interactive processing. For example, consider a credit card billing system with an indexed sequential master file of customer account information. An appropriate key for the file would be the account number of each record. The file could be accessed in batch mode, monthly, to generate customer invoices and to build summary reports of account activity. Each account record would be accessed once in this processing. The bills and the detail lines on the summary report would appear in account number sequence.

The credit card management agency wants to use the master file of account information also to support interactive inquiry of the current credit status of any account. When a customer makes a purchase, the master file will be consulted to determine the credit limit and then to update the remaining credit amount. This kind of processing could not be supported well by sequential access to the customer account file. Rather, the need to access an individual account, given its account number, dictates use of the index of the indexed sequential file organization.

Another example of an application that calls for support by an indexed sequential file is a class records system. Processing requirements for this system include the following:

1. List the names and addresses of all students.
2. Compute the average age of the students.
3. Compute the mean and standard deviation for students' grade point averages.
4. Compute the total number of credit hours for classes in which the students are presently enrolled.
5. Change the classification of a particular student from probational to regular.
6. Display the grade record for a particular student.
7. Insert a record for a new student.
8. Delete the record for a particular student who has withdrawn from the school.

Some of these requirements call for sequential accessibility of the student file; others call for direct accessibility to particular records of the file. The combination of requirements can be satisfied by using indexed sequential file organization. The sort key and the index key for the file would be the student identifier.

B⁺-TREE STRUCTURES

One of the popular techniques for implementing indexed sequential file organization is to use a variation on the basic B-tree known as the *B⁺-tree*.

Fig. 15–2 shows a B⁺-tree that contains the same key values as does the basic B-tree of Fig. 14–4. Examination of this B⁺-tree reveals a new set of pointers: the leaves have been connected to form a linked list of the keys in sequential order. The B⁺-tree has two parts: the *index part* is the interior nodes; the *sequence set* is the leaves. Nodes a through i form the index part; nodes j through y form the sequence set. The linked leaves are an excellent aspect of a B⁺-tree; the keys can be accessed efficiently both directly and sequentially.

A B-tree can also support sequential access to the key values it contains. The tree

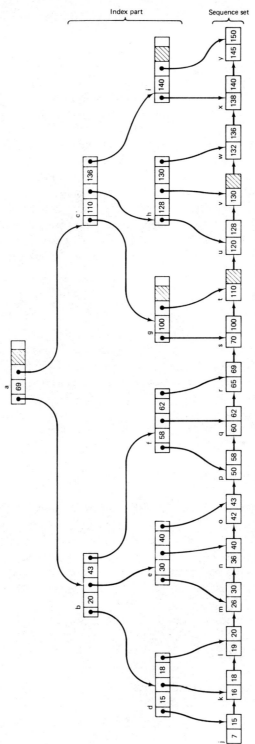

Figure 15-2 A B$^+$-tree containing the same key values as the B-tree of Fig. 14-4.

can be traversed sequentially by visiting the nodes in essentially in-order. Each internal node will be visited more than once since it contains several keys. The subtree associated with each key must be visited before the next key of the node is accessed. In fact, sequential access to the keys of a B-tree does not exhibit very good performance, especially when the memory requirements to trace the paths through the tree are considered. The sequence set of a B^+-tree remedies the problem.

When a B^+-tree is used to provide indexed sequential file organization, the key values in the sequence set are the key values in the record collection; the key values in the index part exist solely for internal purposes of directing access to the sequence set.

We designed this B^+-tree such that pointer P_i in the index points to the subtree containing key values greater than those in the subtree pointed to by P_{i-1} and *less than or equal to* key value K_i. Sometimes B^+-trees are designed such that pointer P_i in the index points to the subtree containing key values greater than those in the subtree pointed to by P_{i-1} and *less than* key value K_i. The leaf containing key value K_i then is in the subtree pointed to by P_{i+1}.

Manipulating a B^+-tree

Inserting a new key value into a B^+-tree is done in almost the same way as insertion of a new key value into a basic B-tree. When a leaf node is split into two nodes, a copy of a low-order key value from the rightmost node is promoted to be the separator key value in the parent node. The new node also must be inserted in the linked list of the sequence set.

Deleting a key value from a B^+-tree is somewhat easier than if the tree were a basic B-tree. When a key value is deleted from a leaf, there is no need to delete that key value from the index of the tree. That key value still can direct searches to the proper leaves.

Searching a B^+-tree

A direct search in a B^+-tree must terminate in a node of the sequence set. If there is a key in the index that matches the sought key, the preceding pointer is followed until eventually the correct leaf is reached. Not every key in the index part need also appear in the sequence set. A key may have been deleted from the sequence set when its corresponding record was deleted from the record collection, but the key may have been retained in the index part of the B^+-tree for purposes of guiding access to the sequence set.

A B^+-tree provides about as good performance for direct searching as does a basic B-tree of the same order. The maximum height of a B^+-tree of order m with n key values is $\left(\log_{\lceil 1/2m \rceil} \frac{n+1}{2} \right)$.

Sequential access to the data indexed by a B^+-tree is provided by scanning the sequence set. Typically, as an indexed sequential file, the sequence set contains not only key values, but also the corresponding data records. If data records are variable length or relatively large, the file alternatively might be structured in a way that the sequence

Example   403

set nodes contain pairs of key value and address that point to the data records stored elsewhere.

EXAMPLE

Figure 15–3 shows an indexed sequential file of animal information, structured using the B$^+$-tree approach. The nodes of the index file are labeled *index blocks*. The nodes of the sequence set are called *data blocks* and reside in the data file.

This example contains N data blocks and three levels of index. Each entry in the index is a pair of lowest key value and pointer. The pointer is to another block in which the key value is the lowest key value that appears. Each level of index block points to all of the blocks that form the next-lower level of the index, except for the lowest-level index blocks, which point to the data blocks. This B$^+$-tree is a 4-way search tree.

Direct Access

When a request for access to a particular record, say the one with key value BAT, is received, the highest level of index (here block 3–1) is searched first. In this example, the pointer from AARDVARK is followed to index block 2–1. The appropriate pointer out of that box is the one found with AARDVARK and leads to index block 1–1. The pointer followed out of that box is the one found with BABOON and leads to data block 2. The data block is then searched for the record with the target key, BAT, and the record is made available.

Sequential Access

A request to access the data in sequential order is serviced by accessing the data blocks in sequential order. The data blocks are the sequence set; they are logically consecutive but are not necessarily physically consecutive.

Inserting Records

Let us now consider a series of requests to insert new animal records. Assume that each data block has space adequate to hold five records.

The requests

> INSERT APE
> INSERT AIREDALE

are easy to do. Only data block 1 is affected, and it results in the contents shown in Fig. 15–4. Note that the entries in the block must be kept in ascending sequential order.

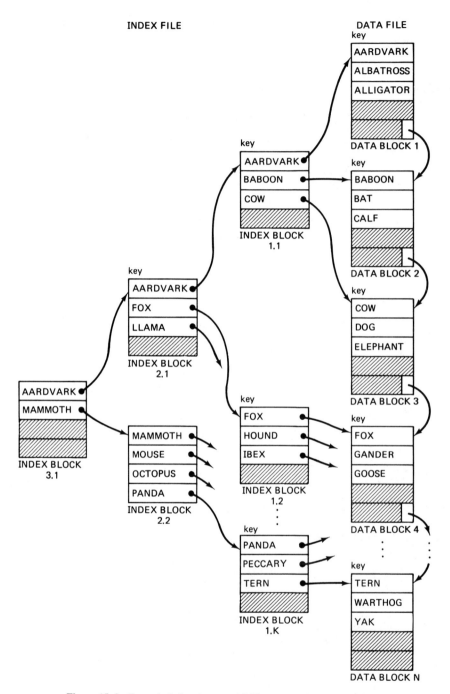

Figure 15–3 Example indexed sequential file structured using a B⁺-tree.

Example   405

Figure 15–4 Data block 1 of Fig. 15–3 after inserting APE and AIREDALE

The request

INSERT ARMADILLO

is a bit more difficult to handle. Search of the index structure reveals that ARMADILLO should reside in data block 1, but that block is already full. This condition necessitates a split of data block 1, with accompanying modification of index block 1–1, as shown in Fig. 15–5. Half of the contents of data block 1 remain there; the other half are moved to the newly created block: data block 1A.

The requests

INSERT CAT
INSERT BEAR
INSERT BOBCAT

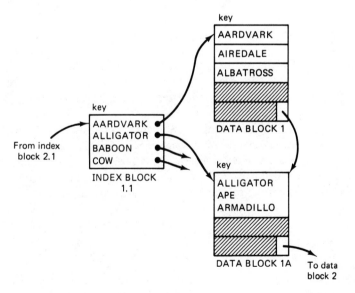

Figure 15–5 Splitting to accommodate insertion of ARMADILLO into data block 1 of Fig. 15–4.

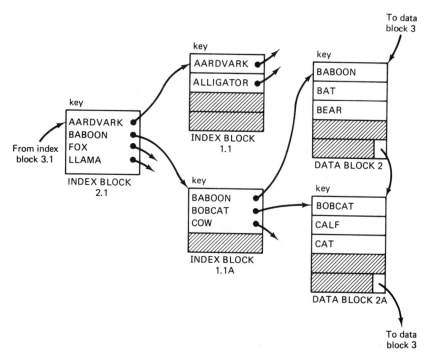

Figure 15–6 Splitting to accommodate insertion of CAT, BEAR, and BOBCAT into data block 2 of Fig. 15–3.

fill data block 2, then cause it to split, forming data blocks 2 and 2A (Fig. 15–6). Index block 1–1 is already full and cannot accommodate a pointer to block 2A, so it also must split, with the change percolating up to index level 2.

When the index block at the highest level (here level 3) becomes full, then splits, a new level is added to the index tree. All direct searches would then require four index block accesses and one data block access.

Use of B^+-trees to implement indexed sequential files is common. For example, it is used in International Business Machine's (IBM's) key-sequenced VSAM files. In VSAM terminology, a data block is referred to as a *control interval*. When the records in a control interval are stored in ascending order by a given key (as they are in an indexed sequential file), the records are said to be in a *key-sequenced data set*.

PHYSICAL-LAYOUT INDEXES

Another approach to implementing the indexed sequential file concept is to base the index structure more on the physical characteristics of storage than on the logical distribution of key values. The index may have several levels, such as a cylinder-index level and a

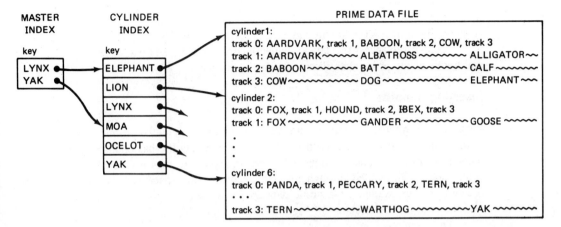

Figure 15–7   Example animal file structured using physical-layout index approach.

track-index level. The data file generally is implemented as two files: a prime area and an overflow area. Fig. 15–7 depicts this type of structure for the indexed sequential file of animal data.

Let us assume that each cylinder of the storage device has four tracks. This particular file has six cylinders allocated to the prime data area. The first track (number 0) of each cylinder contains an index to the record keys on that cylinder. Entries in this index are of the form

> lowest key value, track number.

Within a data track, records are kept in sequence by key value. The first level of index in the index file is called a *master index*. As is shown in Fig. 15–7, entries in this index are of the form

> highest key value, pointer.

The second level of index is called the *cylinder index*. It contains pointers into the prime data file and has entries of the form

> highest key value, cylinder number.

Accessing Data Records

When a request for access to a particular record, say one with key value BAT, is received, the master index is searched first. Because BAT precedes LYNX, the pointer from LYNX is followed into the cylinder index. Because BAT precedes ELEPHANT, the pointer from ELEPHANT is followed to track 0 of cylinder 1. Because BAT follows BABOON and precedes COW, the pointer from BABOON is followed to track 2, which is searched sequentially until BAT is found and made available or is determined not to exist.

A request to access the data in sequential order is serviced by accessing the cylinders and tracks of the prime data file in physical sequence.

Inserting Records

Let us now examine the handling of updates to an indexed sequential file that is implemented in this manner. Assume that each track of the prime data file has enough space for five records. If insertions and deletions to the file are expected, then it would be created with empty spaces distributed through the data records. This space is called *free space* or *padding*. In our example, the prime data area was created with 40% free space as was also the case for the structure of Fig. 15–3.

The requests

       INSERT APE

       INSERT AIREDALE

are easy to do. Only data track 1 of cylinder 1 is affected and it results in the contents shown in Fig. 15–8. Note that the entries in the track must be kept in ascending sequential order.

> cylinder 1
> track 0: no change
> track 1: AARDVARK ∿∿ AIREDALE ∿∿ ALBATROSS ∿∿ ALLIGATOR ∿∿ APE ∿∿
> track 2: no change
> track 3: no change

Figure 15–8   Cylinder 1 of Fig. 15–7 after inserting APE and AIREDALE.

The request

       INSERT ARMADILLO

is a bit more difficult to handle. Search of the index structure reveals that ARMADILLO should reside in track 1 of cylinder 1, but that track is full. This condition necessitates use of the overflow data area. This overflow area is in a separate file from the prime data area but is pointed to by entries in the prime data area. Fig. 15–9 shows the result of adding ARMADILLO. Because ARMADILLO belongs after the five existing entries of track 1 of cylinder 1, it must be placed in the overflow data area. The track index for cylinder 1 must be modified to show that there is now a record in the overflow area that logically should reside at the end of track one; thus the addition of the entry <ARMA-

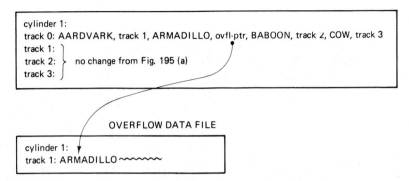

Figure 15–9   Cylinder 1 of Fig. 15–8 with overflow area to accommodate inserting ARMADILLO.

DILLO, ovfl-ptr>, where ovfl-ptr is the <cylinder, track, record> number of the corresponding record.

The requests

> INSERT CAT
>
> INSERT BEAR
>
> INSERT BOBCAT

fill track 2 of cylinder 1 of the prime data area, then cause use of the overflow area (Fig. 15–10). Note that CAT is moved to the overflow area because not only must the entries in a prime track be in sequence, but also those entries must precede any overflow entries from that track.

Now service the request

> INSERT ANT.

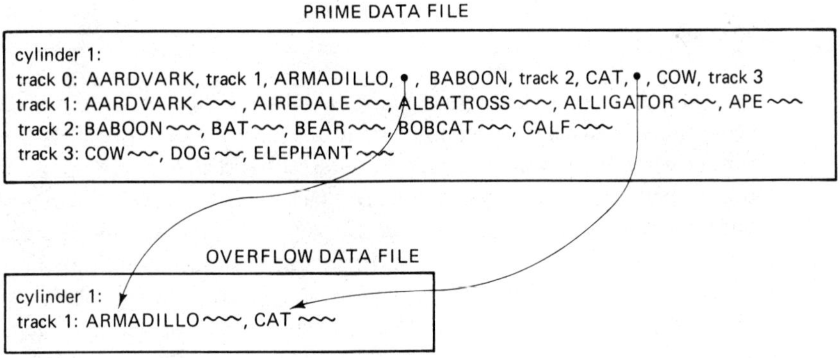

PRIME DATA FILE

```
cylinder 1:
track 0: AARDVARK, track 1, ARMADILLO, •, BABOON, track 2, CAT, •, COW, track 3
track 1: AARDVARK ~~~ , AIREDALE ~~~, ALBATROSS ~~~, ALLIGATOR ~~~, APE ~~~
track 2: BABOON ~~~, BAT ~~~, BEAR ~~~, BOBCAT ~~~, CALF ~~~
track 3: COW ~~~, DOG ~~~, ELEPHANT ~~~
```

OVERFLOW DATA FILE

```
cylinder 1:
track 1: ARMADILLO ~~~, CAT ~~~
```

Figure 15–10   Cylinder 1 of Fig. 15–9 with overflow area after inserting CAT, BEAR, and BOBCAT.

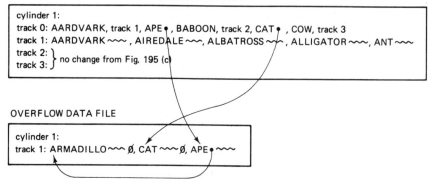

Figure 15–11   Cylinder 1 of Fig. 15–10 with overflow area after inserting ANT.

Search of the index structure reveals that ANT should reside in track 1 of cylinder 1. Again, the proper ordering of keys in the prime area must be maintained, so ANT is placed in track 1 of cylinder 1 and APE is bumped to the overflow area (Fig. 15–11). Track 1 now has more than one entry in the overflow area. To be able to access the records sequentially, and, in fact, to be able to find a record with direct access, the overflow from a track must be chained together in proper sequence. Thus the format of records in the overflow area is

key value, rest of record, pointer to next overflow record for this track

A given track of the overflow area may contain records that represent several prime tracks and that the overflow chain for a particular prime track may span multiple overflow tracks. The file can be defined with either one overflow area per cylinder or a combined overflow area containing records from all the prime cylinders. Entries are made in the overflow area in order by time of insertion. The linked lists in the overflow area show the key sequencing.

Wrinkles

The processes of direct and sequential retrieval from this type of indexed sequential file actually are somewhat more complex than we have presented here. When a request for a particular record is received, the master and cylinder indexes are used to locate the correct cylinder in the prime data area for the target record. The index in track 0 of that cylinder then is searched. The pointer accompanying the key in the track index that is the largest key value not greater than the sought key value is followed. If that pointer is to a track in the prime area, the keys of records on that track are compared in sequence with the target key value. On the other hand, if the pointer is to a record in the overflow area, the linked list of records pointed to is searched. These records will be linked in ascending key value order but may be located physically anywhere in the overflow area.

A request to access the data in sequential order is done by accessing the next prime track and then following its overflow chain, and so forth until the prime and overflow areas have been exhausted.

It is easy to see that with many record insertions, long overflow chains could result. Direct access to a record that resides in the prime area generally requires four I/O-device accesses: two for the index file, one to the track-0 index, and one to the appropriate prime track. Direct access to a record that resides in the overflow area could require as many as $3 + K$ I/O-device accesses: two for the index file, one to the track-0 index, and K to the overflow area, where the target record is K^{th} on the overflow chain. Access to each record on the overflow linked list could require a distinct I/O-device access.

Indexed sequential files that are implemented with prime and overflow data areas are susceptible to degradation of performance over a period of insertion activity. In contrast to B^+-tree structures which are dynamic and self-reorganizing, indexed sequential files based on physical-layout indexes are static and require periodic and explicit reorganization. Usually the old indexed sequential file is read sequentially, then written sequentially to a new indexed sequential file with an expanded prime data area.

Deleting Records

Deletions in this type of indexed file may be handled in two ways. With dynamic deletion, the subject record is physically removed from the file. If it resided in the overflow area, the linked list in which it participated is adjusted to compensate for its removal. If it was the first entry in the linked list, the track-0 entry for the chain is modified to contain the key of the next entry in the linked list and to point to its location. On the other hand, if it resided in the prime data area, the remaining entries in the prime area are "shifted left," one record from the track's overflow chain is brought into the prime area, and the track-0 entry for the chain is modified appropriately.

Another alternative for handling deletion is to mark the subject record as deleted, but not actually to remove it. Retrievals skip over deleted records. A "garbage collection" routine could be processed at intervals to perform the tasks indicated above. An advantage of this approach is that the garbage-collection process need not be paid for with every single deletion. A disadvantage is that the space allocated to "deleted" (but not yet collected) records may not be available for reuse. Searches may extend into the overflow area because of deleted records in the prime area, and chains in the overflow area may include deleted records.

The physical-layout index approach with prime and overflow areas for implementing indexed sequential files was developed before the B^+-tree approach.

INDEXED SEQUENTIAL FILES IN COBOL

Declaring a File

Declaration information for indexed sequential files is supplied in both the ENVIRON-MENT DIVISION and the DATA DIVISION of a COBOL program. The format of the SELECT clause of the FILE–CONTROL paragraph of the INPUT–OUTPUT SECTION of the ENVIRONMENT DIVISION for an indexed sequential file is shown below.

SELECT filename ASSIGN TO implementor-name[,implementor-name2]

$$\left[\text{RESERVE integer } [\begin{array}{c}\text{AREA}\\ \text{AREA}\end{array}]\right]$$

ORGANIZATION IS INDEXED

$$\left[\text{ACCESS MODE IS}\left\{\begin{array}{l}\text{SEQUENTIAL}\\ \text{RANDOM}\\ \text{DYNAMIC}\end{array}\right\}\right]$$

RECORD KEY IS dataname-1

[FILE STATUS IS dataname-2].

The filename is the name by which the file is known in this program. The implementor-name is the name of the device upon which this file resides. Some implementations require specification of two devices here: one for the index and one for the data.

The optional RESERVE and FILE STATUS clauses have the same meanings that they have for sequential and relative files.

The ORGANIZATION IS INDEXED phrase is required for indexed sequential files. If this phrase were omitted, the file would default to having sequential organization.

The ACCESS MODE phrase specifies the manner in which records in the file are going to be accessed: sequentially, directly, or both. The RECORD KEY phrase specifies that dataname-1 contains the key for sequencing and indexing records of the file. This is the key that provides access paths to the file's records. All values of this key field must be unique in the file. The key field must appear as part of the record description in the file's FD; the key field therefore must be contained within the record. It must be defined to be alphanumeric.

ACCESS MODE IS SEQUENTIAL means that records will be accessed (read/written) in order by ascending key value. RANDOM access means that the value of the key field will be used to identify a particular record to be read, written, deleted or modified. DYNAMIC access means that records will be accessed sometimes in SEQUENTIAL mode and sometimes in RANDOM mode by the program.

Each indexed sequential file used in a program must have an associated file description (FD) entry. An FD contains clauses that give information about block size, record size, label records, and data records in the file. The entry is essentially the same for indexed sequential files as for relative files; however the RECORD KEY must be included as a field in the file's record description(s), while the RELATIVE KEY for a relative file does not appear in its record description.

Some nonstandard COBOL compilers that implement the block index and data approach also allow the programmer to specify the sizes of index and data blocks, the percent of padding to leave in index and data blocks when the file is created, and the maximum number of levels that the index tree is allowed to attain.

Other programming languages that support indexed sequential files ask the programmer to specify these same kinds of information to describe the structure of the file.

Creating a File

When an indexed sequential file is created in COBOL, it must be open for OUTPUT. In implementations based on the physical-layout indexes approach, records must be written in sequential order by ascending RECORD KEY value. In some implementations based on the B$^+$-tree approach, this restriction may also be enforced. If it is not, it still is nearly always more efficient to create the file in ascending order. Thus we assume that the file is created with ACCESS MODE IS SEQUENTIAL.

The following form of the WRITE verb is used to store a new record on the file:

<u>WRITE</u> recordname [<u>FROM</u> identifier]
<u>INVALID</u> KEY imperative-stmt.

Prior to execution of the WRITE for a record, that record's RECORD KEY data item must have been given its appropriate value. The INVALID KEY condition is raised if the record's RECORD KEY value is not greater than that of the previously written record.

The data management system takes responsibility for correctly building the file's index structure; the programmer's job is made simple.

Creating a File Using a Utility

Some COBOL compilers do not support the creation of indexed sequential files. In these cases, the programmer uses a system utility supplied for this purpose. Typically, such a utility first asks the programmer a number of questions, such as

What is

- the maximum data record size?
- the data type of the key field?
- the location of the key field in a record?
- the number of records per block in the file to be used as input in creating the indexed sequential file?
- the desired number of records per data block in the indexed sequential file?
- the desired padding in the data blocks?
- the desired number of entries per index block in the indexed sequential file?
- the desired padding in the index blocks?
- the maximum number of data records that the indexed sequential file should be able to contain?
- the name of the indexed sequential file?
- the device to be used for storage of the indexed sequential file?

These utilities generally read a sequential file of sorted records as input and create the index and data parts of the corresponding indexed sequential file. This file can then be input to a COBOL program for retrieval or update processing.

Retrieving Records

When records are retrieved from a COBOL indexed sequential file, the file must be open for INPUT (or for I/O if records are going to also be written). Records can be retrieved from the file either sequentially or directly, using the READ verb. Sequential access may be positioned by the START verb.

If the file has ACCESS MODE IS SEQUENTIAL, only sequential access is supported. The following verb form is used:

READ filename RECORD [INTO identifier]
AT END imperative-statement.

A loop through this statement will access the records in ascending order of the RECORD KEY field value. The AT END condition is raised when the end-of-file is encountered.

The START verb can be used to position subsequent sequential reads. The syntax and semantics of this START are essentially the same as for use with relative files. The verb does have, however, additional functionality when used with indexed sequential files. The data name specified in a START statement need not be the entire RECORD KEY data item but can be a leftmost field subordinate to this data item. This facility allows the programmer to specify a partial key match, also known as a *generic key*.

For example, consider an indexed sequential COURSE–FILE file declared with RECORD KEY COURSE–ID, where COURSE–ID is defined in the file's record description as

```
02  COURSE-ID.
    03  DEPT        PIC X(3).
    03  NUM         PIC X(3).
    03  EXT         PIC X.
```

The statements

```
MOVE 'MIS' TO DEPT OF COURSE-ID.
START COURSE-FILE KEY = DEPT
    INVALID KEY ~~~.
READ COURSE-FILE RECORD INTO WS-CLASS-REC
    AT END ~~~.
```

would cause the first record for courses in the 'MIS' department to be read. Subsequent sequential reads would access the rest of the records whose RECORD KEY fields started with 'MIS' and then would start on the "next" department.

If the indexed sequential file has ACCESS MODE IS RANDOM, only direct access is supported. The following verb form is used for retrieval:

<u>READ</u> filename RECORD [<u>INTO</u> identifier]
<u>INVALID</u> KEY imperative-statement.

Prior to execution of the READ, the key value for the desired record must have been moved to the file's RECORD KEY data item. The record with that value for its RECORD KEY is the record that is retrieved. If there is no such record, then the INVALID KEY condition is raised.

If an indexed sequential file has ACCESS MODE IS DYNAMIC, then both sequential and direct (random) retrieval are supported.

Updating a File

When a COBOL indexed sequential file is updated, it must be open for I/O. New records can be added using the WRITE verb; old records can be removed using the DELETE verb; existing records can be modified using the REWRITE verb.

If the file has ACCESS MODE IS SEQUENTIAL, records must be accessed in sequential order of ascending RECORD KEY value. The START verb can be used to position sequential access. New records are written using the form of the WRITE verb introduced earlier. The sequential form of the DELETE verb is the same as for a relative file:

<u>DELETE</u> filename RECORD.

Execution of the DELETE must have been preceded by a successful sequential READ for the file. The record that was read is deleted.

The sequential form of the REWRITE verb is

<u>REWRITE</u> recordname [<u>FROM</u> identifier]
<u>INVALID</u> KEY imperative-statement.

As for the DELETE, execution of a sequential REWRITE must be preceded by a successful READ. The record that was read is the one that is replaced. The INVALID KEY condition is raised if the value of the RECORD KEY data item in the replacement record does not match the value of the RECORD KEY data item in the last record read from the file. That is, the key value cannot be changed between the execution of the READ and of the REWRITE.

If the file has ACCESS MODE IS RANDOM, then records can be accessed in any order. The direct-access form of the WRITE verb is

<u>WRITE</u> record-name [<u>FROM</u> identifier]
<u>INVALID</u> KEY imperative-statement.

Prior to the execution of the WRITE for a record, that record's RECORD KEY data item must have been given its appropriate value. The INVALID KEY condition is raised if there already is a record in the file with that RECORD KEY value.

The direct-access form of the DELETE verb is

> DELETE filename RECORD
> INVALID KEY imperative-statement.

Prior to execution of the DELETE for a record, the RECORD KEY data item must have been given an appropriate value. The record with that RECORD KEY value is deleted. The INVALID KEY condition is raised if there is no record on the file with that RECORD KEY value.

The direct-access form of the REWRITE verb is

> REWRITE recordname [FROM identifier]
> INVALID KEY imperative-statement.

Prior to the execution of the REWRITE for a record, the RECORD KEY data item must have been given an appropriate value. The record with that RECORD KEY value is replaced. The INVALID KEY condition is raised if there is no record on the file with that RECORD KEY value.

As with other operations, sequential and direct-access update of an indexed sequential file can be intermingled in one program if the file has ACCESS MODE IS DYNAMIC.

Other languages that support indexed sequential files provide the same kinds of facilities for record insertion, access, modification, and deletion. In all cases, the function must be specified, the key value of the target record must be given (for direct access), and the action to be taken if an exceptional condition arises must be identified.

DESIGN OF INDEXED SEQUENTIAL FILES

The primary questions that need to be addressed in designing an indexed sequential file include the following:

1. What is the layout of fields in the record?
2. What is the key field(s) used to identify record occurrences?
3. How extensive are record insertions expected to be?
4. What approach is used locally to implement the indexed sequential construct?

As discussed with the other file organization techniques, the record layout problem is the same as the problem addressed in Chapter 3. Both fixed- and variable-length records can be accommodated by many indexed sequential implementations.

The appropriate field(s) to form the key for an indexed sequential file is determined by the application. The significant restriction of indexed sequential organization is that whatever field forms the key for sequential access of the file must also be the key for indexed access of the file. If this is not the case and different keys seem appropriate for sequential and indexed access, then one of the file organizations introduced in Chapter 16 is more appropriate than is indexed sequential organization.

The extent of expected insertions to the file determines how much free space should be allocated in the file when it is initially loaded. A rough guideline is to leave 40% padding.

Depending upon the approach used to implement the indexed sequential file, other design decisions must be made. Local data management manuals commonly give implementation-dependent guidance on determining parameters such as the following:

1. B$^+$-tree approach
   (a) data block size
   (b) index block size
   (c) number of index levels initially
   (d) maximum number of index levels
2. Physical-layout index approach
   (a) index area size
   (b) levels of index
   (c) prime area size
   (d) overflow area size
   (e) record blocking in the prime area

These parameters are determined by the system's natural block size, the current and expected number of data records, and the usage of the file. The need for rapid direct retrieval implies use of a bushy index; the need for rapid sequential retrieval implies larger data blocks or larger prime data area and blocking factor. The more often data or index blocks must be split, the more expensive is update overhead. In general, the block index and data approach provides better performance in all ways: direct and sequential retrieval as well as update.

SUMMARY

An indexed sequential file supports both sequential access by key value and direct access to a particular record given its key value. This type of file organization is implemented by building an index on top of a sequential data file that resides on a direct-access storage device.

One good implementation approach is to use a B$^+$-tree. Another implementation approach uses prime and overflow data areas and is based more on the physical characteristics of storage. These two approaches differ primarily in their treatment of overflow conditions. When a data or index block in the B$^+$-tree approach overflows, it is split.

When a data track in the second approach overflows, records are placed into a separate overflow area and chained together to maintain logical key sequence order.

The basic concepts required for using an indexed sequential file in COBOL were introduced. Compilers that support indexed sequential files interface with extensive data management facilities that shield the programmer from the details of implementing and maintaining indexed sequential files in storage. Finally, several aspects of the design of indexed sequential files were reviewed.

Indexed sequential files are used extensively when there is the need for both sequential and direct access to records in a file. If only sequential access is needed, sequential file organization generally is cheaper and can utilize tape storage devices. If only direct access is needed, then relative file organization incurs less system overhead since access by logical key sequence order need not be supported.

TERMS

B^+-tree	key-sequenced data set
control interval	master index
cylinder index	overflow data area
free space	padding
generic key	prime data area
indexed sequential file organization	sequence set

SELECTED REFERENCES

ARNOW, D. and A. M. TENENBAUM. "An empirical comparison of B-trees, compact B-trees, and multiway trees," *ACM SIGMOD '84 Proc. of Annual Meeting*, SIGMOD Record, 14(2):33–46, June 1984.

BATORY, D. S. "Optimal file designs and reorganization points," *ACM Trans. on Database Systems*, 7(1):60–81, March 1982.

CHIN, Y. H. "Analysis of VSAM's free-space behavior," *Proc. Intl. Conf. on Very Large Data Bases*, Sept. 22–24, 1975, Framingham, MA, pp. 514–515.

GHOSH, S. and M. SENKO. "File organization: on the selection of random access index points for sequential files," *Jour. ACM*, 16(4):569–579, Oct. 1969.

HENRY, W. R. "Hierarchical structure for data management," *IBM System Jour.*, 8(1):2–15, 1969.

KEEHN, D. G., and J. O. LACY. "VSAM data set design parameters," *IBM System Jour.*, 13(3):186–212, 1974.

LARSON, P. A. "Analysis of index-sequential files with overflow chaining," *ACM Trans. on Database Systems*, 6(4):671–680, Dec. 1981.

LARSON, P-A. "Analysis of index-sequential files with overflow chaining," *ACM Trans. on Database Systems*, 6(4):671–680, Dec. 1981.

LITWIN, W. and D. B. LOMET. "A new method for fast data searches with keys," *IEEE Software*, 4(2):16–24, March 1987.

MULLIN, J. K. "An improved index sequential access method using hashed overflow," *Comm. ACM*, 15(5):301–307, 1972.

NAKAMURA, T., and T. MIZOGUCHI. "An Analysis of storage utilization in block split data structuring schemes," *Proc. 4th Intl. Conf. on Very Large Databases*, W. Berlin, 1978, pp. 489–495.

PFALTZ, J. L., W. J. BERMAN, and E. M. CAGLEY. "Partial-match retrieval using indexed descriptor files," *Comm. ACM*, 20(9):522–528, Sept. 1980.

SCHNEIDERMAN, B. and V. GOODMAN. "Batched searching of sequential and tree structured files," *ACM Trans. on Database Systems*, 1(3):268–275, Sept. 1976.

SUSSENGUTH, E. H. "Use of tree structures for processing files," *Comm. ACM*, 6(5):272–279, May 1963.

REVIEW EXERCISES

1. What is the difference between a B-tree and a B$^+$-tree?
2. What determines the shape of a B$^+$-tree?
3. When would you want to balance a B$^+$-tree?
4. When might you use a B-tree instead of a B$^+$-tree?
5. When might you use a B$^+$-tree instead of a B-tree?
6. When might you use a trie instead of a B$^+$-tree?
7. Consider the B$^+$-tree in Fig. P15–7.

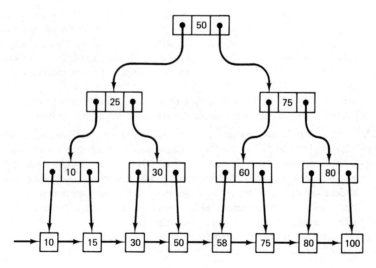

Figure P15–7

    (a) What are the keys of records indexed by this B⁺-tree?
    (b) Show the results of the following activities:
        delete key 30,
        insert key 28,
        insert key 26.

8. Draw a B⁺-tree that corresponds to the set of key values shown in the B-tree of Fig. 14–8.

9. A public utility company has a computerized billing system. Each month meter readings for each customer are fed into the computer. Each month two reports are output from the billing system. One report consists of a billing statement for each customer, showing the date and dollar amount due, meter readings and usage, customer's name, address, and ID number, previous balance due, and taxes. The second report is used internally and shows all of the billing information for each customer for the month. There are two basic files used by the billing system: (1) meter reading data file, and (2) customer data file (name, address, ID number, balance due).
    (a) What should the organization of each file be?
    (b) What should the key of the records on each file be?

10. A retail outfit has a computerized inventory control system. At the end of each day an inventory clerk informs the computer via a terminal of the number of units of each product sold during the day. Such reporting of daily sales by product provides constant inventory updating for each product. When the inventory of any particular item reaches a specified low point, new goods are ordered to replenish the stock. The outputs that are generated by the inventory control system are the following: (1) current inventory after the clerk inputs the desired information for a product on the terminal, (2) a summary report of the day-by-day inventory for each product, generated weekly, and (3) order forms containing supplier's name and address, date, number of units ordered, product number, and unit cost, generated when the reorder point of product is reached.
    (a) What should the organization of the product file be?
    (b) What should the key of the records on the file be?

11. A large restaurant chain maintains records of quantities of the various menu selections that are purchased by its patrons in order to better plan its purchasing of component foods. At each restaurant, information from the meal check is keyed at the time of customer checkout into a data terminal and recorded on a tape cassette. The tape cassettes from all the restaurant outlets are transmitted each morning to a central site where they are batched and input to an analysis system.
    (a) What should be the organization of the file generated at each restaurant outlet?
    (b) What should be the key or identifier of each record on the file?

12. A large hospital has a computerized patient record system. Each nursing station has a terminal with display and key capability. When a patient is admitted, a record containing personal information and medical history is created. The patients' doctors record treatment information as the needs are diagnosed. Nurses access the information that the doctors have stored in the patient's records to determine medication dosages, dietary restrictions, etc. and they also update the records with temperature, pulse, blood pressure, etc., statistics which the doctors later access to brief themselves on patient progress.
    (a) What should be the organization of the patient file?
    (b) What should be the key or identifier of each record on the file?

13. **(a)** Which of the processing requirements in the class records system (described in this chapter) call for sequential accessibility of the student file?

    (b) Which call for direct accessibility to particular records of the file?

14. Why is a B$^+$-tree a better structure than is a B-tree for implementation of an indexed sequential file?

15. Describe the sequence of actions required to access an indexed sequential file sequentially. Describe the sequence of actions required to access a given record directly in an indexed sequential file. Describe the sequence of actions required to insert a record in an indexed sequential file. Describe the sequence of actions required to delete a record from an indexed sequential file. What type of implementation are you using in these descriptions?

16. The physical-layout index approach is being replaced by the B$^+$-tree approach to implementing indexed sequential files. What are the relative advantages and disadvantages of the two approaches?

17. Obtain a listing from your installation of a program that accesses an indexed sequential file. Study the way the file is described and the series of actions taken by the programmer.

18. Propose another method for implementing an indexed sequential file and compare it with the B$^+$-tree and the physical-layout index approaches.

19. Write a program that implements the physical-layout index approach to providing indexed sequential access to data. Be able to handle insertion of new records, deletion of old records, and retrieval of records. Be able to split and merge blocks.

20. Build an indexed sequential file using the language/utility facilities available at your installation. Access the file sequentially and using the index. Insert and delete records.

21. Build several versions of an indexed sequential file using the language/utility facilities available at your installation. Vary design parameters, e.g., block size, padding, index structure, and compare the performance of the resultant files for sequential and direct access and for update activity.

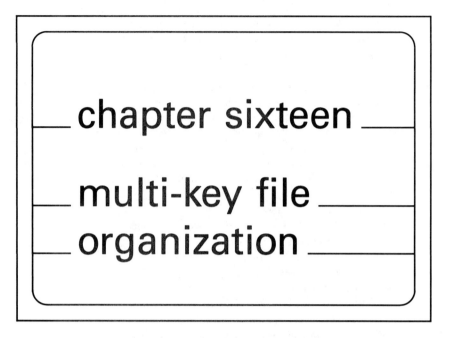

chapter sixteen

multi-key file organization

In this final chapter we introduce a family of file organization techniques that allow records to be accessed by more than one key field. Until this point, we have considered only single-key file organizations: sequential by a given key, relative giving direct access by a particular key, and indexed sequential giving both direct and sequential access by a key (Fig. 16–1). Now we broaden our horizons to include those file organizations that enable a single data file to support multiple access paths, each by a different key. These file organization techniques are at the heart of database implementations.

MULTI-KEY ACCESS

There are numerous techniques that have been used to implement multi-key files. Most of the approaches are based on building indexes to provide direct access by key value. The fundamental indexing techniques were introduced in Chapters 14 and 15. In this chapter we discuss two approaches for providing additional access paths into a file of data records:

- Inversion
- Multi-list organization.

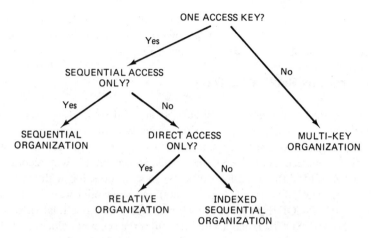

Figure 16–1 Distinguishing among the fundamental file organizations.

Many programming language compilers do not provide built-in capabilities to support multi-key files. Rather, a data processing group generally acquires a data management package that supports multi-key files or writes its own data management system. Language compilers may then interface directly with this file support, or they may generate CALLs to this support. Here, we will introduce the alternate-key indexed sequential facility of COBOL, which provides support for multi-key files.

The chapter closes with a review of the basic trade-offs that should be considered in the design of a multi-key file.

Example: The Need for Multiple Access Paths

Many interactive information systems require the support of multi-key files. Consider a banking system in which there are several types of users: tellers, loan officers, branch managers, bank officers, account holders, and so forth. All have the need to access the same data, say records of the format shown in Fig. 16–2. Various types of users need to access these records in different ways. A teller might identify an account record by its ID value. A loan officer might need to access all account records with a given value for OVERDRAW-LIMIT, or all account records for a given value of SOCNO. A branch manager might access records by the BRANCH and TYPE group code. A bank officer

ACCOUNT

ID	NAME		GROUP-CODE		SOCNO	BALANCE	OVERDRAW LIMIT
	LAST	FIRST	BRANCH	TYPE			

Figure 16–2 Example record format.

might want periodic reports of all accounts data, sorted by ID. An account holder (customer) might be able to access his or her own record by giving the appropriate ID value or a combination of NAME, SOCNO, and TYPE code.

Support by Replicating Data

One approach to being able to support all of these types of access is to have several different files, each organized to serve one type of request. For this banking example, there might be one indexed sequential account file with key ID (to serve tellers, bank officers, and account holders), one sequential account file with records ordered by OVER-DRAW-LIMIT (to serve loan officers), one account file with relative organization and user-key SOCNO (to serve loan officers), one sequential account file with records ordered by GROUP-CODE (to serve branch managers), and one relative account file with user-key NAME, SOCNO, and TYPE code (to serve account holders). We have just identified five files, all containing the same data records! The five files differ only in their organizations, and thus in the access paths they provide.

Difficulties Caused by Replication

Replicating data across files is not a desirable solution to the problem of providing multiple access paths through that data. One obvious difficulty with this approach is the resultant storage space requirements. However, a more serious difficulty with this approach is keeping updates to the replicated data records coordinated. The multi-key file is a classical and often successful solution to the multiple-path retrieval problem; it uses indexes rather than data replication.

Whenever multiple copies of data exist, there is the potential for discrepancies. Assume that you have three calendars. You keep one at home by the telephone, one in your briefcase, and one at your office. What is the probability that those three calendars show the same record of appointments and obligations? The likely situation is that you will post some updates to one copy but forget to enter them in the other copies. Even if you are quite conscientious about updating all three copies, there must be some lag between the times that the updates actually appear in the three locations. The problem becomes more complex if somebody in addition to you, for example your secretary, also updates one or more of your calendars. The same difficulties arise in updating data that appear in multiple files.

The result of incomplete and asynchronous updates is loss of data integrity. If a loan officer queries one file and finds that account #123456 has an overdraw limit of $250, then queries another file and finds that the same account has an overdraw limit of $1000, he or she should question the validity of the data.

Support by Adding Indexes

Another approach to being able to support several different kinds of access to a collection of data records is to have *one* data file with multiple access paths. Now there is only one copy of any data record to be updated, and the update synchronization problem caused by record duplication is avoided. This approach is called *multi-key file organization*.

The concept of multiple-key access generally is implemented by building multiple indexes to provide different access paths to the data records. There may also be multiple linked lists through the data records. We have seen already that an index can be structured in several ways, for example as a table, a binary search tree, a B-tree, or a B$^+$-tree. The most appropriate method of implementing a particular multi-key file is dependent upon the actual uses to be made of the data and the kinds of multi-key file support available.

INVERTED FILE ORGANIZATION

Basic Concepts

One fundamental approach to providing the linkage between an index and the file of data records is called *inversion*. A key's *inversion index* contains all of the values that the key presently has in the records of the data file. Each key-value entry in the inversion index points to all of the data records that have the corresponding value. The data file is said to be *inverted* on that key.

The inversion approach to providing multi-key access has been used as the basis for physical database structures in commercially available database management systems, including several relational systems (IBM's DB2, Relational Technology's Ingres, and Oracle, Inc.'s Oracle), Intel's System-2000, and Software AG's Adabas. These systems were designed to provide rapid retrieval to data records via as many inversion keys as the designer cares to identify. They have user-friendly, natural-language-like query languages to assist the user in formulating inquiries.

Example

A simple inversion index is structured as a table. For example, inverting the example ACCOUNT-FILE on SOCNO results in the inversion index shown in Fig. 16–3. This figure refers to the data records shown in Fig. 16–4 which will be used throughout the chapter.

Fig. 16–3 may bring to mind the index structures that we discussed in the context of relative files (see Fig. 13–6 and 13–7). At that time we referred to an index as a directory. Either term is correct. One difference between the examples in Chapter 13 and the example here is that the data records in the first are not in key-sequence order, because they are organized as a relative file, whereas the data records here are ordered by ID value. In either case, the ordering of the key values in the index need not match the ordering of the corresponding records in the data file.

Variations

This particular inversion index has sorted entries, which facilitates searching for a particular key value, because binary search techniques can be used. Recall from Chapter 9 that a binary search requires $O(\log_2 N)$ comparisons, while a sequential search requires an average

SOCNO	ADDRESS
001234123	6
123456789	5
213823456	14
299167305	16
399042131	4
411625331	13
412631467	7
426135447	20
445062681	17
459463001	1
513014265	8
612305116	9
626311660	18
692122222	12
713214622	3
798392289	15
821346211	2
912346789	19
923146154	11
987654321	10

Figure 16–3   Example index inverting the records of Fig. 16–4 by SOCNO key value.

of $O(N/2)$ comparisons. When N is relatively large, sequential searching significantly slows response time and throughput. Of course when a record is added to the data file, the inversion index must also be updated and maintained in sorted order. Not all inversion indexes are sorted.

A glance at Fig. 13–7 suggests that an inversion index need not be structured as a table but could be structured as a tree, which would provide shorter search times but would be somewhat more complex to manage.

An inversion index can be built on top of a relative file or on top of an indexed sequential file. An inversion index on key SOCNO for a relative file with user-key ID would provide a file that would support direct access by either ID or SOCNO. An inversion index on key SOCNO for an indexed sequential file with key ID would provide a file that would support direct access by either ID or SOCNO and would support sequential access by ID. A sorted SOCNO inversion index could be used to access records in order by SOCNO but would probably be expensive to use.

More Definitions

If one key field is used to determine the storage structure of the data file, it is called the file's *primary key*. Any other access keys are called *secondary keys*.

From a purist's point of view, use of the term *inversion* implies that the indexed data values have been taken out of the data records and reside only in the corresponding

Record Address	ID	NAME LAST	NAME FIRST	GROUP-CODE BRANCH	TYPE	SOCNO	BALANCE	OVERDRAW LIMIT
1	111111	DEAN	JOHN	DT	001	459463001	100.50	0.
2	112131	AMORE	CAROL	NW	001	821346211	2311.20	100.
3	198121	RICE	BESS	DT	002	713214622	−191.87	200.
4	201431	PARKER	OLA	DT	001	399042131	3142.93	100.
5	208432	ANDERSON	BARBARA	NW	001	123456789	95.26	0.
6	291821	ANDERSON	BRENT	NW	002	001234123	146.92	0.
7	300123	HART	ALLISON	NE	002	412631467	3000.00	100.
8	310103	TAHOE	SERENA	DT	001	513014265	243.63	0.
9	324196	BONES	IGOR	EA	001	612305116	0.02	0.
10	335812	BEE	VERA	DT	002	987654321	88.72	0.
11	386132	ARC	JEAN	WE	002	923146154	−89.98	100.
12	387122	ELLS	JOSHUA	WE	002	692122222	10.95	0.
13	415631	BELLE	ELLIE	NE	001	411625331	426.86	100.
14	486212	MATTHERS	ANN	DT	002	213823456	893.92	100.
15	511211	SNUGGS	JOHN	NW	001	798392289	2814.12	250.
16	534216	LOOMIN	TIM	EA	001	299167305	296.12	250.
17	535218	ELLSWORTH	NANCY	EA	001	445062681	2814.12	250.
18	641230	WELLS	CHUCK	DT	002	626311660	−98.14	100.
19	686116	SWORTH	LAUREN	DT	001	912346789	3216.16	100.
20	696123	GUNNESS	MARION	NE	002	426135447	95.93	25.

Figure 16-4 Example data file.

427

inversion index. The data records shown in Fig. 16–4 thus would not include a SOCNO field. A *completely inverted* file has an inversion index for every data field. If the corresponding values have been removed from the data records, the logical result is that a completely inverted file need have no data records! If a file is not completely inverted but has at least one inversion index, it is said to be a *partially inverted* file.

While taking an inversion key's values out of the data records conserves space, it can make processing more difficult. For example, the request: What is the SOCNO for the account with ID = '335812'? would require the following steps:

- Determine the address of the record with ID = '335812' in the data file (the technique used depends on how the file is organized).
- Search the SOCNO inversion index for the entry with that address. (Note that the SOCNO value is *not* in the data record.)

A sequential search of the SOCNO inversion index could be required, because inversion indexes usually are structured by their inversion key values, not by data record addresses.

Indexing with Indirect Addresses

An attractive variation on the inversion index structure is to use indirect addressing, as illustrated for our example file in Fig. 16–5. Rather than accompanying each SOCNO value with the address of the corresponding data record, index entries are in the form of

SOCNO	ID
001234123	291821
123456789	208432
213823456	486212
299167305	534216
399042131	201431
411625331	415631
412631467	300123
426135447	696123
445062681	535218
459463001	111111
513014265	310103
612305116	324196
626311660	641230
692122222	387122
713214622	198121
798392289	511211
821346211	112131
912346789	686116
923146154	386132
987654321	335812

Figure 16–5   Index inverting the records of Fig. 16–4 by SOCNO key value, using indirect addressing.

secondary key-primary key pairs. This approach allows the data file to be reorganized and restructured physically without forcing changes to the index files. The trade-off is that extra work is required to actually find the data record with a given secondary-key value, since the corresponding primary-key value must be translated to the data record's address.

Non-Unique Key Values

In our example, SOCNO values are unique; each entry in the SOCNO inversion index has one corresponding data record. Inversion can also be used with keys that do not have unique values. Fig. 16–6 shows a tabular index for the GROUP-CODE key. As with the SOCNO index, the following index design questions are raised:

- Should key value entries be ordered?
- How should the index itself be structured?
- Should direct or indirect addressing be used?

When a secondary key can have duplicate values, its inversion index must be able to cope with variable numbers of pointers for each key value. There are several alternatives:

- Manage variable-length index entries.
- For each value, allocate space to accommodate the maximum number of entries for any value and manage fixed-length index entries.
- Make one entry in the index for each secondary key-primary key pair; thus if key value x appears in 12 data records, there will be 12 index entries for value x.

With any of these approaches, the question arises of how to order the primary-key entries for a given key value. In Fig. 16–6, entries for a key value are ordered by ascending ID value. Keeping the primary-key entries sorted can make record retrieval faster but incurs overhead when updating records.

GROUP-CODE BRANCH TYPE		ID
DT	001	111111, 201431, 310103, 686116
DT	002	198121, 335812, 486212, 641230
EA	001	324196, 534216, 535218
NE	001	415631
NE	002	300123, 696123
NW	001	112131, 208432, 511211
NW	002	291821
WE	002	386132, 387122

Figure 16–6 Index inverting the records of Fig. 16–4 by GROUP-CODE value, structured as a table.

Existence Queries

One attractive feature of an inverted file is that some types of queries can be answered without accessing the data file. For example, the following requests can be processed just using the inversion indexes of Figs. 16–5 and 16–6.

1. Is there an account for SOCNO = '414556233'?
2. How many accounts are there with GROUP-CODE = 'EA001'?
3. How many accounts are there at BRANCH = 'NE'?
4. How many different types of accounts are there at BRANCH = 'NE'?
5. Does BRANCH = 'WE' have any TYPE = '001' accounts?
6. List the ID values for accounts in GROUP-CODE = 'DT002'.
7. List the ID values for accounts of TYPE = '002'.
8. Does ID = '696123' have an account of TYPE = '002'?
9. Does SOCNO = '426135447' have an account of TYPE = '002'?

MULTI-LIST ORGANIZATION

The other basic approach to providing the linkage between an index and the file of data records is called *multi-list organization*.

The multi-list approach to implementing multi-key access has been the basis for physical database structures in many of the commercially available network and hierarchic database management systems, including the CODASYL family of systems, Cincom's TOTAL, and IBM's IMS.

Basic Concepts

Like an inverted file, a multi-list file maintains an index for each secondary key. There is one entry in the secondary key's index for each value that the secondary key presently has in the data file. The multi-list organization differs from inversion in that while the entry in the inversion index for a key value has a pointer to *each* data record with that key value, the entry in the multi-list index for a key value has just one pointer to the *first* data record with that key value. That data record contains a pointer to the *next* data record with that key value, and so forth. Thus there is a linked list of data records for each value of the secondary key. Multi-list chains usually are bi-directional and occasionally are circular to improve update performance.

Example

Figures 16–7 and 16–8 illustrate the multi-list indexes for secondary keys GROUP-CODE and OVERDRAW-LIMIT respectively in our example file. Fig. 16–9 shows the corresponding data file. Note that while inversion did not affect the data file, use of the multi-

GROUP–CODE BRANCH TYPE		ID
DT	001	111111
DT	002	198121
EA	001	324196
NE	001	415631
NE	002	300123
NW	001	112131
NW	002	291821
WE	002	386132

Figure 16–7 Multi-list index for GROUP-CODE secondary key and the data file in Fig. 16–9.

OVERDRAW LIMIT	ID
0.	111111
100.	112131
200.	198121
250.	511211

Figure 16–8 Multi-list index for OVERDRAW-LIMIT secondary key and the data file in Fig. 16–9.

list organization does. Each record must have space for the pointers that implement the secondary-key accessibility.

The same kinds of design decisions must be addressed as were required with inversion:

- Should key value entries be ordered?
- How should the index itself be structured?
- Should direct or indirect addressing be used?
- Should data record entries for a given key value be ordered?

Here we have ordered key values, used tabular index structures with indirect addressing, and have linked data records by ascending ID value.

Note the result of building a multi-list structure to implement a secondary key that has unique values! If there are N data records, there will be N value entries in the index, each of which points to a linked list of length one. (See Fig. 16–3.) The index is the same as had the secondary key been implemented using inversion.

One attractive characteristic of the multi-list approach is that index entries can be fixed-length. Each value has associated with it just one pointer.

Record Address	ID	NAME		GROUP-CODE		NEXT	SOCNO	BALANCE	OVERDRAW LIMIT	NEXT
		LAST	FIRST	BRANCH	TYPE					
1	111111	DEAN	JOHN	DT	001	201431	459463001	100.50	0.	208432
2	112131	AMORE	CAROL	NW	001	208432	821346211	2311.20	100.	201431
3	198121	RICE	BESS	DT	002	335812	713214622	-191.87	200.	0.
4	201431	PARKER	OLA	DT	001	310103	399042131	3142.93	100.	300123
5	208432	ANDERSON	BARBARA	NW	001	511211	123456789	95.26	0.	291821
6	291821	ANDERSON	BRENT	NW	002	0	001234123	146.92	0.	310103
7	300123	HART	ALLISON	NE	002	696123	412631467	3000.00	100.	386132
8	310103	TAHOE	SERENA	DT	001	686116	513014265	243.63	0.	324196
9	324196	BONES	IGOR	EA	001	534216	612305116	0.02	0.	335812
10	335812	BEE	VERA	DT	002	486212	987654321	88.72	0.	387122
11	386132	ARC	JEAN	WE	002	387122	923146154	-89.98	100.	415631
12	387122	ELLS	JOSHUA	WE	002	0	691222222	10.95	0.	0.
13	415631	BELLE	ELLIE	NE	001	0	411625331	426.86	100.	486212
14	486212	MATTHERS	ANN	DT	002	641230	213823456	893.92	100.	641230
15	511211	SNUGGS	JOHN	NW	001	0	798392289	2814.12	250.	534216
16	534216	LOOMIN	TIM	EA	001	535218	299167305	296.12	250.	535218
17	535218	ELLSWORTH	NANCY	EA	001	0	445062681	2814.12	250.	696123
18	641230	WELLS	CHUCK	DT	002	0	626311660	-98.14	100.	686116
19	686116	SWORTH	LAUREN	DT	001	0	912346789	3216.16	100.	0.
20	696123	GUNNESS	MARION	NE	002	0	426135447	95.93	250.	0.

Figure 16–9 Example data file with multi-list structure, corresponding to data in Fig. 16–4.

Processing

The multi-list approach provides the same type of secondary-key accessibility as does the inversion approach, but processing of the two types of files differs. For example, to respond to the following questions posed in connection with Figs. 16–5 and 16–6:

2. How many accounts are there with GROUP-CODE = 'EA001'?
3. How many accounts are there at BRANCH = 'NE'?
6. List the ID values for accounts in GROUP-CODE = 'DT002'.
7. List the ID values for accounts of TYPE = '002'.
8. Does ID = '696123' have an account of TYPE = '002'?

the data records themselves must be accessed. (These queries could be answered by index access only in the example inverted file.) In order to be able to answer some types of "counting-queries" (such as 2 and 3), each value entry in the multi-list index may have stored with it not just a pointer to the first record with that key value, but also the length of the entry's linked list of records. Figs. 16–10 and 16–11 show this variation for the GROUP-CODE and OVERDRAW-LIMIT indexes.

This length information is also useful for identifying the best access paths for some types of requests. For example, there are three potential access paths that could be used to respond to the request

GROUP-CODE BRANCH TYPE		ID	LENGTH
DT	001	111111	4
DT	002	198121	4
EA	001	324196	3
NE	001	415631	1
NE	002	300123	2
NW	001	112131	3
NW	002	291821	1
WE	002	386132	2

Figure 16–10 Variation on index of Fig. 16–7, showing lengths of linked lists.

OVERDRAW LIMIT	ID	LENGTH
0.	111111	7
100.	112131	8
200.	198121	1
250.	511211	4

Figure 16–11 Variation on index of Fig. 16–8, showing lengths of linked lists.

List the IDs of accounts of GROUP-CODE = 'EA001'
with OVERDRAW-LIMIT = 100.

The data file could be searched sequentially, the GROUP-CODE index could be used, or the OVERDRAW-LIMIT index could be used. Which of these is the best choice? Sequential search requires access to 20 data records, use of the GROUP-CODE index means access to 3 data records, and use of the OVERDRAW-LIMIT index means access to 8 data records. GROUP-CODE is the most desirable option. For each of the accessed records with GROUP-CODE = 'EA001', it is necessary only to check the value of the OVERDRAW-LIMIT field.

Variations

Two variations on the basic multi-list structure are the controlled-length multi-list and the cellular multi-list structures. In a *controlled-length multi-list* file, a maximum length is imposed upon the linked lists of data records. If a secondary-key value is possessed by more data records than that length allows, then the key value would appear more than once in the index and there would be more than one linked list of data records with that value.

In a *cellular multi-list* file, the list structures are determined in part by the characteristics of storage. For example, a cell could be defined as a cylinder, as a track, or as a page. A linked list is not allowed to cross cell boundaries. If there are records in three cylinders that have the same secondary-key value, then there would be three index entries and three linked lists for that value. This multi-list variation can be useful in reducing disk arm-movement requirements and I/O accesses.

ALTERNATE-KEY INDEXED SEQUENTIAL FILES

COBOL provides multi-key file support by building upon the indexed sequential file organization that we discussed in Chapter 15. In addition to the index and sequential data files used to implement the already-discussed sequential concept, another index is maintained (by the data management system, not by the programmer) for each defined secondary key.

Example

Consider an example which is a subset of the banking application introduced earlier. We will use this example throughout the chapter. Assume that we need to be able to access account records in the following ways:

- Sequential by ascending ID value
- Direct by ID value

- Direct by SOCNO value
- Direct by GROUP-CODE value.

For expository purposes, assume that a person can have only one account, that is, SOCNO and ID values both will be unique. The first two requirements alone would suggest use of an indexed sequential file with key ID. The other two requirements suggest building additional index structures for access to the data file. COBOL calls such a multi-key file an alternate-key indexed sequential file.

Declaring a File in COBOL

The SELECT clause for an alternate-key indexed sequential file is the same as for an ordinary INDEXED file, with the addition of one or more ALTERNATE RECORD KEY phrases. Each data item specified by an ALTERNATE RECORD KEY phrase becomes a secondary key for the file. For our example, the following SELECT clause would be appropriate:

```
SELECT ACCOUNT-FILE ASSIGN TO DISK
    ORGANIZATION IS INDEXED
    ACCESS MODE IS SEQUENTIAL or RANDOM or DYNAMIC
    RECORD KEY IS ID
    ALTERNATE RECORD KEY IS SOCNO
    ALTERNATE RECORD KEY IS GROUP-CODE
        WITH DUPLICATES.
```

The WITH DUPLICATES phrase on the second ALTERNATE RECORD KEY entry indicates that GROUP-CODE values need not be unique. The absence of this phrase on the first ALTERNATE RECORD KEY entry indicates that the SOCNO values must be unique. Recall that primary key values (here values of ID) must be unique in an INDEXED file.

The proper ACCESS MODE phrase for a file in a program is determined by the way that the program accesses the file by its primary key, not by secondary key values. ACCESS MODE SEQUENTIAL means that records are accessed by ascending value of the primary key. Sequential access by a secondary key implies use of ACCESS MODE RANDOM, since that access order probably does not match primary-key order.

Just as the primary key must be an alphanumeric field that appears in the record description for the file, so must any secondary key be alphanumeric and appear in the file's record description. The primary record key and alternate record keys are referred to collectively as *record keys*.

Creating a File

The creation of an alternate-key indexed sequential file proceeds in the same way as does the creation of an indexed sequential file without secondary keys. If the file is created with ACCESS MODE SEQUENTIAL, then records must be written in order by ascending value of the primary key. The "system" builds not only the index for the primary key, but also an index for each secondary key. Either inversion or multi-list organization can be used to tie indexes to the data file.

Retrieving Records Sequentially

Retrieval of records from an alternate-key indexed sequential file may be relative to the primary key or any secondary key. Unless otherwise specified, sequential retrieval is relative to the primary key, as discussed in Chapter 15. Sequential retrieval by an alternate key must be preceded by a START statement. The format of the START verb is

$$\underline{\text{START}} \text{ filename} \left[\underline{\text{KEY}} \text{ IS} \begin{Bmatrix} \dfrac{\underline{\text{EQUAL}} \text{ TO}}{=} \\ \dfrac{\underline{\text{GREATER}} \text{ THAN}}{>} \\ \dfrac{\underline{\text{NOT}} \underline{\text{LESS}} \text{ THAN}}{\underline{\text{NOT}} <} \end{Bmatrix} \text{dataname} \right]$$

$$\underline{\text{INVALID}} \text{ KEY imperative-statement.}$$

If the KEY phrase is omitted, then the START positions the file relative to the primary key's value. Otherwise, dataname must be either a record key (primary or alternate) or a component of a record key, sharing its left boundary in storage (see our earlier discussion of generic keys).

Following are several examples of COBOL code for sequential retrieval by alternate record key for the ACCOUNT-FILE. The first section of code retrieves the records of the account file in order by ascending SOCNO value. There should be no duplicates.

```
MOVE ZERO TO SOCNO.
START ACCOUNT-FILE
    KEY GREATER THAN SOCNO
    INVALID KEY . . . .
READ ACCOUNT-FILE RECORD INTO WS-ACCOUNT-REC
    AT END MOVE 'Y' TO EOF-ACCOUNT-FILE-SW.
PERFORM PROCESS-NEXT
    UNTIL EOF-ACCOUNT-FILE.
    . . .
PROCESS-NEXT.
    . . .
    READ ACCOUNT-FILE RECORD INTO WS-ACCOUNT-REC
        AT END MOVE 'Y' TO EOF-ACCOUNT-FILE-SW.
```

The next section of code retrieves the records for accounts in the 'DT' branch, in order by ascending TYPE values (since alternate key GROUP-CODE is composed of BRANCH and TYPE). There may be more than one record with BRANCH = 'DT' and a given TYPE value; these "duplicates" are retrieved in the order in which they were written to the file initially.

```
MOVE 'DT' TO BRANCH OF GROUP-CODE.
START ACCOUNT-FILE
    KEY EQUAL TO BRANCH OF GROUP-CODE
    INVALID KEY. . . .
READ ACCOUNT-FILE RECORD INTO WS-ACCOUNT-REC
    AT END MOVE 'Y' TO EOF-ACCOUNT-FILE-SW.
PERFORM PROCESS-NEXT
    UNTIL EOF-ACCOUNT-FILE
        OR BRANCH OF GROUP-CODE NOT = 'DT'.
    . . .
PROCESS-NEXT.
    . . .
    READ ACCOUNT-FILE RECORD INTO WS-ACCOUNT-REC
        AT END MOVE 'Y' TO EOF-ACCOUNT-FILE-SW.
```

The INVALID KEY condition is raised on the START if there are no records with BRANCH = 'DT'. The looping through the account records has two stopping conditions: reaching end-of-file and encountering the next BRANCH value after 'DT'. Without the second condition, the sequential read would continue until the file were exhausted. A sequential read based on an alternate key does not recognize breaks in the key's value.

The key of reference for retrieval can be changed from one record key to another by use of a START (specifying the desired record key), by a WRITE, or by a command that specifies random (i.e., direct) access to records of the file.

Retrieving Records Directly

The direct form of the READ verb for alternate-key access is

```
READ filename RECORD [INTO identifier]
     [KEY IS dataname]
     INVALID KEY imperative-statement.
```

If the KEY phrase is omitted, the READ is relative to the primary key for the file. If the KEY phrase is included, then dataname must be a record key for the file.

To access the account record for the customer whose SOCNO value is '123456789', the following statement is used.

```
MOVE '123456789' TO SOCNO.
READ ACCOUNT-FILE RECORD INTO WS-ACCOUNT-REC
    KEY IS SOCNO
    INVALID KEY DISPLAY 'NO RECORD FOR SOCNO'
        SOCNO.
```

To retrieve the records for accounts in the 'DT' branch, in order by ascending TYPE values, starting with TYPE = '001', the following section of code could be used.

```
MOVE 'DT001' TO GROUP-CODE.
READ ACCOUNT-FILE RECORD INTO WS-ACCOUNT-REC
    KEY IS GROUP-CODE
    INVALID KEY. . . .
PERFORM PROCESS-NEXT
    UNTIL EOF-ACCOUNT-FILE
        OR BRANCH OF GROUP-CODE NOT = 'DT'.
    . . .
PROCESS-NEXT.
    . . .
    READ ACCOUNT-FILE RECORD INTO WS-ACCOUNT-REC
    AT END MOVE 'Y' TO EOF-ACCOUNT-FILE-SW.
```

Compare this section of code with that given earlier (two examples previous) to retrieve records for accounts in the 'DT' branch, in order by ascending TYPE values. There the START was used with generic key BRANCH; here the entire alternate-key value is specified.

Thus direct retrievals can be used to access data by any record-key value. The name of the record key in use is given in the READ's KEY phrase. Subsequent sequential READs proceed from that position according to the same record key, until changed by a START, a random READ, or other random-access verb action on the file.

Updating Records

The update of an alternate-key indexed sequential file is governed by the primary record key. The INVALID KEY condition is raised on a WRITE or REWRITE if the insertion or replacement would violate a constraint on duplicates.

COMPARISONS AND TRADE-OFFS

Both inverted files and multi-list files have

- An index for each secondary key.
- An index entry for each distinct value of the secondary key.

In either file organization

- The index may be tabular or tree-structured.
- The entries in an index may or may not be sorted.
- The pointers to data records may be direct or indirect.

The indexes differ in that

- An entry in an inversion index has a pointer to each data record with that value.
- An entry in a multi-list index has a pointer to the first data record with that value.

Thus an inversion index may have variable-length entries whereas a multi-list index has fixed-length entries. In either organization

- The data record pointers for a key value may or may not appear in some sorted order.
- Keeping entries in sorted order introduces overhead.

The data record file

- Is not affected by having an inversion index built on top of it.
- Must contain the linked lists of records with identical secondary key values in the multi-list structure.

Some of the implications of these differences are the following:

- Index management is easier in the multi-list approach because entries are fixed in length.
- The inverted file approach tends to exhibit better inquiry performance. Many types of queries can be answered by accessing inversion indexes without necessitating access to data records, thereby reducing I/O-access requirements.
- Inversion of a file can be transparent to a programmer who accesses that file but does not use the inversion indexes, while a multi-list structure affects the file's record layout. The multi-list pointers can be made transparent to a programmer if the data manager does not make them available for programmer use and stores them at the end of each record.

Additionally, the multi-list structure has proven useful in linking together occurrences of different record types, thereby providing access paths based upon logical relationships. It is also possible to provide multiple sort orders through a single data collection, by linking the records together in order by various keys.

FILE DESIGN SUMMARY

We have now discussed the basic approaches to structuring collections of records so that the files can support our information systems' requirements. File design is a complex problem, in part because there are so many parameters that should be considered. (Fig. 16–12).

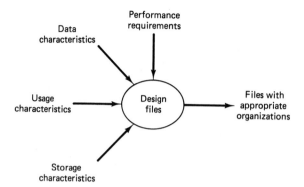

Figure 16–12 Basic parameters that should be considered in designing files.

Data characteristics include

- Record length.
- Record format: fixed or variable.
- Maximum record length.
- Primary key and its value distribution.
- Secondary keys and their value distributions.
- Average number of records with given secondary key value.
- Logical structure of data.

Usage characteristics include

- Frequency of query.
- Frequency of update.
- Growth expected.
- Volatility of data values.
- Batch versus interactive access.
- Random versus sequential access.
- Record orderings needed.
- Clustering of accesses to subsets of records.
- Variety of types of transactions.
- Priorities of requirements.

These characteristics are typically the most difficult to specify, especially since the answers tend to change as time goes by.

Storage characteristics include

- Type of storage devices available.
- Block sizes.

- Average random access times.
- Average sequential access times.
- Cost of I/O access.
- Main memory availability for buffers.
- Cost of storage.
- Available file organization methods.
- Available access methods.

The performance of a particular design can be judged on the basis of factors such as

- Expected and worst case response times.
- Expected and worst case update times.
- Transaction throughput.
- I/O-access requirements.
- Storage space requirements.
- Complexity of required support.
- Maintenance requirements.
- Availability of required support.

Of course, the relative importance of each of these factors is application-dependent.

CLOSING WORDS

Data structuring and file organization are two important factors in determining the performance of a system. The systems programmer and applications programmer alike must design the appropriate structures to meet data processing requirements. Data need to be managed both for the life of a particular program and also more permanently. This book has introduced you to some of the powerful data structuring and file organization techniques that the data processing community has developed. Researchers and practitioners will continue to add to the store of possibilities. As database management systems become increasingly prevalent, some of the burden of structuring files for permanent storage will shift from application programmers to database administrators. I hope that your study of this book will prove instrumental in preparing you to be continually successful in your data management endeavors. Bonne chance!

TERMS

alternate key   B-tree
alternate-key indexed sequential   B$^+$-tree
binary search tree   cellular multi-list file

completely inverted file
controlled-length multi-list file
direct addressing
indirect addressing
inversion index
inverted-file organization

multi-key file organization
multi-list file organization
partially inverted file
primary key
record key
secondary key

SELECTED REFERENCES

ANDERSON, H. D. and P. B. BERRA. "Minimum cost selection of secondary indexes for formatted files," *ACM Trans. on Database Systems*, 2(1):68–90, March 1977.

BENTLEY, J. L. and J. H. FRIEDMAN. "Data structures for range searching," *ACM Computing Surveys*, 11(4):397–409, 1979.

CARDENAS, A. F. "Analysis and performance of inverted data base structures," *Comm. ACM* 18(5):253–263, May 1975.

CARDENAS, A. F. "Evaluation and selection of file organization: a model and system," *Comm. ACM*, 16(9):540–548, Sept. 1973.

COMER, D. "The difficulty of optimum index selection," *ACM Trans. on Database Systems*, 3(4):440–445, Dec. 1978.

FEDEROWICZ, J. "Database performance evaluation in an indexed file environment," *ACM Trans. on Database Systems*, 12(1):85–110, March 1987.

HATZOPOULOS, M. and J. G. KOLLIAS. "On the optimal selection of multilist database structures," *IEEE Trans. on Software Engineering*, SE-10(6):681–687, Nov. 1984.

IP, M. Y. L., L. V. SAXTON, and V. V. RAGHAVAN. "On the selection of an optimal set of indexes," *IEEE Trans. on Software Engineering*, SE-9(2):135–143, March 1983.

KRIEGEL, H. P. "Performance comparison of index structures for multi-key retrieval," *ACM SIGMOD '84 Proc. of Annual Meeting, SIGMOD Record*, 14(2):186–196, June 1984.

ROTHNIE, J. B. and T. LOZANO. "Attribute based file organization in a paged memory environment," *Comm. ACM*, 17(2):63–69, Feb. 1974.

SCHKOLNICK, M. "Secondary index optimization," *Proc. ACM-SIGMOD 1975 Intl. Conf. on Management of Data, May 14–16, 1975, San Jose CA*, 186–192.

SEVERANCE, D. G. "Identifier search mechanisms: a survey and generalized model," *ACM Computing Surveys*, 6(3):175–194, Sept. 1974.

STONEBRAKER, M., B. RUBENSTEIN, and A. GUTTMAN. "Application of abstract data types and abstract indices to CAD databases," *Engineering Design Applications, ACM/IEEE Database Week, May 23–26, 1983, San Jose CA*, pp. 107–114.

VALLARINO, O. "On the use of bit maps for multiple key retrieval," *Proc. Conf. on Data: Abstraction, Definition, and Structure, March 22–24, 1976, Salt Lake City UT, ACM SIGPLAN Notices*, 2(Spec. Iss.):108–114, 1976.

WELCH, J. W. and J. W. GRAHAM. "Retrieval using ordered lists in inverted and multilist files," *Proc. ACM-SIGMOD 1976 Intl. Conf. on Management of Data, June 2–4, 1976, Washington DC*, pp. 21–29.

REVIEW EXERCISES

1. Discuss the trade-offs that should be considered in designing an inversion index for a multi-key file.

2. Discuss the trade-offs that should be considered in designing an index for a multi-list file.

3. Why do most implementations of the alternate-key indexed sequential structure use an inverted approach rather than a multi-list approach?

4. Describe the kinds of requests that can be serviced by the index alone in an inverted file.

5. In some multi-list files, each index entry includes the length of the corresponding linked list. What kinds of requests would benefit by having this information available?

6. Discuss the advantages and disadvantages of giving the application programmer the responsibility for designing the files used in his or her programs, versus having another person bear the responsibility.

7. Discuss the relative advantages and disadvantages of using an inverted approach and of using a multi-list approach to provide access to a file via a secondary key that may appear a variable number of times in each record of the file. Which approach would you use in this situation?

8. Find out what procedures and guidelines are followed in designing files at your installation.

9. Who has the responsibility for designing files at your installation?

10. Write a program to implement a multi-key file. Build several versions of the file, using different design parameters in each. Document the variations and compare the performance of the several versions.

11. Write a program that builds a multi-key file using inversion. Maintain your own inversion indexes. Write another program that builds a multi-key file using multi-lists. Maintain your own indexes and linked lists. Compare the performance of the resultant files with various types of activity, including record retrieval, insertion, and deletion.

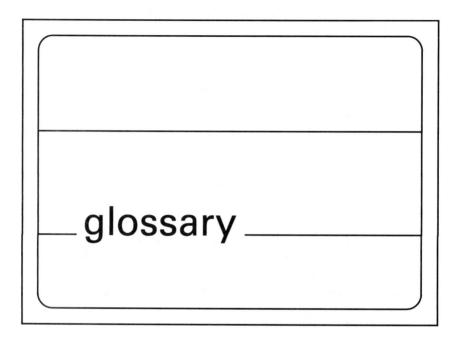

glossary

ABSOLUTE ADDRESSING.   A technique for mapping records to storage where the key value is the record's actual address. Compare with *relative addressing*.

ACCESS MECHANISM.   The means for reading and/or writing data representations from and/or to a storage medium.

ACTIVITY GRAPH.   A graph representing the precedence required and parallelism possible among a set of activities or tasks; often the nodes of the graph represent activities and the edges represent precedence requirements.

ACYCLIC GRAPH.   A graph that has no cycles. See *cycle*.

ADJACENCY MATRIX.   A matrix used to represent the structure of a graph; $A(i,j) = 1$ if and only if edge (v_i, v_j) is in the set of edges for the graph, and 0 otherwise, where v_i and v_j are nodes of the graph.

ALMOST-COMPLETE BINARY TREE.   A binary tree with K ($K \geq 2$) levels, where levels 0 through $K - 2$ are full and level $K - 1$ is being filled left to right.

ALPHABET.   A set of elementary symbols, which in combination form the words of a vocabulary.

ALTERNATE KEY.   See *secondary key*.

ALTERNATE-KEY INDEXED SEQUENTIAL.   A COBOL multi-key file organization which builds secondary-key indexes upon an indexed sequential file.

ANTICIPATORY BUFFERING. A buffer management technique whereby data are read into a buffer before they are actually requested by a program. Compare with *demand buffering*.

ARC. See *edge*.

ARRAY. Finite, ordered set of homogeneous elements; a two-dimensional array is commonly referred to as a table.

ASCII. (American Standard Code for Information Interchange). A 7-bit character-encoding scheme developed as a standard for data transmission and now widely used for data representation in volatile and nonvolatile storage.

AUXILIARY MEMORY. See *secondary storage*.

AVL TREE. A height-balanced binary tree; for each node R_i of the tree, the height of the left subtree of R_i and the height of the right subtree of R_i differ by at most 1.

BALANCED MERGE. A merge technique that uses an equal number of input devices and output devices.

BASE LOCATION. The starting address of a data structure.

BATCH MODE. The processing of transactions accumulated over a period of time. Compare with *interactive mode*.

BB TREE. See *bounded-balance tree*.

BINARY SEARCH. A search technique that is applied to a list of ordered keys. At each step of the search the list is partitioned into two equal parts, with the selection of the appropriate partition to probe in the next step made on the basis of relative key values.

BINARY SEARCH TREE. A binary tree where for each node R_i, all keys of nodes in the left subtree of R_i precede the key labeling R_i, and the key labeling R_i precedes all keys of nodes in the right subtree of R_i. A special case of *m*-way search tree, where $m = 2$.

BINARY TREE. A tree where the maximum out-degree of each node is 2, and leftness and rightness are imposed upon the subtrees of each node.

BIT STRING. A finite sequence of symbols derived from the alphabet $\{0,1\}$.

BLOCK. A collection of contiguous records recorded as a unit; sometimes called a *physical record*.

BLOCK MULTIPLEXOR CHANNEL. A channel that can execute one instruction of the channel program for one device, then can switch to perform an instruction of another device's channel program. Compare with *selector channel* and *multiplexor channel*.

BLOCKING FACTOR. Number of records per block, also sometimes number of characters per block.

BOOLEAN. A primitive data structure with value taken from the set *{true, false}* and with fundamental operators: *not, and,* and *or*. Also called *logical*.

BOOLEAN OPERATOR. An operator with one or more boolean operands; the fundamental boolean operators are defined by Table 2 in Chapter 1 of the text.

BOUNDED-BALANCE TREE (BB tree). A binary tree in which a designer-selected bound value (β) constrains the difference between the number of nodes in any node's left subtree and its right subtree, for $0 < \beta \leq \frac{1}{2}$.

BREADTH-FIRST. A method of graph traversal in which one node is selected as the starting point, it is visited, then all nodes adjacent to that node are visited, then nodes adjacent to those nodes are visited, and so on until the entire graph has been traversed. Compare with *depth-first.*

B*-TREE. A special case of B-tree in which each node is at least two-thirds full instead of at least one-half full.

B$^+$-TREE. A tree resembling a B-tree but in which there is a linked list connecting the leaf nodes. When a B$^+$-tree is used as an index, indexed key values appear in the leaf nodes; the interior nodes provide relatively direct access to the leaf nodes.

B-TREE OF ORDER m. A special case of m-way search tree in which each nonroot and nonleaf node have between $\lceil \frac{1}{2}m \rceil$ and m subtrees, the root has either zero or at least two subtrees, and all leaf nodes are on the same level.

BUBBLE SORT. An internal sort in which each key floats up to its proper position through a series of pairwise comparisons and exchanges with adjacent key values; requires $O(N^2)$ comparisons to sort N key values.

BUCKET ADDRESSING. A technique for managing records on storage where a record's key value is mapped to an area of space (bucket) that can hold multiple records.

BUFFER. An area of storage reserved for use in performing input/output operations, into which data are read and from which data are written; used to compensate for a difference in the rate of flow of data between devices.

CASCADE MERGE. A merge technique that uses a decreasing number of input devices at each phase of a pass, temporarily retiring intermediate output files to be input at the start of the next pass.

CELLULAR MULTI-LIST FILE. A multi-list file in which no linked list crosses a boundary between physical cell areas (e.g., a cell may be a disk cylinder).

CHANNEL. A device that connects the processing unit and main memory with the I/O control units.

CHANNEL PROGRAM. The instructions that are executed by a channel to access devices and control data pathways.

CHARACTER. A primitive data structure with value taken from an alphabet; the basic element of the string data structure.

CIRCULARLY LINKED LIST. A linked list in which the last node points to the first node or the head node of the list.

CIRCULAR QUEUE. A queue implemented such that its last element immediately precedes its first element, when the queue is full.

COLLATING SEQUENCE. Ordering of characters, for use in comparing bit patterns to determine which of two is larger.

COLLISION. Situation occurring when two unequal key values map to the same address.

COLLISION RESOLUTION TECHNIQUE. A technique applied to determine an alternative address for a key value when a collision occurs.

COLUMN-MAJOR ORDER. An array-linearization technique that stores all the elements from one column, before storing any elements from the next column.

Subscripts are varied left-to-right; that is, the left-most subscript is varied fastest. Compare with *row-major order.*

COMPLEMENT REPRESENTATION. An approach used to represent integer values, where a non-negative integer X is represented in its true form (i.e., X) and a negative integer $-X$ is represented in its complement form (i.e., $R - X$) for some complementation constant R. The complement representations of all integers are non-negative. Compare to *sign-and-magnitude representation.*

COMPLETE BINARY TREE. A binary tree that contains the maximum number of nodes possible for its height.

COMPLETELY INVERTED FILE. A file structure which includes an inversion index for every field of the records. Compare with *partially inverted file.*

CONCATENATION. An operator with two string operands, producing a string result. If $S = 'a_1a_2 \ldots a_N'$ and $S^0 = 'b_1b_2 \ldots b_M'$, CONCAT (S,S^0) is $'a_1a_2 \ldots a_Nb_1b_2 \ldots b_M'$.

CONNECTED GRAPH. A graph that cannot be partitioned into two graphs without removing at least one edge.

CONTROL INTERVAL. A data block in an IBM VSAM (indexed sequential) file.

CONTROLLED-LENGTH MULTI-LIST FILE. A multi-list file in which no linked list exceeds a specified length.

CONTROLLER. A device that controls input/output operations at one or more devices.

CRITICAL PATH. The longest path in an activity graph.

CROSS-SECTION. A subset of an array, obtained by holding one (or more) of the subscripts at a constant value while varying the remaining subscripts through their entire ranges of values.

CYCLE. A path in a graph where both (1) no edge appears more than once in the sequence of edges, and (2) the initial node of the path is the same as the terminal node of the path.

CYLINDER. In a disk pack, the set of all tracks with the same distance from the axis about which the disk pack rotates; the tracks of a cylinder can be accessed without repositioning the access mechanism.

CYLINDER ADDRESSING. A technique for addressing the data records on a disk, where a record's address is its cylinder number, surface number, and record number. Compare with *sector addressing.*

CYLINDER INDEX. In an indexed sequential file, an index to the key values stored on each cylinder allocated to the file.

DATABASE. A collection of logically related data that supports controlled shared access by multiple users and programs.

DATABASE MANAGEMENT SYSTEM (DBMS). An interface between programs and file systems, with responsibility for defining, representing, storing, organizing, and protecting data, as well as for interfacing users with the database.

DATA STRUCTURE. A class of data characterized by its logical organization and the operations that are defined on it. Also known as *data type.*

DATA TYPE. See *data structure.*

DEDICATED DEVICE.   A device that is suitable for access by only one user at a time. Compare with *shared device, virtual device.*

DEGREE.   Characteristic of a graph node; the number of edges incident at the node; the sum of the node's in-degree and out-degree.

DEMAND BUFFERING.   A buffer management technique whereby data are read into a buffer only when they are actually requested by a program. Compare with *anticipatory buffering.*

DENSE INDEX.   An index that contains all the key values of the data collection being indexed. Compare with *sparse index.*

DEPTH-FIRST.   A method of graph traversal in which one node is selected as the starting point, it is visited, then all nodes on one path leading from that node are visited, then all nodes on another path leading from the start node are visited, and so on until the entire graph has been traversed. Compare with *breadth-first.*

DIRECT ACCESS.   The ability to access any of a collection of records without necessitating access to physically preceding records. Compare with *serial access.*

DIRECT-ACCESS STORAGE DEVICE (DASD).   A storage device that supports direct access. Commonly refers to magnetic disk storage.

DIRECT ADDRESSING.   Addressing or indexing that maps a record's key value directly to a corresponding relative or absolute address. Compare with *indirect addressing.*

DIRECTED GRAPH.   A graph in which directionality is assigned to the edges; an edge has its source in one node and terminates in another node; each node then has both an in-degree and an out-degree.

DIRECTORY.   (a) See *index* (b).

(b) A structure used to manage identification and location information about files or records.

DIRECTORY LOOKUP ADDRESSING.   A technique for managing access to records whereby an index is used as an intermediary between key values and record addresses.

DISK DRIVE.   A mechanism for moving a disk pack or single magnetic disk and for controlling its movements.

DISKETTE.   A thin, flexible magnetic disk and a semirigid protective jacket in which the disk is permanently enclosed. Also called *floppy disk.*

DISK PACK.   An assembly of magnetic disks.

DIVISION-REMAINDER HASHING.   An address-calculation technique whereby the key value is divided by an appropriate number and the remainder is used as the record's relative address.

DOUBLE BUFFERING.   A buffer management technique whereby two buffers are allocated to accommodate the input/output activity for a file.

DOUBLE HASHING.   A collision resolution technique whereby a second hash function is applied to the key value. Compare with *linear probing.*

DOUBLY LINKED LIST.   A linked list in which each node points to both the next node and the prior node in the list; a doubly linked list is not necessarily circular.

DYNAMIC HASHING.   A virtual hashing technique that uses a binary tree index structure to keep track of buckets and to guide access to records. Compare with *extendible hashing.*

EARLIEST START TIME.   The earliest possible trigger time for a node in an activity graph. Compare with *latest start time*.

EBCDIC (Extended Binary Coded Decimal Interchange Code).   An 8-bit character encoding scheme widely used for both data storage and data transmission purposes.

EDGE.   An elementary component of a graph, providing a connection between two nodes; depicted by a line. Also called *arc*.

ELEMENTARY ITEM.   A field that is not decomposable to component fields.

END-OF-TAPE MARK.   A mark on a magnetic tape used to indicate the end of the area where recording is permissible.

EQUIVALENCE CLASS.   A set of key values that are synonyms.

EQUIVALENT TREES.   Trees that have the same structure and node contents. Compare with *similar trees*.

EVEN PARITY.   A technique in which an extra bit is appended to the representation of each character and is set such that the number of 1-bits for the character is even. Compare with *odd parity*.

EXCHANGE SELECTION SORT.   A variation on a straight selection sort in which the selected key value is moved to its final position by being exchanged with the key initially occupying that position; sorts in place; requires $O(N^2)$ comparisons to sort N key values.

EXCHANGE SORT.   One of a family of internal sort algorithms in which pairs of key values are compared and exchanged if they are not in the proper relative positions.

EXTENDIBLE HASHING.   A virtual hashing technique that uses a tabular directory based on a degenerate trie structure to keep track of buckets and to guide access to records. Compare with *dynamic hashing*.

EXTERNAL LABEL.   A label affixed to the exterior of a storage medium, used to identify the medium to humans.

EXTERNAL SORT.   A method for arranging a collection of keys into a specified order, where the collection resides on an auxiliary storage device. Read/write time is a significant factor in determining sort performance. Also called a *file sort*. Compare with *internal sort*.

FIELD.   A specified area of a record used to represent a particular kind of information.

FILE.   A collection of logically related record occurrences that are treated as a unit and are persistent, i.e., independent of the execution of a particular run-unit.

FILE ACTIVITY RATIO.   The ratio of the number of records with activity during the period to the total number of records on the file.

FILE ORGANIZATION.   The technique used to represent, structure, and store the records on a file.

FILE SORT.   See *external sort*.

FILE SYSTEM.   A set of routines that manage directories, device accesses, and buffers, enabling programs to access files without being concerned with details of physical storage characteristics and device timings.

FIRST-IN-FIRST-OUT (FIFO).   A method of linear list management in which the first element into the list will be the first element taken out of the list; defines the mode of operation of a queue. Compare with *last-in-first-out*. See also *queue*.

FIXED-HEAD DISK.   A disk in which there is one read/write head per track; the access mechanism never has to be moved. Compare with *movable-head disk*.

FLOPPY DISK.   See *diskette*.

FOREST.   A collection of rooted trees.

FREE SPACE.   Memory allocated to a file but not containing meaningful records. See also *padding*.

FRONT.   The element that has been in a queue the longest. Also, the next element to be removed from a queue.

GENERATION FILE.   One of multiple versions of a file created during successive cycles of processing.

GENERIC KEY.   The leading portion of a key field.

GRAPH.   A collection of nodes and edges, where each edge connects a pair of nodes.

GRAPH ORDER.   The number of nodes in a graph.

GROUP ITEM.   A field that is decomposable into component elementary and/or group items.

HASH FUNCTION.   Calculation applied to a key value to obtain an address.

HASHING.   An address calculation technique. Also known as *hash table method, direct addressing technique, key-to-address transformation method, randomizing technique, scatter storage technique*.

HEAD CRASH.   Situation occurring when a read/write head comes into contact with the recording surface of a disk.

HEAD NODE.   The distinguishable first node of a list. It may or may not contain meaningful data.

HEAP.   An almost-complete binary tree, in which the records are arranged such that for each node i, $key (i) \leq key (j)$, where node j is the father of node i.

HEIGHT-BALANCED TREE.   See *AVL tree*.

HIT RATIO.   The percentage of records read or written by a given request or set of requests.

HOME ADDRESS.   The address to which a key value hashes.

IN-DEGREE.   The number of edges directed into a node in a directed graph. Compare with *out-degree*.

INDEX.   (a) See *subscript*.

                (b) A collection of key value, address pairs, used to facilitate access to a collection of records.

INDEXED SEQUENTIAL FILE ORGANIZATION.   A file organization technique that supports both sequential and direct access to records by a key field.

INDIRECT ADDRESSING.   Addressing or indexing that maps a key value to an intermediary value which is then mapped (sometimes via indexing) to a record's relative or absolute address. Compare with *direct addressing*.

INFIX NOTATION.   A method of representing an arithmetic expression whereby a binary operator appears between its operands. Compare with *postfix* and *prefix notations*.

IN-ORDER TRAVERSAL.   A method of visiting all the nodes of a binary tree, recursively defined by first traversing the left subtree in in-order, then visiting the root, then traversing the right subtree in in-order. Compare with *pre-order* and *post-order traversals*.

INPUT FILE A file that is read, but not written, by a program. Compare with *output file* and *input/output file*.

INPUT/OUTPUT FILE. A file that is both read from and written to by a given program. Compare with *input file* and *output file*.

INSERTION SORT. One of a family of internal sort algorithms in which the next entry in the unsorted list is inserted into its proper relative position in a growing sorted list.

INTEGER. A member of the following set of numbers:

$$\{\ldots, -(n + 1), -n, \ldots, -2, -1, 0, 1, 2, \ldots, n, n + 1, \ldots\}$$

INTERACTIVE MODE. The processing of transactions as they occur. Compare with *batch mode*.

INTERBLOCK GAP. The space between two consecutive blocks on a storage medium.

INTERNAL LABEL. A record of identifying information recorded with a file on a storage medium.

INTERNAL SORT. A method for arranging a collection of keys into a specified order, where the collection resides entirely in main memory. Read/write time is not significant in determining sort performance. Compare with *external sort*.

INTERNAL SORT PHASE. In an external sort, the phase in which an internal sort technique is used to sort records into several runs and to distribute those runs onto two or more storage devices.

INTERRUPT. A temporary halt in the execution of a process, with a switch to the execution of another. When the second has terminated, control may or may not return to the first to resume its execution.

INVERSION INDEX. An index containing all the values that a primary or secondary key has in the data file and (direct or indirect) pointers to all of the data records that have the corresponding values.

INVERTED FILE ORGANIZATION. A multi-key file organization technique that uses inversion indices.

ITERATIVE PROCEDURE. A procedure that repeatedly executes a series of steps but that does not invoke itself; compare with *recursive procedure*.

KEY. (a) The identifying field of a record.
(b) The field whose value is used to place a collection of records into a sorted ordering.

KEY-SEQUENCED DATA SET. The data records in an indexed sequential file; a control interval containing records in ascending order by a given key.

LABELED TAPE. A tape that includes an internal label.

LAST-IN-FIRST-OUT (LIFO). A method of linear list management in which the element most recently added to the list will be the next element to be taken out of the list; defines the mode of operation of a stack; compare with *first-in-first-out*. See also *stack*.

LATENCY. See *rotational delay*.

LATEST START TIME. The latest possible trigger time for a node in an activity graph, where the entire graph will complete in its shortest possible time. Compare with *earliest start time*.

LEAF NODE. A node of a tree or graph with out-degree zero.

LEFT THREAD. A link from a node in a binary tree to its predecessor node in a traversal ordering. Compare with *right thread*.

LEVEL. A characteristic of a node in a tree; a node's level is the length of the path from the root to that node.

LEVEL-NUMBER. In COBOL, a designation used to show the hierarchic structure of fields in a record.

LINEAR LIST. A general data structure comprised of an ordered set of nodes; for each node there is a single "next" node; Compare with *tree*.

LINEAR PROBING. A collision resolution technique in which a search for an empty location proceeds serially from the record's home address. Compare with *double hashing*.

LINEAR SEARCH. A technique applied to find the record of a collection with a particular key value; views the collection as a linear list and starts at the beginning of the linear list, sequentially comparing each record's key value with the sought key value until the target record is found or the end of the list is reached; requires $O(N)$ comparisons to search a collection of N key values. Also known as a *sequential search*.

LINKED LIST. A data structure in which the ordering of nodes is indicated by the use of direct or indirect pointers rather than by physical sequentiality.

LOAD FACTOR. The percentage of the space allocated to a file that is actually in use holding records.

LOAD POINT. The beginning of the permissible recording area on a reel of magnetic tape.

LOGICAL. See *boolean*.

LOOP. An edge that connects a node in a graph to itself.

LOWER BOUND. The minimum value that a subscript may validly have; compare with *upper bound*.

LOWER-TRIANGULAR ARRAY. An array in which all elements above the diagonal are zero. If the diagonal is also zero, the array is strictly lower-triangular. Compare with *upper-triangular array*.

MAGNETIC DISK STORAGE. A direct-access storage device in which data are recorded by magnetic means on the surfaces of one or more flat, rotating disks.

MAGNETIC TAPE STORAGE A serial-access storage device in which data are recorded by magnetic means on the surface of a tape that moves longitudinally.

MAIN MEMORY. See *primary storage*.

MASS STORAGE. Very large-capacity storage device.

MASTER FILE. A file that contains relatively permanent data; each record represents the status of some aspect of an organization's business at a point in time.

MASTER INDEX. In an indexed sequential file, an index to the key values indexed by each cylinder index.

MERGE.   The combination of records in two or more sorted files to form one sorted file.

MERGE DEGREE.   The number of files input to a merge.

MERGE PHASE.   In an external sort, the phase in which the sorted runs are combined to form a single sorted run.

MINIMAL SPANNING TREE.   A minimum cost spanning tree for a graph. See *spanning tree*.

MOVABLE-HEAD DISK.   A disk in which there is one read/write head per recording surface; the access mechanism must be moved from cylinder to cylinder. Compare with *fixed-head disk*.

MULTIGRAPH.   A graph that is not simple. The graph has at least one loop or there is at least one pair of nodes n_i and n_j such that there are two or more edges connecting the pair.

MULTI-KEY FILE ORGANIZATION.   A file organization technique that supports direct access to records by two or more key fields.

MULTI-LIST FILE ORGANIZATION.   A multi-key file organization technique that maintains an index for each key. The index contains all values that the key has in the data file and a pointer to a linked list of data records with that key value.

MULTIPLEXOR CHANNEL.   A channel on which several devices can be active simultaneously, but which must complete execution of the channel program for one device before starting another device's channel program. Compare with *selector channel* and *block multiplexor channel*.

M-WAY SEARCH TREE.   A tree in which each node has out-degree $< = m$, each node is composed of a set of pointers and key values, and the key values are arranged in a specific manner that facilitates searches through the pointer structures. See *binary search tree* for a special case.

NATURAL MERGE.   A merge technique that uses one output device and a constant number of input devices.

NODE.   An elementary component of a list, graph, or tree.

NONVOLATILE STORAGE.   A storage device whose contents are not lost when power is removed. Compare with *volatile storage*.

NULL.   The value given to a pointer variable that is empty, i.e., that points nowhere; also called *nil* in Pascal.

NULL GRAPH   A graph with no nodes.

O(N).   "on the order of N"—approximately N.

O(N^2).   "on the order of N^2"—approximately N squared.

O($N\log_2 N$).   "on the order of $N\log_2 N$"—approximately N times the log base 2 of N.

ODD PARITY.   An error-control technique in which an extra bit is appended to the representation of each character and is set such that the number of 1-bits for the character is odd. Compare with *even parity*.

OPEN ADDRESSING.   An approach to collision resolution whereby synonyms are all stored in the file's primary address space. Compare with *separate-overflow addressing*.

ORDER.   Characteristic of a graph; the number of nodes it comprises.

OUT-DEGREE.   The number of edges coming out of a node in a directed graph. Compare with *in-degree*.

OUTPUT FILE.   A file that is written, but not read, by a program. Compare with *input file* and *input/output file*.

OVERFLOW DATA AREA.   An auxiliary file that contains records that do not fit in the area originally allocated to a file. Compare with *prime data area*.

PACKED-DECIMAL REPRESENTATION.   A scheme for storing numeric data values, where two digits occupy 8 bits; compare with an *unpacked representation*, whereby the two digits would occupy 16 bits.

PACKED-STRING REPRESENTATION.   A scheme for storing string data values, whereby each of the successive codes for the characters of a string are placed in successive words of storage, with as many of the characters as possible in any given word. Compare with *unpacked-string representation*.

PADDING.   (a) Space inserted into a record for purposes of ensuring the correct alignment of fields on appropriate word boundaries. Also called *slack bytes*.

(b) Allocated space intentionally left empty when a file is created, for purposes of accommodating future additions to the file. Also called *free space*.

PARALLEL HEAD-PER-TRACK DRIVE.   A fixed-head disk drive in which one head on each of the surfaces can be active simultaneously.

PARITY.   An error-control technique by which one redundant bit is appended to the representation of each character. See *odd parity* and *even parity*.

PARTIALLY INVERTED FILE.   A file structure including an inversion index on one or more, but not all, fields of the records. Compare with *completely inverted file*.

PARTITION-EXCHANGE SORT.   An exchange sort. At each step of the sort the list is partitioned into two parts such that the key values in one partition are all less than a particular key value and key values in the other partition are all greater than that paticular key value; the partitions are then treated independently in following steps of the sort. Also called *quicksort*.

PATH.   A sequence of one or more edges that connects two nodes in a graph.

PATH LENGTH.   The number of edges in a path; a measure of the number of comparisons required to use the tree.

PHYSICAL RECORD.   See *block*.

POINTER VARIABLE.   A variable whose value must be an address or null.

POLYPHASE MERGE.   A merge technique that uses a constant number of input devices and recycles each output device as an input device in the next phase of a pass.

POP.   To remove an element from a stack; see also *last-in-first-out*. Compare with *push*.

POSTFIX NOTATION.   A method of representing an arithmetic expression whereby a binary operator appears after its operands. Compare with *infix notation* and *prefix notation*.

POST-ORDER TRAVERSAL.   A method of visiting all the nodes of a binary tree whereby the left subtree is first traversed in post-order, then the right subtree is traversed in post-order, then the root is visited. Compare with *in-order* and *pre-order traversals*.

PREFETCHING. See *anticipatory buffering*.

PREFIX NOTATION. A method of representing an arithmetic expression whereby a binary operator appears before its operands. Compare with *infix* and *postfix notations*.

PRE-ORDER TRAVERSAL. A method of visiting all the nodes of a binary tree whereby the root is visited first, then the left subtree is traversed in pre-order, then the right subtree is traversed in pre-order. Compare with *in-order* and *post-order traversals*.

PRIMARY KEY. The main key field of a multi-key file. In an alternate-key indexed sequential file, the field for which direct and sequential access are supported.

PRIMARY STORAGE. A storage device with the property that the time required to access the contents of one location is the same as the time required to access the contents of any other location of the memory. Also called *main memory*. Compare with *secondary storage*.

PRIME DATA AREA. The main space allocated to a file. Compare with *overflow data area*.

PRIMITIVE. A data structure that cannot be decomposed to other data structures.

PROGRAM FILE. A file that contains instructions for processing.

PUSH. To add an element to a stack; see also *last-in-first-out*. Compare with *pop*.

QUERY LANGUAGE. An end-user-oriented language for retrieving selected data from a file or database.

QUERY PROCESSOR. Software that translates a user's requests (phrased in a query language) into instructions that can be used directly for file or database access.

QUEUE. A linear list in which elements are added only to the rear of the list and are removed only from the front of the list; see also *first-in-first-out*.

QUEUEING THEORY. A formal analytic body of knowledge about the behavior of systems that involve queues.

QUICKSORT. See *partition-exchange sort*.

RADIX. The base of a system of numbers. For example, the radix of the decimal system is 10; the radix of the hexadecimal system is 16.

RANGE. (a) Of an array: the number of elements in the array.

(b) Of a subscript: the set of values that the subscript may validly have.

REACHABILITY MATRIX. A matrix used to represent the paths that exist between each pair of nodes in a graph; $R(i,j) = 1$ if and only if there is a path between nodes v_i and v_j in the graph. See also *transitive closure*.

REAR. The element most recently placed on a queue. Also, the last element that will leave a queue.

RECORD. (a) A finite, ordered collection of possibly heterogeneous elements (fields) that are treated as a unit. Also called a *structure*.

(b) A collection of logically related fields treated a unit.

RECORD KEY. A primary or secondary key.

RECURSIVE PROCEDURE. A procedure in which each step makes use of the results of earlier steps, generally by invoking execution of some part of itself; compare with *iterative procedure*.

RELATIVE ADDRESSING. A technique for mapping records to storage whereby a key value is mapped to the record's ordinal position in the file. Compare with *absolute addressing.*

RELATIVE FILE ORGANIZATION. A file organization technique that supports access directly to records by a key field.

REPORT FILE. A file containing data that are formatted for presentation to an end-user.

REPORT-WRITER PACKAGE. A software product that translates a user-oriented request for a report into instructions that are used to create that report from accesses to a master file or database.

RESPONSE TIME. CPU time or elapsed time required to process a transaction.

RIGHT THREAD. A link from a node in a binary tree to its successor node in a traversal ordering. Compare with *left thread.*

ROOTED TREE. A tree in which one node (called the root) is distinguished from the other nodes.

ROTATION. A type of restructuring applied to a tree to return it to a state of balance.

ROTATIONAL DELAY. The time required for an addressed block to appear under the read/write head of a rotating disk.

ROW-MAJOR ORDER. An array-linearization technique that stores all the elements in one row before storing any elements from the next row. Subscripts are varied right-to-left; that is, the rightmost subscript is varied fastest. Compare with *column-major order.*

RUN. A sorted sequence.

SEARCH ARGUMENT. The key value of a record that is being sought.

SEARCHING. The process of trying to find the record or records that meet a given criterion.

SECONDARY KEY. In a multi-key file, any key field except the primary key.

SECONDARY STORAGE. A storage device with the property that the time required to access the contents of one location may be different from the time required to access the contents of another location on the same device; generally slower and cheaper per bit than a primary storage device. Also called *auxiliary memory.*

SECTOR. That part of a track on a disk that can be accessed by the read/write heads in the course of a predetermined rotational displacement of the particular device.

SECTOR ADDRESSING. A technique for addressing the data records on a disk, whereby a record's address is its sector number, record number. Compare with *cylinder addressing.*

SEEK TIME. The time required for the read/write heads of a disk to be positioned at the appropriate cylinder.

SELECTION SORT. One of a family of internal sort algorithms in which the next logically sequential key in the unsorted list is selected and placed in the next position in a growing sorted list.

SELECTOR CHANNEL. A channel that can manage data flow between main memory and only one device at a time.

SEPARATE-OVERFLOW ADDRESSING. An approach to collision resolution whereby all records that cannot be stored at their home addresses are stored in a separate file from the file's primary address space. Compare with *open addressing*.

SEQUENCE SET.   The leaves of a B$^+$-tree.

SEQUENTIAL FILE ORGANIZATION.   A file organization technique that supports serial access to records.

SEQUENTIAL SEARCH.   See *linear search*.

SERIAL ACCESS.   Access in physically consecutive order. Compare with *direct access*.

SERIAL-ACCESS DEVICE.   A storage device that supports serial access. Compare with *direct-access storage device*.

SHARED DEVICE.   A device that supports concurrent access by multiple users. Compare with *dedicated device, virtual device*.

SIGN-AND-MAGNITUDE REPRESENTATION.   A human-oriented approach for representation of numeric values, where a number is represented by a sign (+ or −) and a string of digits that represent its absolute value (i.e., its magnitude). Compare with *complement representation*.

SIMILAR TREES.   Trees that have the same structure, but not necessarily the same node contents. Compare with *equivalent trees*.

SIMPLE GRAPH.   A graph that has no loops and in which no pair of nodes is connected by more than one edge. Compare with *multigraph*.

SIMULATION.   The use of programming techniques to represent certain features of the behavior of a physical or abstract system.

SLACK BYTES.   See *padding* (a).

SORTED FILE.   A file in which the records are ordered logically by value of a sort key.

SORTING.   The process of arranging a collection of keys (and records) into a specified order.

SORT KEY.   A field (elementary or group item) whose value is used to order records of a collection.

SORT/MERGE.   See *external sort*.

SPANNING TREE.   A tree that contains all the nodes of a graph and no other nodes; its branches are a subset of the graph's edges.

SPARSE ARRAY.   An array with a relatively high density of elements with value zero.

SPARSE INDEX.   An index that contains a proper subset of the key values of the data collection being indexed. Compare with *dense index*.

SPOOLING.   The use of buffers on auxiliary memory to reduce the effects of timing differences between the central processing unit and peripheral equipment, commonly printers.

STABLE SORT.   A sort in which the original ordering of records that have equal keys is preserved in the sorted ordering of those records.

STACK.   A linear list in which elements are added to and removed from only the top of the list; see also *last-in-first-out*.

STORAGE MEDIUM.   Physical material that holds data representations.

STRICTLY TRIANGULAR ARRAY.   An upper-triangular array or a lower-triangular array in which the elements on the diagonal all have value zero.

STRING.   A finite sequence of symbols taken from an alphabet.

STRING LENGTH.   The number of symbols (i.e., characters) in a string; length is a fundamental attribute of a string.

STRUCTURE.   See *record* (a).

SUBSCRIPT.   A value that designates the ordinal position of an element in an array. Also called an *index* (a).

SUBSTRING.   An operator with one string operand and two integer operands, producing a string result. If $S = {}'a_1, a_2, \ldots, a_N'$, then substr (S, i, j) is $'a_i, a_{i+1}, \ldots, a_{i+j-1}'$.

SYNONYM CHAINING.   An approach to collision resolution in which access to synonyms is facilitated by maintaining a linked list of the records in an equivalence class.

SYNONYMS.   Two or more unequal key values that hash to the same home address. See also *equivalence class*.

SYNTAX.   Grammar; rules for the formation of the allowable strings of a vocabulary.

TABLE.   A two-dimensional array. See also *array*.

TAPE DRIVE.   A mechanism for moving a magnetic tape, controlling the tape's motion, and reading/writing on the tape.

TEXT FILE.   A file of alphanumeric and/or graphic information created and changed using a text editor.

THREADED TREE.   A tree that includes a linked list of the nodes according to a tree traversal ordering.

THROUGHPUT.   The number of transactions or volume of work that a system can process in a given time period.

TOP.   The element most recently inserted in a stack. Also, the element next to be removed from a stack.

TOURNAMENT SORT.   An internal sort; a repeated selection sort in which each sublist consists of no more than two keys; the sublists are organized into a binary tree for purposes of determining the elements in the next subject sublist. Also called *tree-selection sort*.

TRACK.   (a) An area on a single surface of a rotating disk that can be read without repositioning the read/write head.

(b) An area on a magnetic tape for storing single bits in sequence from the beginning to the end of the tape.

TRANSACTION.   An event or action that changes the status of something tracked in a master file or database.

TRANSACTION FILE.   A file of transactions to be processed against a master file or database.

TRANSITIVE CLOSURE.   The sum of all powers of a graph's adjacency matrix; see also *reachability matrix*.

TRANSPOSE.   Of a two-dimensional array: the array obtained by reversing the subscript positions. The transpose of an N-by-M array is an M-by-N array.

TREE.   An acyclic, simple, connected graph.

TREE HEIGHT. One plus the number of the highest level on which the tree has non-null nodes, where the root is on level zero.

TREE-SELECTION SORT. See *tournament sort*.

TREE TRAVERSAL. A method for visiting all the nodes of a tree, whereby each node is visited once and only once. See also *in-order*, *post-order*, and *pre-order* traversals.

TREE WEIGHT. The number of leaf nodes in a tree.

TRIANGULAR ARRAY. An array in which all elements either above or below the diagonal have value zero. See also *lower-triangular array*, *upper-triangular array*, *strictly triangular array*.

TRIE. A general tree structure in which the node structure is based on the radix of the key values and searches through the tree are based upon representations of key values as sequences of characters rather than as key values themselves.

UNDIRECTED GRAPH. A graph in which edges do not have directionality. Compare with *directed graph*.

UNPACKED-STRING REPRESENTATION. A scheme for storing string data values, whereby each of the successive codes for the characters of the string are placed in successive words of storage, with one character per word. Compare with *packed string representation*.

UPPER BOUND The maximum value that a subscript may validly have. Compare with *lower bound*.

UPPER-TRIANGULAR ARRAY. An array in which all elements below the diagonal are zero. If the diagonal is also zero, the array is *strictly upper-triangular*. Compare with *lower-triangular array*.

VECTOR. A one-dimensional array. See *array*.

VERTEX. See *node*.

VIRTUAL DEVICE. A device that does not physically exist, used to make a dedicated device appear to be shared.

VIRTUAL HASHING. Any hashing technique that may dynamically change its hash function.

VOCABULARY. The set of all possible strings that can be obtained from an alphabet. The vocabulary that is derived from alphabet A is denoted $A*$ (contains the null string) or A^+ (all strings have length greater than zero).

VOLATILE STORAGE. A storage device whose contents are lost when power is removed. Compare with *nonvolatile storage*.

WEIGHT-BALANCED TREE. A binary tree in which the balanced state is determined by the number of nodes in the left and the right subtrees of each node. Compare with *height-balanced tree*.

WINCHESTER DISK. A form of magnetic disk storage in which the recording surfaces, access mechanism, and read/write heads are manufactured together and packaged in a sealed cartridge.

WORK FILE. A temporary file, typically used to store large volumes of data during the execution of a program.

answers to selected review exercises

Chapter 1

1. Measurement, collection, transcription, validation, organization, storage, aggregation, update, retrieval, protection.

   Most expensive: collection and transcription, because this is where human labor commonly is used extensively.

2. 1, 10, 2, −6, 0, and so forth.

3. True, false.

4. (a) False, (b) false, (c) true, (d) true, (e) true, (f) true, (g) false, (h) false, (i) true, (j) true, (i) false.

5. (a) 5, (b) 6, (c) MAGICPIE, (d) EEL, (e) MAGPIE, (f) MAG WHEEL, (g) PIE, (h) PIE, (i) PILE, (j) MIC, (k) EELPIE.

6. $-7 = 100$, $-6 = 1001$, $-5 = 1010$, $-4 = 1011$, $-3 = 1100$, $-2 = 1101$, $-1 = 1110$, $+0 = 0000$, $+1 = 0001$, $+2 = 0010$, $+3 = 0011$, $+4 = 0100$, $+5 = 0101$, $+6 = 0110$, $+7 = 0111$.

7. (a) 21, (b) 201.

8. (a) 32 ($R = 2^5$), (b) 256 ($R = 2^8$).

9. N.

10. N.

11. (a) $+16$, -15, (b) $+128$, -127, (c)2^{N-1}, $-(2^{N-2} - 1)$.

12. (a) $+15$, -15, (b) $+127$, -127, (c)$2^{N-1} - 1$, $-(2^{N-1} - 1)$.

19. MAGPIEPIEMAGENTA ; MAGPIEMAGENTA ; MAGPIEξPIEξMAGENTAξ

PTR1S PTR2S PTR3S   PTR1S PTR2S PTR3S   PTR1S   PTR2S   PTR3S

20. Overlaying strings conserves storage but can greatly complicate processing when the values of string variables are changed.

21. Packing strings conserves storage but complicates processing when the values of string variables are modified.

22. A and B both allow overlaying of strings; C does not. C requires a smaller table than does A or B. A and B both require some processing to find the end of a string.

23. An object-oriented programming language requires a declaration of the operations valid for a data structure. The compiler and run-time environments enforce the restriction that only these operations may be performed on the data structure.

Chapter 2

1. 70.

2. An array linearized in row-major order first stores the elements of its first row, then its second row, and so forth until all elements are stored. An array linearized in column-major order first stores the elements of its first column, then its second column, and so forth until all elements are stored.

3. $(B - A + 1) * (D - C + 1)$.

4. N; $3(N + 1)$.

5. 16.

6. (a) 1911; (b) 8578.

7. $B + 318 * S$.

8. If stored in row-major order:

$(i - B) * (A - B + 1) * n + (j - D) * n$.

If stored in column-major order:

$(j - D) * (C - D + 1) * n + (i - B) * n$.

9. (a) $(B - A + 1) * (D - C + 1) * (F - E + 1)$, (b) correct answer depends upon the order of linearization of the three dimensions.

10. 3.

11. 1200.

12. See Fig. 2–16.

13. In Pascal:

```
var original: array [1..N,1..M] of real;
    newone: array [1..N,1..M] of real;
    i, j: integer;
```

```
begin for i = 1 to N do
         for j = 1 to M do
                 newone [j,i] = original [i, j]
 end;
```

14. Original sparse array:

Row	Column	Value
1	3	1
2	1	2
2	5	3
3	4	9
3	6	1
4	2	16

Transpose array:

Row	Column	Value
3	1	1
1	2	2
5	2	3
4	3	9
6	3	1
2	4	16

16. See Fig. 2–13 and Fig. 2–14.

17. Trade-off of saved space and program complexity to locate individual elements; programmer has to calculate correct subscript values. Positive indicators are Primary: both arrays will stay triangular (otherwise they have to move out of shared space); and Secondary: both arrays are approximately same dimensions (otherwise will suboptimize space usage).

18. 1st row: N
2nd row: N − 1
Nth row: 1

$$\text{Total} \quad \sum_{i=1}^{N} (N - i + 1) = \frac{N(N+1)}{2}$$

23. They use a constant offset for the elements of the array.

26. (a) 18

(b) Q(−1,1,1), Q(−1,1,2), Q(−1,1,3), Q(−1,2,1),
Q(−1,21), Q(−1,2,3), Q(0,1,1), Q(0,1,2),
Q(0,1,3), Q(0,2,1), Q(0,2,2), Q(0,2,3),
Q(1,1,1), Q(1,1,2), Q(1,1,3), Q(1,2,1),
Q(1,2,2), Q(1,2,3).

(c) Q(−1,1,1), Q(0,1,1), Q(1,1,1), Q(−1,2,1),
Q(0,2,1), Q(1,2,1), Q(−1,1,2), Q(0,1,2),
Q(1,1,1), Q(−1,2,2), Q(0,2,2), Q(1,1,2),
Q(−1,1,3), Q(0,1,3), Q(1,1,3), Q(−1,2,3),
Q(0,2,3), Q(1,2,3).

Chapter 3

1. The elements of an array must be of the same type, while the elements of a record can be of different types. Yes. Yes.

2. To be able to refer to and manipulate the component fields.

3. The first program apparently has no need to refer to the component fields of phoneno while the second program does.

4. FORTRAN does not have a facility for explicit declaration of record structures; these are important in file processing, which is ubiquitous in business data processing.

5. The COBOL SYNC feature insulates the programmer somewhat from physical implementation details, thereby improving program maintainability. However, other programming languages (such as Pascal, PL/I) do not have a SYNC feature, making brute-force padding or no padding the only alternatives. Padding improves execution times but increases space requirements. Padding increases program development times.

9. If there are multiple record types on a single file, (1) program logic must be able to distinguish between them, (2) a greater volume of data may need to be read than program logic warrants, increasing I/O costs, (3) the number of file open and closes may be minimized, reducing I/O costs. If the STUDENT and CLASS records are both accessed by the application, then a mixed file may be appropriate.

Chapter 4

2. (a) Error condition; (b) i; (c) undefined or null; (d) i; (e) 0.

3. (a) True; (b) false; (c) error condition.

4. i.

5. S.

6. House the stack in an array and keep an integer variable whose value is the subscript of the stack's top element.

7. See the Push algorithm in the chapter.

8. See the Pop algorithm in the chapter.

9. Push a sequence of elements onto the stack.

10. Examples: inventory lists, identifiers of windows in a screen management system, menu picks in a hierarchical menu management system.

11. Overflow occurs when a stack gets too large for its containing array. Underflow occurs when a stack gets negative size. Both can cause writing outside of a stack array's boundaries, potentially corrupting neighbor data structures. Overflow might appropriately result in a message to the user that system size limits have been exceeded. Underflow might result in a message that an illegal Pop operation has been requested.

12. (a) $AB * CD + - EF - FHI \uparrow / + G +$; (c) $AB \uparrow C * D - EF/GH + / +$

13 See the Pop algorithm in the chapter.

Chapter 5

1. Similarities: special cases of linear list, can be housed in arrays.
Differences: where insertion and deletion occur (queue is FIFO, stack is LIFO).

2. Rear, front.

3. So that the storage space can be more fully used.

4. No. Its base never needs to move; only its top.

5. Draw a picture, carefully label the queue slots, and hand-simulate the algorithm.

6. When slots are numbered starting at 0.

7. The test is determined by the way that you establish and manage the pointers.

Chapter 6

1. FIRST = 2
AVAIL = 3

	INFO	NEXT
1	PEACH	0
2	APPLE	4
3		0
4	CHERRY	5
5	GRAPE	1

2. FIRST = 4
AVAIL = 7

	DATA	NEXT
1	G	3
2	D	5
3	J	0
4	B	2
5	E	6
6	F	1
7		8
8		9
9		0

3. FIRST = 8
AVAIL = 0

	DATA	NEXT
1	G	3
2	D	5
3	J	9
4	B	7
5	E	6
6	F	1
7	C	2
8	A	4
9	Z	0

4. This algorithm requires sequencing through the nodes of the singly linked list, counting until the jth node is found. Be careful not to fall off the end of the list if it has fewer than j nodes.

5. The list T can be added to the beginning or end of the Avail list (or anywhere in between). Adding to the beginning can be done with the following procedure:
   (a) Find the last node in T list. Change its Next pointer to point to the first node in the Avail list.
   (b) Find the last node in the Avail list. Change its Next pointer to point to the first node in T list.
   (c) Avail : = T

6. *P*.

7. (a) Get space for the new node and make NEW point to it.
   (b) Info (NEW) : = '1234'
   (c) Next (NEW) : = Next (X)
   (d) Next (X) : = NEW

8. (a) Q : = Prior (X)
   (b) Prior (X) : = S
   (c) Prior (S) : = Q
   (d) Next (Q) : = S
   (e) Next (S) : = X

9. Singly linked list:
   (a) S1 : = S
   (b) Q : = Next (S)
   (c) Do until Q = Null
       (c1) R : = Next (Q)
       (c2) Next (Q) : = S
       (c3) S : = Q
       (c4) Q : = R
   (d) Next (S1) : = Null

   Doubly linked list
   (a) S1 : = S
   (b) Q : = Next (S)
   (c) Do until Q = Null
       (c1) R : = Next (Q)
       (c2) Next (Q) : = S
       (c3) Pior (Q) : = R
       (c4) S : = Q
       (c5) Q : = R
   (d) Next (S1) : = Null

10. The algorithm to get a node from an Avail queue is the same as for an Avail stack. The algorithm to free a node, adding it to an Avail queue is simplified by ready access to the tail of the queue. This is usually done by keeping a pointer to the tail.

11. At least 2.

12. See the Getnode and Freenode algorithms for an Avail stack.

13. See the Getnode and Freenode algorithms for an Avail queue.

14. (a) Find the last node in list a, and make LAST point to it.
    (b) Next (LAST) : = B

15.

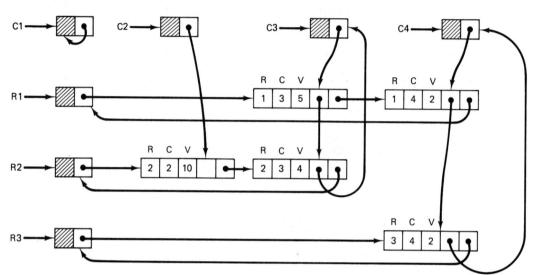

16.

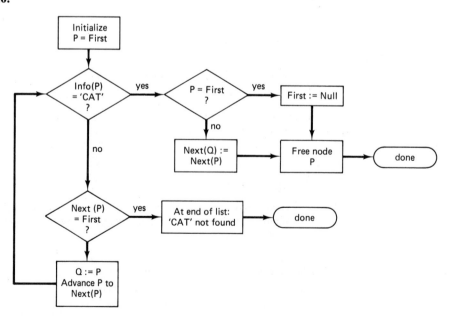

17. (a) If Next (FIRST) = FIRST then done, empty list.
    (b) P : = FIRST
    (c) Do until Info (P) = 'BAT'
       (c1) P : = Next (P)
       (c2) If P = first then done, 'BAT' not in list.
    (d) Q : = Next (P)
    (e) If Info (Q) not = 'CAT' then done, 'CAT' doesn't follow 'BAT.'
    (f) Get node from Avail list and make CATFIRST point to it.
    (g) Next (CATFIRST) : = Q
    (h) Next (P) : = FIRST
    (i) R : = Q
    (j) Do until Next (R) = FIRST
       (j1) R : = Next (R)
    (k) Next (R) : = CATFIRST

19.

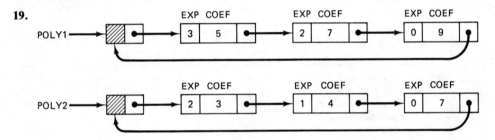

20.

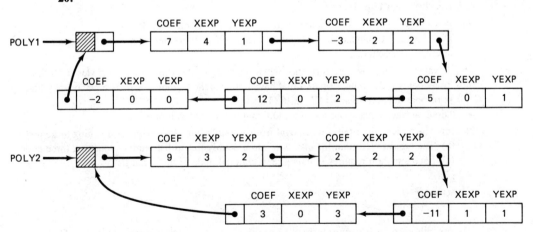

21. Sequence though the list nodes, adding to a counter as you proceed. The counting stops when the end of the list is reached. Depending on the list structure, the end may be signalled by a null Next pointer (non-circular list), by the Next pointer equal to the pointer to the first node of the list (circular list), or by the Next pointer reaching to the list's head node.

22. Final state.

	Author	Next-author	Title	Next-title	Stock-no	Next-stock-no	Prior-stock-no	Next-avail
1	F. Stop Fitzgerald	4	Creative . . .	10	53526	10	5	0
2	Linus Type	0	Newspaper . . .	4	98374	0	10	0
3								11
4	Lowen Maner	10	The Longest	0	23764	9	6	0
5	Ascent Agu	6	La Marke de . . .	2	49261	1	9	0
6	Dr. Frank Annstein	1	Beer Basted	9	19822	4	8	0
7								3
8	Artie Abacus	5	Computer . . .	1	17760	6	0	0
9	Denn M. Stretcher	2	Betsy Wore . . .	8	38641	5	4	0
10	C. Sanders	9	Finger . . .	5	73920	2	1	0
11								12
12								13
13								14
14								15
15								0

Headings: First-Author = 8
                First-Title = 6
                First-Stock-No = 8
                Last-Stock-No = 2
                Avail = 7

23. Advantages: Helps in finding the end of a circular list; can be used to store information describing the list.
Disadvantage: Uses space.

24. Advantage: Helps in sequencing from any node to any other in the list.
Disadvantage: Can make the end of the list more difficult to detect than if the last node contained a null Next pointer.

25. Advantages: Improves performance when inserting or deleting particular nodes from the list, by reducing the number of nodes that have to be touched. Improves performance when finding prior node relative to any node in the list.
Disadvantage: Uses space for one additional pointer in each node.

26. (a) The typical algorithm for removal from a doubly linked list requires touching three nodes.
     (b) The typical algorithm for insertion into a doubly linked list requires touching three nodes.
     (c) Each situation requires touching an additional node in the Avail list.

Chapter 7

1. (a) sum $graph(j,i)$ varying j from 1 to n; (b) sum $graph(i,j)$ varying j from 1 to N.

3. Yes;

5. Sparse matrix, typically using a multi-list representation.

Chapter 8

3. No, by definition of equivalence.

4. No, since every subtree must have a root node.

5. 2^I.

6. 2^I for $I < K - 1$ and a maximum of 2^I for $I = K - 1$.

7. Impossible; 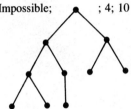 ; 4; 10

8. Nodes in a binary tree have a fixed number of subtrees, whereas nodes in a general tree may have widely varying numbers of subtrees.

9. (a) A B D G L P E H M Q I C F J K N O; (b) P L G D Q M H I E B J N O K F C A; (c) P L G D B H Q M E I A C J F N K O

10. True

11.

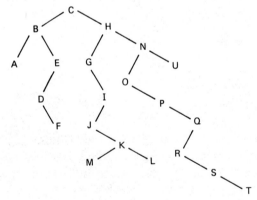

12.

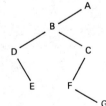

13.
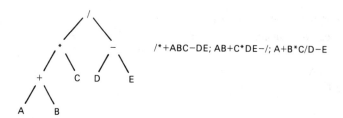

14.
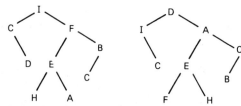

/*+ABC−DE; AB+C*DE−/; A+B*C/D−E

15.
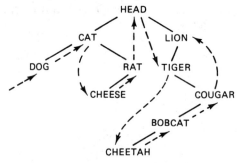

16. Keep inserting the ''middle'' key next.

18.

HEAD

CAT LION

DOG RAT TIGER

CHEESE COUGAR

BOBCAT

CHEETAH

19. In-order.

22. LEFT RIGHT INFO IN-ORDER THREAD POST-ORDER THREAD.

23. No; usually only one traversal order is appropriate for the type of data stored in the tree.

35. Balanced tree: left and right subtrees have equal numbers of nodes; height-balanced tree: left and right subtrees have nearly equal maximum path lengths.

Chapter 9

2. (a).01; (b) 3.45; (c)

key(i)	prob(i)	(d) 2.35
12	.32	
2	.26	
10	.21	
4	.15	
8	.05	

3. The move-to-the-front method promotes a key to the front of the list when it is the target of a search. The transposition method promotes a key to the next higher position when it is the target of a search. Both are based on the idea that searching for a particular key raises the probability that that key will be sought again. The transposition method is more conservative than the move-to-the-front method.

4. Move-to-the-front in an array requires moving all preceding elements of the list. In a linked list, only the links in the old first and new first elements and their immediate neighbors need to be changed.

5. Transposition in an array requires switching two elements' positions. In a linked list, the links in the two elements and their immediate neighbors need to be changed.

6. A sort "in place" requires space for n (sometimes $n + 1$) entries. If sorting is not done in place, then space is required for $2 * n$ entries.

12. There are no advantages to applying the binary search technique to a linked list of data.

13. The $O(n \log_2 n)$ sorts repeatedly reduce (by approximately one-half) the number of keys remaining to be compared with each other, while the $O(n_2)$ sorts do not repeatedly partition the keys into sublists.

20. $O(n\log n)$ performance would result from a sort that repeatedly reduces the number of keys remaining to be compared with each other to a third. This would be a ternary search. $O(n\log n)$ performance would result from a k-ary search, which repeatedly partitions the remaining keys into k independent sublists.

23. See answer to question 12. A sequential search is nearly always used, unless there are auxiliary indexes into the list.

Chapter 10

1. Permanence of storage, independent of a particular program's run-unit; size; selective access requirements.

2. A variety of file structuring requirements must be satisfied; no one file organization is flexible enough to meet all needs with acceptable performance.

9. Restructuring operations include changing field widths, adding fields to records, allocating more space to the file, balancing an index tree, resequencing records in the file, and so forth. Reorganization operations change the file's fundamental organization structure. Both restructuring and reorganization are maintenance activities.

10. A file system's responsibilities typically include maintaining file directories, establishing paths for data flow between main memory and secondary storage, coordinating communication between the CPU and secondary devices, buffering data for delivery to the CPU or secondary devices, preparing files for use, and cleaning up after I/O operations.

11. A file system's directory typically contains file identifiers, file attributes (record length, block size, kind of organization), file boundaries, error counts and flags, file status) and so forth.

12. A channel is a processor that interfaces the CPU with secondary storage devices. It offloads from the CPU responsibilities for building data paths between primary and secondary storage and coordinates the CPU and device controller actions.

13. A selector channel manages one device at a time. A multiplexor channel can switch between several devices, but cannot interleave the execution of channel programs, which a block multiplexor can do.

14. A virtual device is a disk file that is camouflaged to appear to a program as a real device. When the real device is ready, a spooler copies the disk file to the real device.

15. Record blocking allows multiple records to be brought into main memory in a single access to secondary storage, thus reducing the number of device accesses required to read a file. Same for writing.

16. Anticipatory buffering can reduce program wait times caused by I/O requests.

17. Yes, one buffer is being filled while the other is being used.

18. (a) 0; (b) 1; (c) n; (d) 1; (e) output; (f) flag $= 0$ if the buffer is empty, $= 1$ otherwise; (g) 1.

19. Code generated by the compiler for a READ does not have to check if this is the first READ.

20. Buffer space allocated to the file may be freed prior to run-unit termination.

25. A database management system typically uses a file system. The database management system adds functions like enhanced security checking (at the record or field level rather than the file level), concurrency control, backup and recovery, performance monitoring and turning, report writer, query processor, language preprocessors, and so forth.

Chapter 11

1. To eliminate erroneous records as early as possible in the process; to reduce the sort volume.

2. Processing control might be simplified if the transaction file were stored on disk; thus the master files would always be on tape. This run's updated master is next run's old master.

3. 40%

4. High rate of data change, high file activity ratio, and high urgency for current data suggest frequent file update. Large size suggests infrequent update. Frequent update increases processing costs but improves data quality.

5. Probability of need to access old data for recovery purposes and historic reporting requirements should be considered.

6. The COBOL programmer can declare the file's internal and external names, whether or not the file is required, the number of buffers to allocate, the file organization method and access technique, the name of a variable to contain I/O status information, the location of the file on a multi-file tape, the sizes of blocks and records, the kind of labels on the file, and the record formats.

7. Sort the transaction file first!

19. (a) 011010; (b) 100101.

20. Users have a variety of storage needs; higher-cost devices tend to be faster than lower-cost devices; some devices support only serial access while others support direct access.

21. (a)
$$\frac{2400 \frac{ft}{tape} * 12 \frac{in}{ft}}{5 \frac{rec}{block} * \frac{80 \frac{char}{rec}}{1600 \frac{char}{in}} + .6 \frac{in}{gap} * 1 \frac{gap}{block}} = 33,882 \frac{blocks}{tape}$$

which is 169,411 records.

(b)
$$\frac{2400 \frac{ft}{tape} * 12 \frac{in}{ft}}{15 \frac{rec}{block} * \frac{80 \frac{char}{rec}}{1600 \frac{char}{in}} + .6 \frac{in}{gap} * 1 \frac{gap}{block}} = 21,333 \frac{blocks}{tape}$$

which is 320,000 records.

22. (a)
$$\frac{33,882 \frac{blocks}{tape} * .25 \frac{in}{block}}{200 \ in/sec} + 33,882 \frac{blocks}{tape} * \frac{.004 \ sec}{gap} * \frac{1 \ gap}{block}$$

$$= 178 \ sec/tape.$$

(b) 165 sec.

23. Permanence, size, selective access requirements, data independence.

24. A variety of file structuring requirements must be satisfied.

Chapter 12

1. Tournament sort generates long runs relative to the amount of main memory space that it uses. This improves performance of the file sort.

2. Number of copies reflects I/O requirements, while number of comparisons reflects CPU requirements. In most file sorting environments, I/O activity is "more expensive" than is CPU activity.

Chapter 13

1. Seek time (arm movement time) is zero for a fixed-head disk, which has one head per track and therefore always has an access head positioned at the requested track. Seek time is greater than zero for a movable-head disk.

2. *b*.

3. *c*.

10. Division-remainder.

11. 75% to 80%.

14. (a) to calculate an address for a record with a given key value; (b) to resolve a collision; (c) to resolve a collision; (d) to improve access times to synonyms.

Chapter 14

1. Binary search tree allows a maximum of two-way branching; *m*-way search tree allows a maximum of *m*-way branching.

2. True.

3. B-tree.

4. 15 key values; 16 pointers to subtrees, 15 pointers to records (1 per key value) if the tree is an index.

5. 1 key value; 1 pointer to a subtree if the node is not a leaf, 1 pointer to a record if the tree is an index.

6. 121 nodes; 242 key values.

7. 512 nodes; 1023 key values.

8. $\lceil \log_3 242 \rceil = 5$; $\lceil \log_3 1023 \rceil = 7$.

9. $\lceil \log_4 242 \rceil = 4$; $\lceil \log_4 1023 \rceil = 5$.

10. 15 key values; 16 pointers to subtrees, 15 pointers to records (1 per key value) if the tree is an index.

11. 7 key values; 8 pointers to subtrees if the node is not a leaf, 7 pointers to records (1 per key value) if the tree is an index.

12. 0.143.

13. See answer to question 8.

14. $O\left(\log_8 \dfrac{n + 1}{2} \right)$.

24. A B*-tree is a B-tree in which each node is at least two-thirds full instead of at least half full. The insertion and deletion algorithms differ.

25. Search through a B-tree is based on key values, while search through a trie is based on representations of key values.

26. The distribution of key values

27. A trie cannot be balanced without control of the key-value distribution.

28. Ten pointers per node; four levels

Chapter 15

1. In a B^+-tree the leaves are linked together to form a sequence set; interior nodes exist only for purposes of indexing the sequence set (not to index into data records). The insertion and deletion algorithms differ slightly.

2. The order of the tree (How many ways of branching?).

3. A B^+-tree is by definition in balance.

4. When sequential access to the key values is never required.

5. When both sequential and direct access to the key values are required.

6. When rapid unsuccessful searches are important.

7. (a) 10, 15, 30, 50, 58, 75, 80, 100.

9. (a) Both sequential; (b) customer ID number or name.

10. (a) Relative (the weekly summary report could be generated from a sequential file derived from sorting the relative file) or indexed sequential; (b) product number.

11. (a) Sequential (it's stored on a tape cassette); (b) records will be on the file sequentially by time of customer checkout; each record would include the keys of the pertinent menu selections.

12. (a) Relative; (b) patient identifier.

13. (a) (a) − (d); (b) (e) − (h).

14. Sequential access to the keys of a B-tree is much slower than is sequential access to the keys of a B^+-tree, since the latter are linked in sequential order by definition.

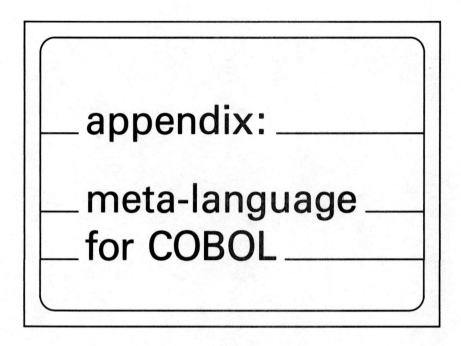

appendix:

meta-language for COBOL

The following notation is used in the description of the syntax of COBOL-language statements:

Required reserved words are upper-case and underscored, e.g. <u>READ</u>

Optional reserved words are upper-case, e.g., RECORD

Programmer-supplied data-names are lower-case, e.g. filename

Optional phrases are enclosed in square-brackets, e.g.

[AT <u>END</u> imperative-statement]

Select at least one alternative of phrase choices that are given in curly braces, e.g.

SORT filename ON $\begin{Bmatrix} \underline{ASCENDING} \\ \underline{DESCENDING} \end{Bmatrix}$ KEY dataname1 [,dataname2]. . .

Repeat the phrase preceded by ellipses (. . .) zero or more times (e.g. see above).

index